中国商务文化读本 BUSINESS CULTURE IN CHINA

The First Touch of E-commerce in China

中国电子商务初体验

■ 华迎 编

中国出版集团
中译出版社

图书在版编目(CIP)数据

中国电子商务初体验：汉英对照 / 华迎编． —北京：中译出版社，2019.7

（中国商务文化读本）

ISBN 978-7-5001-5996-4

Ⅰ.①中… Ⅱ.①华… Ⅲ.①电子商务－研究－中国－汉、英 Ⅳ.①F724.6

中国版本图书馆 CIP 数据核字（2019）第 129243 号

出版发行 / 中译出版社
地　　址 / 北京市西城区车公庄大街甲 4 号物华大厦 6 层
电　　话 / (010) 68359827, 68359376（发行部）；53601537（编辑部）
邮　　编 / 100044
传　　真 / (010) 68357870
电子邮箱 / book@ctph.com.cn
网　　址 / http://www.ctph.com.cn

出 版 人 / 张高里
总 策 划 / 贾兵伟
出版统筹 / 胡晓凯
责任编辑 / 范祥镇　王馨敏
封面设计 / 潘　峰

排　　版 / 北京竹页文化传媒有限公司
印　　刷 / 北京玺诚印务有限公司
经　　销 / 新华书店

规　　格 / 787毫米×1092毫米　1/16
印　　张 / 22.75
字　　数 / 370千字
版　　次 / 2019年7月第一版
印　　次 / 2019年7月第一次

ISBN 978-7-5001-5996-4　定价：62.00元

版权所有　侵权必究

中译出版社

序

　　商业与互联网的结合催生了信息时代新的商业模式——电子商务，近年来互联网和信息技术的迅猛发展，推动全球电子商务进入规模化发展阶段。电子商务已经广泛渗透到社会生活的方方面面，覆盖各个领域及产业，成为全球经济增长和一体化的关键动力。中国电子商务起步于20世纪90年代，2006年开始进入高速发展阶段，自2010年之后更是以强劲的势头飞速发展，目前已经成为全世界电子商务规模最大的国家，占据全球电子商务市场份额的40%，其发展模式极具代表性。本书作为帮助海外读者以及旅居中国的外国朋友快速了解中国电子商务业环境和运作模式的商务系列读本之一，以通俗易懂的方式向广大读者介绍中国电子商务的发展状况和特点，通过生动形象地方式，带领读者分别以"买家"和"卖家"身份体验中国典型电子商务网站的交易流程和使用方法，为读者快速了解并开展电子商务探索提供帮助指引。

　　本书得以顺利完成，需要感谢在此过程中给予关心、帮助和支持的各位朋友、同仁。首先，作者要感谢的是参与本书初稿资料收集和撰写工作的对外经济贸易大学的学生。其次要感谢国际商务汉语教学与资源开发基地韩红主任、李荣荣老师和国际合作交流处霍媛副处长的大力支持推进。再次要感谢中译出版社的各位编辑。本书撰写于2015年，由于电子商务正处于飞速发展时期，更新变化较快，加之作者水平所限，难免有疏漏和不足之处，敬请广大读者批评指正。

华 迎

2018 年 10 月 26 日

PREFACE

The combination of commerce and the Internet has given birth to a new business model in the information age: electronic commerce. In recent years, with the rapid development of Internet and information technology, the global e-commerce has entered the stage of large-scale development. E-commerce has penetrated into all aspects of social life, covering all fields and industries, and has become the key driving force of global economic growth and integration. China's e-commerce started in the 1990s, and began to enter the stage of rapid development in 2006. Since 2010, it has developed even more rapidly. Now, China has become the world's largest e-commerce country, whose market share of e-commerce accounts for 40% of the global, and whose development model is extraordinarily of representative. As one of the business series that helps readers oversea and foreign friends living in China understand quickly the environment and mode of operation of China's e-commerce industry, this book presents the development and characteristics of e-commerce in China to readers in an easy-to-understand manner, and vividly leads the reader as the "buyer" and the "seller" respectively to experience the transaction flow and usage method of the typical e-commerce websites in China, providing help and guidance for readers to quickly understand and carry out e-commerce exploration.

The book is completed successfully and gratitude should be offered to friends and colleagues for their concern, help and support in this process. First of all, I would like to thank the students from University of International Business and Economics who participated in the collection and writing of the first draft of this book. Secondly, I would like to thank Han Hong, director of Institute of International Business Chinese Education and Resources Development, Li Rongrong, and Huo Yuan, deputy director of the Office of International Cooperation and Exchange, for their strong support and promotion. This book was written in 2015 and due to the rapid development of e-commerce, the fast update in the field and my limited professional knowledge, there are inevitably omissions and deficiencies which I respectfully ask the readers to criticize and correct.

Hua Ying
26th October, 2018

目录

第一章 / 001
第一节　中国电子商务背景介绍　/ 001
第二节　初步了解本书框架　/ 008

第二章 / 011
第一节　你准备好了么？/ 011
第二节　你要买什么？/ 023

第三章 / 047
第一节　先比价，再下单　/ 047
第二节　终于到付款啦　/ 064

第四章 / 082
第一节　等待，再等待　/ 082
第二节　我要退换货！/ 088
第三节　确认收货和评价　/ 094

第五章 / 102

第一节　开店构思　/ 103

第二节　开店申请　/ 114

第三节　网店商品展示　/ 121

第四节　营销推广　/ 130

第六章 / 137

第一节　做好"抓住"顾客的售前服务　/ 137

第二节　买卖做起来！/ 147

第三节　评价投诉那些事儿　/ 158

第四节　打造贴心的售后服务　/ 165

CONTENTS

Chapter 1 / 175
1.1 Background of China's E-commerce / 175
1.2 The Framework of This Book / 182

Chapter 2 / 185
2.1 Are You Ready? / 185
2.2 What Do You Want to Buy? / 197

Chapter 3 / 222
3.1 Compare Prices, Then Order / 222
3.2 To Pay Finally / 239

Chapter 4 / 257
4.1 Wait and Wait / 257
4.2 I Want to Return It! / 263
4.3 Confirm Receipt & Evaluate / 269

Chapter 5 / 277
5.1 Conceiving / 278
5.2 Application for Opening a Shop / 289
5.3 Displaying Products / 296
5.4 Marketing and Promotion / 305

Chapter 6   / 313

6.1   "Attract" Customers Through Good Pre-service   / 313

6.2   Do Business!   / 324

6.3   Evaluating Complaints   / 336

6.4   Provide Considerate After-sale Service   / 344

第一章

第一节　中国电子商务背景介绍

在这一节中，你将……
- ✓ 了解中国电子商务的发展情况
- ✓ 了解中国网络购物的发展情况
- ✓ 了解中国电子商务未来发展趋势

谈及"电子商务"，你一定不会感觉到陌生。随着互联网的飞速发展，各类电子商务网站层出不穷，模式也逐渐多样化，电子商务已经渗透进了我们生活的方方面面。相信生活在互联网浪潮中的你，扳起手指头随口就能说出几个国际性电子商务网站的名字：亚马逊，eBay，阿里巴巴……

在中国，电子商务在人们生活中的渗透更为明显：零食、衣物、包包、化妆品、家居用品等等直接上购物网站就能买到，订外卖也有专门的O2O（在线—离线服务）外卖平台。出门只带了手机而没有带钱包，没关系，手机支付可以解决你日常生活中遇到的绝大多数付款问题。出门旅游，路线规划、机票住宿，还在不停地查阅资料？还在打电话咨询售票点？那你就out啦，在线旅游网站分分钟解决你的旅游出行问题。部分海外大牌商品在中国国内买不到？这也不是件难事，如今有各类全球购网站前来助阵，全球各国商品将以最快的时间送达到你的手中……中国电子商务正以难以想象的强劲势头飞速发展着。不信？请跟着我们往下看。

中国电子商务发展现状知多少

中国的电子商务起步于二十世纪九十年代，2006年开始崛起并进入高速发展阶段。自2010年起中国电子商务进入了新元年，尤其是2014年9月阿里巴巴在纽交所的上市，更是让全世界都知道了阿里巴巴的名字，见证了中国电子商务发展的生命力。

据艾瑞咨询发布的报告显示，2014年中国电子商务市场交易规模达12.3万亿元人民币（下同），同比增长21.3%；其中，B2B电子商务市场占比超七成，网络购物占比超两成，网络购物占比有明显提升；中小企业B2B电商市场营收增长超三成；网络购物年度线上渗透率首次突破10%；移动购物市场规模增速超200%。[1]

2011年至今，中国电子商务交易规模逐年增大，且增长率相对稳定，在未来几年内，将继续保持良好的势头平稳快速增长，中国电子商务的发展是极具潜力的。

图1-1-1[2]

---

[1] 数据来源：艾瑞咨询
[2] 图片来源：艾瑞咨询

艾瑞咨询报告分析认为，中国电子商务市场细分领域中，移动购物市场发展迅速，未来几年将保持48%的复合增长率，成为网络购物市场快速发展的主要推动力。此外，在线旅游和O2O未来几年也将保持20%以上的复合增长率，发展快速。其中，移动购物和O2O将成为未来几年电子商务市场中发展最快的细分领域。[1]

中国电子商务主要细分市场未来发展预期

大类别	小类别	2014年规模（亿元）	2018年规模（亿元）	CAGR（2014-2018年）
B2B电子商务	中小企业B2B电子商务	61358.6	116627.3	17.4%
	规模以上企业B2B电子商务	28782.6	42140.1	10.0%
网络购物	网络购物（移动+PC）	28145.1	73000.0	26.9%
	移动网络购物	9297.1	45039.7	48.4%
	PC网络购物	18848.0	27960.7	10.4%
在线旅游	在线机票	1607.3	3250.0	19.2%
	在线酒店	636.1	1620.0	26.3%
	在线度假	426.5	1286.7	31.8%
O2O	餐饮O2O	941.9	2127.3	22.6%
	休闲娱乐O2O	660.0	1521.5	23.2%
	婚庆O2O	45.2	227.1	49.7%
	亲子O2O	55.7	135.9	25.0%
	美容美护O2O	54.1	88.7	13.2%

来源：综合企业财报和专家访谈，根据艾瑞统计模型核算。
©2015.1 iResearch Inc.　　　　　　　　　　　　www.iresearch.com.cn

图1-1-2[2]

网上购物——生活在中国必备的技能之一

你若生活在中国，那么你一定会与电子商务亲密接触的，其中，与你接触最频繁的一定非网上购物莫属了。中国人喜欢在网上买各种各样的东西，可以

---

[1] 资料来源：钛媒体
[2] 图片来源：艾瑞咨询

说，只有你想不到的，没有网上买不到的。很神奇吧，所以如果你生活在中国却不懂网上购物，那可就有点跟不上时尚潮流了。

中国的网上购物风潮究竟有多盛行呢？我们用数据来说话。

艾瑞咨询发布的报告显示，2014年中国网络购物市场交易规模达到2.8万亿元，增长48.7%，仍然维持在较高的增长水平。根据国家统计局2014年全年社会消费品零售总额数据，2014年，网络购物交易额大致相当于社会消费品零售总额的10.7%，年度线上渗透率首次突破10%。报告分析认为，随着移动购物市场的飞速发展、典型电商企业向三四线城市甚至农村市场的扩张及国际化战略的布局，未来几年，中国网络购物市场仍将保持27%左右的复合增长率。[1]

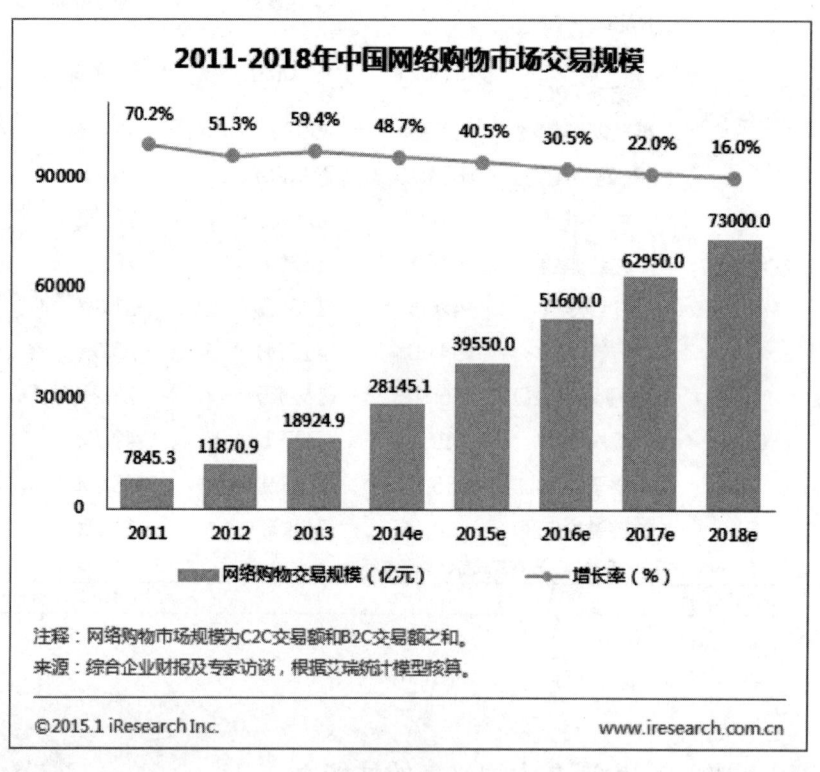

图1-1-3[2]

目前，中国的网络购物市场主要是C2C市场与B2C市场在平分天下。C2C市

---

[1] 资料来源：钛媒体
[2] 图片来源：艾瑞咨询

场体量大，产品品类齐全，在满足网购用户差异化及个性化需求方面有一定优势，未来仍将维持稳定增长。相较于 C2C 市场发展的稳定、中小企业或个人商家成长空间的有限，B2C 市场中有众多国内外品牌商／制造商企业进入，存在较多的市场机会，未来也将有较大的发展空间。从消费者方面看，随着网络购物的逐步发展与成熟，网络购物用户的消费观念逐渐发生改变，对商品品质的诉求不断提升，与 C2C 相比，B2C 在信誉和质量保障方面更能满足网络购物用户的消费诉求。[1] 所以，在产品品质及服务水平逐渐成为影响网络购物用户购买决策的重要因素的情况下，从整个宏观市场来看，B2C 市场在网络购物整体中的占比将持续提升。

以阿里巴巴为例，其旗下有诸多电子商务产品，淘宝网是 C2C 模式，而天猫是 B2C 模式。淘宝与天猫都会是你在中国最常用的购物网站，其使用流程我们将在后面的章节中做具体的介绍。除了淘宝与天猫以外，中国人常用的购物网站还包括京东、1 号店、聚美优品等等。

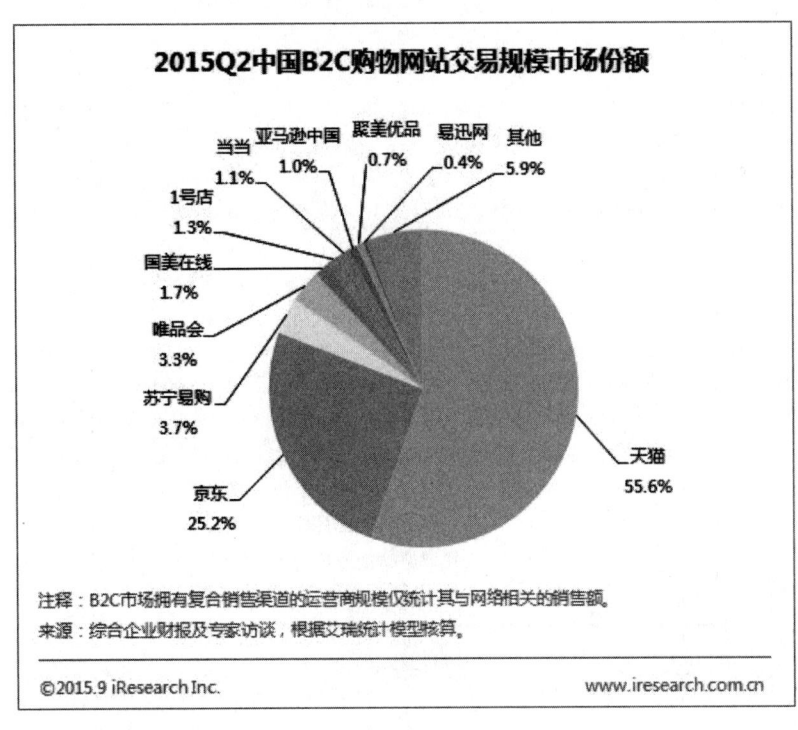

图 1-1-4[2]

[1] 资料来源：艾瑞咨询《2014 年中国电子商务行业年度检测报告简版》
[2] 图片来源：艾瑞咨询

从 2015 年二季度网络购物 B2C 市场看，天猫市场份额占比为 55.6%，京东占比超过 25%。（见图 1-1-4）其余 B2C 企业中苏宁易购、唯品会的同比增速均高于 B2C 市场整体增速。从自主销售为主 B2C 市场来看，京东占比接近 60%，苏宁易购、唯品会占比近 10%，其他项中小米手机官网继续保持平稳快速增长。[1]

从市场份额中我们可以看出，在网络购物 B2C 市场中占有不可撼动地位的仍旧是阿里巴巴集团旗下的天猫。

随着近些年跨境电商的兴起以及本土极具经验的电商巨头的创新开拓，中国网络购物市场交易规模正逐渐扩大，大有远超美国的猛烈势头。艾瑞数据显示，2013 年中国网络购物市场交易规模 18409.5 亿元，同期美国网购市场交易规模 15997.9 亿元。（见图 1-1-5）2013 年中国移动网购市场交易规模 1696.3 亿元，美国移动网购交易规模 2559.7 亿元，预计 2015 年中国移动网购市场将超过美国。[2]

图 1-1-5[3]

---

[1] 资料来源：钛媒体
[2] 资料来源：艾瑞咨询《2014年中国电子商务行业年度检测报告简版》
[3] 图片来源：艾瑞咨询

展望中国电子商务未来发展趋势

趋势一：跨境电商发展机遇

经过几年的沉淀发展，中国跨境电商已逐渐形成一条涵盖营销、支付、物流和金融服务的完整产业链，行业格局日渐稳固。政府也从政策层面对跨境电商提供支持，除了出台一系列跨境电商利好政策，还先后批准上海、重庆、杭州等十几个城市成为跨境电商试点城市，在政府政策的大力支持及全球电商快速发展和中国电商全球化的大趋势下，中国跨境电商将会迎来高速发展时期。

趋势二：移动电商市场潜力巨大。其中移动购物将推动网络购物市场快速发展，在线旅游和O2O发展迅速

艾瑞咨询发布的报告分析认为，中国电子商务市场细分领域中，移动购物市场发展迅速，未来几年将保持48%的复合增长率，成为网络购物市场快速发展的主要推动力；此外，在线旅游和O2O未来几年也将保持20%以上的复合增长率，发展快速。其中移动购物和O2O将成为未来几年电子商务市场中发展最快的细分领域。[1]

趋势三：不同类型增值服务的份额会越来越大，成为B2B平台未来的营收重点

由于B2B在线交易的单笔交易额相对较大、支付安全有待提升、用户在线交易习惯仍需继续培育等原因，并非所有企业都接受在线交易形式；因此，支付、担保、认证、供应商贷款等一系列服务未来还有待进一步完善，企业用户在线交易习惯也有待深入培养。总体而言，会员费、交易佣金、广告费、增值服务费等短期内仍会是中小企业B2B电子商务平台的主要盈利方式，而不同类型增值服务的份额会越来越大，成为B2B平台未来的营收重点，并且成为企业竞争的核心优势。[2]

总结

- 中国电子商务发展情况

中国电子商务起步于二十世纪九十年代，2006年开始崛起并进入高速发展阶段。

---

[1] 资料来源：钛媒体
[2] 资料来源：钛媒体

当前，B2B 电子商务市场占比最大。

2011 年至今，中国电子商务交易规模逐年增大，且增长率相对稳定，在未来几年内，其将继续保持良好的势头平稳快速增长，中国电子商务的发展是极具潜力的。

- 中国网络购物发展情况

中国网络购物市场交易规模逐年增大，随着移动购物的持续发展，中国网络购物市场发展空间与潜力是巨大的。

B2C 市场占比越来越大，其中天猫仍旧占据网络购物 B2C 市场的领军地位。中国网络购物市场规模将超越美国。

- 中国电子商务未来发展趋势

趋势一：跨境电商发展机遇。

趋势二：移动电商市场潜力巨大。其中移动购物将推动网络购物市场快速发展，在线旅游和 O2O 发展迅速。

趋势三：不同类型增值服务的份额会越来越大，成为 B2B 平台未来的营收重点。

第二节　初步了解本书框架

在这一节中，你将……

✓ 了解本书框架

随着信息技术的高速发展和广泛应用，社会逐步信息化。在这样的信息化大潮中，商业与互联网的结合催生了信息时代新的商业形式——电子商务。中国电子商务起步于二十世纪九十年代，之后迅速发展，从 2006 年至今，电子商务保持着稳定的增长速度，像一股浪潮席卷了整个中国。

由于中国独特的社会经济环境，中国的电子商务也有自己的特色，为了帮助一些旅居中国的外国朋友了解中国的电子商务发展状况，我们以一些比较具有代表性的电子商务网站为例，介绍中国电子商务的使用方法和中国电子商务的一些特点。

本书分别以"买家"和"卖家"的身份视角出发，详细介绍了代表性网站的使用方法。

从第二章到第四章是"买家"部分，主要叙述在中国的电子商务网站以买家身份进行购买交易的主要流程和方法。

第二章——购物前，你必须要知道的事。在这一章中，我们分为两节，在第一节中介绍了在中国电子商务网站购物的一般性流程以及在开始正式购物之前所需做的一些准备。第二节中则叙述了中国典型电子商务网站的一些特点和适应性。这一章主要是带领着我们的读者入个门。

第三章——购买和付款。第三章是"买家"部分的主要重点，分为两小节，分别主要叙述"购买"和"付款"相关流程。在"购买"一节中，我们从商品的挑选到与卖家沟通到最后的下单都进行了详细的介绍，还提出了贴心的小提示。在"付款"一章中，针对中国与国外不同的支付特点，我们也特别进行了介绍。阅读第三章，你可以了解到网上购物的主要流程，作为"买家"，不可错过。

第四章——售后问题全解读。这一部分，主要是对于下单后，物流查询、收货退货相关环节的一些介绍。良好的购物体验与良好的售后服务密不可分，如果在下单后有什么疑问，一定要记得参考第四章。

第五章和第六章是"卖家"部分，主要叙述在中国的电子商务网站以卖家的身份进行交易活动的方法。

第五章主要是讲述了开店前所需的准备事项，从构想店铺理念，到申请店铺，开业后如何上新并进行营销和推广，在这一章都有介绍。

第六章则开始关注店铺建立起来后，进一步的扩张推广。如何营销吸引更多的顾客，如何提供贴心的服务，如何完善售后保留住更多的回头客，都是在这一章将要叙述的内容。

整本书至此，大致结束。

◆ **总结**

在这一章中，主要分为两节。

在第一节中,我们概述了中国电子商务的发展状况,总体上介绍了中国电子商务的特点。

第二节对全书的内容进行了梳理和概括,帮助读者了解全书的脉络内容。

第二章

第一节　你准备好了么？

在这一节中，你将……
- ✓ 了解网上购物前需要准备哪些东西
- ✓ 了解怎样准备这些东西
- ✓ 了解中国网络购物流程

约翰是一名来自美国的留学生，今年刚来到中国 A 大学就读，需要置办一些学习和生活用品。由于人生地不熟，他只好求助相邻的中国学生李军。李军告诉他，在中国，电子商务非常方便，而且及时可靠，几乎所有东西都可以通过互联网购买。可是约翰是个网络购物（以下简称"网购"）新手，不了解中国的网购流程和所需准备工作。那么，网上购物前究竟需要准备些什么呢？在中国网络购物的流程又是什么样的呢？下面就让我们一起了解一下吧。

你需要的硬件设施

- 电子设备（台式电脑、智能手机或平板电脑）

你可以通过电子设备上的浏览器来访问购物网站。或者，你也可以在智能手机或平板上下载安装 APP（一般大型的购物网站都推出了可在移动设备上运行的客户端应用），通过 APP 来访问购物网站。

- 互联网

当然了，进行网上购物需要你将电子设备接入到互联网中。如果你想使用移动设备，最好通过 Wi-Fi（无线网络）连接到互联网，或者使用移动运营商提供的3G/4G网络（比较耗费流量）。

- 支付工具

一张开通网上银行服务的中国银行卡

虽然现在很多网上购物平台都支持货到付款，但大部分的网上交易还是需要在线支付，所以为了减少不必要的麻烦，一张开通了网上银行服务的银行卡是必不可少的。首先，你需要携带个人身份证件（如护照），去中国境内的银行网点申办一张银行卡，银行卡可以分为储蓄卡（借记卡）和信用卡。对于网购来说，一张储蓄卡必不可少。办好或你已经持有中国发卡行提供的银行卡，开通网上银行业务比较方便快捷，只需要携带身份证件在银行柜台填写一些申请表格即可。如果习惯使用信用卡进行网上支付，则需在银行柜台申办信用卡，由于信用卡的申请有一定的条件限制，所以最好事先致电银行客服进行电话咨询。

与MASTER与VISA类似，China Unionpay中国银联是一个银行卡联合组织，它联合了中国的各家银行制定行业标准加强合作，为消费者提供方便。

在中国生活，一张银联卡是必不可少的，它会减少生活中许多的不便。现在银联也已走向世界，当你离开中国，在世界上150多个国家也是可以使用的。

目前基本在中国的任何一家银行都可以办理银联卡，不知道你有没有听说过"工农中建"四大银行。这是中国老百姓们比较熟悉的几家主要的大银行，如果对中国银行不了解，就从中选择一家好了。

- 国际信用卡

目前中国电子商务网站上的部分交易，可以使用国际信用卡（如 Visa, MasterCard, Discover, JCB 等）进行支付，所以如果你已经持有国际信用卡，则可在这类网站直接支付。

以中国最大的购物网站——淘宝网为例，目前淘宝网平台实物类商品交易可使用全球（除美国华盛顿州）发卡机构发行的 Visa/MasterCard/JCB 卡支付，但买家需支付 3% 的手续费；而且仅支持个人类型的银行卡，不支持公司类型的银行卡。其他购物网站对国际信用卡也有不同程度的支持，具体内容可以从网站说明中获得，这里就不一一列出了。

使用网上银行的一些注意事项

1. 谨防钓鱼网站。其实，真正由于银行安全漏洞造成钱财失窃的事情是少数，更多的人是因为上了钓鱼网站的当才不幸中招。当我们打开银行首页时，可以将正确的网址收藏起来，避免通过"超链接"进入到虚假银行系统。

2. 保护好网上银行登录账号和密码。

3. 定期查询交易明细。

4. 使用杀毒软件。将电脑的防火墙设置到高级别，及时升级杀毒软件，避免"网银大盗"的入侵。

使用国际信用卡支付的具体内容，详见第三章第二节。

你需要的软件设施

- 试着开通一个第三方支付账号吧！

第三方支付，是具备一定实力和信誉保障的第三方独立机构，采用与国内外各大银行签约的方式，借助银行卡等卡基支付工具或虚拟账户、虚拟货币等网上支付工具，提供与银行支付结算系统衔接的交易支持平台[1]。在通过第三方

---

[1] 《中国第三方支付产业市场前瞻与投资战略规划分析报告》。

支付平台的交易中,买方选购商品后,使用第三方平台提供的账户进行货款支付,由第三方通知卖家货款到达、进行发货;买方检验物品后,就可以通知付款给卖家,第三方再将款项转至卖家账户。因为第三方支付平台集成了很多家银行,所以比较常用的第三方支付平台的应用范围很广。在中国,人们最常用的第三方支付平台是支付宝,类似于国外的 Paypal。所以下面就以支付宝为例,介绍注册开通第三方支付账号的步骤。

在浏览器地址栏输入 https://www.alipay.com 进入支付宝首页。

图2-1-1

点击页面右上方"免费注册",根据提示,输入信息,进行新用户注册。

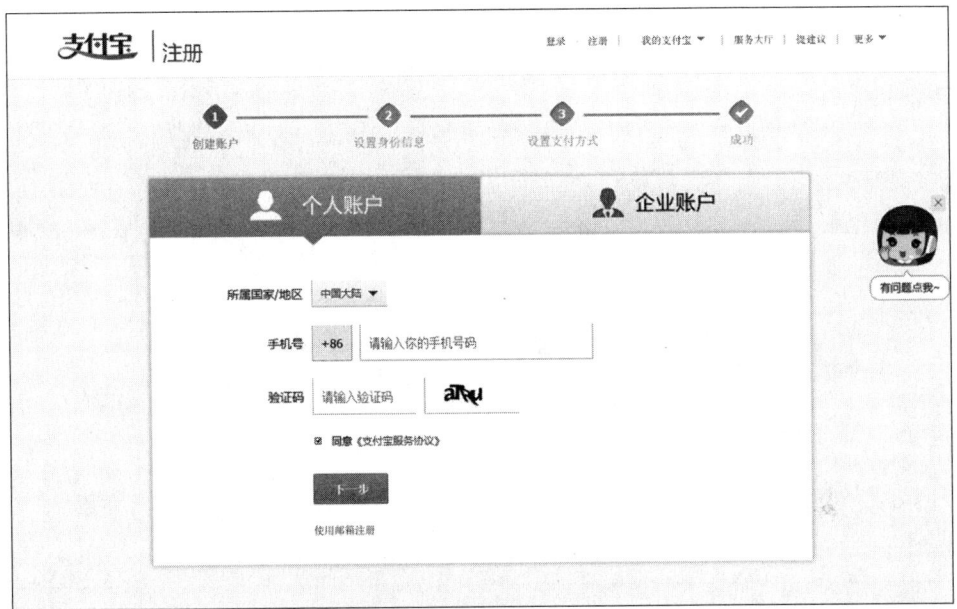

图2-1-2

注册可选择邮箱注册或者手机注册。手机注册需要输入手机短信验证码:

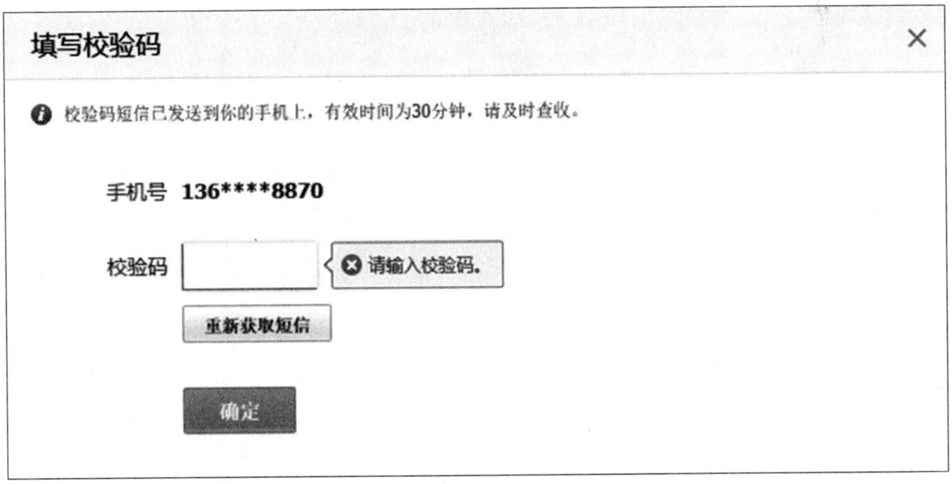

图2-1-3

邮箱注册需要验证邮箱：

图2-1-4

此后只需要继续设置自己的账户信息就可以完成注册了。

注意事项

1. 一定要记清自己的支付宝支付密码和登录密码，如果将它们记错，付款的时候很可能会出现层出不穷的麻烦。如果实在害怕记混，可以考虑把两个密码设置成相同的。

2. 使用第三方账号要注意安全。如果推荐你安装安全数字证书，一定要安装，它可以保护你在一台PC机上的支付安全，避免密码被盗用。如果不是必要，还是不要在账户里放太多钱，这样即使丢了也不会造成太大的损失。

- 与卖家沟通的桥梁——阿里旺旺

我们在浏览商品时可能会有一些问题需要询问卖家，因此，在进行网购时，我们还需要一个能与卖家进行实时交流的工具。不同的购物网站用不同的方式解决这一问题，有的使用网页客服，有的提供QQ账号。其中，阿里旺旺是淘宝提供的免费网上商务沟通软件。在淘宝网、天猫商城购物时，你可以使用阿里旺旺与卖家沟通（如咨询商品信息、讨价还价、商量运费等）。同时，阿里旺旺上面的聊天记录也是你发起投诉或维权时的有效法律依据。

关于阿里旺旺的使用，详见第三章第一节。

好了，以上就是你开启网购新世界所需的主要装备啦。从一个可以进行网购的设备开始，连上互联网，准备好支付的银行卡与软件，你就可以真正开始网购了！

不过，在此之前，你可以先简略地看看在中国网购的主要流程。

简单了解一下中国网购的流程

在中国，有许多提供网上购物服务的网站，虽然它们服务的侧重点略有不同，但主要购物流程都大同小异。网购的主要流程可以概括为：注册——登录网站——查找想买的商品——挑选自己心仪的商品——加入购物车——提交订单并付款——追踪物流信息——确认收货——评价。

下面将以日常使用最多的淘宝网为例，进行说明。

- 注册及登录网站

在浏览器地址栏输入 www.taobao.com，进入淘宝网首页。

图2-1-5

淘宝网首页内容五花八门，是不是觉得注册的地方特别难找呢？其实它就在页面的左上方。点击"免费注册"，根据提示输入信息就可以进行新用户注册了。

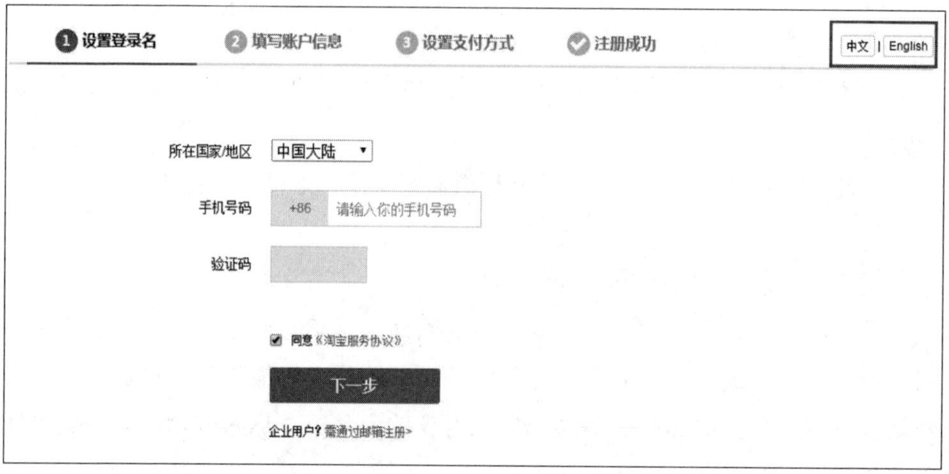

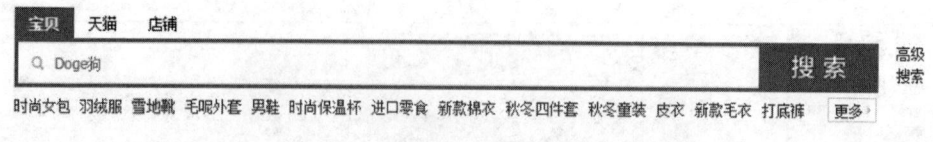

图2-1-6

 注册页面的右上角有中英文的切换，如果你不习惯中文页面，那么就切换至英文注册页面吧。

- 查找想买的商品

淘宝网主页的正上方有一个搜索栏，你可以在搜索栏中输入任何你想要购买的商品，当然，如果你是某个淘宝店铺或者品牌的忠实粉丝，你也可以在搜索栏里查找相应的店铺。

图2-1-7

- 挑选自己心仪的商品

使用搜索栏搜索自己想要的商品后，淘宝网就会将搜索结果页面呈现给你。

在搜索结果页面中，如果你觉得搜索结果太多眼花缭乱了，那么你可以选择例如品牌等条件来进行进一步的筛选，也可以对当前的搜索结果按不同条件进行排序。

当你在搜索结果页面中有看见满意的商品时，就毫不犹豫地点击图片或者文字链接去看一看关于该商品的详细介绍吧。

• 加入购物车

如果你浏览完商品的详细信息后决定购买，你只需要继续选择你想要的颜色、款式、数量等，点击"立即购买"即可进入支付页面。如果你还想继续浏览其他商品，则需点击"加入购物车"将该商品加入购物车，然后继续选择其他商品最后一起下订单。

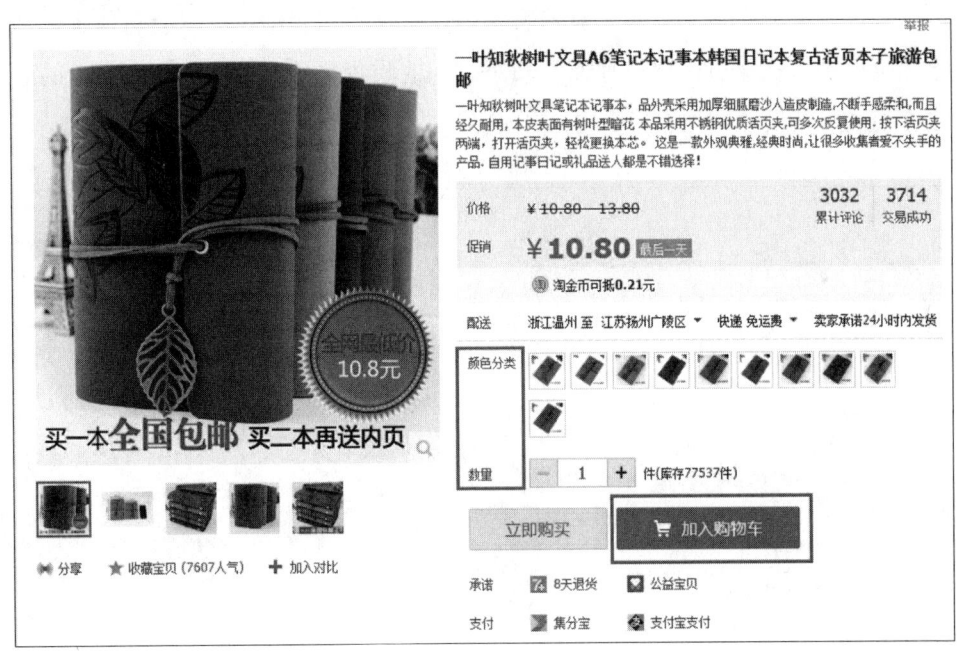

图2-1-8

• 提交订单并付款

如果现在你已经选好了想买的商品，那么就点击网页右上方的"购物车"进行商品的结算和付款吧。

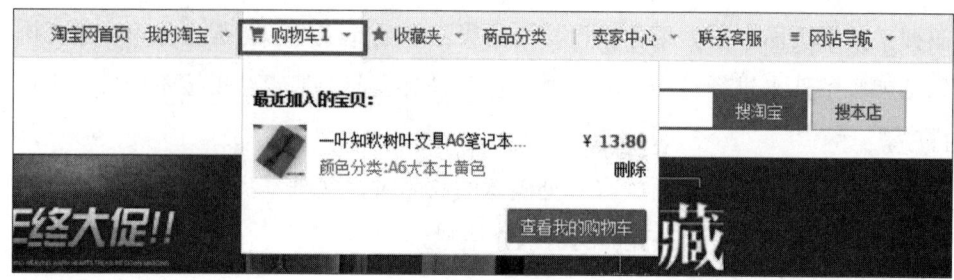

图2-1-9

你所有加入购物车的心仪商品现在全都排列在购物车页面啦。如果你发现，"哎呀，我一下子加入的东西太多了"或者"最近手头有点紧，有些东西还是不要买了"，那么在购物车页面中你可以将不想要的商品删除掉；如果你打算将它们全部都收入囊中，那就不要犹豫直接结算吧。点击"结算"就会出现确认订单的页面了。在该页面中，你需要填写详细的收货地址，这样你心心念念的商品才会准确无误地到达你的手中。

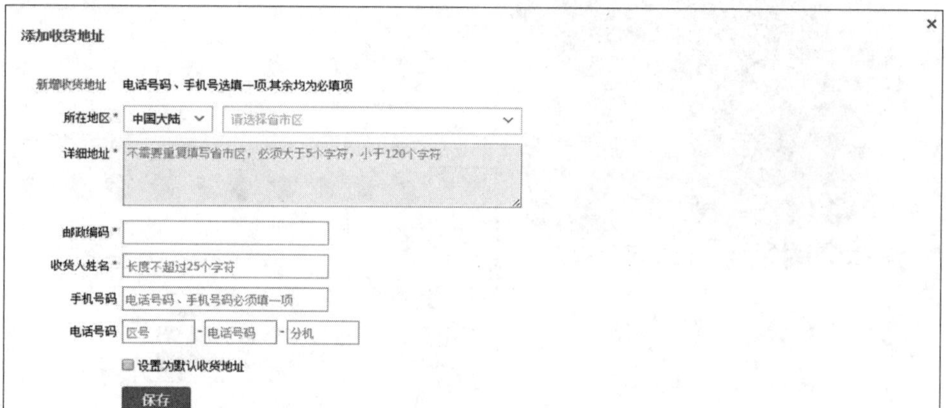

图2-1-10

填写好你的收货地址并且确认好相应的商品信息后，你就可以提交订单了。提交订单后，淘宝网会自动连接到支付宝付款页面。如果没有直接进入到付款页面又或者是你不小心关闭了付款页面，那也不用担心，只需要点击网站页面右上方"我的淘宝"——"已买到的宝贝"则可进入到你已经提交的所有订单的页面。

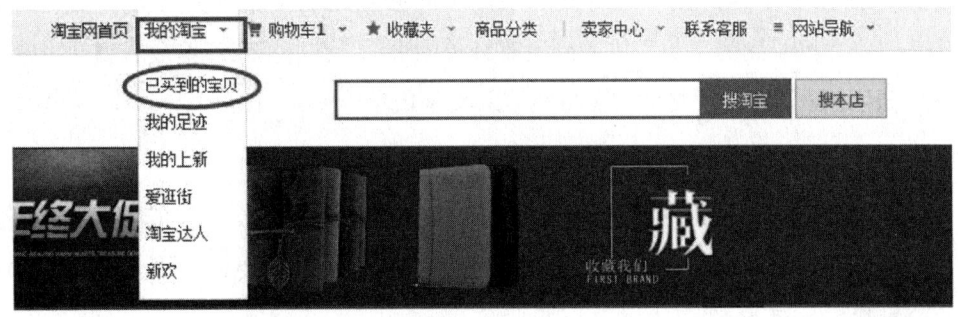

图2-1-11

只要点击订单最右侧的"立即付款"就可以进入到付款页面了。

图2-1-12

- 追踪物流信息

商品购买完毕，剩下的就是焦急等待商品送货上门的过程了。在这一过程中，你一定很想知道你的商品被运送到哪儿又是否离自己更进一步了吧？此时，只要点击网站页面右上方"我的淘宝"——"已买到的宝贝"进入到所有订单的页面，点击相应订单右侧的"查看物流"就可以轻松便捷地查看商品的物流信息。

- 确认收货及评价

焦急等待多天的商品终于到手了，仔细检查一下发现没有什么大问题，也和自己的预想基本一致，这时候登录淘宝网并且点击网站页面上方"我的淘宝"——"已买到的宝贝"进入到所有订单的页面，点击相应订单最右侧的"确认收货"，操作成功后支付宝会将钱汇入卖家账户。

在没有收到商品之前，或者你在收到商品之后有打算退换商品的想法，记得千万不要去点"确认收货"按钮，不然你就钱货两空了。

如果你收到商品后过于兴奋以至于将确认收货这件事抛到九霄云外了，也不用担心，在一定天数之后，淘宝网系统会自动确认收货。

确认收货完毕，你可以对购买的商品进行满意与否的评价。至此，你在淘宝网的购物就圆满画上句号了。

看了这么多，是不是觉得有点复杂又难以记住呢？没关系，本部分只是希望你对网购的流程有个初步的认识。在后面的章节里，你将会详细地了解到上述网购流程中的每一步具体操作以及尚未提到的退换货流程的操作。相信通过后面的讲述，你会成功地由一个网购新手蜕变成一个网购达人的。

总结

- 网购前需要准备的东西

硬件设施：电子设备（电脑、智能手机或平板）、互联网、支付工具

软件设施：拥有第三方支付的账号、阿里旺旺

- 网购的主要流程

注册——登录网站——查找想买的商品——挑选自己心仪的商品——加入购物车——提交订单并付款——追踪物流信息——确认收货——评价。

第二节 你要买什么?

在这一节中,你将……
- ✓ 了解从中国电子商务网站上能买什么
- ✓ 了解中国典型电子商务网站的特点和类别

约翰在了解到在中国网购需要的设施之后,一一地进行了准备。电脑、网络、银行卡等都已备好,就等着在网上"血拼(shopping)"一番。但是,他看着自己长长的购物清单,却一下子犯了难。室友们今天拖进来一个"1号店"的大箱子,里面都是吃的,明天又抱进来一个箱子写着"聚美优品",里面都是护肤品;而他要买的东西这么多,吃穿用什么都需要,中国又好像有很多购物网站,页面都差不多,他中文又不好,浏览起来极费时间。快开学了,急用的东西到底要从哪里买呀?

你是不是也像约翰一样遇到了这种窘境,不知道不同商品在哪里买合适呢?下面,我们就来讲讲购物网站的选择问题。

中国人一般都从网上买什么

在了解中国人在网上买什么之前,我们先来看看中国人使用网络购物的状况。用数字来说,2014年,中国电子商务交易规模为3.19万亿元(超过了美国和全球平均水平),而其中"网上购物"占到了近30%。预计到2020年,中国电子商务交易规模将逼近50万亿元,有望成为全球第一大电子商务交易市场,其中网络零售交易额将超过10万亿元,占社会零售总额比重达到16.3%。[1] 同时,中国物流体系也在不断发展,尤其在北京、上海等资源丰富的一线城市,在某些大型购物网站上常常第一天下单,第二天货便可到家,甚至上午下单、

---

[1] 数据来源:《2014—2018年中国网络购物市场分析及前景预测报告》,No. 701670,2015年1月,中国报告大厅。

下午到货也是有可能的。

这些表明在中国网购可能比你想象中还要普及和便利,甚至可以说中国的电子商务文化已经开始渗透到中国城镇居民的日常生活中。一位全职太太说,以前,她的家人习惯于在每周末抽出一个晚上的时间,全家人一起开车去小区附近的大型超市进行采购,买回一周的消耗品。但是自从开始网上购物,小到食品保鲜袋、卫生卷纸,大到电饭锅、洗衣机,统统从网上买,第二天就能派上用场。家在天津的她还经常在网上给远在四川的老父亲买东西,直接寄送到父亲家里,这下就不用怕腿脚不方便的父亲自己去市场了。

所以说,中国人已经在网上买卖各种各样的东西了,你不用担忧东西能不能从网上买到,大型购物网站上的商品肯定比你家附近的小超市丰富。不信?我们可以看一下两家大型综合购物网站首页上的商品分类:

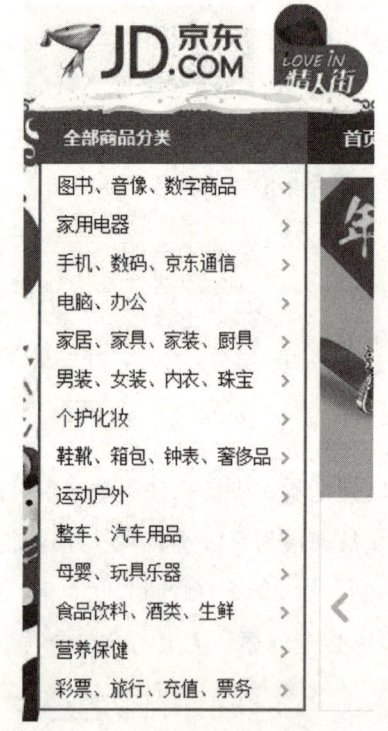
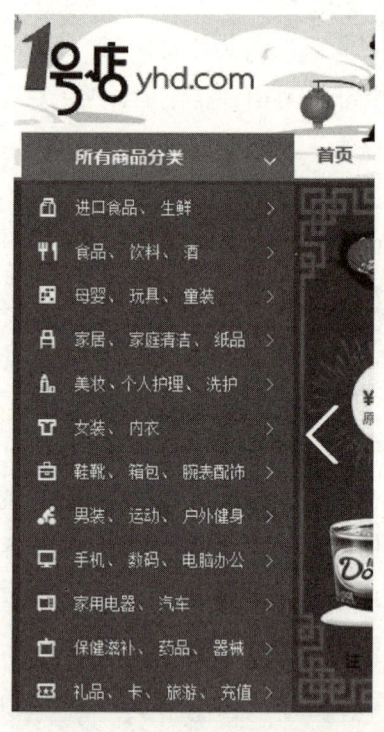

图2-2-1 京东商城的商品分类　　　图2-2-2 1号店的商品分类

怎么样?综合起来看,商品的覆盖范围够广泛吧?

当然,虽然他们都是综合性购物网站,但是根据主打售卖的商品不同有所侧重。提到购买电子设备和电器产品，我们一般都会去京东，而说到买吃的，我们第一反应是去1号店。这从上面两家网站商品分类的排序就可见一斑。

下面，我们就根据电子商务网站的一般分类以及你可能购买的商品类型，介绍几家中国典型的购物网站。

中国典型的电子商务网站

- B2C 类型

B2C 是电子商务的模式之一，它的全称是 Business to Customer，即商家（泛指企业）对消费者的电子商务模式。通俗地讲，就是商业零售，企业直接面向消费者销售产品和服务。B2C 是中国最早产生的电子商务模式，很多购物网站——网上综合商城、百货商店、垂直商店和品牌店——都属于 B2C 模式。下面介绍几家大型且常用的 B2C 网站。

➢ 囤点儿粮食，上"1号店"

1号店是国内首家网上超市，由戴尔公司前高管于刚和刘峻岭联合在上海张江高科技园区创立。2008年7月成立以来，凭着一个"比超市更便宜的网上超市"的想法，1号店持续保持高速的增长势头。2013年底，1号店已拥有5700万的注册用户，并拥有超过1500万的移动端注册用户。目前，它已成为国内最大的 B2C 食品电商。

1号店的网站地址为 http://www.yhd.com/。

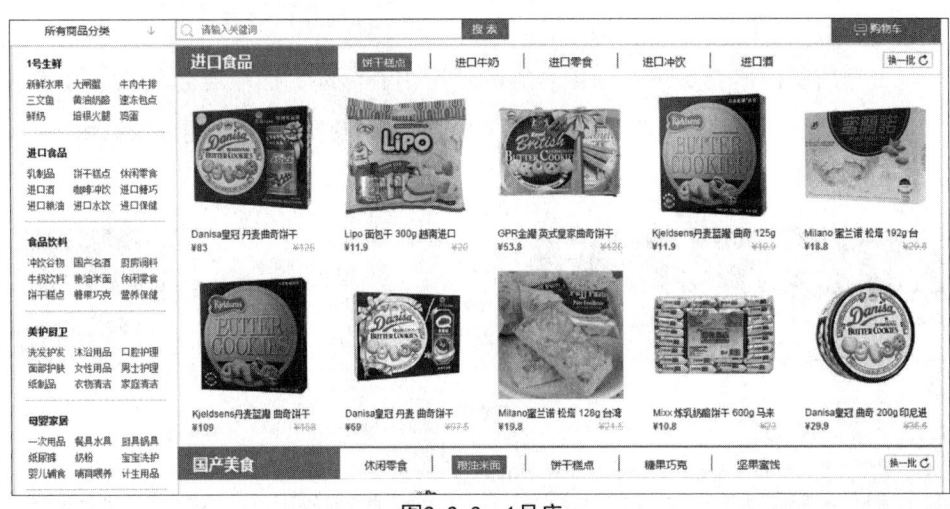

图2-2-3　1号店

在1号店上的购物流程和大多数电子商务网站差不多,在此不再赘述。

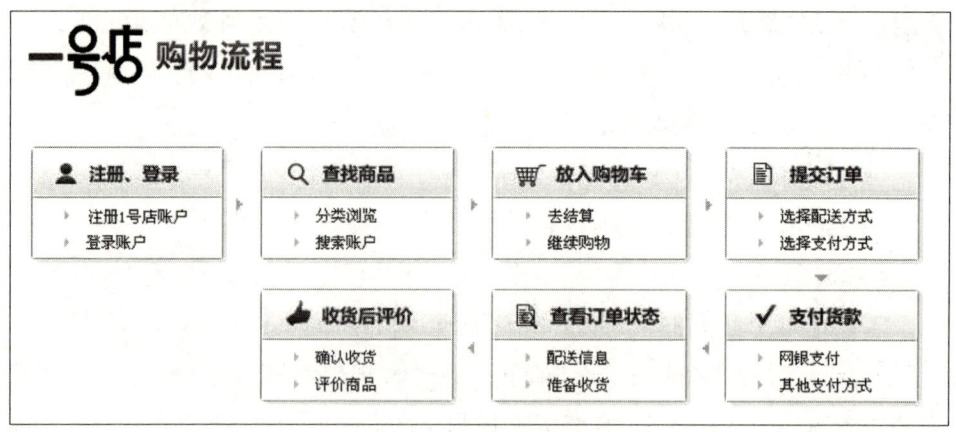

图2-2-4　1号店购物流程[1]

比较特别的是,1号店提供了如下几项服务:

定日达

订单在每日20:00前提交成功(在线支付需付款完成),顾客可选择当日起7天内的任意一天进行收货。

准时达[2]

订单在每日20:00前提交成功(在线支付需付款完成),顾客可选择当日起7天内的指定时段进行收货,最准可精确到1小时,1号店将保证在此时间段内为顾客送货上门。

试用中心

1号店的注册会员可参与1号店的试用中心活动。已注册会员从1号店网页右上方点击"网站导航",从下拉菜单栏中选择"0元试用",便进入试用中心。

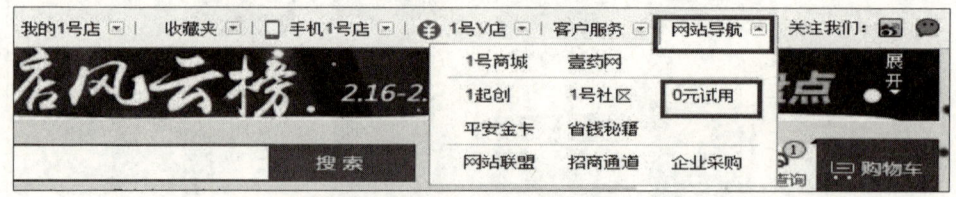

图2-2-5

---

[1] 图片来源:http://cms.yhd.com/cms/view.do?topicId=24091
[2] 定日达/准时达服务仅限1号店自配送区域,仅支持1号店自营商品的订单。服务说明详见http://cms.yhd.com/cms/view.do?topicId=24111

试用活动分为两种形式——"免费试用"和"付邮试用"。顾名思义,"免费试用"是指会员可以完全免费地获取试用品的活动,并免运费。活动期间,会员申请试用活动,在活动结束的10个工作日内从所有申请人中选出获得试用资格的一部分顾客,商家或者供应商发送试用品。通常,"免费试用"投放产品为精品正装,数量少,单价高。

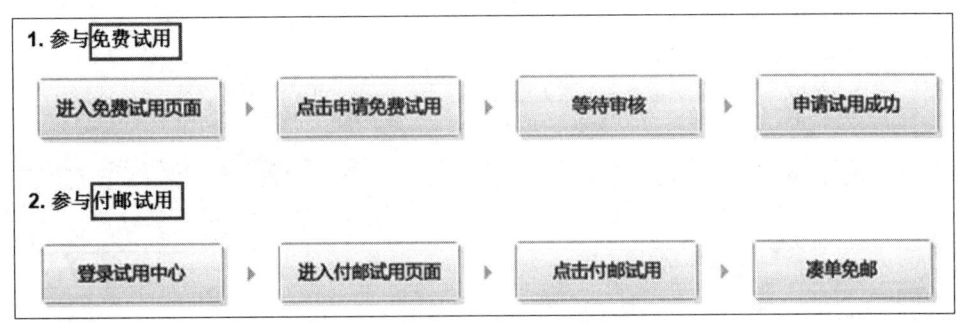

图2-2-6[1]

"付邮试用"是指顾客支付一定运费,0元领取商品的方式。但若顾客订单满足了一定规则,则随单获得试用品,不用额外支付运费。比如说,商家店铺满59免运费,顾客在该店铺买了60元商品,则可以随单领取该商家试用活动的商品,不用再支付运费。"付邮试用"投放产品为小样或者低单价正装,数量多,单价低。

在中国各大电子商务平台竞争如火如荼之时,诸如1号店提供的定日达、准时达、试用中心等众多花样百出的特色服务,可以说是这些电子商务平台招揽生意、扩大客源的"小心机"了。当然,我和你作为消费者,尽可"坐享渔翁之利",提升自己的购物体验!所以,下一次在1号店购物时,不要忘记享受这些特色服务了!

> 买数码产品、家用电器,上"京东"

京东是中国最大的自营式电商企业,2014年5月22日,京东在纳斯达克挂牌,成为仅次于阿里巴巴、腾讯、百度的中国第四大互联网上市公司。

---

[1] 图片来源:http://cms.yhd.com/cms/view.do?topicId=24170

作为一个综合的一站式购物平台，京东商城提供的网络零售服务覆盖范围广泛：计算机、手机及其他数码产品、家电、汽车配件、服装与鞋类、奢侈品、家居与家庭用品、化妆品与其他个人护理用品、食品与营养品、书籍与其他媒体产品、母婴用品与玩具、体育与健身器材以及虚拟商品等，共 13 大类 3150 万种 SKU[1] 的商品。

京东的网址为：http://www.jd.com/。

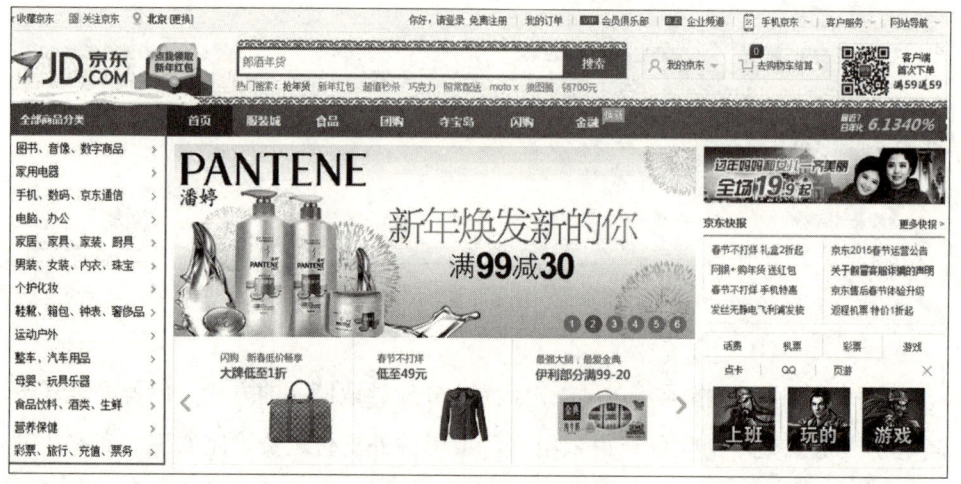

图2-2-7 京东商城

在中国消费者的心目中，在京东商城买电子产品、家用电器这些产品比较靠谱。针对家电数码产品，京东提供了正品保障以及相对完善的售后服务政策，比如，为大家电提供配送和上门安装，可申请返修和退换货等等。所以，与在实体店购买相比，在京东上购买，消费者权益并不会遭受损失。

---

[1] SKU=Stock Keeping Unit（库存量进出单位）。针对电商而言，SKU有另外的注解：SKU是指一款商品，每款都有出现一个SKU，便于电商品牌识别商品。一款商品多色，则是有多个SKU，例如一件衣服，有红色、白色、蓝色，则SKU编码也不相同，如相同则会出现混淆，发错货。

售后特色服务	
服务名称	具体描述
7天无理由退货	客户购买京东自营商品7日内（含7日，自客户收到商品之日起计算），在保证商品完好的前提下，可无理由退货。（部分商品除外，详情请见各商品细则）
售后上门取件	客户购买京东自营商品15日内（含15日，自客户收到商品之日起计算）因质量问题提交退换申请且审核通过，在京东自营配送范围内，京东提供免费上门取件服务。法定节假日、停电、天气等不可抗力情况除外。
售后100分	客户购买京东自营商品15日内（自客户收到商品之日起计算）如出现故障，京东售后服务部收到故障品并确认属于质量故障（以国家三包法等有关法律、法规为准）开始计时。在100分钟内（工作时间每周一至周五，上午9:00至12:00，下午13:00至18:00，法定节假日、停电等无法正常处理情况除外）处理完客户的售后问题，处理完的标志为已经为客户提交了换新订单、补发订单、补偿申请或者退款申请（通过邮政等退款要依赖于第三方退款平台服务速度）。注：如客户不同意以上解决方案，协商时间另计。如以上承诺京东未做到，除故障商品全额退款外再给予客户京东账户1000个京豆作为补偿。
售后到家	自商品售出一年内，如出现质量问题，京东将提供免费上门取送及原厂授权维修服务。 温馨提示： A. 售后到家服务仅针对部分指定商品，具体以客户下单订单详情为准； B. 此服务仅限京东自营商品（京东销售和配送）； C. 法定节假日、停电、天气等不可抗力情况除外。

注：
京东自营商品指在商品详情页明确标识为"京东发货并提供售后服务"的商品，此外为第三方卖家商品。

图2-2-8　京东商城售后特色服务[1]

> 买图书，上"当当网"

当当网成立于1999年11月，以图书零售起家，已发展成为领先的在线零售商：中国最大图书零售商、高速增长的百货业务和第三方招商平台。当当网于2010年12月8日在纽约证券交易所正式挂牌上市，是中国第一家完全基于线上业务、在美国上市的B2C网上商城。

在图书品类，当当网占据了线上市场份额的50%以上，同时占据全国图书零售市场份额的三分之一。当当网的图书订单转化率高达25%，远远高于行业7%的平均值，这意味着每四个人浏览当当网，就会产生一个订单。

当当网地址为：http://www.dangdang.com/。

---

[1]　图片来源：http://help.jd.com/help/question-149.html#help1710

图2-2-9 当当图书

➢ 专业美妆护肤品，去"聚美优品"和"乐蜂网"

聚美优品是一家化妆品限时特卖商城，由陈欧、戴雨森等创立于2010年3月，本质上是一家垂直行业的B2C网站。2014年5月16日，聚美优品在纽约证券交易所正式挂牌上市，成为中国首个赴美上市的垂直化妆品电商[1]。

聚美优品的网址为http://www.jumei.com/。

图2-2-10 聚美优品

---

[1] 垂直电商：垂直电子商务是指在某一个行业或细分市场深化运营的电子商务模式。垂直电子商务网站旗下商品都是同一类型的产品。

聚美优品坚持从品牌厂家、正规代理商、国内外专柜等进货渠道采购商品，它提供的正品保障，在一定程度上会打消你在网上购买化妆品的疑虑，争取消费者的信任。2013年底，聚美优品首家线下旗舰店开业，开创了中国垂直美妆类B2C正式布局O2O（Online to Offline：线上到线下）的先例。其CEO陈欧解释道："因为电子商务开设门槛太低，消费者对于线上化妆品有种天然的不信任，选择此时切入线下，将有利于解决消费者信任的问题。"

目前，聚美优品正在着力发展"海外购"，主要以日韩化妆品为主，欧美品牌为辅。具体说来，通过行邮保税模式，聚美将在国外采购的货品备至郑州保税区，然后再进行质检和销售。在价格上，化妆品类较高的行邮税[1]由聚美承担。因此，对顾客来说，聚美提供的价格接近于免税店。所以在中国想要以更实惠的价格买到海外品牌化妆品的你，可以考虑聚美优品的"极速免税店"哦！

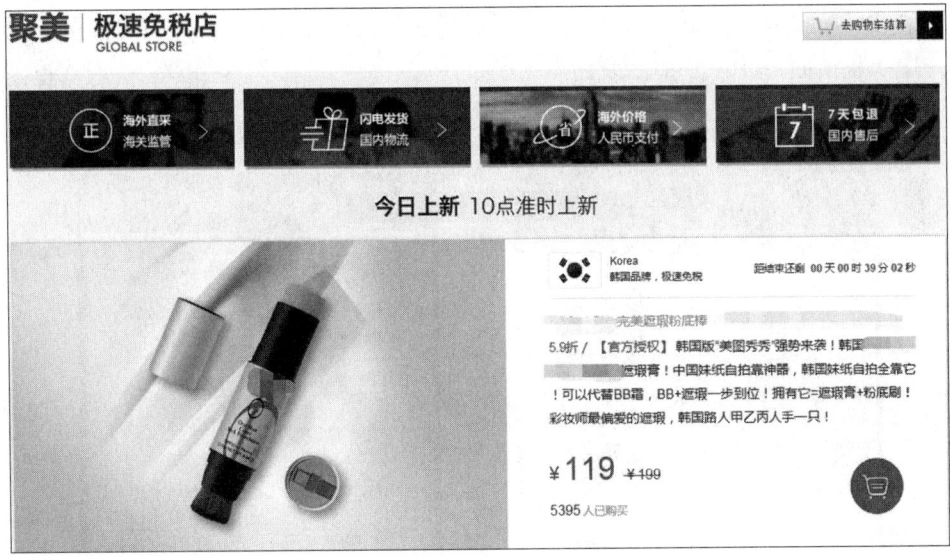

图2-2-11　聚美优品"极速免税店"

---

[1] 行邮税是行李和邮递物品进口税的简称，是海关对入境旅客行李物品和个人邮递物品征收的进口税。《中华人民共和国进出口关税条例》第五十六条规定："进境物品的关税以及进口环节海关代征税合并为进口税，由海关依法征收。"

图2-2-12 乐蜂网

乐蜂网也是一家垂直化妆品电商，由知名电视人李静于2008年创办，以提供"亿万中国女性优质生活的首选入口"为目标，是中国第一个拥有专家明星进驻和品牌授权、实施"100% 行货正品"策略的B2C网站。乐蜂网的特别之处在于它推出明星达人品牌，签约一个明星达人，就会推出一个相应的自有品牌。

乐蜂网的地址为http://www.lefeng.com/。

图2-2-13 乐蜂网明星品牌

图2-2-14 乐蜂网明星品牌

从知名度、销售额、会员数量等方面综合看，乐蜂网和聚美优品是中国最大的两家化妆品垂直电商，业内竞争在所难免；自2013年起，乐蜂网和聚美优品就出现了多次"促销大战""价格大战"。你不妨亲身体验一下两家的服务，从中再选择自己更为偏好的一家。

> 网络上的奥特莱斯（outlet）——"唯品会"

有别于其他购物网站，唯品会定位为"一家专门做特卖的网站"，每天上新品，以低至1折的折扣及充满乐趣的限时抢购模式，提供一站式的优质购物体验。每天有多达100个品牌在唯品会上授权特卖，商品囊括时装、配饰、鞋、美容化妆品、箱包、家纺、皮具、香水、3C、母婴等。2012年3月，唯品会成功登陆纽约证券交易所。

唯品会的货源直接来自品牌厂方，省去了中间多级的销售渠道，价格自然低很多，甚至可以优惠至最基本的成本费！

唯品会的网站地址为：http://www.vip.com/。

图2-2-15　唯品会

因为唯品会每天"10点上新"的特卖模式，很多唯品会会员，都养成了每天10点前坐在电脑前准备"开抢"的习惯。还有很多热心的抢购达人，撰写"唯品会抢购秘籍攻略"供大家分享。如果你有一直中意的品牌，不妨时常关注一下唯品会的特卖活动,说不定就能买到性价比高的品牌产品哟!

• C2C 类型

C2C 指的是 Customer to Customer,即消费者对消费者的电子商务模式,为买卖双方提供一个在线交易平台,使卖方可以主动提供商品,而买方可以自行选择商品进行购买。中国最大的 C2C 网站应属淘宝网,其在中国 C2C 市场的份额占到了 60% 以上。由于本书从第三章起,将会详细介绍淘宝网的购物流程和使用方法,所以不在这里过多介绍。

除淘宝网外,很多大型的综合型购物网站除了提供自营的 B2C 服务外,还鼓励第三方卖家入驻,建立 C2C 平台。在上文提到的 B2C 网站中,乐蜂网、聚美优品、唯品会这三家属于垂直类型的 B2C,而 1 号店、京东、当当,虽然各有侧重,但都属于综合型的购物网站,并且都建立了 C2C 渠道。

以京东为例,我们来试试看。当你在京东搜索某品牌彩色铅笔时,会得到多个类似的搜索结果,例如:

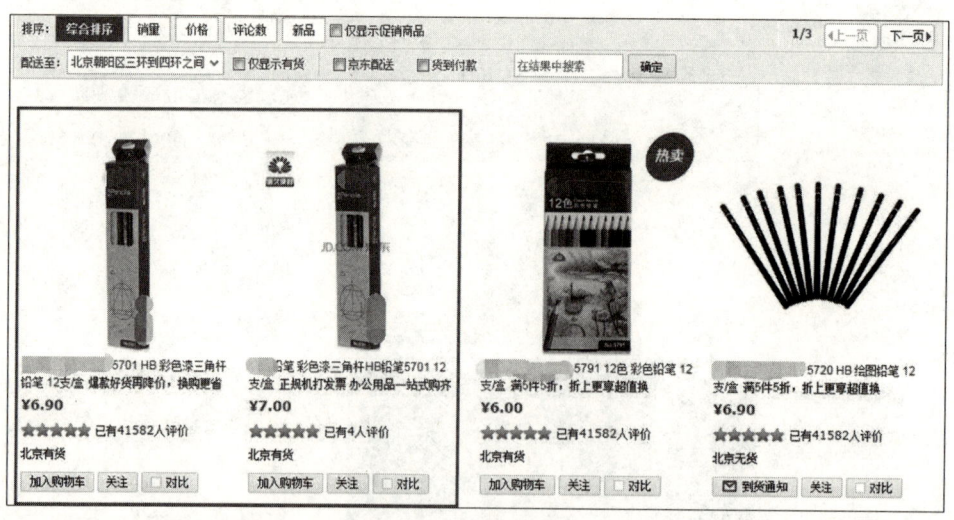

图 2-2-16 搜索结果

当你看到同种商品价格不同,当然会点开查看详情,第一款商品是这样的:

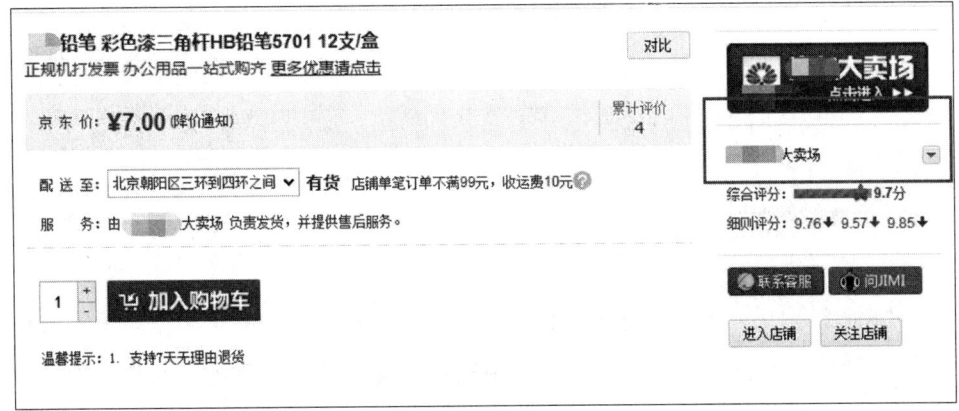

图2-2-17　商品详情

第二款商品是这样的：

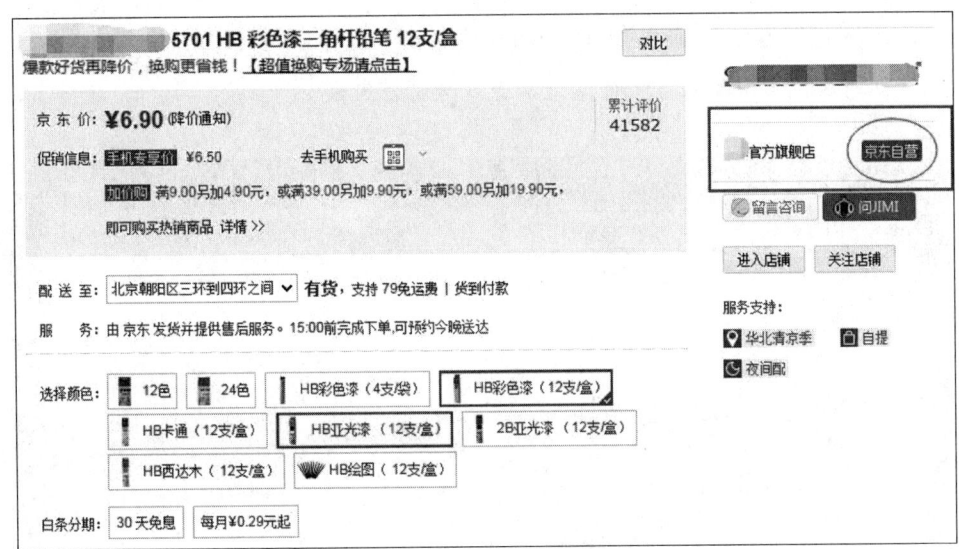

图2-2-18　商品详情

在页面的右侧，可以看到商品来自于哪家店铺。第一款商品来自"XX大卖场"，第二款来自"XX官方旗舰店"。而且你可以注意到，第二款商品的店铺名称右边，注明了"京东自营"，而第一款商品的店铺名称右边则没有，说明"XX大卖场"这家店是第三方卖家，而不是京东自己经营的。

在使用京东、当当、1号店购买的时候，一定要注意一下要买的商品是该网站自营的还是来自第三方。自营商品和来自第三方卖家的商品在价格、发货速度、运费上面会有一些差异，并不是孰优孰劣，而是需要根据你自己的偏好来挑选。

- O2O 类型
  - 叫外卖——饿了么

饿了么是中国最大的餐饮 O2O 平台之一，创立于 2009 年 4 月。饿了么整合了线下餐饮品牌和线上网络资源，用户可以方便地通过手机、电脑搜索周边餐厅，在线订餐、享受美食。它被称为"外卖订餐领域的淘宝"。

由于外卖网站的使用方法在流程上面与 B2C 网站稍显不同，所以在此简单向你介绍一下饿了么网站的使用。

1. 选择所在城市和地址

在浏览器地址栏输入 http://www.ele.me/，进入饿了么网站。根据提示，选择你所在城市，输入你所在地址，进入网站首页。

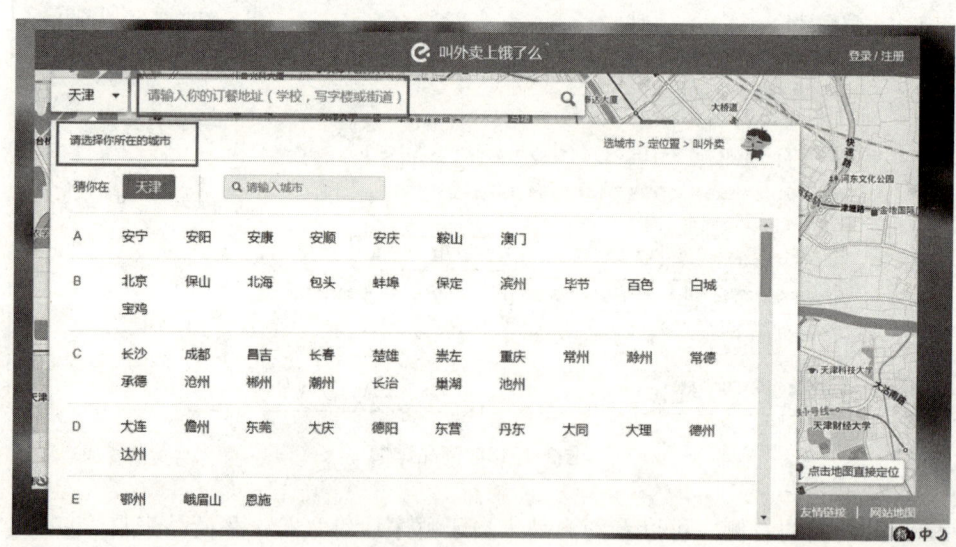

图2-2-19

图2-2-20 饿了么

2. 用户注册及登录

点击页面右上方的"登录/注册",根据提示输入信息,进行新用户注册。

图2-2-21

3. 浏览餐厅及菜单

注册登录完成后,你可以开始选择想吃的菜肴了。你可以在首页选择一家你感兴趣的餐厅，浏览该餐厅菜单。

图2-2-22

你也可以在页面上方的搜索栏，搜索感兴趣的餐厅、美食。

图2-2-23

4. 将美食加入美食篮子

选择好菜品之后，点击价格按钮，即可将该菜品加入美食篮子。

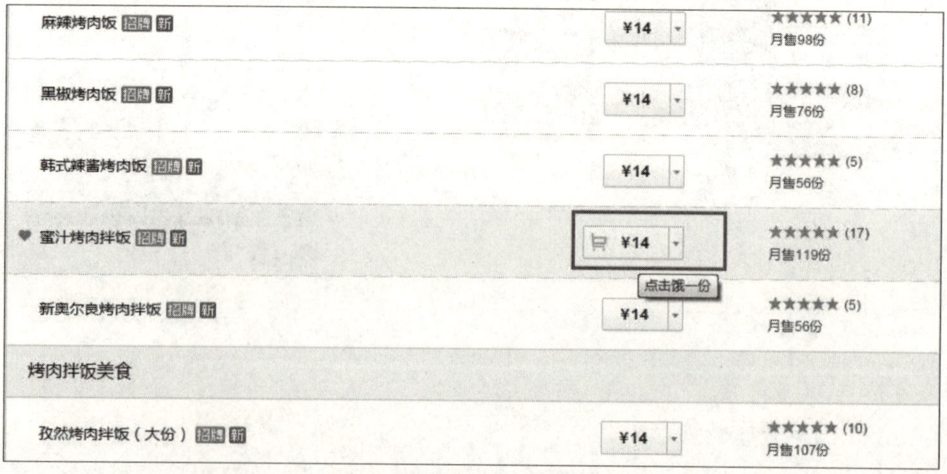

图2-2-24　点击价格按钮

5．订单确认及支付

点击美食篮子右下方的"去买单"按钮，确认订单信息。

图2-2-25 订单确认

在订单确认页面，根据提示信息，输入送达地址，选择送达时间和支付方式。如果你有什么特殊要求，比如没有零钱、不要辣、多放蔬菜等，可以在留言框内给餐厅留言。

图2-2-26 确认订单信息

点击"确认下单"，选择一个你合适的付款方式，在30分钟内完成支付，否则你的订单将会被取消。

图2-2-27　确认并完成支付

6．查看订单状态

支付完成后，就等待你的外卖上门吧。你可以在首页上方点击"我的饿单"，查看你的订单状态。

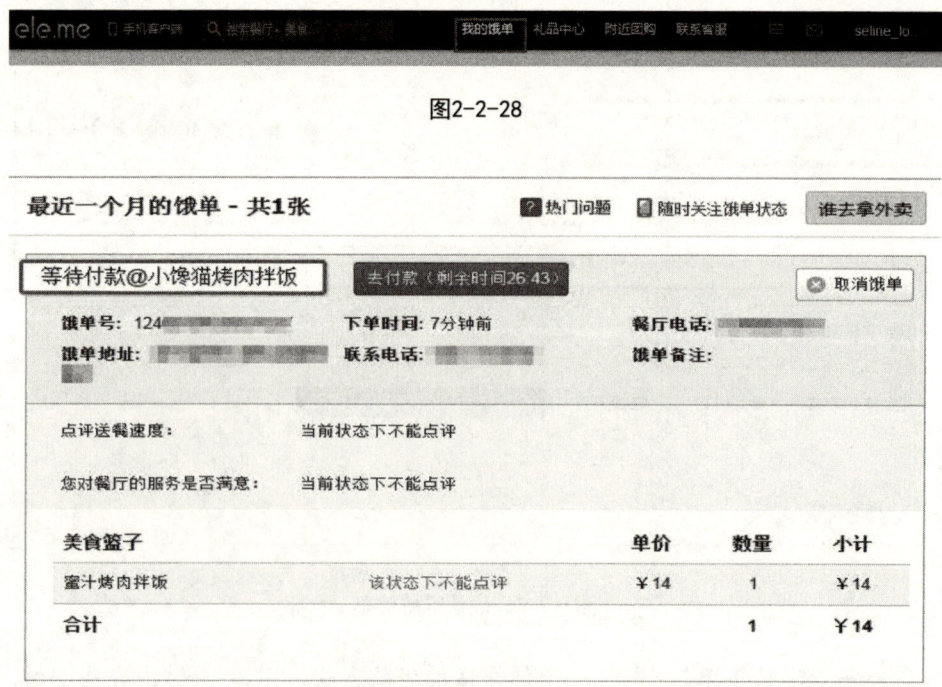

图2-2-28

图2-2-29　查看订单状态

类似饿了么这样的餐饮O2O网站还有很多，比如美团外卖（waimai.meituan.com）、百度外卖（waimai.baidu.com）。各大平台面对竞争，经常推出一些满减优惠活动，建议你在根据个人喜好选择合适外卖网站的同时，不要忘记留意一下有没有优惠活动。

外卖　下一场O2O大战主战场？

又到了"出门晒死，不出门闷死"的炎热夏季，吃饭也成了一件难事，自己做汗流浃背，出门吃晒到无食欲。于是外卖的生意也随着这天气一起火热了起来。不过，收集小卡片、打电话预定的行为早已落伍了，今年流行的是：APP定外卖……

手机下单　外卖送上门

在高新路上班的徐良，每到夏天便为怎么吃午饭而发愁，公司周边的小饭馆每到中午便是人山人海，连门外也放满了餐桌。"烈日下坐等一碗面的功夫，身上的汗出得就跟洗了个澡似的。"这对于一直在"微胖界"苦苦煎熬的他来说确实是件极其痛苦的事情。公司旁边也有许多环境舒适，可以吹着空调美餐一顿的地方，但对于工薪族来说，那些地方只能偶一为之，"不然一个月赚的钱只够吃饭的了。"

不过今年夏天，徐良的日子好过了许多。"美团、百度都推出了外卖APP（手机应用），提前半小时下个单，等下班饭就送到公司来了。"虽然每单都需要几块钱的外卖费，但三五同事一起凑个单，每人也就多瓶冰峰的钱，"蹭着公司空调吃外卖，完事再好好睡一觉。多美！"

就跟打车APP一样，外卖APP似乎也在一夜之间"火"遍全国众多城市；不过同样受到互联网巨头资金"加持"的外卖似乎比打车更为刚需，因为相比打车软件持续至今的烧钱送补贴行为，迟至去年才纷纷上线的外卖类APP目前除了首单优惠外，已经很少有优惠了。"看来外卖大家更需要，所以补助就没打车爽了。"徐良一边享受着外卖的方便，一边"埋怨"补助不给力。

各取所需　商家多一份生意

其实外卖本不是什么新鲜事，无论是高校学生门缝里插着的订餐小卡片，还是品牌餐饮公布的订餐电话，"定份外卖"已经成为许多年轻人解决就餐问题的选项之一。甚至外卖APP，也早在数年前就被某国外快餐品牌推送上线了。

就跟打车不是新鲜事却被互联网玩新鲜了一样，菜还是那些菜，店还是那几家店，外卖APP改变的只是让更多没钱雇派送工或者开发APP的街头小店也能开展起外卖业务。"那天我看到楼下一家只有六张桌子的面馆也挂上了'美团外卖'的牌子。"在徐良的印象里，这家面馆是典型的"夫妻店"：老板做饭，老板娘收钱，一个伙计收拾店面。加入外卖，肯定让生意更红火。

袁航前段时间在凤城五路附近开了家凉皮店，虽然灯箱、卡座的店内装饰并不比连锁的中式快餐店差，但装修加上房租几乎已经用尽了积蓄，所以吧台两人、后厨三人和服务员两名已经是他能请得起的人数上限了。"现在的人工成本太高了。开店前我们就想着要不要送外卖，但人实在太难招了。没干过快递的，没一个月连周围楼盘都记不清；干过快递的，人家的工资咱又付不起。"

所以在开业后那段因为天气较凉而生意冷淡的时候，当有人上门推荐可以加入美团外卖时，他便爽快地答应了。"我接单子卖饭，美团帮我配送。我赚我的饭钱，他赚他的快递费，多好。"

方便背后　互联网巨头的暗战

"丰富的商家选择、良好的用户体验和客服系统"——号称最大外卖平台的美团外卖对记者介绍道，这是其之所以区别于传统外卖平台的特点，"为消费者提供一站式的优质本地生活服务，是美团一直以来的目标。"

不过，这番话在一名大学生创业者袁征（化名）听来却是另一番滋味。因为他和他的小伙伴们早在2009年便开始了外卖创业，甚至一度将业务拓展到周边15所大学和5个CBD。"争取5年内在全国100个城市展开业务",曾是他们的梦想,但梦想照进现实时,却难免碰壁;由于自有资金有限,他们的业务模式还只停留在将商家信息挂上网,用户下单后由商家提供配送。

这个只提供信息对接的平台,既没有令人心动的优惠,也难解决商家招聘派送员的成本之痛,所以不仅对商家难以像美团、百度等外卖平台一样要求健康证,甚至连自身的盈利也只在规划中。

所以当美团、百度等外卖平台挟互联网巨头投资强势来袭之时,袁征的处境便可想而知。就像打车APP迅速取代各地叫车平台一样,外卖APP也将本地外卖平台冲击得七零八落。

不过新模式内部的厮杀也未停止,在互联网巨头BAT之间的暗战才刚刚开始,百度有百度外卖;阿里不仅占有美团股份,更在日前成立了口碑外卖;而腾讯则通过追加持股25%的大众点评投资外卖O2O平台饿了么。

更为重要的是,不同于打车APP,无论是专车、快车还是顺风车,都还只是在一辆轿车上玩游戏。外卖平台已经将自己的触角,从最为刚需的"吃饭",延伸到了鲜花、水果、蔬菜、百货甚至药品等更多的日用百货零售行业中。

"隔壁的小王"之前是一家水果店的店员,当了解到个人也可以申请加入外卖平台后,他便辞职自己创业了。"其实就是在APP上把我能卖的水果照片挂上去,然后有人下单,我就去胡家庙进货给人送过去。"由于此前的打工经历,让他可以在胡家庙水果批发市场低价拿货,然后自己赚个差价,"赚得也不多,但比打工强。"

互联网就此将服装、家电大卖场和柴米油盐杂货店"一网打尽"。所以美团外卖敢于豪气地说出:"凡是未被互联网改变的行业,都将被互联网改变。"

记者:裴磊

来源:西安日报(西安)2015年7月31日

➢ 参与团购——美团网

团购（Group purchase）这种消费模式在中国兴起于 2010 年。简单来说，团购就是消费者组团购物。认识或不认识的消费者联合起来，加大与商家的谈判能力，以求得最优价格。根据薄利多销的原理，商家可以给出低于零售价格的折扣和单独购买得不到的优质服务。

美团网是中国的第一家团购网站。

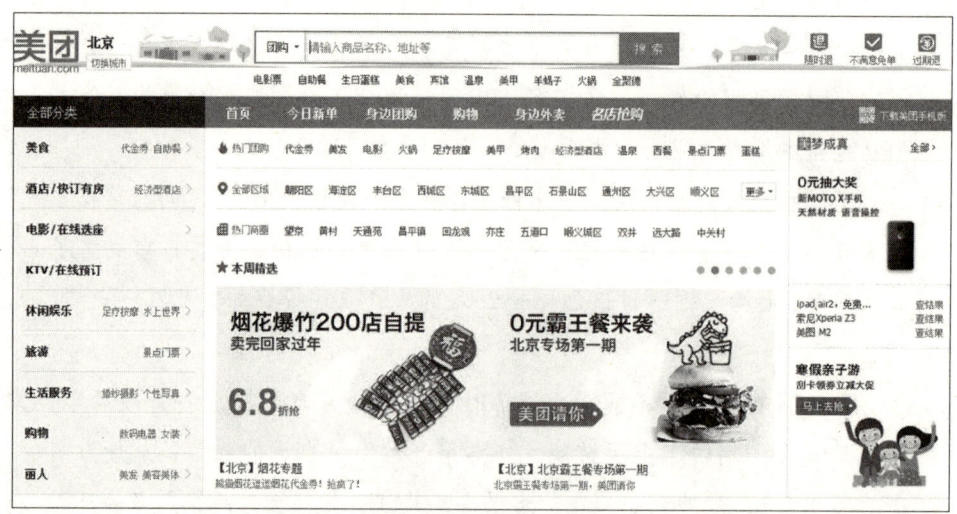

图2-2-30　美团网首页

图2-2-31　美团网上的美食

在美团网购物的流程和一般网购没有太大的区别，最大的不同是，当你对某一商家的可团购产品感兴趣，并通过支付宝或者银联卡付钱下单后，你收到的并不是商品，而是美团网发送的短信密码消费券，凭此短信密码可直接到商家的实体店铺里消费。

图2-2-32 美团网购物流程[1]

---

1 图片来源：http://www.meituan.com/help/tutorial?mtt=1.help%2Fnewbie.0.0.i67gyka1

图2-2-33 团购商品种类丰富

除了实体商品外,团购网站还提供多种类型的服务型产品。如果你想做头发、看电影、拍写真,从美团网上"团"一个,确实是省钱的好方法!类似的团购网站也有许多,如百度糯米(http://www.nuomi.com/)、大众点评团购(http://t.dianping.com/)、拉手网(http://www.lashou.com/)等,模式相似,不再详述。

◆ 总结

- 了解从中国电子商务网站上能买什么

只有你想不到的,没有网上买不到的

- 了解中国典型电子商务网站的特点类别

B2C 类型:1号店、京东、当当网、聚美优品、乐蜂网、唯品会

C2C 类型:淘宝网、1号店、京东、当当网

O2O 类型:饿了么、美团网

第三章

第一节　先比价,再下单

在这一节中,你将……
- ✓ 了解如何在淘宝网上进行商品的检索和排序
- ✓ 了解怎样货比三家
- ✓ 了解如何使用阿里旺旺
- ✓ 了解物流方式的选择
- ✓ 了解商品下单流程

约翰准备好了网购所需要的一切东西,也了解了中国网购的流程和诸多购物网站的特点,现在,他准备正式开启他的网购之旅了。环顾宿舍,约翰觉得宿舍太空旷了,缺少了些许家的温馨,于是他决定买些墙纸装饰一下宿舍,顺便再买一些家居用品。可是这些东西上哪儿买比较方便实惠呢?这时候,约翰想起了舍友之前所提到的淘宝网。便捷的淘宝网提供了那么多种类的商品、那么多特色的店铺以供挑选,约翰已经迫不及待地想要登录淘宝网,将所需的商品全都收入囊中了。可是当约翰登录淘宝网进行商品的挑选时却傻了眼,淘宝网上有许多家店铺提供了类似的商品甚至是同一种产品,只是价格上略有不同。这可愁坏约翰了,难道要挑最便宜的买吗?可是,最便宜的不一定是最好、最适合的呀!

相信从未有过网购经验的你一定会遇到和约翰一样的情境,那么,究竟怎样才能在淘宝网上买到真正物美价廉的商品呢?让我们一起往下看吧。

快速准确地发现心仪商品——商品的检索以及排序

在第二章第一节中已经教给你注册淘宝网的方法,现在你就去试着注册一个淘宝账号吧!淘宝账号可是相当于你在淘宝网网购的通行证,没有它,你在淘宝网的网购中将寸步难行。

同样是在第二章第一节中,我们初步了解了搜索的功能,那么现在就将它运用到实践中去吧。比如你和约翰一样,想在淘宝网上购买墙纸装饰一下宿舍,那么就在搜索栏中输入"墙纸"进行搜索。

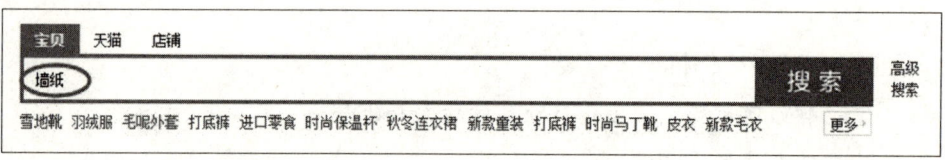

图3-1-1

你会发现出来的搜索结果竟有几十万条!是不是陡然产生一种大海捞针的感觉了呢?随手翻几页是不是就已经觉得看花了眼,但却还没有找到心仪的墙纸呢?这个时候页面最上方的筛选功能就派上一定用场了。如果你对品牌有偏好,那么你可以直接选择你喜欢的品牌;如果你对风格有自己的喜好,那么你也可以选择你喜欢的风格。以风格为例,你是不是觉得淘宝网提供的这些风格有些少呢?其实,秘密在于后面的"更多"。点击"更多"你会发现又出现了许多种风格供你选择。这下,你是不是觉得有好几种风格都是你心仪的呢?那么点击后面的"多选"来选择多种风格吧。

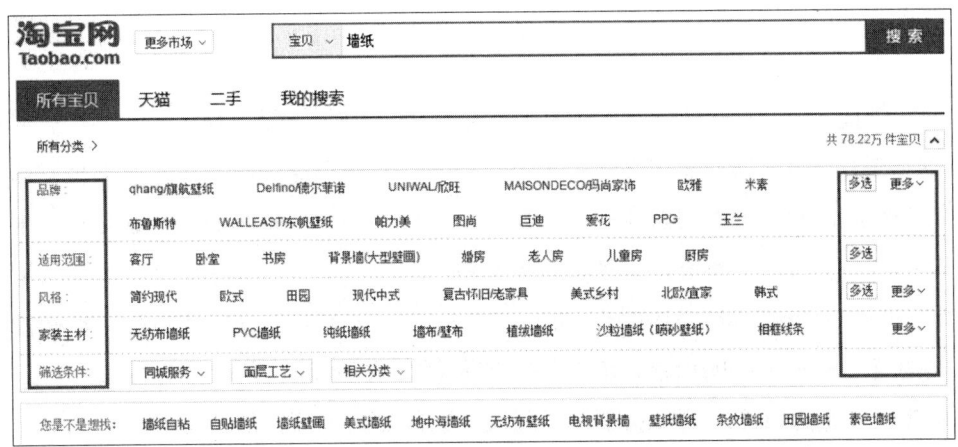

图3-1-2

利用上面的筛选，你已经离心仪的目标商品又近一步了。接下来，使用一下筛选下方的排序功能试试看吧。排序功能可是会大大筛选掉不符合你心意的商品，省去你不少时间呢！淘宝网提供了"综合排序""人气""销量""信用""价格"五种排序方法。在进行排序前，如果你心中对商品有个预期价格，那不妨给出一个价格范围再做排序吧。

"综合排序"是由淘宝网综合卖家商品的各个方面进行的排序结果，输入检索词后直接出来的搜索结果是综合排序的结果；"人气"顾名思义指的是商品的受欢迎程度，受欢迎程度不一定是说这个商品买的人一定多，有可能是点击率较高或者收藏数较多的商品；"销量"就是商品具体卖出的数量多少啦；"信用"排序指的是按照卖家的信誉来排序（有关"卖家的信誉"内容将在下文进行介绍）；"价格"排序是根据价格高低排列。

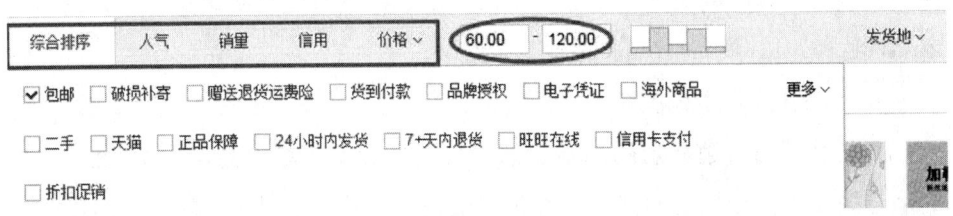

图3-1-3

以上几种排序方式，没有一个是最优的选择，它们各有优缺点，所以你就按照自己的实际情况选择自己喜欢的排序方式吧。

货比三家——看商品介绍、看卖家信誉、看商品评价

好了,通过以上操作你一定很快地找到了一些心仪的商品了。同样是以墙纸为例,你看中了很多漂亮的墙纸,可是你总不能全都将它们买回家吧?一来浪费钱,二来也不需要那么多。如果你想直接挑一个价格最便宜的买,那么请等一等!中国有一句俗语叫作"便宜没好货",这里的意思自然不是指价格便宜的就一定不是好的商品,而是说一般价格便宜的商品更容易出现质量问题,毕竟网购是虚拟活动,你总不希望收到实物以后再为商品的售后而头疼吧。下面针对"如何比较这些商品并挑出最优的那一个"这个问题给你支上几招。

• 方法一:看商品介绍

随便点开一个商品链接,在该商品页面的宝贝详情中你可以了解到商品的具体信息。在宝贝详情中,卖家不仅介绍了商品的品牌、产地、规格等基本信息,而且放上了商品的实拍图、效果图、细节图,给你一个商品的直观印象。

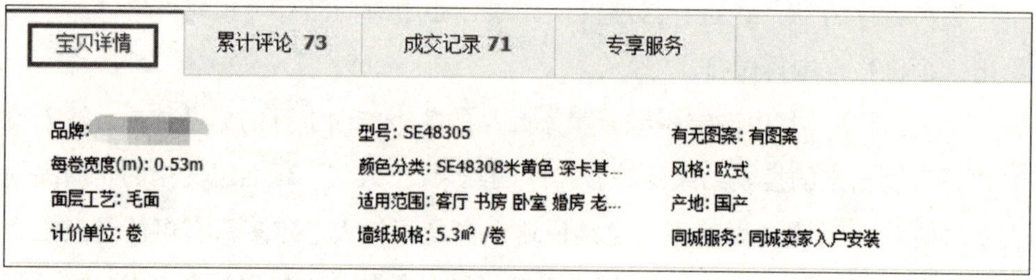

宝贝详情	累计评论 73	成交记录 71	专享服务
品牌:	型号: SE48305	有无图案: 有图案	
每卷宽度(m): 0.53m	颜色分类: SE48308米黄色 深卡其...	风格: 欧式	
面层工艺: 毛面	适用范围: 客厅 书房 卧室 婚房 老...	产地: 国产	
计价单位: 卷	墙纸规格: 5.3㎡/卷	同城服务: 同城卖家入户安装	

图3-1-4

如果你买的是衣服或者鞋子一类的商品,那么这些商品的具体尺码对照表是放在宝贝详情中的。购买商品的时候一定要仔细对照尺码表选择适合自己的商品,这样可以减少退换货的麻烦。

• 方法二:看卖家信誉

商品页面的右边显示的就是卖家信息了。卖家信息中会显示卖家的信誉、商品与描述相符合程度的评分、对卖家服务态度的评分以及卖家发货速度的评分(满分均为5分)。

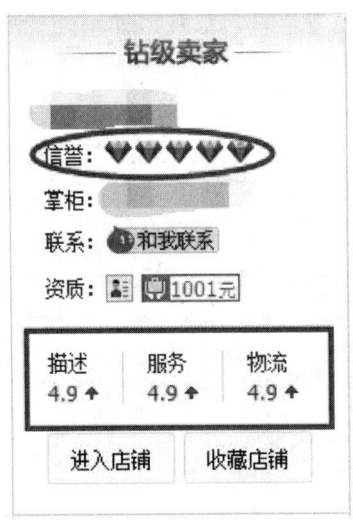

图3-1-5

卖家信用等级划分

淘宝会员在淘宝网每使用支付宝成功交易一次,就可以对交易对象做一次信用评价。评价分为"好评""中评""差评"三类,每种评价对应一个信用积分,具体为:"好评"加一分,"中评"不加分,"差评"扣一分。

4分-10分	♥
11分-40分	♥♥
41分-90分	♥♥♥
91分-150分	♥♥♥♥
151分-250分	♥♥♥♥♥
251分-500分	💎
501分-1000分	💎💎
1001分-2000分	💎💎💎
2001分-5000分	💎💎💎💎
5001分-10000分	💎💎💎💎💎
10001分-20000分	👑
20001分-50000分	👑👑
50001分-100000分	👑👑👑
100001分-200000分	👑👑👑👑
200001分-500000分	👑👑👑👑👑
500001分-1000000分	👑
1000001分-2000000分	👑👑
2000001分-5000000分	👑👑👑
5000001分-10000000分	👑👑👑👑
10000001分以上	👑👑👑👑👑

图3-1-6

信用等级自然是越高越好，皇冠最佳。如果是皇冠，那说明这家店有许多人光顾且好评不断。如果你点击一下信誉后面的钻石或皇冠标志，你还会看到半年内该卖家与同行业其他卖家的比较以及店铺三十天内的服务情况。

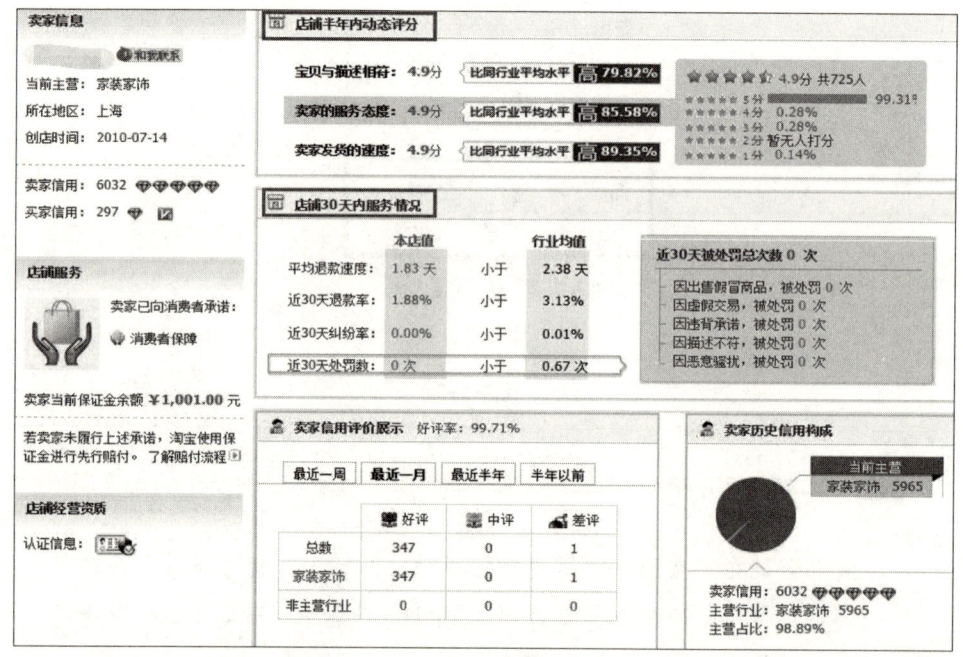

图3-1-7

- 方法三：看商品评价

在"宝贝详情"标签页的旁边你会发现"累计评价"。点击一下就会出现商品的评价页面。该页面上宝贝与描述相符程度的评分是综合了所有评价的买家的打分给出的一个平均分，五分为满分，越接近满分说明该商品越符合用户期望值。

在商品评价页面，你可以浏览到购买过该商品的买家对于商品的评价。大多数买家的评论还是相对客观公正的，相比较卖家的一面之词，买家的评价更具有参考价值。许多买家会在评论中附上自己的实拍照片，相较于卖家在宝贝详情中附上的图片，买家实拍图更为真实客观，也将色差、细节等披露得更为全面。

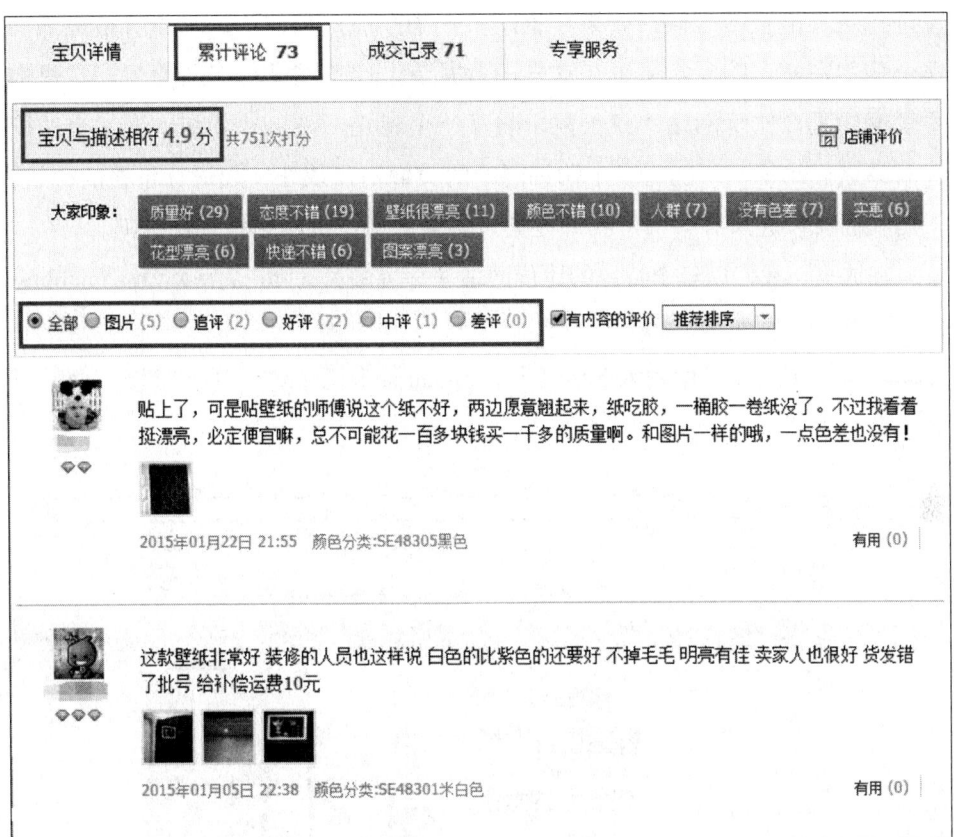

图3-1-8

货比三家另一利器——比价网站

当然,你可能会觉得上述货比三家的过程比较烦琐,但熟能生巧,网购经历多了之后,你一定会找到适合自己的货比三家的实用途径。况且为了买到最优最心仪的东西,付出些努力也是在所难免的。

虽然我们一直说价格不是决定是否购买这件商品的必要因素,但是在实际生活中,大部分购物者的选择还是与价格大大相关的。如果影响你购物选择的因素仅仅只是价格,并且对于在什么样的网购平台上购买没有一点偏好的话,那么在这里我就要向你推荐一个非常好用的货比三家的途径——比价网站。

电子商务的普及产生了大量的网上商店,如 B2C 和 C2C 的网站。用户在进行网上消费的时候，如果希望购买一个产品，往往会选择去价格最低的那个购物网站上购买，所以在这样的背景下，比价网站就应势而生。这里需要说明的是，比价网站不仅仅限于将某一个特定网站（比如淘宝网）上的同种商品进行比价，还能将多个购物网站的类似商品放在一起进行价格的比较。下面我们就一起来看一下，我们究竟该怎么利用比价网站进行比价吧。

在这里，我们以一个特定的比价网站——慢慢买（http://www.manmanbuy.com/）为例。

首先，在地址栏中输入http://www.manmanbuy.com/，进入慢慢买网站页面。

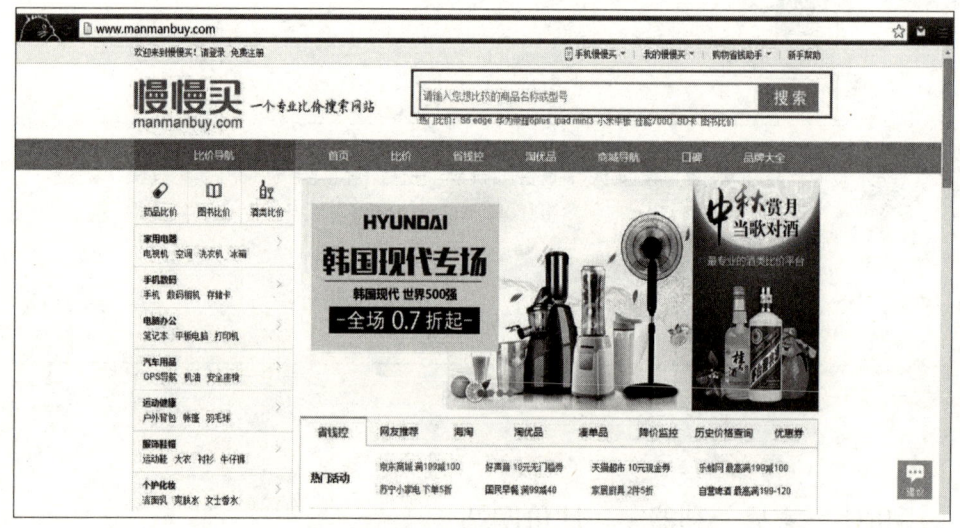

图3-1-9

然后，无须注册登录的步骤，你可以直接在搜索栏中搜索你想要进行比价的商品，比如"iPhone6"，点击"搜索"。

这时候，慢慢买网站会对各大购物网站中符合条件的商品进行搜索，在结果页面中呈现出各大网站中iPhone6的售价。

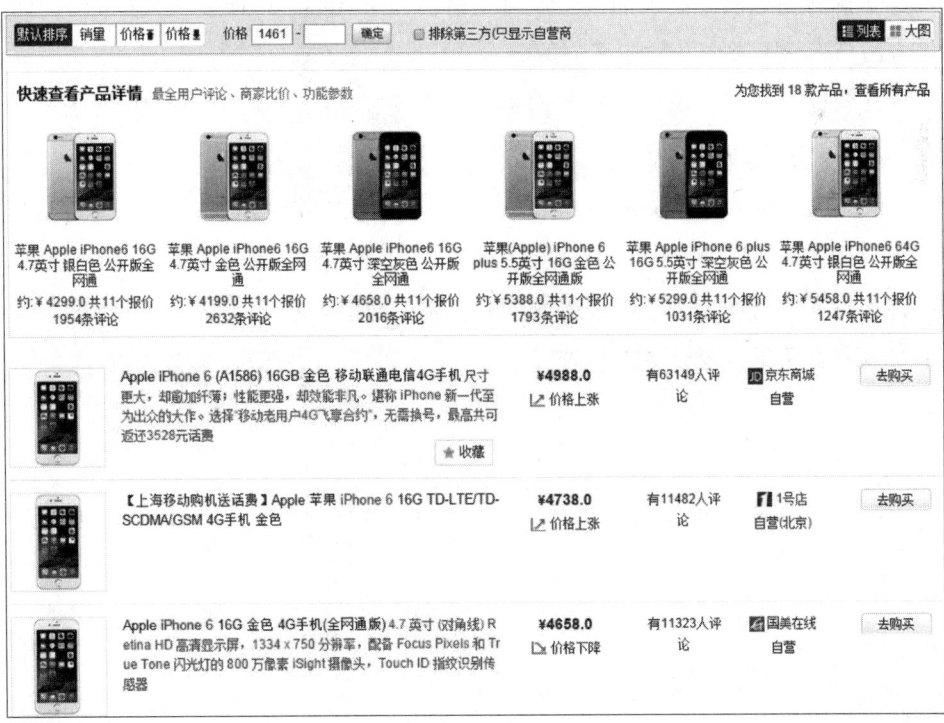

图3-1-10

最后，你只需要选择合适的商品，轻轻点击，网页就会自动跳转至所选商品所在的购物网站，可以进一步查看相关信息以及进行购买（当然，也可以顺便利用上文中我们所讲述的货比三家的三种方法再次进行比较筛选）。

比价网站的好处在于可以进行跨平台的比较，它可以将京东、1号店等我们在第二章第二节中提及的诸多网站的同种商品放在一起比较价格，给你提供的选择将更多，而不是拘泥在某一个特定平台中。但与此同时，这也带来了一个问题，你可能会通过不同的网购平台购买不同商品，这也就需要你拥有多个平台的注册账号以及密码，并且熟悉各个网站的购物流程和规则。

总而言之，比价平台是不是足够便捷，是不是一定要使用比价网站先比价再购物，在这点上就仁者见仁智者见智啦。还是那句话，自己用得好的才是真的好！

阿里旺旺的安装和使用

千挑万选选出了心仪的宝贝，可是有色差怎么办？一次多买几样商品想要店家减免运费？路上货物出了问题怎么和店家联系？

从售前到售后，无论何时我们都有和店家联系的需求，而满足这个需求的神器，就是阿里旺旺。

阿里旺旺分为网页版和客户端版，网页版阿里旺旺功能比较有限，还经常出现发送不了消息，或者发送失败的情况，而客户端版的阿里旺旺功能完善，用起来也非常简便。为了保证购物的好心情，提高购物的效率，我们还是一起来安装阿里旺旺的客户端软件吧！

【安装步骤】

1. 在浏览器地址栏输入 http://wangwang.taobao.com/，进入阿里旺旺下载页面。

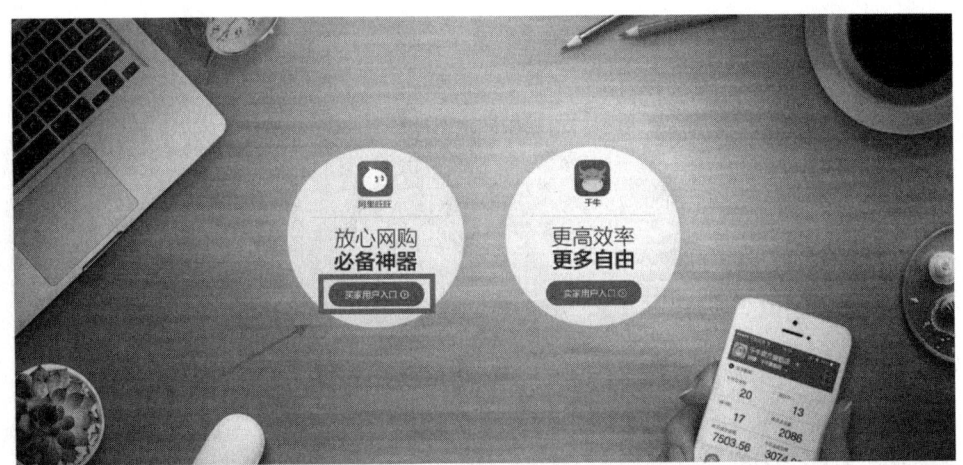

图3-1-11

我们是要进行购物,所以选择左边的"买家进入入口",当你成为卖家后,你就可以翻到第六章看看从"卖家用户入口"进入的安装教程了。

2. 在页面右上角,根据自己电脑/移动设备的操作系统版本选择不同的下载版本。

图3-1-12

3. 选择下载"阿里旺旺"。

图3-1-13

使用 Windows 8 操作系统会直接跳转到应用商店,点击"安装"即可。其他版本的操作系统可以先将软件包下载下来。

4. 点击安装包进行安装。

图3-1-14

- 点击"自定义安装"选择安装路径,然后点击"立即安装"。

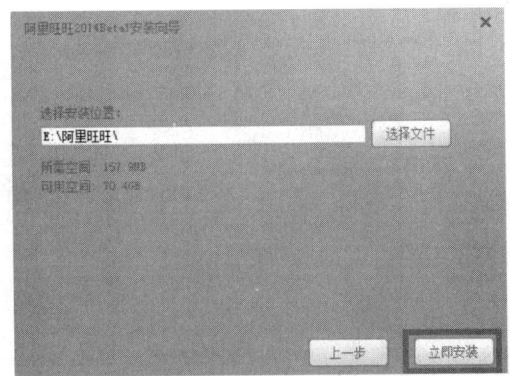

图3-1-15

- 立即体验"阿里旺旺"选择左边的"立即体验",否则选择"完成"。

图3-1-16

终于安装完了,现在,让我们进入"阿里旺旺"的使用体验吧!

【使用指南】

1. 首先,登录自己的账号,"阿里旺旺"账号和"淘宝"账号是绑定为一体的,只要输入自己的淘宝账号和密码就可以了,然后点击"登录"。

图3-1-17

2. 进入了主页面，可以发现联系人区分为四页，分别为"最近会话""好友""群""我的应用"，比较常用的是前两项。

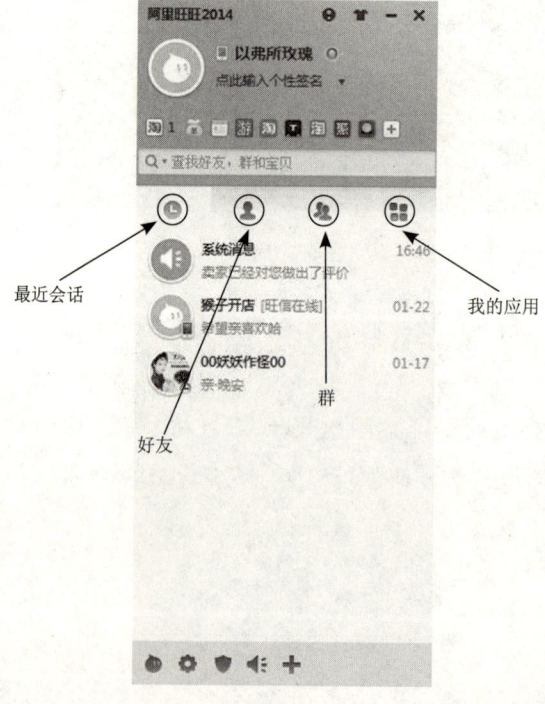

图3-1-18

3. 大多数情况下，我们在网页上浏览过商品后，想要与店家联系时，只要找到"阿里旺旺"的标志，点击一下，就可以转到客户端与商家沟通交流了。

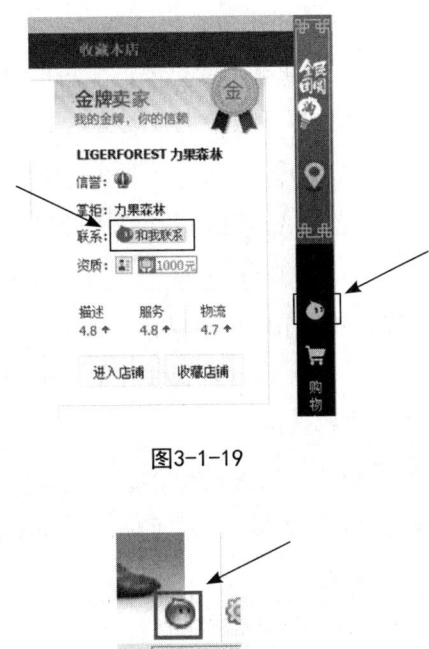

图3-1-19

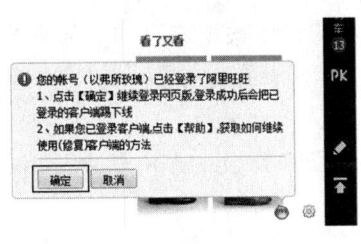

图3-1-20

注意，网页版"阿里旺旺"和客户端有时会产生冲突。

图3-1-21

这时，点击"确定"即可。

之后，我们就可以与店家自由畅谈了。对于有疑问的地方或者其他需要与卖家沟通的问题，比如确认商品细节、免运费、送个小礼品之类的，你都可以在阿里旺旺上与卖家进行沟通。

谁送宝贝上路？——物流方式选择

网上购物，大部分的商品都要跨过山河大海，千里迢迢传送到顾客手里，这时候选择一个可靠的物流企业就十分重要，之后的章节中我们将对中国的主要的物流公司进行一些介绍，以便读者大致了解这些物流公司的特点。

不过近些年来，很多情况下大部分电商网站的物流方式都不需要顾客来选择。比如京东商城、天猫超市这样的 B2C 网站大多数建立了自己的物流渠道，以网站的信誉保证了配送服务的质量和速度。而淘宝网基本都是由卖家来选择物流企业，这一点和 B2C 网站不同，所以在下单前买家需要与卖家沟通确认一下，尽量选择对卖家寄件、买家收件都很便捷的物流公司，以免出现买家所在地物流公司没有设置工作点等情况。

关于物流方式的查看确认，主要有两个途径。

1. 在商品详情或店铺主页查看。部分商家会在店铺主页公告位置或商品详情中标明主要的物流合作公司。

2. 通过与商家交流沟通获取物流公司信息。如果在以上两处位置都没有找到自己想要知道的信息，就可以通过阿里旺旺从商家处确认并协商。如果本地没有商家默认的物流公司，也可以及时和商家协商更换物流企业。

确认过物流企业的信息后，如果发现本地有此企业的快递营业点，那么就可以放心地下单了。值得注意的是，在下单的过程中，有一步是可以在"快递"和"EMS"间选择。如图，可以根据自己的实际需要进行选择，一般情况下因考虑费用和到货时间的原因，选择快递的居多。

运费　　江苏常州 至 北京∨ 快递: 10.00 EMS: 30.00

图3-1-22

万事俱备，只差下单！——下单流程

当你熟练网购之后的某一天，你一定会发现，"下单"一定是你学得最快的一步。毕竟马上就可以将宝贝收入囊中，谁都会既心急又期待吧？

那么我们马上就开始！

挑选好商品以后，进入商品的主页面，点击"立刻购买"。

图3-1-23

进入订单界面。

首先要选择确认收货地址：

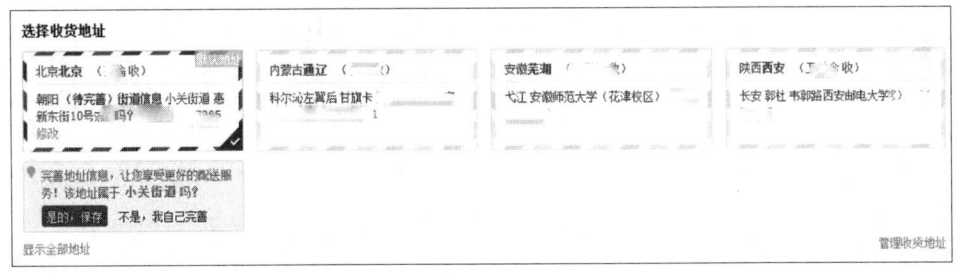

图3-1-24

可以从现有的地址中选择，也可以点击右下角的"管理收货地址"添加或删除地址。

之后是确认订单的具体信息。

可以选择购买运费保险来避免买家承担退货的运费，还可以在左下角给卖家留言。最后，只要点击红色的"提交订单"，下单的过程就完成啦！接下来便是付款环节。

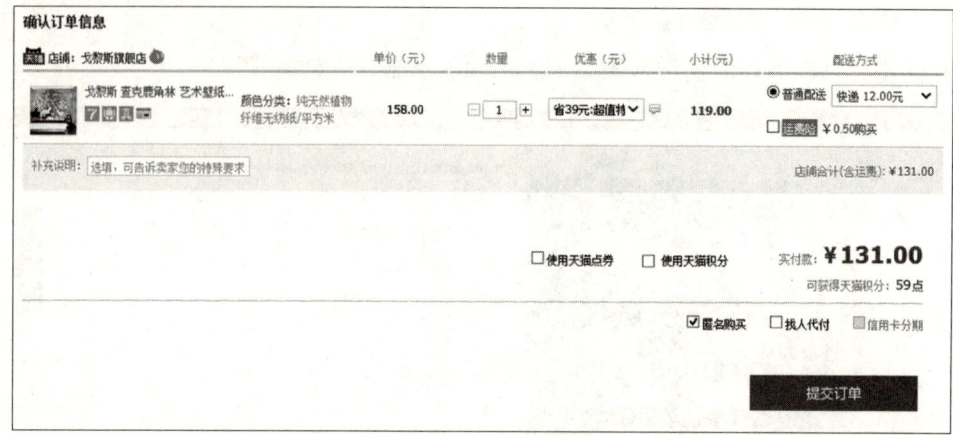

图3-1-25

总结

- 淘宝网商品的检索及排序：

综合排序、按人气高低排序、按销量多少排序、按信用高低排序、按价格高低排序

- 货比三家：看商品介绍、看卖家信誉、看商品评价、利用比价网站进行比价
- 使用阿里旺旺：从官方网站下载安装软件；实时互动沟通交流
- 选择物流方式：在商品详情或店铺主页查看；通过与商家交流沟通获取物流公司信息
- 下单：编辑或选择自己的地址；确认订单信息；提交订单；完成支付

第二节 终于到付款啦

在这一节中，你将……
✓ 了解在淘宝网购物的付款流程
✓ 了解不同的支付方式

经过千挑万选,约翰终于在淘宝网上选出了自己心仪的商品,加入购物车并且成功下单了。完成下单操作的约翰感觉松了一口气,毕竟他的淘宝网网购之旅的线上购物环节已经快接近尾声了。下单之后网站自动连接到了付款页面,这时候约翰盯着付款页面再次傻了眼。淘宝网向消费者提供了支付宝、银行卡等多种支付方式,约翰心想:怎么会有这么多的方式呢?即使自己没有选择恐惧症,也对这些自己并不了解的支付方式无从选择啊。约翰决定先请教一下有网购经验的室友再来进行付款操作。

其实,付款的操作很简单,三步即可轻轻松松结束线上购物环节,只是其中多种支付方式的选择会让你觉得无从下手而已。那么,淘宝网所提供的这些支付方式有什么区别呢?让我们一起来看一下吧。

线上购物最后一环——商品的付款

商品的付款操作非常简单,一般情况下,在你提交订单之后,淘宝网会自动连接到付款页面,这时候你只需要选择你倾向的支付方式,再输入你的支付宝支付密码(注意:在付款页面中无论你选择的是何种支付方式,在下面的方框中输入的一定是支付宝支付密码,而不是你的银行卡密码或者其他密码哟),最后点击"确认付款"即可成功完成付款操作,坐等商品送上门啦。

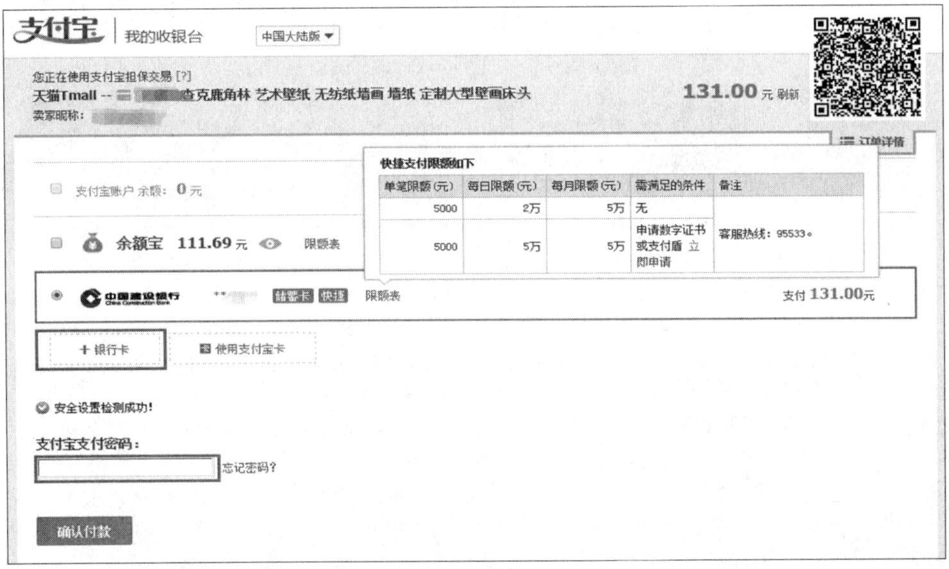

图 3-2-1

如果你不小心关闭了付款页面，又或者是和约翰一样暂时不想进行付款操作因而关掉了付款页面，那也不要产生"付款页面没了，又要完全重复刚才的购物过程"这样的担忧。只要从淘宝网页面的右上方"我的淘宝"——"已买到的宝贝"进入，就可以找到尚未完成付款操作的订单，点击订单最右侧的"立即付款"，就可以重新进入到付款页面去完成付款操作。

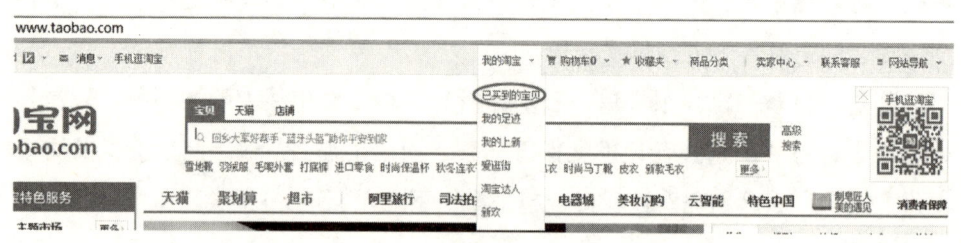

图 3-2-2

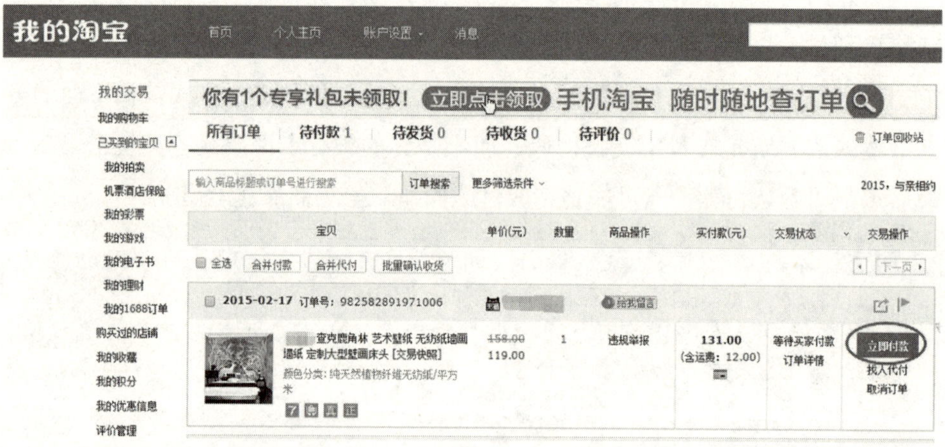

图 3-2-3

多种支付方式，我该选择哪一种？

淘宝网提供了找人代付、支付宝账户付款、银行卡快捷支付、网上银行支付（以下简称"网银支付"）、支付宝卡支付、网点支付、消费卡支付等多种支付形式，为了让你选择出最适合自己的支付方式，下面我们将一一地来了解它们。

• 找人代付

适用场合：不熟悉网上支付的新用户，或者自己账户里余额不足的用户，前提是有一个愿意为你买单的小伙伴。

找人代付，顾名思义就是你买东西而让别人替你买单。如果你和约翰一样是个网购新手，还不太熟悉网上支付，正好你又有一个既会支付操作又乐于助人的小伙伴，那么恭喜你，你可以暂时不必为支付方式的选择而苦恼了。

现在你已经找到了愿意为你买单的人，那么接下来你该如何进行找人代付的操作呢？首先从淘宝网页面的右上方"我的淘宝"——"已买到的宝贝"进入，找到尚未完成付款操作的订单，点击订单最右侧"立即付款"下方的"找人代付"就可以进行找人代付的操作了。

进入到代付页面后，你只需要输入好友的账户（支付宝账户／淘宝账户昵称），点击"请他付款"就可以轻轻松松结束找人代付的操作，剩下的付款事宜就交给你的那位好友啦。

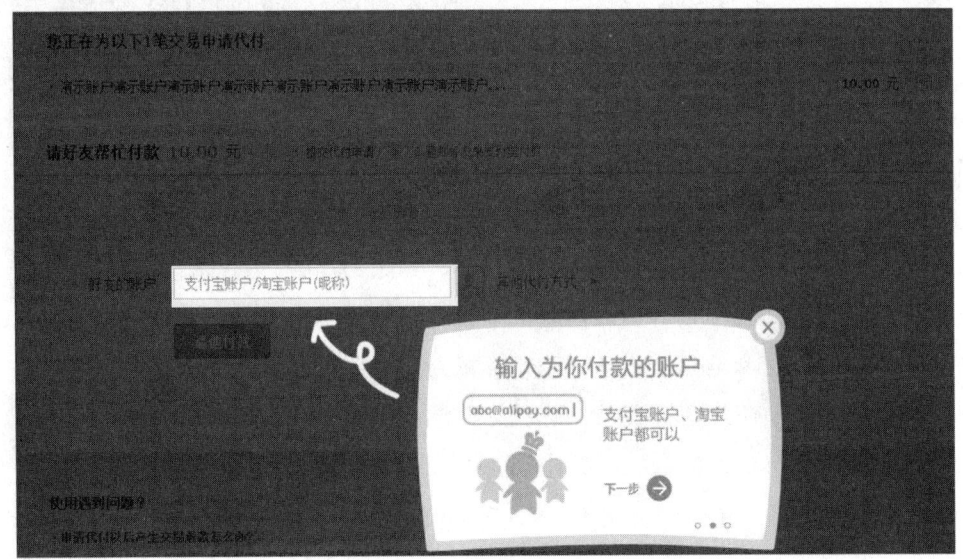

图 3-2-4

可是，如果你只找到了愿意帮你付款的人，可是你并不知道他的账户，这时候又该怎么办呢？不用担心，你可以选择其他代付方式，淘宝网可以生成付款的链接，只需要将付款的链接发给你的好友，他也可以帮你成功完成付款操作的。

但是，请注意，找人代付之前一定要和你的好友说明，而且代付操作完成后也一定要告知诉你的小伙伴，如果你的好友并不知道你找他代付或者一不小心遗忘了这件事，那么你的代付请求很可能被你的好友给无视掉从而造成付款失败。

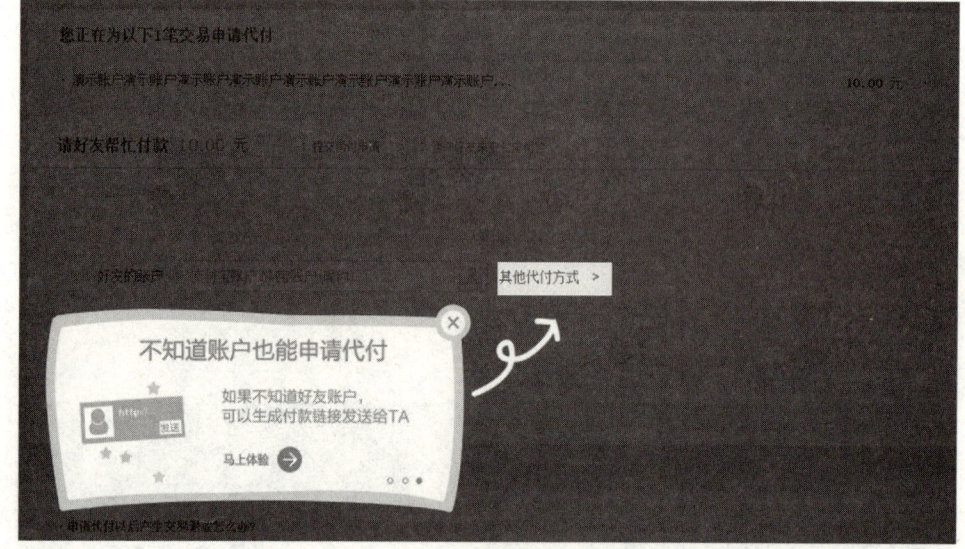

图3-2-5

看到这里，你是不是觉得找人代付是很方便的操作呢？找人代付固然方便，但是方便你的同时却也给他人造成了不便。换位思考一下，如果有人总是找你代付，你会不嫌麻烦且乐此不疲吗？答案当然是否定的。所以，偶尔找人代付是可以的（比如在自己的银行卡账户或者支付宝账户余额不足的情况下），但不能总是使用。对新手来说，寻找适合的付款方式并且亲自付款才是上上之策。

- 支付宝账户付款（推荐！）

适用场合：拥有支付宝账户，且支付宝账户与淘宝账户绑定。

在前面的章节中，你已经知道如何拥有一个支付宝账户了。支付宝和淘宝网一样都是阿里巴巴旗下的网站，因而支付宝账户是可以直接和淘宝网账户进行绑定的。

绑定的操作很简单，只要登录淘宝网并点击右上方的"我的淘宝"，在新页面中的"账户设置"里选择"支付宝绑定"，按照指示即可完成支付宝账户和淘宝账户的绑定。绑定成功后，以后的每次付款都会有支付宝账户付款的选择，在支付宝账户余额充足的情况下，可以输入支付密码轻松完成付款操作。

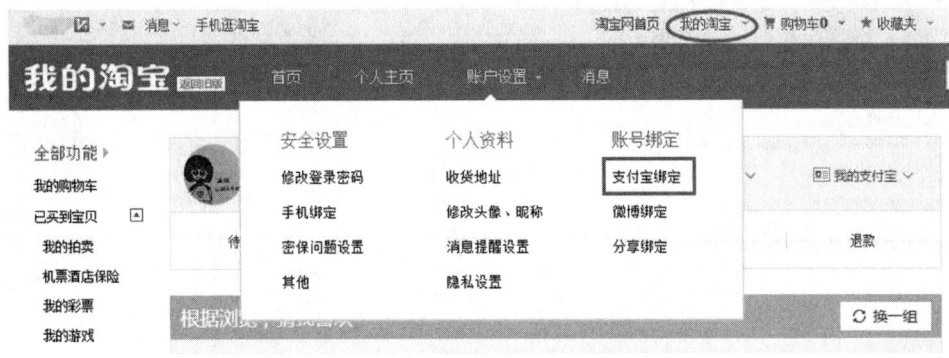

图 3-2-6

那如果我的支付宝账户没有钱，这时候该怎么办呢？答案当然是需要我们去给账户进行充值啦。充值操作也十分容易，首先进入支付宝网站 https://www.alipay.com/ 并登录。

图 3-2-7

然后选择"充值"操作，按照指示进行账户的充值即可（新用户需要按照指示先绑定银行卡）。

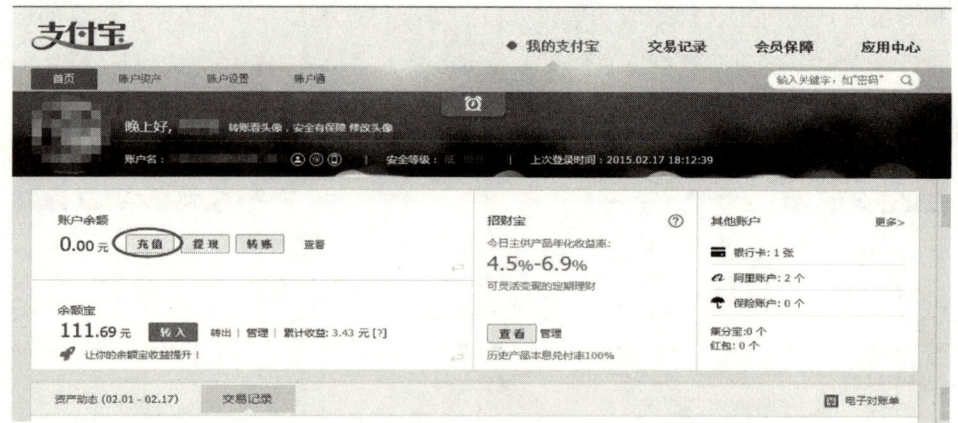

图 3-2-8

账户里有钱了,就再也不用担心付款的问题了。唯一需要注意的是,支付宝有一个默认的设置,当支付金额大于 200 元时,它会向你的手机发送短信验证码。如果遇到这样的情况,你只要将手机接收到的验证码填入网页相应位置再点击"确认付款"就可以了。短信验证码是保障账户安全的一项有力措施。当然,如果你的购买金额总是较高,每次都要输入短信验证码于你而言可能觉得比较烦琐,这时候你可以选择取消短信验证码的服务。

取消短信验证码的方式很简单,首先进入支付宝网站 https://www.alipay.com/ 并进行登录,再选择页面右上方的"安全中心",在出现的页面中你就可以自由选择是开通还是关闭"短信校验服务"啦。

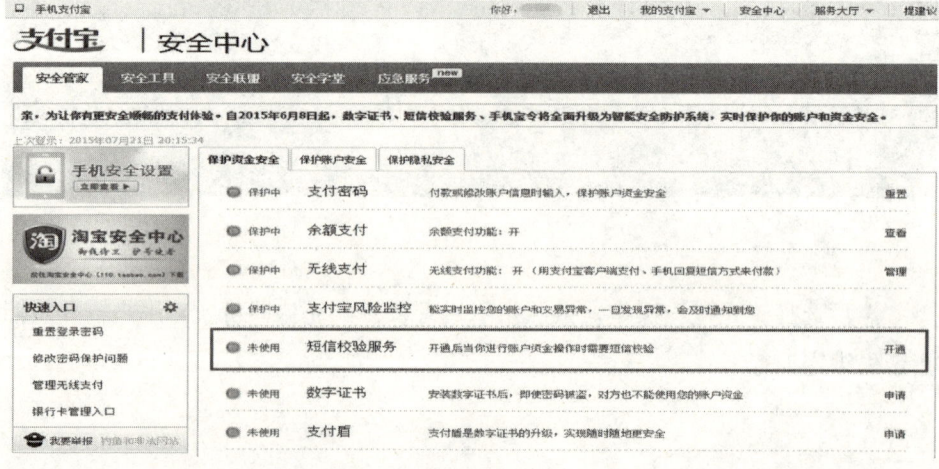

图 3-2-9

支付宝与 PayPal

相信来自其他国家的你，对于 PayPal 是有一定了解的吧。其实呢，中国的支付宝和国际中常用的 PayPal 是具有一定的相似之处的，它们都是网上支付工具，属于第三方支付形式。如果你有一定的 PayPal 使用经验，那么对于支付宝的使用，你可以不用过于担心。

但是，支付宝与 PayPal 有两个最大的不同点值得注意：

一是两者的服务领域不同。PayPal 只负责外贸的收款，它接受美元、加元、欧元、英镑、澳元和日元等 26 种国际主要流通货币，但是不收人民币；而支付宝只收人民币，是中国国内的最主流支付方式之一。

二是卖家收到款项的方式不同。支付宝主要是买家收到卖家的货后，点击"已收到货物"后，款项才会实实在在进入卖家的账户；但 PayPal 只要买家一汇钱，不需要客户点"已收到货物"的按钮，钱是直接到账的。

总而言之，支付宝账户支付是一种较为安全、省心和方便的支付方式，在此强烈推荐给你！

- 银行卡快捷支付（推荐！）

适用场合：支付宝绑定了银行卡

银行卡快捷支付是目前最为方便的线上支付方式，只要绑定使用了银行卡一次，以后就无须再绑定，直接选择即可使用。

第一次绑定使用的步骤如下：

1. 进入付款页面，选择"+银行卡"，直接输入你的银行卡卡号，信用卡、储蓄卡等均可，点击"下一步"。

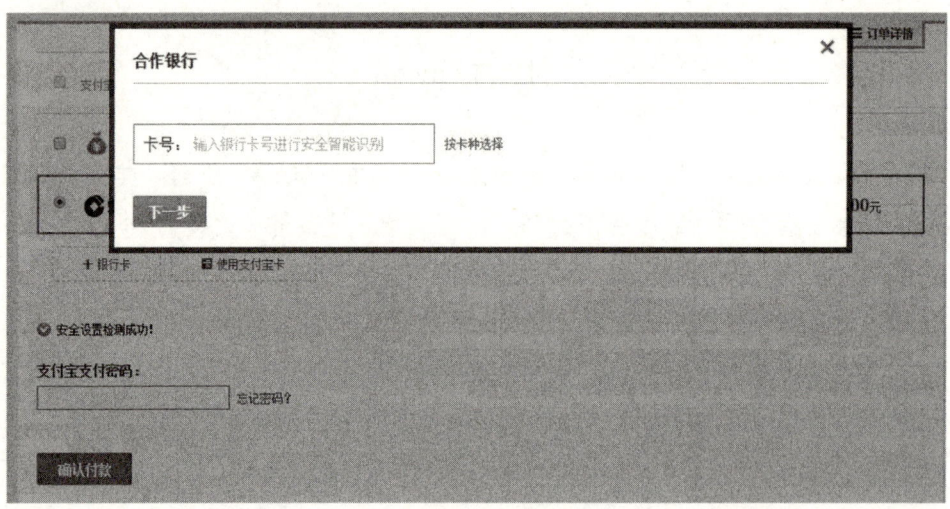

图 3-2-10

2. 选择"快捷支付",点击"下一步"。

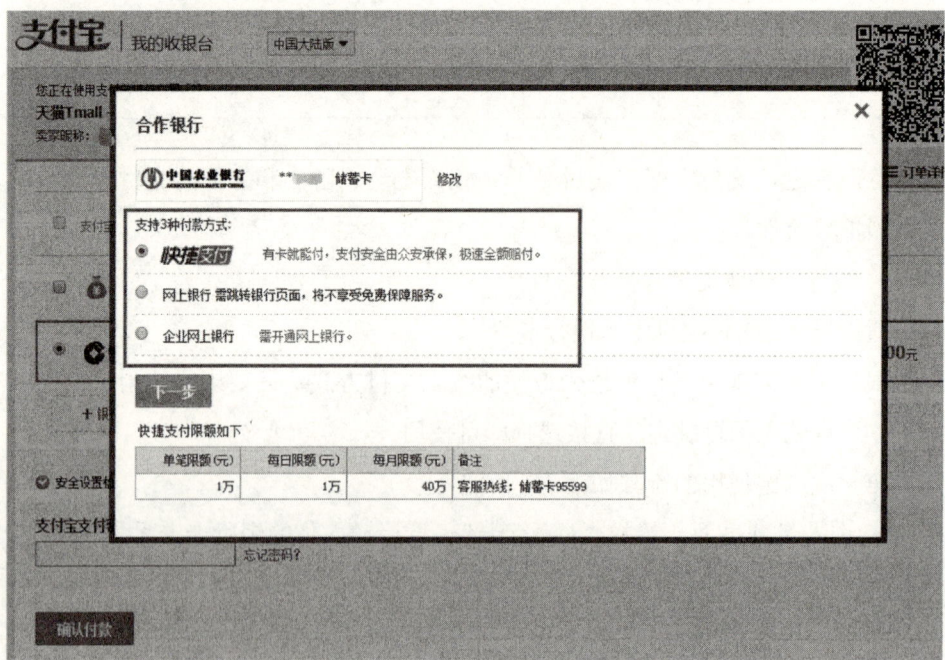

图 3-2-11

3. 按要求填写个人信息并付款。个人信息必须与你当时在银行开户时的信息一致。

图 3-2-12

银行卡快捷支付也是非常便捷省心的支付方式，同样推荐给你！

- 网银支付（网上银行支付）

适用场合：拥有 U 盾，且必须在电脑上进行支付

进行网银支付的前提是你已开通了网上银行服务，而想要成功完成网银支付操作则必须要借助 U 盾。

U 盾

U 盾是用于网上银行电子签名和数字认证的工具，它外形酷似 U 盘，安全性能如一面盾牌，意为 U 型的盾牌，所以取名："U 盾"。U 盾的作用主要是确保网上交易的保密性、真实性、完整性，保护着网上银行资金安全，规避黑客、假网站、木马病毒等各种风险。

当你去银行开通网上银行服务时，银行工作人员就会将 U 盾给你。

每一次在进行付款操作之前,你都必须将U盾插入你的电脑,并保证它运行正常。然后,进入到商品的付款页面,同银行卡快捷支付的操作一样,你得先选择"+银行卡"并且输入你的银行卡卡号,再点击"下一步"。在图3-2-11的付款方式中选择"网上银行"。

网银付款将直接使页面跳转到相应银行的网上银行页面,按照指示就可以成功完成付款操作,操作完成后要记得拔掉U盾。

以前中国的网购消费者中,使用网银支付的人数还是较多的。但是现在使用网银进行网购的人数在逐渐下降。因为在快捷支付兴起后,凭借着方便快捷的操作,不需要借助U盾等原因,快捷支付受到越来越多消费者的喜爱。

• 国际信用卡支付

适用场合:拥有支付宝账户,拥有国际信用卡

对于一些刚到中国的外国人来说,可能还没有时间去新办中国境内银行卡,这时候随身而带的国际信用卡可以在这时候解除支付困境。

下面就来介绍一下国际信用卡的支付流程:

1. 在提交订单后,在支付宝收银台重新选择收银台的地区版本,选择【海外其他地区版】或者【香港版】,这两个版本都可以通过国际信用卡进行支付。

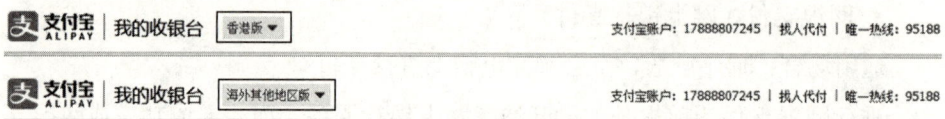

2. 在页面输入支付信息,即可使用国际信用卡进行支付。

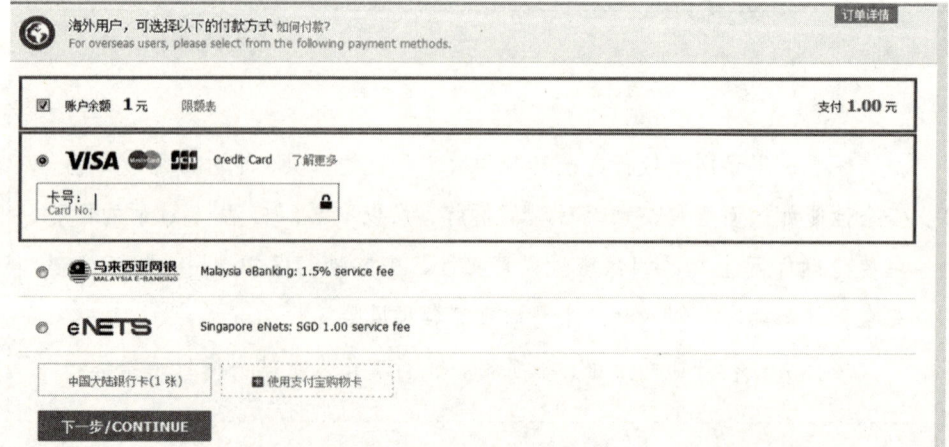

要验证用户 3D 服务密码，则需要输入 3D 验证码。否则，跳过本步骤，直接显示支付结果。

```
Enter Verified by Visa One-Time Password

Verified by Visa One-Time Password (OTP) has been sent to
your mobile phone number in our record (last 4 digits 1010).
Please enter OTP in the field below.
            Merchant: ALIPAY (WWW.ALIPAY.COM)
              Amount: CNY 50.00
                Date: 06/12/2011
       Credit Card Number: XXXX XXXX XXXX 3005
      One-Time Password: ajB3-
                     Submit
Resend OTP?   Cancel OTP   Mobile Number Changed?   ? Help
```

点击【确认付款】，完成支付。

- 支付宝卡支付

适用场合：拥有支付宝卡

支付宝卡是由支付宝发行的预付卡，在淘宝天猫购物时可以直接使用，卡内资金可以在支付宝网站"账户资产——支付宝卡"中查询。支付宝卡不记名、不挂失、不予提现，有多种面值，使用有效期为 36 个月。支付宝卡逾期可付费延期，延期后也可继续使用。[1]

支付宝卡目前仅可在江苏、上海、四川、广东、江西、河北、浙江、福建、黑龙江九个省市购买。在支付宝卡网页 https://card.alipay.com/pcardprocess/shopChannel.htm 中，你可以查询到支付宝卡的代销点。

---

[1] 参考支付宝网站。

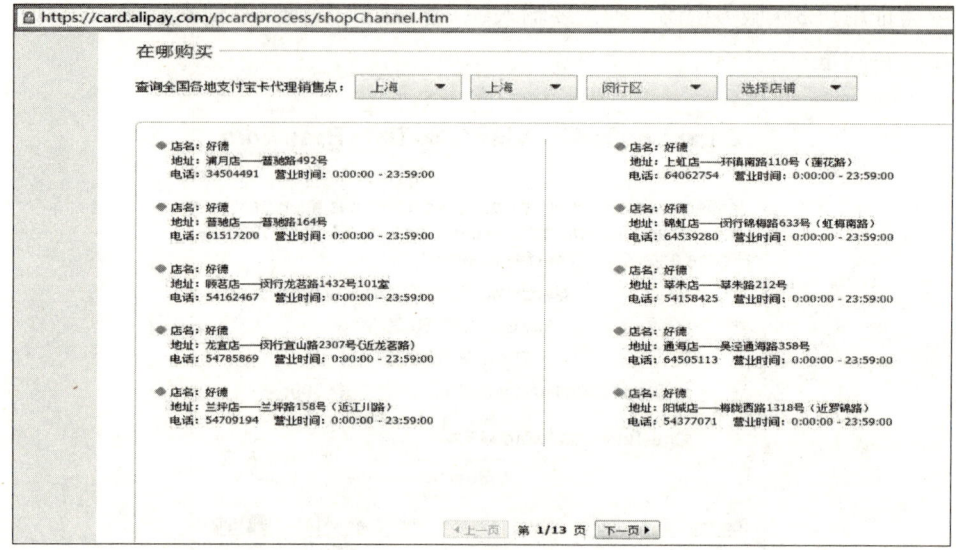

图 3-2-13

对于大多数买家来说,购买支付宝卡是极其不方便的。抛去购买这一限制因素,支付宝卡的使用还是相对简单的。同样是进入到付款页面,选择"使用支付宝卡",在弹出的页面中填入卡号和密码就可以使用了。但是这里要注意的是,你在使用支付宝卡的同时也将支付宝卡与你的支付宝账号关联了,该张支付宝卡以后就只能给你的支付宝账户使用了。

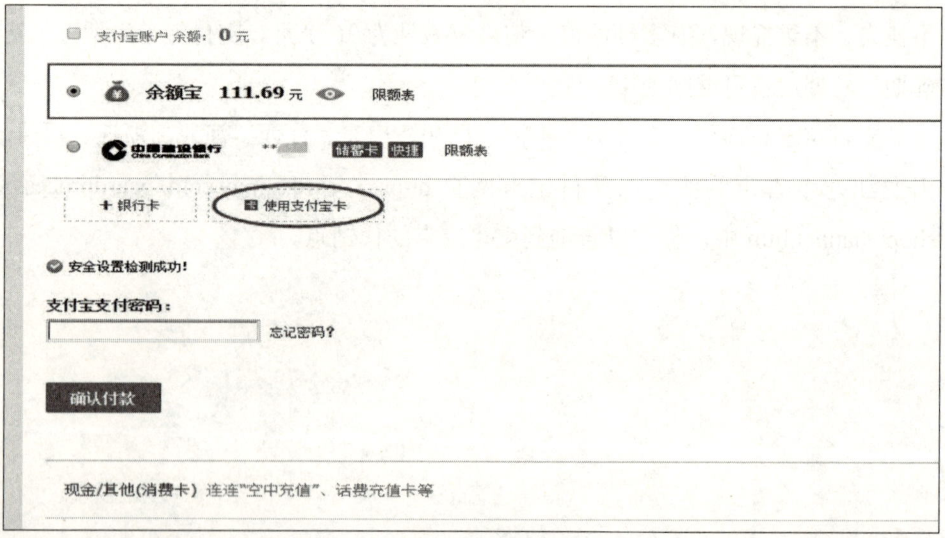

图 3-2-14

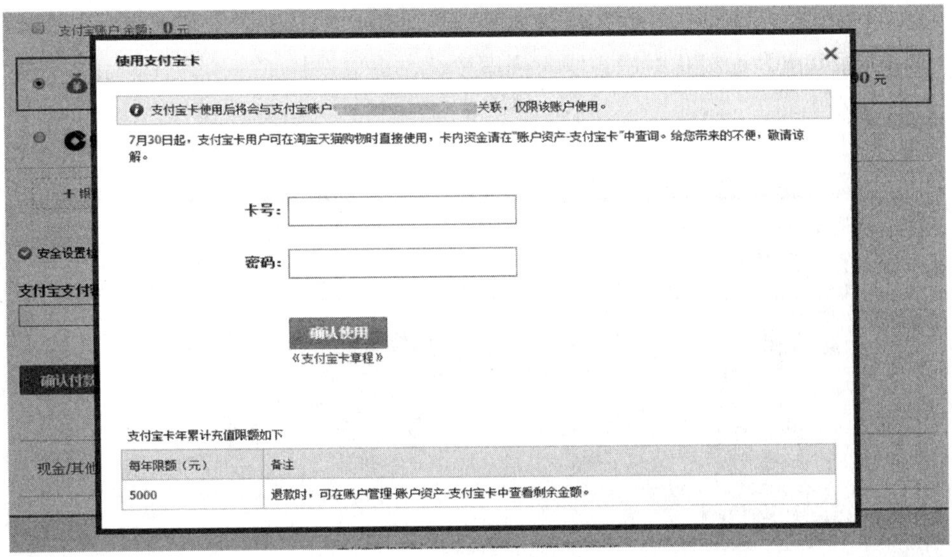

图 3-2-15

- 网点支付

适用场合：附近有支付宝的合作机构网点，没有办法做到线上成功付款、必须进行线下付款的情况

网点支付就是线下的现金或刷卡付款方式，它是支付宝新开通的一种付款方式，适合没有支付宝账户也没有网银的用户使用。网点支付最基本的要求是我们附近必须有支付宝的合作机构网点。

网点支付需要我们先在线上提交交易信息，具体流程如下：

进入到商品的付款页面，在付款页面中点击"现金／其他（消费卡）"。

图 3-2-16

在新弹出的页面中选择你的所在地,如果所在地显示正确则不用进行选择。选择合作网点。如果你对网点支付尚不了解,可以选择下方的"查看如何付款"进行操作。

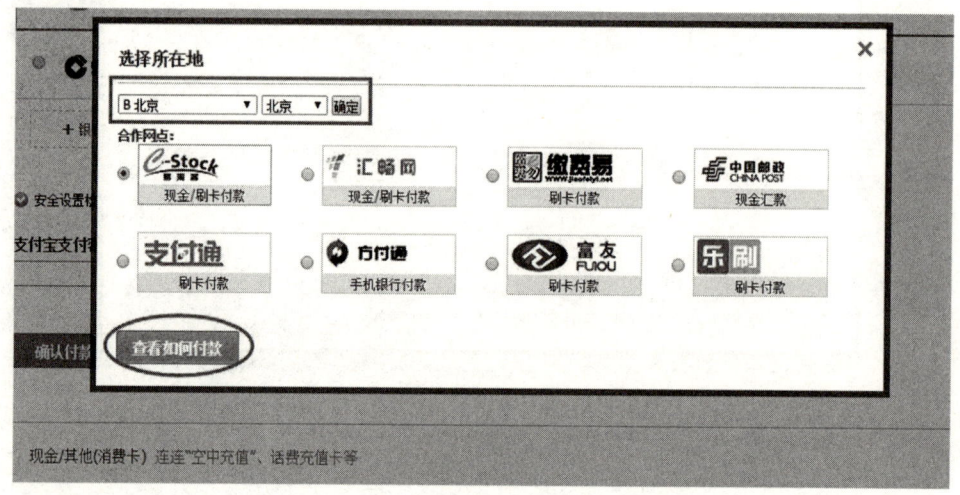

图 3-2-17

操作完成后记得保存好你的交易号和交易金额,然后到附近的合作网店交给柜员办理。

对于在第三章早就准备好支付宝账户和银行卡账户的你而言,这种烦琐的网点支付就可以直接抛弃啦。

• 消费卡支付

适用场合:拥有消费卡,且订单金额较小

消费卡支付主要是以话费充值卡为主,目前仅支持100元以下(不含100元)的话费充值卡。在消费卡支付之前,你需要去移动、联通、电信营业厅或者售卖这三家中任一家话费充值卡的地方购买一张话费充值卡。

拥有了一张话费充值卡后,在付款页面中点击"现金/其他(消费卡)"。在新弹出的页面中选择"其他"——"话费卡",然后点击"下一步"。

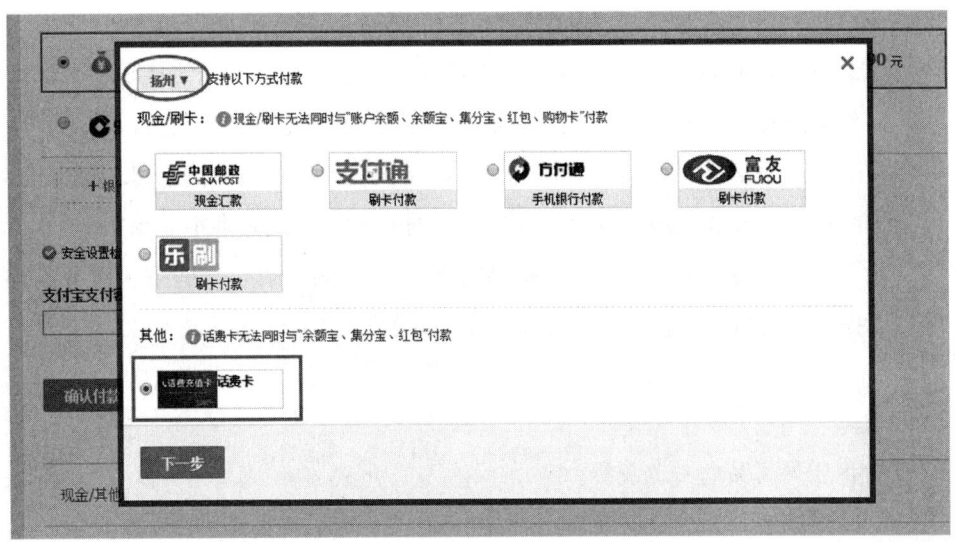

图 3-2-18

按照要求选择话费充值卡的面值,输入话费充值卡的卡号和密码,点击"确认"就可以完成付款操作了。

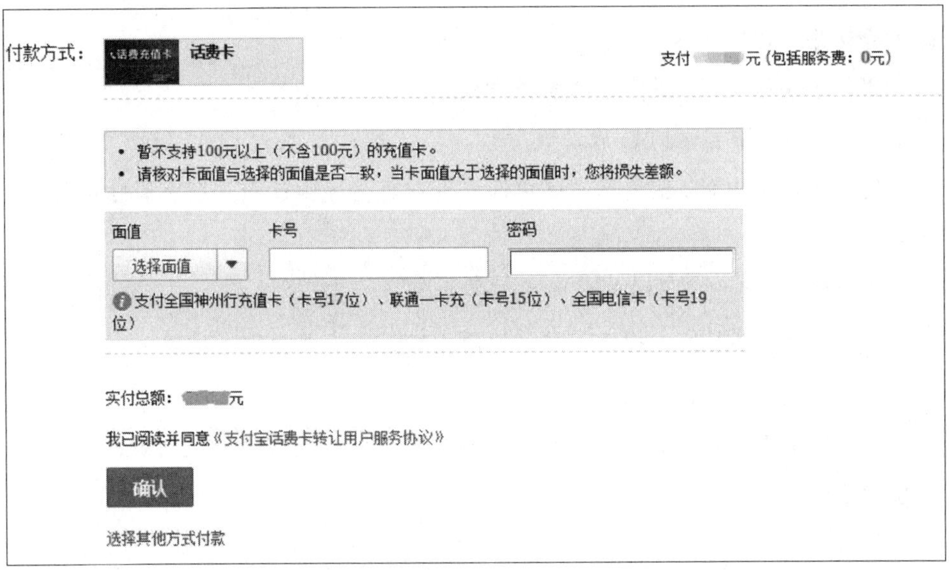

图 3-2-19

消费卡支付一般适用于小额支付,且使用消费卡付款将收取 5% 的手续费,因而不建议使用这种支付方式。毕竟,手续费的钱也是钱,既然有更好的方式可供选择，为什么要选择这种麻烦还要收手续费的支付方式呢？

到这里，我们对于淘宝网的这七种支付方式已经有了一定的认识啦。那么现在，你会选择哪一种支付方式呢？约翰那位有网购经验的舍友告诉约翰，绝大多数中国人通常是采用支付宝账户支付以及银行卡快捷支付进行付款操作的，因为这两种支付方式是最为安全便捷的，省时省力的方式有谁不爱呢？

除了上面所提到的支付方式外，淘宝网的部分店家以及一些电子商务购物网站还提供货到付款的支付方式以供消费者选择。

总结

- 淘宝网商品的付款流程

"我的淘宝"——"已买到的宝贝"——立即付款——选择付款方式——输入支付宝支付密码——确认付款

- 淘宝网提供的多种支付方式

找人代付：方便自己，麻烦别人

支付宝账户支付：支付宝账户与淘宝账户绑定，只要支付宝账户里有余额即可轻松完成付款操作

银行卡快捷支付：最方便的支付方式

网银支付：需要借助 U 盾

国际信用卡支付：适用于刚来中国、没有办当地银行卡只拥有国际银行卡的人

支付宝卡支付：需要在特定的代售点购买支付宝卡

网点支付：需要去支持线下支付的网点进行刷卡或者现金付款

消费卡支付：付款将收取 5% 的手续费

淘宝网的部分店家以及一些电子商务购物网站还会提供货到付款的支付方式供消费者选择。

◆ 总结

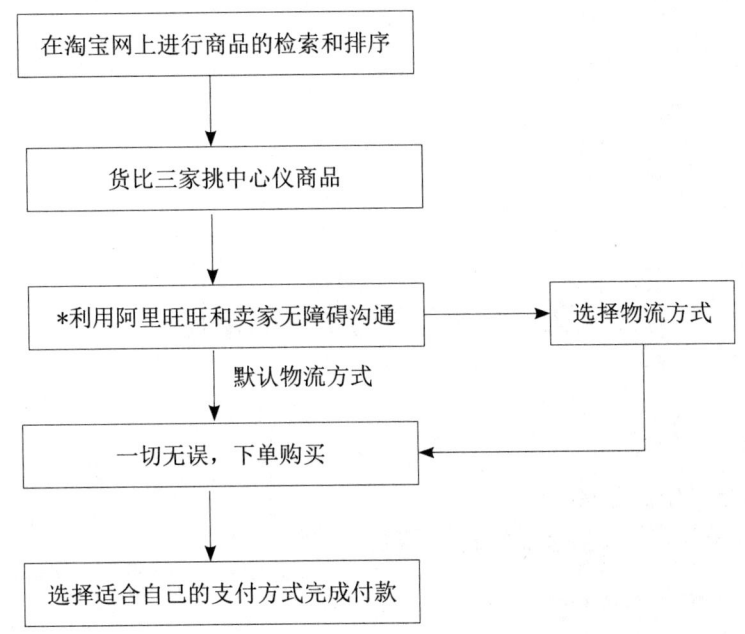

在这一章中，你在淘宝网的购物之旅正式拉开帷幕。你知道了怎样在淘宝网上进行商品的检索与排序，怎样货比三家选出性价比最高的心仪商品，知道了如何利用阿里旺旺和卖家沟通，如何选择物流方式，如何顺利下单购买，如何选择最适合自己的支付方式并成功付款，从而给自己的线上购物之旅画上圆满的句号。

首先，淘宝网的搜索功能将带你进入你想买的商品的世界，巧用筛选和排序功能（五种排序方法包括综合排序、按人气高低排序、按销量多少排序、按信用高低排序、按价格高低排序）避免大海捞针，离心仪商品更进一步。其次，货比三家（可以看商品介绍、看卖家信誉、看商品评价，也可以利用比价网站）准确无误将心仪商品收入囊中；如果有任何问题想要与卖家沟通，不要犹豫，快使用阿里旺旺，尺码不确定、卖萌求包邮……卖家与你沟通无障碍！最后，确认好商品的物流方式，眼疾手快下单后，记得选择最适合自己的支付方式完成商品的付款，在这里，向你强烈推荐的支付方式包括支付宝账户支付以及银行卡快捷支付。

走完这章，线上的购物流程相信你已经熟记于心啦。

第四章

第一节　等待,再等待

在这一节中,你将……
- ✓ 了解如何查看订单的状态
- ✓ 了解如何查询物流状态

拍下商品付款后,等待令人心焦。泰戈尔说"等待是最初的苍老。"要是不知道订单状况如何,物流到了哪里,那一定会老得更快!幸好大部分的电商网站都提供了物流状态查询的功能,我们就来一起看看怎么使用吧!

查看订单状态

大多数情况下,订单的处理要经过"买家下单——买家付款——卖家发货——买家确认收货"这一过程。只有每一步都圆满达成,最终才能完成一个双方都满意的交易。

这一系列过程虽然看起来复杂,其实并不会特别费心费力。在第三章中我们已经完成了下单和付款的流程,那么下一步就是卖家发货了。在这一步,作为上帝的你,只需要监督一下。

1. 首先打开淘宝界面,登录自己的账号。

2. 点击网页上方的"我的淘宝"——"已买到的宝贝"

图4-1-1

3. 在这个页面，可以看到自己买过的所有商品，想要查看哪一个订单的状态，只要查看订单右侧的状态栏中的第一个就对啦。在我们挑选的例子中，可以看到，这笔交易已经成功，也就是说所有的交易过程已完成，买家收到了货品，卖家也已经收到了货款。

图4-1-2

在这一阶段，可能出现的订单状态有三种：

• 买家已付款

这种情况，是买家已经下单并付款，但货物还在卖家手中，并没有发货交给物流公司。

卖家的发货速度是对卖家的服务质量的重要评判标准之一。大部分的卖家会在下单后 48 小时内发货。如果等待多日卖家迟迟不发货，可以通过阿里旺旺和卖家沟通，沟通失败也可申请退货（你可以在本章第二节找到怎么做），并进行相应的卖家评价。

• 卖家已发货

与上面的状态相对应，这时卖家已经把货品交给物流公司，货物已经在运送途中，收货人只需耐心等待。但如果你还是想要知道商品在哪里，咨询卖家可就找错人了。这时你应该转向物流公司查询物流信息，这个接下来就会介绍。

• 交易已完成

上面图 4-1-2 里的例子里的订单状态就是"交易已完成"。这个状态意味着你的货品已经收到，卖家也收到了付款，这个状态就是我们的终极目标。

查看完订单状态，如何看物流状态呢？我们马上开始对物流状态进行探索。

我买的商品到哪里了？

查询物流状态和查询订单状态的操作相似，仍是"登录——我的淘宝——已买到的宝贝"到达图 4-1-3 的页面，见页面右侧下方。

```
和我联系                                        ¥  ↑  ▶  🗑

申请售后          65.00              交易成功          追加评论
投诉卖家         (含运费：0.00)        订单详情          再次购买
                                    查看物流
                                    双方已评
```

图4-1-3

点击"查看物流"之后，会出现一个新的页面（图 4-1-4），在这个页面就可以查看自己的宝贝到哪里了。

```
物流动态

2015-01-18 17:29:25    卖家已发货
2015-01-18 22:57:11    由【银川】发往【西安分拨中心】
2015-01-18 22:58:28    快件已到达【银川】扫描员是【秦晋红】上一站是【银川兴庆区西门】
2015-01-19 09:39:32    【银川兴庆区西门】的收件员【张俊峰】已收件
2015-01-19 21:02:38    快件已到达【西安分拨中心】扫描员是【称重扫描】上一站是【银川】
2015-01-19 22:33:16    【西安分拨中心】正在进行【装袋】扫描
2015-01-21 02:28:20    快件已到达【北京分拨中心】扫描员是【秦占全】上一站是【西安分拨中心】
2015-01-21 02:38:57    【北京分拨中心】已进行【拆袋】扫描，【】
2015-01-21 20:10:37    【北京分拨中心】正在进行【装袋】扫描
2015-01-23 15:48:25    快件已到达【中心】扫描员是【装】上一站是【北京分拨中心】
2015-01-24 09:00:17    ■■■■已收入
2015-01-24 09:00:17    ■■■■的派件员■■■正在派件
2015-01-24 15:58:40    ■■■■■■■■■■■■■■■■■■■■■
                       信息来源：国通快递  运单号：5107933112

💡 以上部分信息来自第三方，您可以点击展开每条信息并查看其来源
```

图4-1-4

有时候，因为网站信息更新不及时的问题，有的物流信息可能从电子商务网站上查询不到。这时候，你也可以追本溯源通过快递公司查询。

1. 找到要查询物流状态的订单，点击"查看物流"文字链接，打开物流详情页面。

2. 在页面左侧物流编号下方，找到"运单号码"并复制。

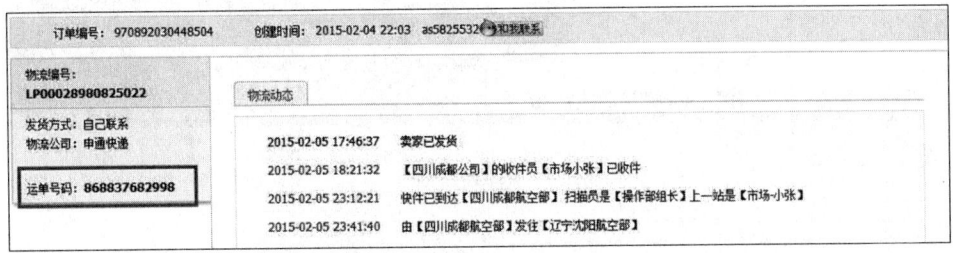

图4-1-5

3. 在物流状态栏中，点击物流方的快捷链接，进入相应物流公司官方网站查询页面。不同卖家会采用不同的物流公司，所以不同的宝贝订单有可能打开不同的物流方查询页面。

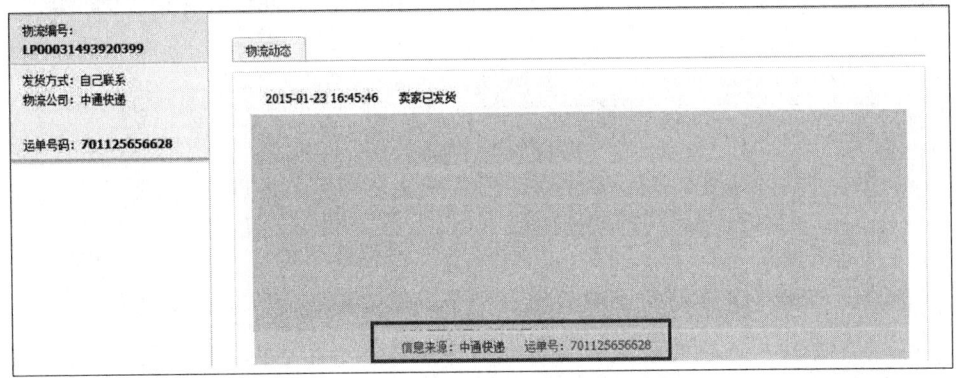

图4-1-6

4. 打开查询页面后，在订单号输入框中粘贴运单号码，点击"确定"按钮。

图4-1-7

5. 之后会打开一个新页面显示订单的跟踪状态，包括日期、时间、订单当前地点等信息。如果订单查询结果中没有任何记录，而订单又是已发货状态，有可能是物流方还没有发出商品，可以拨打客户服务电话咨询。

好了，现在你会查看订单和物流状态了吧？要知道，物流是电子商务中十分重要的一部分。在物流产业，中国也可以说发展出了具有自身特色的物流配送系统，一起来看看吧！

中国特色物流公司

目前在中国，物流公司之间的竞争可谓格外激烈。中国快递业已经连续三年保持了超过两位数的增长，且长期增速超过50%，无论从哪一方面来看，其产生的商业影响和经济价值都是不容小视的。从网上舆论也可看出快递在网民网购生活中的重要作用。

如果你住的地方周围有个快递送货点，你就可去溜达一圈看看主要都有哪些快递公司。最常见的比如圆通、申通、中通；规模小一点的天天、百世汇通、小红帽、宅急送；快递里的战斗机顺丰，虽然贵但又快又安全；

或者邮政快递服务——EMS。我们就来看看这些快递公司各自的特点。

首先是"三通一达",即"圆通、申通、中通和韵达"。这四家快递公司里,韵达最便宜,圆通价格也不贵。申通的安全性相对最好。中通价格和速度都比较平庸。

接着来介绍顺丰。顺丰快递应该是目前中国口碑最好的快递品牌,以快速、安全著称,适合在买比较贵重的、比较急用的东西的时候选用。顺丰的工作人员素质高,丢件率也比较低,被称为快递里的战斗机。当然价格也就相对较高了。

EMS(即"Express Mail Service"),是中国邮政提供的一种快递服务。虽是中国邮政提供的服务,但价格相对较高,速度也没有什么优势。不过在寄往一些很偏远的地区时,私营的快递公司往往没有营业点而无法送达,EMS就变成了必然选择。

我们刚才也提到了一些相对较小的快递公司,如天天、小红帽、百世汇通……他们最大的特点就是价格相对便宜。但是一分价钱一分服务,在丢件率和送货速度上和更好一点的快递公司还是有差别的。不过在买几块钱或十几块的小东西的时候,如果不想出现快递费比商品价格还高的情况,选择这些快递也是没有问题的!

总结

- 查看订单状态:登录淘宝,点击"我的淘宝",点击"已买到的宝贝"。
- 查看物流状态:"查看物流",根据快递单号从快递公司官网查询物流最新动态。

第二节 我要退换货！

在这一节中，你将……
✓ 了解退换货的条件
✓ 了解淘宝网商品的退换货流程

约翰盼星星盼月亮，可算是把自己的包裹给盼到了。签收完快递回到宿舍后，约翰就迫不及待地拆开了包裹。墙纸和卖家在淘宝网上描述得一致，真的质量又好又漂亮。可是将墙纸整个摊开以后，约翰却发现墙纸中间的图案有所损坏，如果是边边角角倒还好，可偏偏在中间，这就影响美观了。作为网购新手的约翰，一直觉得退换货听着就是一件很麻烦的事情，不到万不得已他还真不想退换货。虽然商品有些小瑕疵，但是他实在是喜欢，思来想去半天，约翰最终决定向卖家要求换货。可是，如何进行换货操作呢？约翰又开始发愁了，要不要先给卖家打个电话商量一下呢？

很多买家都有和约翰一样觉得退换货很麻烦的心理，因而觉得将就一下就好，但大多数时候的将就不仅浪费金钱而且影响心情。其实很多网络购物平台如淘宝网都提供了很完善的退换货机制，退换货并没有想象中那么难，遇到问题不要担心，不信的话，就让我们一起往下看。

什么样的商品可以退换货？

尽管包括淘宝网在内的多数大型电商平台都向买家提供退换货服务，但并非所有的商品都能进行退换货。有些电商明确表示，数码产品、食品药品、母婴用品及个护（个人护理）化妆等商品，无质量问题不接受退货；有些电商认为贵金属、手表、珠宝首饰及个人配饰类产品，不应在退换货范围内；还有电商称贴身用品如内衣裤、泳装、袜子等一经签收，非质量问题不予退换货。不过，也有"另类"电商对退货看得很淡，如聚美优品保证30天内即使开封使用也支持退换。

那么,就淘宝网而言,淘宝网默认所有预定商品或订制特殊尺码的商品、鲜活易腐类商品、在线下载的数字化商品、服务性质的商品以及部分收藏类属性的商品是不予退换的。除此以外,商品是否接受退换货是由卖家自行决定的,如若商品不享受退换货服务,一般卖家都会在介绍商品时给予明确说明。

一般来说,可退换的商品必须满足以下要求:

1. 商品如要进行退换货,一定不能点击"确认收货"(除非已提前与卖家沟通协商好);

2. 商品收到时就有质量问题(不包括人为产生的商品问题)可以进行退换货;若非质量问题且商品无 7+ 退换承诺,需要与卖家商量能否退换货;拥有 7+ 退换承诺的商品可以在规定日期内,在不影响商品二次销售的前提下,无理由退换货(任何不喜欢 / 不想要的主观理由均可成立);

3. 退换货要求商品外包装、配件、吊牌等完好,无使用痕迹,不影响二次销售;购买物品被洗过、穿过、人为破坏或标牌拆卸的不予退换。[1]

7+ 退换承诺

1. 消费者在签收货物后超过 7 天(8 天 -15 天),在不影响二次销售的前提下,都可以申请无理由的退换货;

2. 卖家可以自行规定退换货承诺的有效时限(最少 8 天,最多十五天)以及退货 / 换货的运费由谁承担;

3. 申请金额仅以买家实际支付的商品价款为限;

4. 买家的申请在形式上必须符合相关法律法规的规定。

拥有 7+ 退换承诺的商品会在搜索页面中相应商品的下方显示"7+"的图标。

---

[1] 来源于《大连晚报》。

图4-2-1

你可以点击图标，查看卖家对于商品具体的7+退换承诺的描述，包括商品享受几天内退换服务以及运费由哪一方承担等内容。

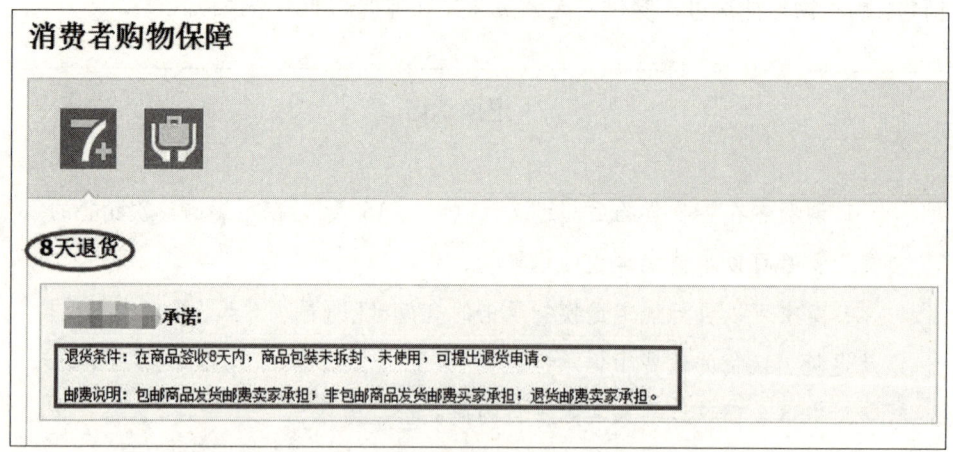

图4-2-2

在掌握了以上知识以后，你就可以开始着手退换货了。在此先给你一个小小的建议，如果你实在对商品退换货的权限和流程等方面存在困惑，或者觉得完全没有头绪，那么准备退换货的时候要记得及时联系卖家，甚至在购买前就向卖家确认好该种商品是否能够退换货以及退换货的相应条件是什么，未雨绸缪。

下面，我们将介绍具体的退换货流程，赶快来学习一下吧。

收到的商品不满意，退货换货来帮你

- 淘宝网的退货流程

（1）登录淘宝网，点击页面右上方"我的淘宝"——"已买到的宝贝"。

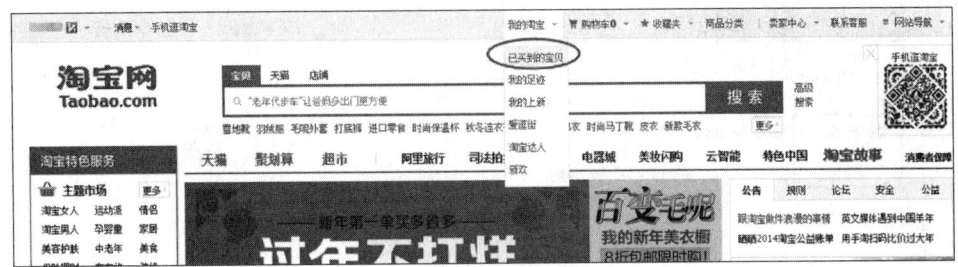

图4-2-3

（2）选择需要退货的宝贝，点击"退款/退货"。

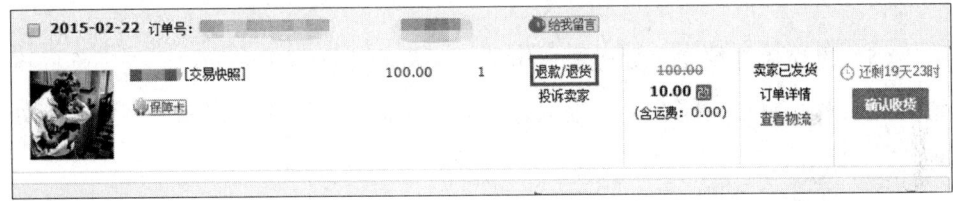

图4-2-4

（3）选择"退货退款"。

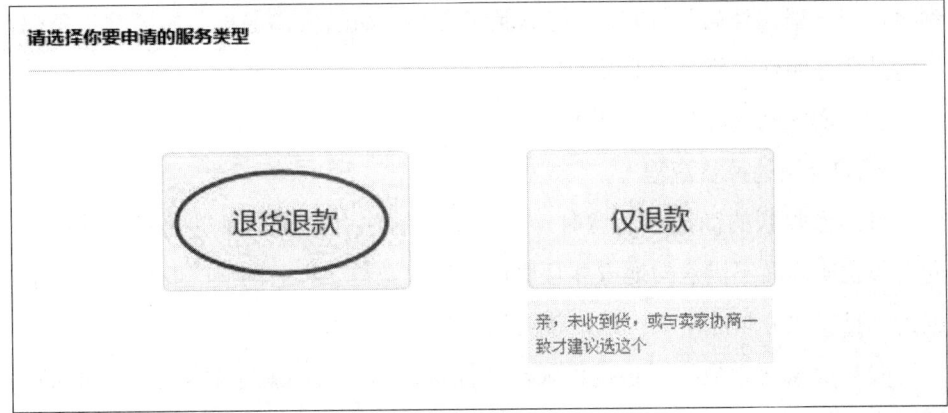

图4-2-5

（4）选择退货退款原因（必选），并输入退款金额（必填），同时可以输入退款说明以及上传凭证（如展示出商品存在质量问题的照片等），然后点击"提交申请"。

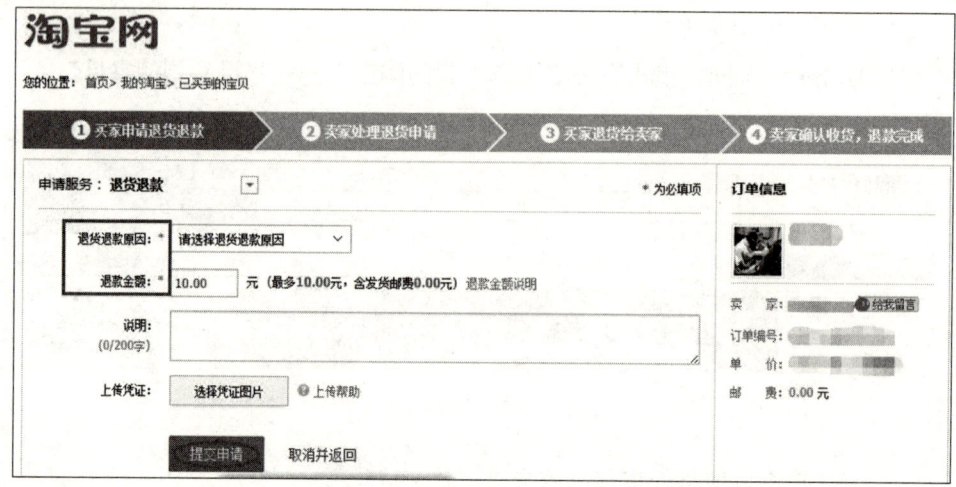

图4-2-6

（5）提交后等待卖家处理退货申请。如果卖家在规定时间内不处理你的申请，那么系统将自动退款。如果双方就此产生问题，可以申请淘宝客服介入处理。

（6）卖家处理申请完毕，将通过阿里旺旺向你提供商品的退货地址。（若卖家没有主动联系你，那么身为买家的你一定要记得主动向卖家索要退货地址）

（7）你需要根据地址将商品寄回给卖家。一般卖家会要求不得使用平邮和到付，用一般快递寄回即可。（切记保留寄回商品的快递底单，如果发生争端，这将是能证明你已经寄回商品的证据）

（8）卖家确认收货，退款成功。

- 淘宝网的换货流程

（1）当收到的商品不满意时，身为买家的你可以通过阿里旺旺联系卖家，向客服说明商品不满意的地方并且要求换货。（记得保存好阿里旺旺的聊天记录，因为一旦发生分歧达不成一致，聊天记录将会是有力证据）

（2）卖家同意换货后将提供邮寄地址，你需要做的就是根据地址将商品寄回给卖家。

（3）卖家收到退回的商品后将重新发货。如果卖家迟迟不再发货，而系统又将到期自动确认收货，你可在已买到的宝贝中打开"订单详情"申请延长收货时间。

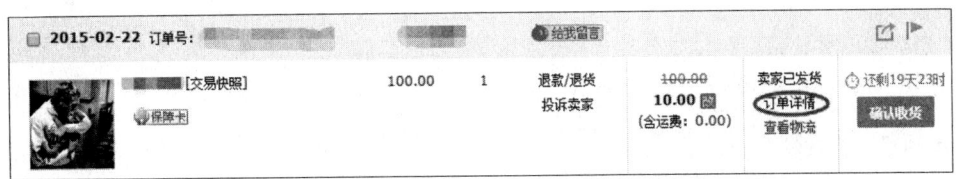

图 4-2-7

图 4-2-8

（4）签收商品，完成换货。

通过上述介绍，你是不是发现退换货的流程并没有想象中那么复杂呢？所以，当你以后像约翰一样在网上买到不合适的东西时，记得利用退换货哟，我们要拒绝"将就"。

总结

- 商品退换货的条件：

（1）商品尚未"确认收货"

（2）商品收到时就有质量问题（不包括人为产生的商品问题）可以进行退换货；

非质量问题且商品无 7+ 退换承诺，需要与卖家商量能否退换货；

拥有 7+ 退换承诺的商品可以无理由退换货

（3）要求商品外包装、配件、吊牌等完好，无使用痕迹，不影响二次销售

- 淘宝网商品的退货流程

申请退货——卖家发送退货地址给买家——买家退货并填写退货物流信息——卖家确认收货，退款成功

- 淘宝网商品的换货流程

联系卖家要求换货——寄回需要换货的商品——卖家重新发货——签收商品，完成换货

第三节　确认收货和评价

在这一节中，你将……

✓ 了解确认收货的流程

✓ 了解如何给卖家评价

经历了漫长的等待和复杂的退换货过程，约翰终于心满意足地拥有了漂亮美观又质量上乘的墙纸。他的网购过程到这里基本就可以结束了，但是，还有一个小小的收尾——确认收货并针对卖家给出评价。

确认收货

确认收货的大体流程为"点击确认收货——确认订单信息——确认支付宝转款给卖家——交易成功"。

首先登录淘宝网账户，点击网站页面上方"我的淘宝"——"已买到的宝贝"进入到所有订单的页面。找到相应订单，点击最右侧的"确认收货"。

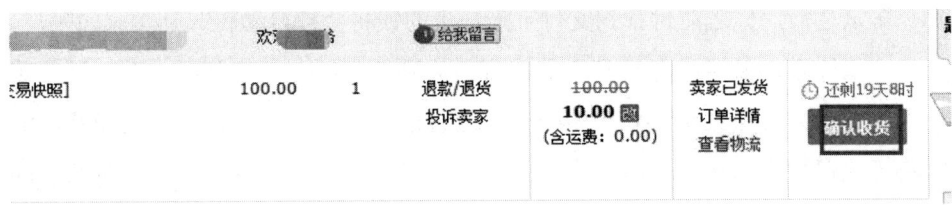

图4-3-1

页面跳转,请再次确认订单信息是否正确。

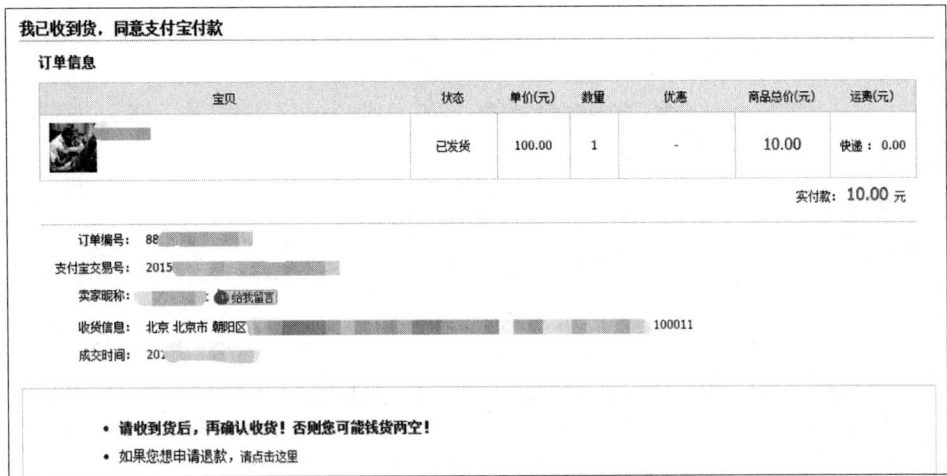

图4-3-2

根据提示,输入支付宝支付密码和验证码,点击"确定"。

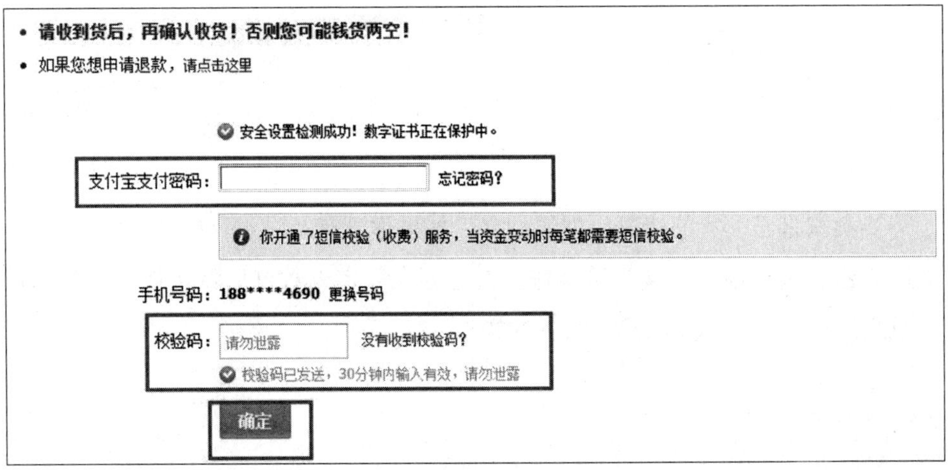

图4-3-3

确认之后，你之前付款到支付宝账户里的钱将会被自动转入到卖家的账户。所以，请注意，如果没有收到商品或者你收到的商品有任何问题，万万不要确认收货！因为确认收货代表着整个交易过程的顺利完成，一旦再想退换货，淘宝将无法保护你的权益，卖家也没有义务满足你的要求，你将面临钱货两空的风险！

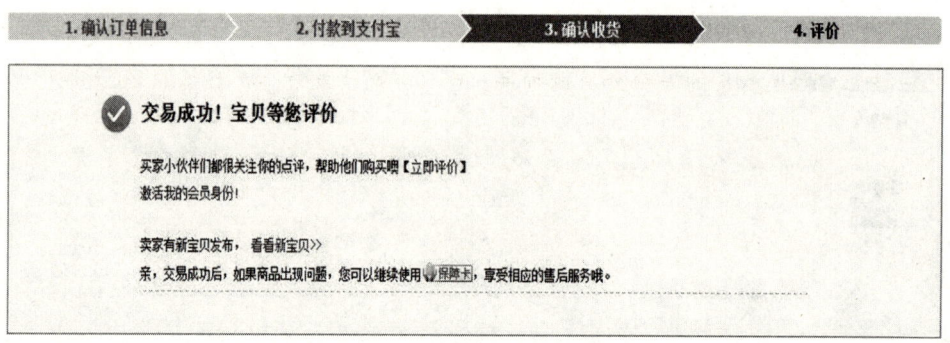

图4-3-4

确认收货完成后，此时，交易状态变更为交易成功。

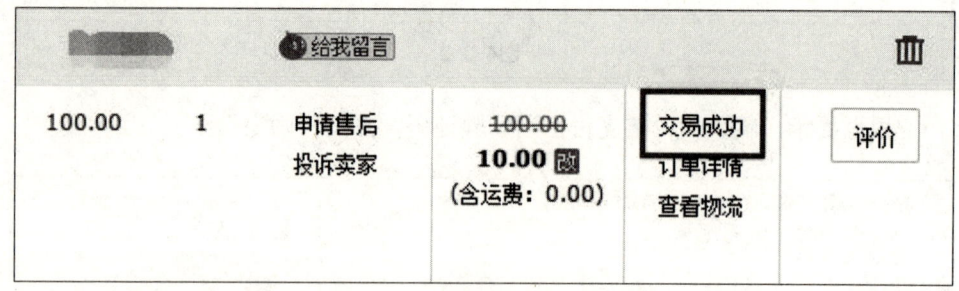

图4-3-5

当卖家将已发货的情况反馈给淘宝，如果你没有及时进行确认收货的操作，同时也没有进行申请退换货等操作，淘宝会在一定天数过后默认你已经收到货并且很满意，会自动完成确认收货的操作。

多长时间不确认收货系统会自动打款给卖家？

1. 购买实物商品

1）如果购买时选择的物流方式为"快递、EMS、不需要物流"，自"卖家已发货"状态起的 10 天后，系统会自动确认收货。

2）如果购买时选择的物流方式为"平邮"，自"卖家已发货"状态起的 30 天后，系统会自动确认收货。

3）如果购买的是海外直邮商品，自"卖家已发货"状态起的 20 天后，系统会自动确认收货。

2. 购买虚拟商品

1）如果买的是自动充值商品 [自动充值]，完成支付宝付款后，系统会马上自动确认收货。

2）如果买的是自动发货商品 [自动发货]，自"卖家已发货"状态起的 24 小时后，系统会自动确认收货。

3）如果买的是虚拟物品 [虚拟物品]，部分类目的虚拟物品自"卖家已发货"状态起的 3 天后，系统会自动确认收货。

3. 如果没有收到货物，可以让卖家帮助延长交易超时。

4. 可以进入"我的淘宝"——"已买到的宝贝"页面找到具体的订单，点击"订单详情"查看该笔交易超时时间。

给卖家评价

在第三章第一节中，其他买家的评论，有效地帮助了你做出购买决策。作为合格的买家，收到商品后无论是否满意，都可以主动和广大淘宝网友分享宝贝的使用心得，并对商品质量和卖家的服务做出客观的评价。

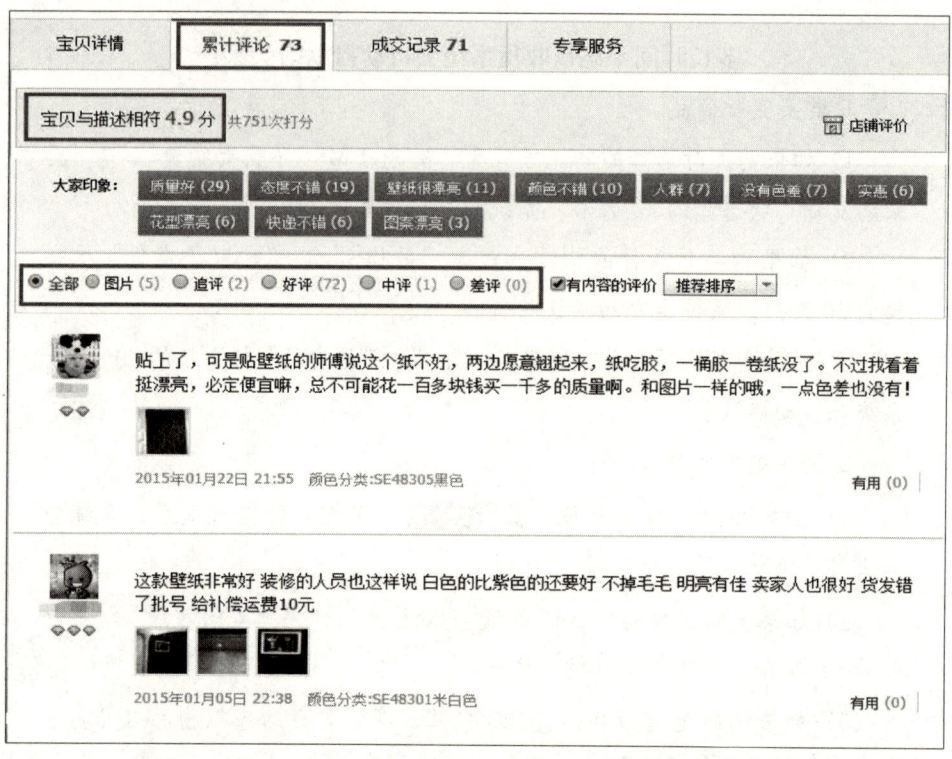

图4-3-6　买家评价

那么如何给卖家做评价呢？

在你确认收货后，订单的交易状态会显示"交易成功"，此时即可对商品和卖家做出评价。点击相应订单最右侧的"评价"。

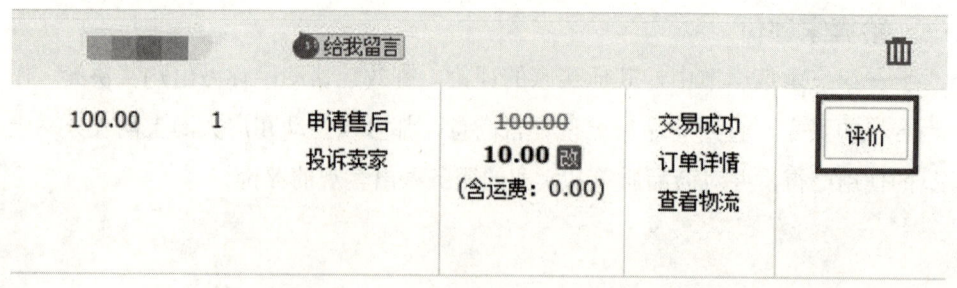

图4-3-7

根据商品状态、自己的购买体验和满意程度选择"好评"（红色花）、"中评"（黄色花）或"差评"（黑色花）。还可以写下自己的评价意见，上传商品的实拍图，给其他买家做参考。你还可以自己选择是匿名评价或是公开你的账号作为评论人。

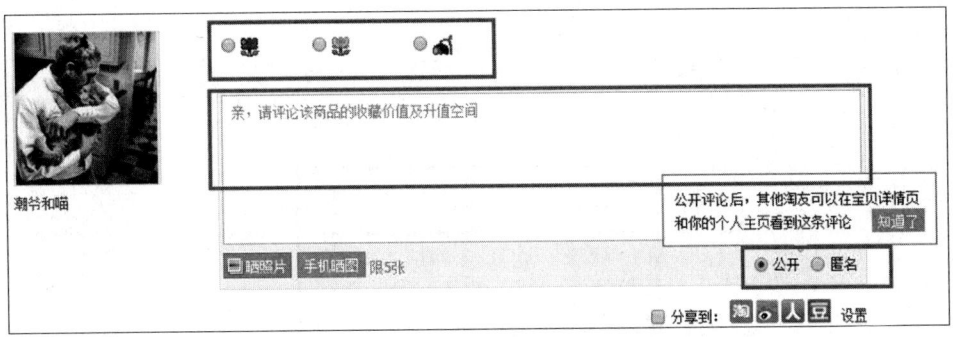

图4-3-8

下一步，请你根据商品与描述相符度、卖家的服务态度、卖家发货速度、物流发货速度四项为卖家店铺打分。

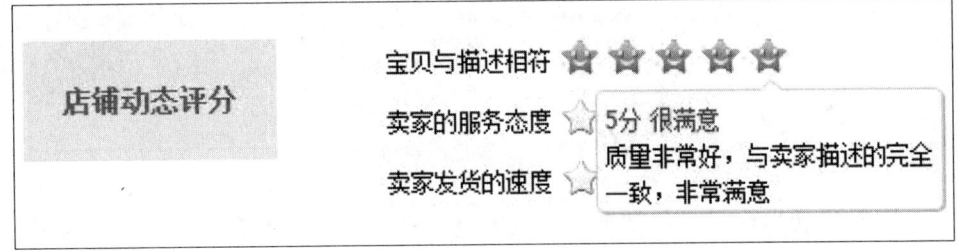

图4-3-9

对卖家评价之后，卖家的信用等级将会被影响。同时，卖家对你也会做出评价。

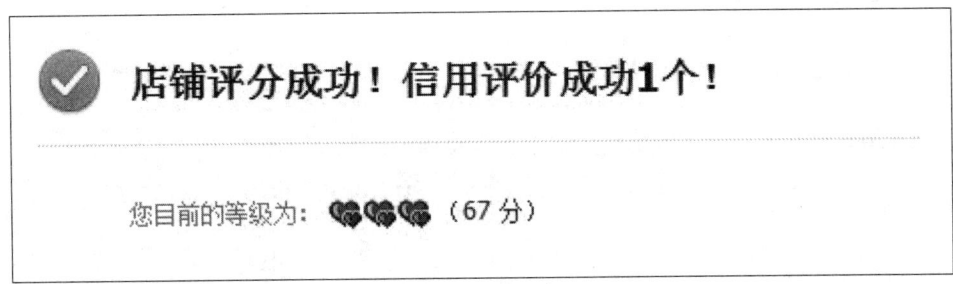

图4-3-10

买家信用等级划分

交易双方在淘宝每交易成功一个订单都可以获得相应的评价。订单交易成功后,卖家可针对其中的每一项宝贝给买家做出如实的评价。评价分为"好评""中评""差评"三类,"好评"加一分、"中评"不加分、"差评"减一分。

4分-10分	♥
11分-40分	♥♥
41分-90分	♥♥♥
91分-150分	♥♥♥♥
151分-250分	♥♥♥♥♥
251分-500分	◆
501分-1000分	◆◆
1001分-2000分	◆◆◆
2001分-5000分	◆◆◆◆
5001分-10000分	◆◆◆◆◆
10001分-20000分	👑
20001分-50000分	👑👑
50001分-100000分	👑👑👑
100001分-200000分	👑👑👑👑
200001分-500000分	👑👑👑👑👑
500001分-1000000分	👑
1000001分-2000000分	👑👑
2000001分-5000000分	👑👑👑
5000001分-10000000分	👑👑👑👑
10000001分以上	👑👑👑👑👑

图4-3-11　买家信用等级划分

有时候会出现另一种情况,买到的商品在刚拿到时没有使用之前很满意,你给该商品打了很高的分数;但是使用了一段时间之后发现质量、耐用性等方面远低于原文描述及期望值,大大出乎你的意料,而已给出的评价无法更改,怎么办?没关系,你可以"追加评论",它就在相应订单的最右侧。点击"追加评论"文字链接,在弹出的新页面中,你就可以补充使用感受啦!

	给我留言			
100.00	1	申请售后 投诉卖家	~~100.00~~ 10.00 (含运费: 0.00)	交易成功 订单详情 查看物流 我已评价	追加评论

图4-3-12

到这里，你已经完成了在淘宝网上购买商品的完整流程——得到了心仪的商品，成功付款，买卖双方相互给予了评价，更新了信用等级。现在，你不能再说自己是新手啦！但是，实践出真知，在真正的网购中会出现各种超出我们预料的问题，只有亲自上手，才能了解在中国网购到底是什么样的体验。感悟中国的电子商务文化，就从你在淘宝网上亲自下一笔订单开始吧！

总结
- 了解确认收货的流程

点击确认收货——确认订单信息——确认支付宝转款给卖家——交易成功
- 了解如何给卖家评价

为商品评分、写意见——为卖家店铺评分——追加评论

第五章

2014年9月19日,阿里巴巴集团(以下简称"阿里")在纽约证券交易所上市,这一dot-com公司上市的盛大状况不必过多描述,网络上铺天盖地的新闻报道和评论足够你看三天三夜!当然,阿里旗下的淘宝和天猫——两大综合性购物网站,恐怕没有几个触网的中国人不知道啦!中国的电子商务究竟发展到了什么程度呢?我们实在不好描述,那么就看一组数据吧!仅2014年第三季度(Q3),中国网络购物市场交易规模达6914.1亿元,在社会消费品零售总额中占比10.6%,相比去年同期交易规模,增长49.8%[1]。或许你对中国的数据并不敏感,没关系,这是一个很大的数字。你只需要知道,网络购物在中国普及率很高,发展迅猛,前景十分广阔。

看到如此大好的发展机会,你是不是也心动了呢?我们的外国朋友迈克,来自斯里兰卡,在中国北京读书几年之后,今年要回国了。临走前,他有很多闲置物品想要处理。将这些东西带回国又太远,扔掉又浪费。身边的中国朋友建议他通过网店的形式寻找合适的买家,这样做不但能快速处置货品,物尽其用,而且可以避免一定的经济损失。迈克经过一番考虑,觉得这个主意还不错,自己的一些闲置物品,也可以通过网店渠道处理,便决定尝试开一家网店。

只是,这网店究竟该怎么开呢?

说到这里,读者们肯定已经猜到我们这一部分的内容了!没错,就是手把手教你如何在中国开一家网店!具体会涉及哪些内容,让我们从新的一章来学习一下吧!

---

[1] 数据来源:艾瑞咨询

第一节 开店构思

在这一节中，你将……
- ✓ 了解开网店的优势
- ✓ 了解开网店的常用平台
- ✓ 了解开网店的必要准备

开网店，优势有哪些？

图5-1-1　天猫店铺

如今这个时代，走在路边，随便问几个人，恐怕都能说出几条开网店的优势吧？别着急，我们把这些主要优势汇总一下：

1. 网上开店，前景广阔

在这个几乎全民触网的时代，恐怕没有人不承认这一点了。包括我们在这一部分综述中提到的网络购物交易规模年增速 49.8%，无限可能的互联网平台，将推动网络购物交易量持续增长。对于开网店的前景，你没什么可担忧的啦！

2. 成本低

像淘宝网等大型网购平台，网上开店是完全免费的，没有店铺租金；如果你的货物比较少，根据顾客订单进货，那么开店就既不需要仓库，也不需要特定管理人员；网店的装饰，属于虚拟装饰，几乎不耗费资金；其他诸如水电费、燃煤费自然也节省了……如此算下来，开网店的成本，真的很低！

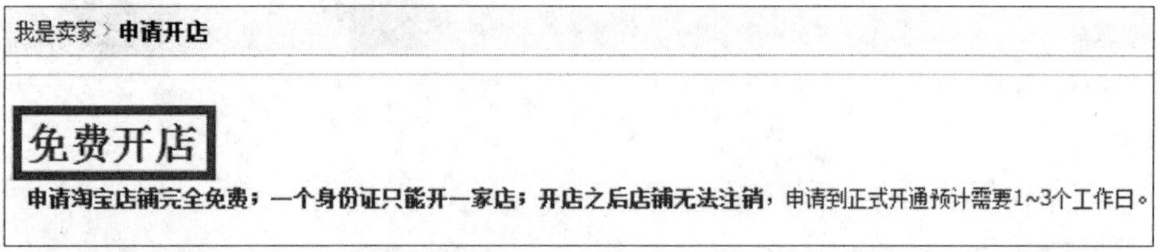

图5-1-2　淘宝网免费开店

3. 网店消费者群体广泛

网店的消费群体广泛，这是一个不争的事实。首先，网店打破了时间和地域的限制，随时随地，想买就买！其次，中国有数亿网络用户，他们都可以自主地上网、浏览网店，成为潜在消费者。

图 5-1-1 中的优衣库（UNIQLO），是大家耳熟能详的服装品牌，相信它的口碑和消费者的认可度也不错。在北京、上海等大城市，优衣库几乎是大型购物广场的标配；然而，在一些规模较小、经济发展水平一般的城市，如潍坊市，优衣库的数量则十分有限，仅有一家。地理位置、数量，都在一定程度上限制着一个实体店所覆盖的消费群体。

图5-1-3 优衣库 北京

图5-1-4 优衣库 潍坊

然而，优衣库网店的开通，大大改善了这一状况。只要你可以接入网络，实体店不能做到的，网店都可以——男装、女装、童装、婴儿装，网店中一应俱全；实体店没有的尺码，可以在网店中选择和预定；即使身处异地，全国物流也可以将货物送到你门前……与实体店相比，网店显然有着更为广泛的消费群体。

图5-1-5　优衣库网店

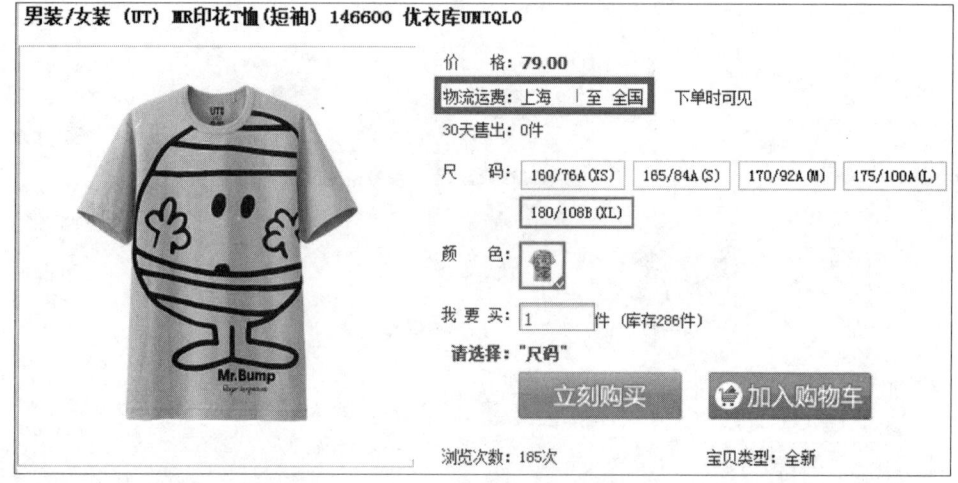

图5-1-6　全国物流

网店的经营模式：
- 如上文中提及的优衣库，是实体店和网店相结合的经营模式。
- 还有一类纯网店经营模式，仅设有网店，不设任何实体店，淘宝和天猫存在大量此类网店。在这一经营模式下，有些人开网店将其作为主业，专职经营；有的人却只将网店作为自己的副业，兼职经营。

4. 经营时间灵活

经营一家网店的时间是十分灵活的。你当然可以给自己制定上下班时间、休假日期。但电子商务平台并不在乎你是否在休假或已下班，一天 24 小时、一年 365 天，只要顾客想下单，就随时都接受下单付款，时时刻刻处于营业状态，即开启的是 24*7 模式。而作为卖家的你，却不必时时刻刻看守店铺，也不必担心天气状况对店铺经营的影响。什么？有急事？有急事卖家您就去处理，时间就是这么灵活！

开网店的优势，基本总结如以上几点，还记得在综述部分的问题么——迈克的中国朋友为什么建议迈克开网店？以上几点，便可解答这一问题了。

哪些平台能开网店？

目前，中国主要有三大 C2C 平台支持开通网店——淘宝网、易趣网、拍拍网。这三大平台均支持以用户注册的方式申请开通网店。

1. 淘宝平台

网址：http://www.taobao.com/

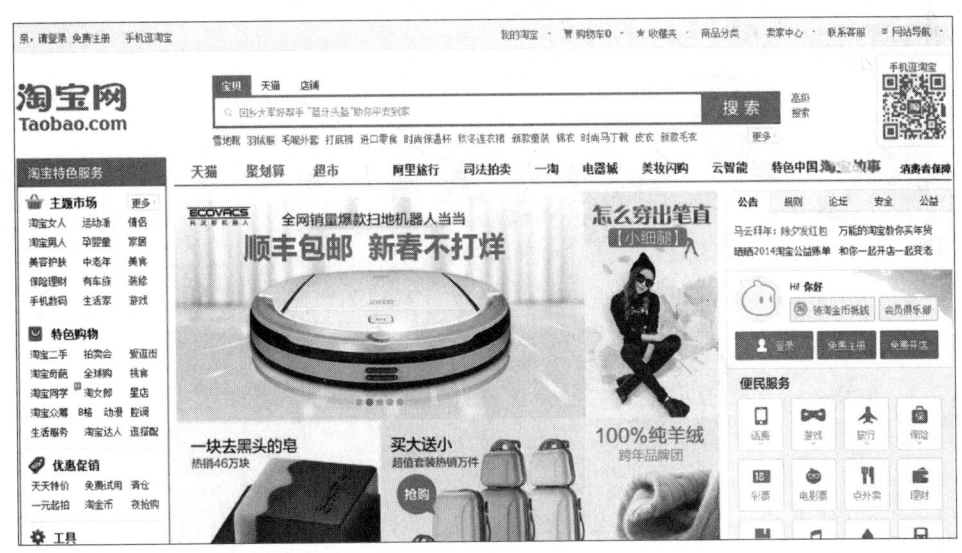

图5-1-7　淘宝网

本书前面的章节中，主要从买家角度对淘宝网进行了详细的介绍。淘宝网最主要的功能，便是作为 C2C 平台，为个人卖家和个人买家提供交易场所。举一个简单的例子，迈克可以在批发市场低价买进一批水杯，放到淘宝网店（免费开店），以高于批发价的价格，卖给顾客，赚取差价。在这一过程中，淘宝网便是迈克与他的顾客间交易的平台。

当然，这个平台的功能也是很强大的，即时聊天工具（阿里旺旺）、支付工具（支付宝）、消费者保障等，各类支持非常全面，卖家和买家都可以放心使用。

值得一提的是，淘宝网是目前中国最受欢迎的 C2C 网络零售平台，它的用户数量、店铺数量、商品种类、交易规模等在中国同类平台中，均居于首位。而自阿里巴巴上市以来，淘宝网及其创始人马云等一直备受关注，从关注度来看，也没有哪一个平台能像淘宝一样被大家如此广泛地关注、讨论！

2. 易趣网

网址：http://www.eachnet.com/

图5-1-8　易趣网

1999 年 8 月，易趣网在上海创立。主营电子商务。易趣用户量早在 2005 年便突破千万，在拍卖市场遥遥领先。2002 年，易趣与 eBay 结盟，更名为 eBay 易趣，并迅速发展成国内最大的在线交易社区。易趣网秉承"帮助几乎任何人在任何地方能实现任何交易"的宗旨,不仅为卖家提供了一个网上创业、实现自我价值的舞台;而且其品种繁多、价廉物美的商品资源,也给广大买家带来了全新的购物体验。

易趣网主打"全球集市"的理念,从上图我们也可以看到,易趣网区分了"中国馆""美国馆""加拿大馆"。易趣网的用户可以通过易趣网购买到来自海外的中意产品。

若想在易趣网卖东西,则可以选择发布单件产品拍卖(或定价卖出),产品有一定的上架下架时间;当然也可以开通店铺,将产品发布在店铺中出售。易趣网也为用户提供了类似支付宝的第三方支付平台——安付通,同时还有用于协调买卖中纠纷的纠纷投诉机制、保护消费者权益的违规举报机制等。

3. 拍拍网

网址:http://www.paipai.com/

图5-1-9　拍拍网

拍拍网是原腾讯电商旗下业务(现被京东战略收购)。拍拍网于2005年9月12日上线,2006年3月13日正式运营。拍拍网致力于打造一个卖家和买家互联互通的C2C平台,通过提供包括服装服饰、母婴、食品和饮料、家居家装和消费电子产品等在内的产品,来全面满足消费者的需求。同时,拍拍网也为第三方卖家提供数据挖掘和分析等增值服务，这些增值服务将帮助卖家对消费者和市场做出精准分析，并为其产品规划和开展精准营销提供支持[1]。

看过以上三大平台的介绍，不知你更倾向于哪一个呢？由于淘宝网目前用户量最大，使用频率最高，所以在之后开网店相关章节的介绍中，我们都将以在淘宝网开店的流程为例进行说明。其他平台的网店开通步骤与淘宝类似，各位读者可以自己进行探索！

开网店前，准备点儿什么？

为了能够帮助你充分准备好此次开店之旅，我们来细细盘点一下，开网店前，都有哪些准备吧！

1. 你需要哪些硬件设备？

- 电脑

毫无疑问，申请店铺、发布商品、装修店铺、与买家沟通……这些工作，哪一项都离不开一台运转良好的电脑！

- 互联网

开通网店，是一定要接入互联网的，无论是有线网络（需要电脑插入网线）还是无线网络。网络接入问题可咨询你所在地的通信服务提供商（如你所在地的中国移动、中国联通营业服务厅）。

- 联系电话

有时候，仅通过网络是不能解决全部问题的，还需要联系电话来帮忙。卖家通常需要在网店中给出电话联系方式，以方便买家与你进行电话沟通。这个联系电话，既可以是固定电话，也可以是移动电话。不过在这个移动通信普及的时代，推荐使用移动电话哦！

- 像素高的相机

对网购有些许了解的朋友都会知道，网店中的商品直观信息主要以图片的形式展现在顾客面前。所以，你也要有一台像素高的相机，将你的实物拍成图

---

[1] 参考自百度百科。

片放到网店中，供顾客了解商品和进行挑选。

• 打印机

订单量比较少时，可以手填物流发货单。如果业务发展到一定阶段，订单量多起来，统一格式打印发货单会更省时省力，此时，打印机就派上用场啦！

• 网银

由于网店的交易基本在网络上展开，包括支付和收款环节；因此，网银在你的网店交易中是必备的！如何申请银行卡以及如何为银行卡开通网银等相关细节，请参考前面章节中的详述。

2. 你需要哪些软件设备？

• 电子邮箱

相信当前每个人至少拥有一个 E-mail 地址，电子邮箱可以用来申请淘宝账号，这一部分在前面的章节中也已提及。此外，邮件还是一种很重要、很正式的沟通方式，无论在与平台提供者、平台管理者还是买家的沟通中，都有可能会用到。

• 实时沟通工具：阿里旺旺

它是淘宝网为用户提供的一款即时聊天工具，有网页版，也可以下载应用程序到 PC 端或移动端（移动端名为"旺信"）使用，大大方便了买卖过程中买家和卖家的沟通交流。

• 图像处理软件

有如下两幅图片（图 5-1-10），若你是一位买家，面对这两件衣服，会如何选择呢？恐怕大部分买家都会选择前者吧。这是同一品牌的 2015 春款服装，当在网店中呈现在买家眼前时，却是完全不同的感觉。精美光彩的图片是吸引买家的第一步，所以对实物图片进行必要的处理，再美美地放到网店中，才能更好地吸引买家。当前最流行的、功能较为全面的图像处理软件便是 Adobe Photoshop。

图5-1-10 对比图

3. 你需要准备哪些信息资料?

- 护照

图5-1-11 护照

- 入境证明(或《外国人永久居留证》/外国人居留许可)

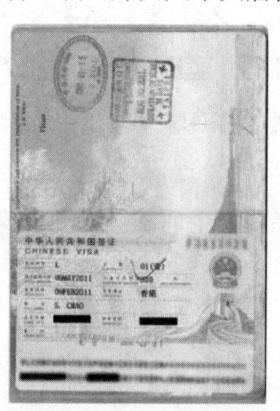

图5-1-12 入境证明

图5-1-13　外国人居留许可

注意事项
- 提供的证件必须为彩色原件电子版（可使用数码相机拍摄或彩色扫描仪扫描）。
- 图片一定要完整，不可以对图片进行任何的修改。

- 在中国的银行账户

无论在哪一平台开网店，你都需要一张银行卡。在淘宝网上，这一银行账户就是你进行交易的结算账户，需要和支付宝绑定。目前，淘宝网上开店支持申请认证的银行卡由以下15家银行发行，一定要认准这15家银行。

建设银行	中国农业银行	兴业银行
中国民生银行	浦发银行	中国工商银行
招商银行	交通银行	中国银行
广发银行	中信银行	光大银行
杭州银行	中国邮政储蓄银行	平安银行

总结

看到这里，这一节的内容便基本结束了。在这一节中，我们共解决了三个问题，并详细列举了开网店前需要做的若干准备，希望对你有所帮助！

1. 开网店的优势
   - 前景广阔
   - 成本低
   - 消费群体广泛
   - 经营时间灵活
2. 开网店的常用平台
   - 淘宝网
   - 易趣网
   - 拍拍网
3. 开网店前的若干准备
   - 硬件准备：电脑、互联网、联系电话、相机、打印机、网银
   - 软件准备：电子邮箱、阿里旺旺、图像处理软件
   - 材料准备：护照、入境证明、在中国的银行账户

第二节　开店申请

在这一节中，你将……
✓ 了解网店的申请步骤

中国有一句古话"读万卷书，行万里路"，意思是在学习理论的同时要加强实践，学以致用。在前面一节中，我们已经对网上开店有了理论上的认识，下面就让我们实践起来，开一个属于自己的网店吧。

这里我们以淘宝 www.taobao.com 为例进行逐步的讲解。

首先，你需要有一个属于自己的淘宝账号。如果你还没有，赶快去申请一个吧。

图5-2-1　淘宝首页

登录自己的账号后，找到屏幕右下角的橘色按钮，点击免费开店。

进入之后，为了保证操作的安全性，淘宝网通常会要求你再次输入密码。输入后，便可进入卖家中心了。

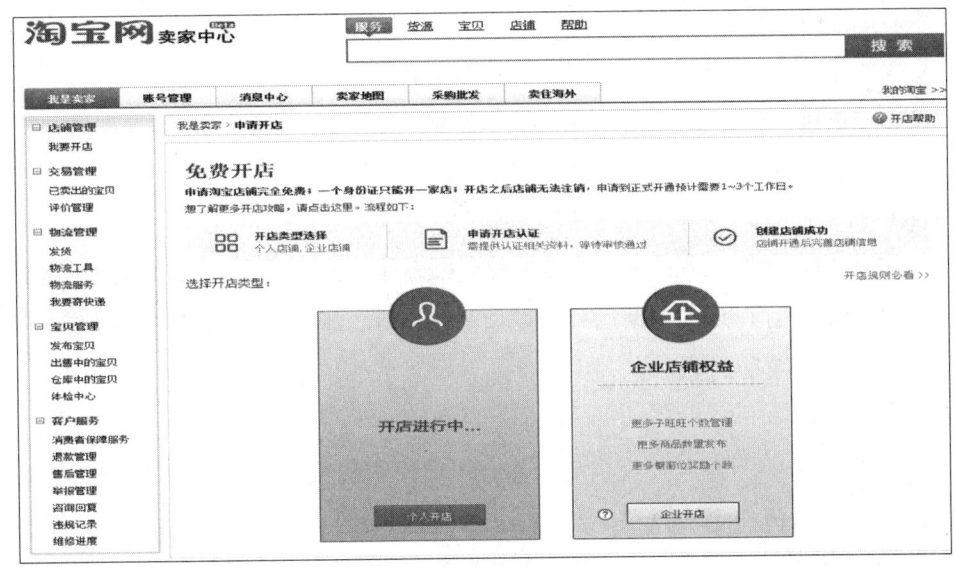

图5-2-2　免费开店

上图就是淘宝网的卖家中心页面，在屏幕的上方提供了简单的搜索服务，你可以在这里搜索货源、货品、店铺等相关信息。屏幕下方展示了分门别类的信息，这些信息涵盖了网上卖货的方方面面，我们将在接下来的讲解中一一介绍。

进入这个页面后，最中心的部分是醒目的彩色开店按钮，有个人开店和企业开店两种开店模式供你选择。如果你是以个人的名义开店，那么请选择个人开店，如果你是以一个团体企业的名义开店请选择企业开店。不同的开店模式在申请流程上会有所不同。在这里，我们选择"个人开店"。点击橙色按钮就可以直接进入开店申请流程了，不过在此之前，我们可以先了解下开店的规则。点击免费开店中"点击这里"的蓝色字样即可进入说明区。

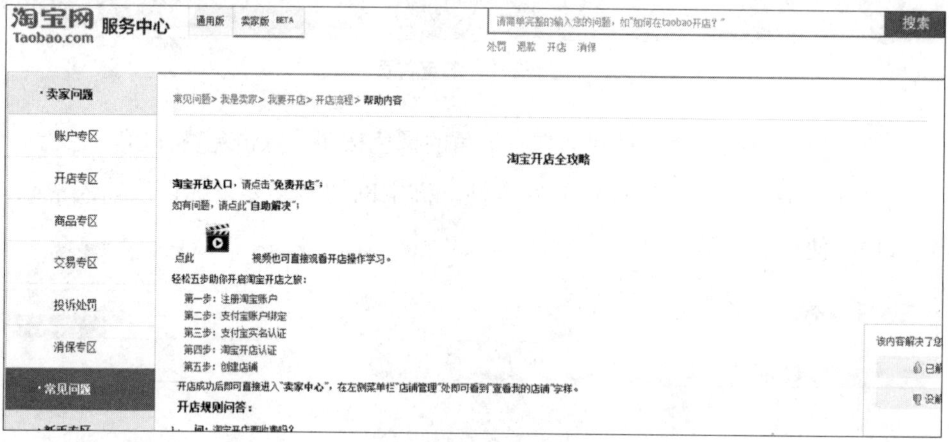

图5-2-3　服务中心

进入后，我们来到了服务中心，这里涵盖了网上开店的各个流程的所需要了解的信息，你可以在申请店铺之前读一读，等正式开店之后也可以到这里来查看解答不了解的问题。

在服务中心阅览相关规则后，你会对申请的流程有宏观上的理解和把握，在后续申请阶段将更加顺利。当然，直接跳过查阅信息这一步的朋友也不用担心，结合网站和本书的步骤，你的开店申请一定会非常顺利。

得到你所需知识后回到卖家中心首页，点击"免费开店"。

点击进入后，淘宝网会自动检测你的账号，查看你是否符合开店条件，如果符合，那将会直接进入到开店认证环节。

在这个环节里，你还要进行两次认证，只有两次认证全部通过才可以顺利开店。这两次认证分别是：支付宝实名认证和淘宝开店认证。

支付宝实名认证的目的：
- 支付宝实名认证是为了核实会员身份信息和银行账户信息。通过支付宝实名认证后，您就相当于拥有了一张互联网身份证，有了这张身份证后您可以在淘宝网等众多电子商务网站开店、出售商品，提高支付宝账户拥有者的信用度。

在支付宝账户认证环节中，要注意支付宝的账户地址必须与您的所在地地址相一致。如果你还没有注册支付宝账户，那就赶快注册一个吧，在本书的第二章有具体说明。

图5-2-4　开店认证

完成支付宝实名认证之后，就要进行淘宝开店认证了，点击"立即认证"。

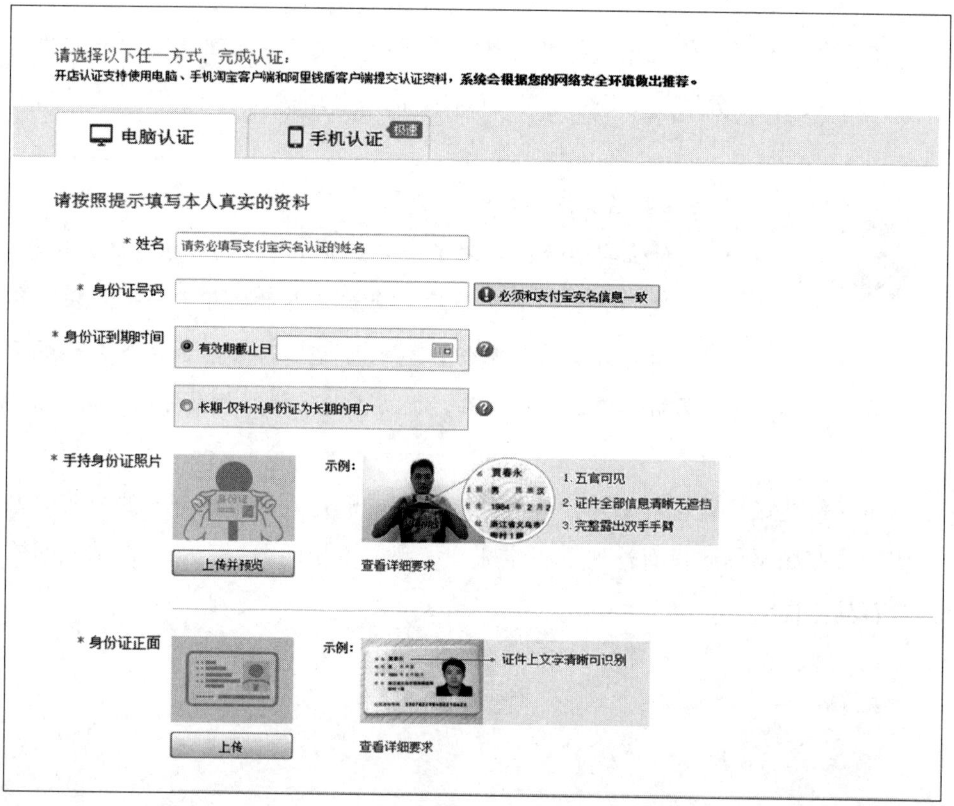

图5-2-5　电脑认证

在身份认证这个步骤中，淘宝网提供了两种认证方法：电脑认证和手机认证。

如果你选择"电脑认证"，那么你需要上传相关的证件并按照其规则上传你的真人照片，另外还要填写地址和手机号信息。

如果你选择"手机认证"，那么你需要在与电脑认证相类似的两个步骤之前安装阿里钱盾并进行扫描认证。

图5-2-6　手机认证

下载完相关安全软件之后，后续的操作流程基本与电脑认证相一致。

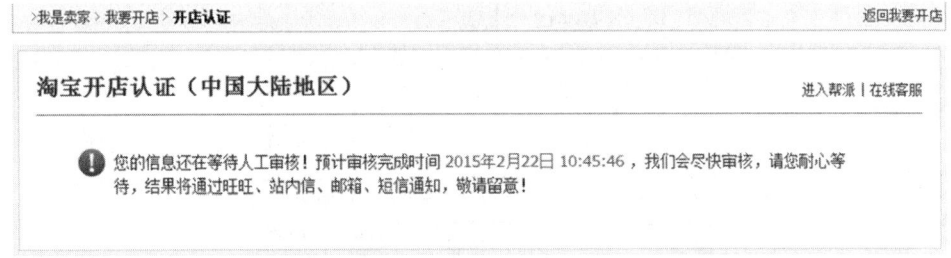

图5-2-7　人工审核

在你提交了申请材料之后，要经过人工审核才能顺利开店，人工审核的时间一般比较长，网站会将预计审核完成时间告诉你，你可以随时关注。

某一天，当你打开网站，你会欣喜地发现，审核成功，你可以创建店铺了！

点击"创建店铺",开始开店吧!

图5-2-8　创建店铺

总结

在这一节中,我们为你详细讲述了申请网店的步骤,希望对你有所帮助!下面是从这一节中提炼的申请流程图,来看一看,让你的申请变得更容易吧!

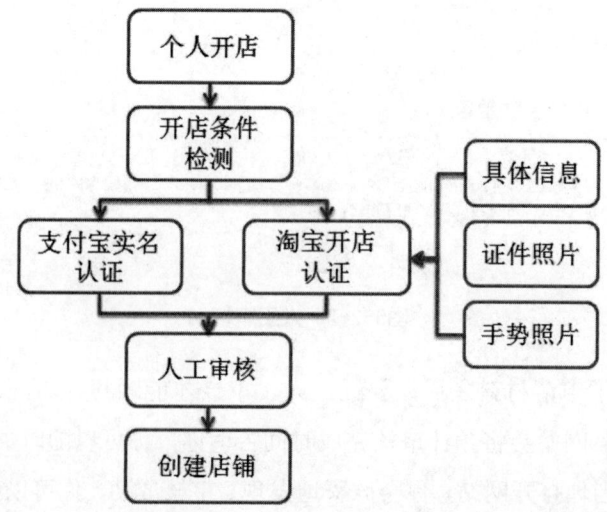

第三节　网店商品展示

在这一节中，你将……

✓ 了解网店发布商品步骤

✓ 了解网店"装修"步骤

发布商品

在淘宝网导航栏中，点击"卖家中心"便可以进入你的网络小店了。

有了梦寐以求的小店，咱们开始发布商品吧。

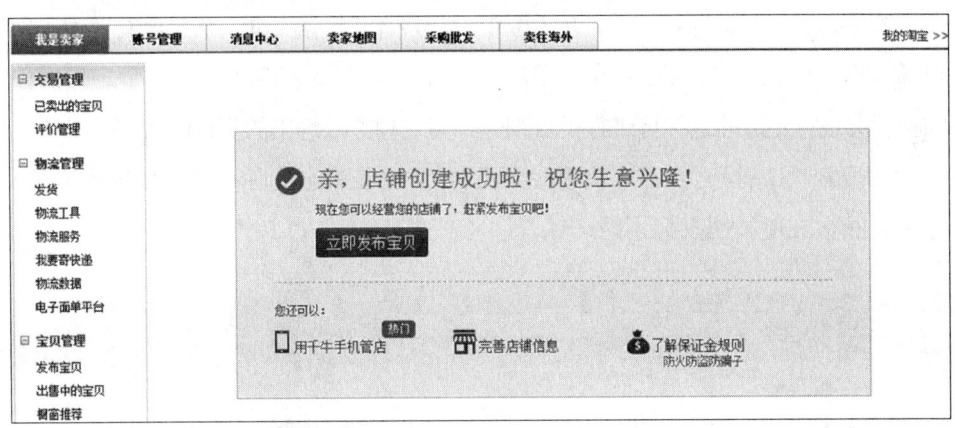

图5-3-1　发布宝贝

你可以在店铺创建成功页面直接选择绿色方框"立即发布宝贝"，也可以选择左侧菜单栏"宝贝管理"中的"发布宝贝"。

图5-3-2　选择分类

你可以通过类目菜单来选择分类，也可以通过类目搜索来查找类目。这里为大家简单介绍一下类目查找栏。在上图中，一共有三栏搜索框，从左至右搜索类别逐渐缩小具体化。最左边是最高一级分类，先在这里进行选择。选定了之后后面的一栏会根据左边的选择再进行类目细分。用这种方法选出的类目既规范又准确。

如搜索"U盾"，点击"快速找到类目"，系统就会为你寻找最佳匹配类目。这种方法很方便，朋友们不妨一试。

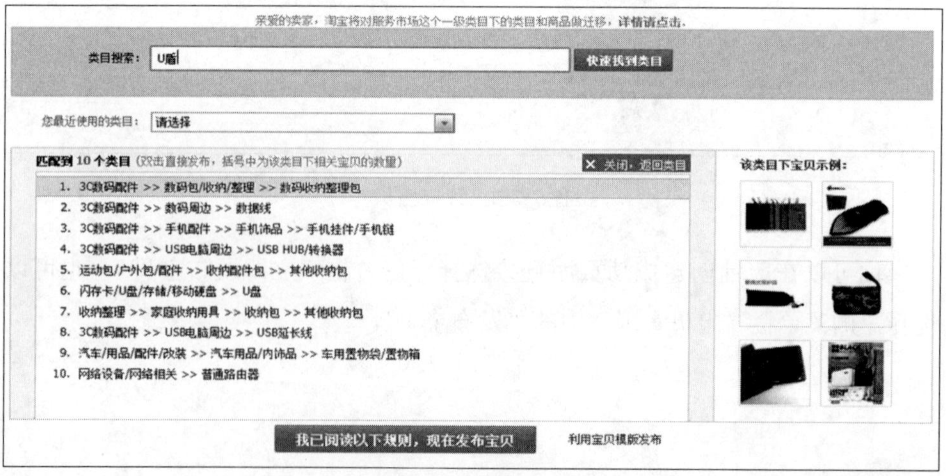

图5-3-3　类目搜索

在设置类目的时候要注意不要随便设置，尽量保证类目的准确有效。这样更方便顾客快速准确地找到你的货品。

确认分类之后点击发布宝贝，你就进入了宝贝（在淘宝网中，为了显得亲切，习惯性将商品称为宝贝）发布前的设置页面。

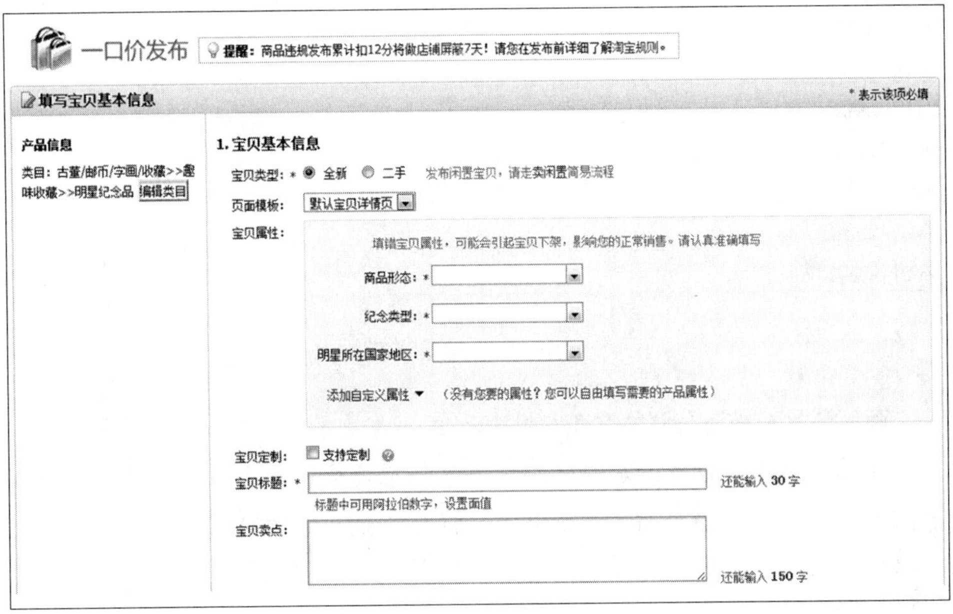

图5-3-4　宝贝信息

在设置页面中，你需要设置宝贝信息、物流和售后等一系列信息。这些信息至关重要，要认真填写。

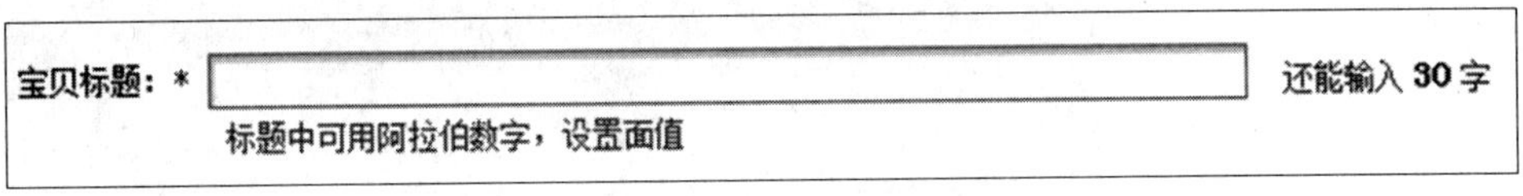

图5-3-5　宝贝标题

商品的标题是顾客得到的关于你的商品的第一个信息，这个信息对访问量和购买量都有着很大的影响。你可以在填写之前看看同类型的商品是如何写标题的。还有一种方法，是将你要发布的商品名称填入淘宝网首页搜索栏里，它会自动出现一些关于这个商品的关键词，这些关键词就是顾客常会搜索的热词，你可以根据这些热词来确定自己商品的标题。

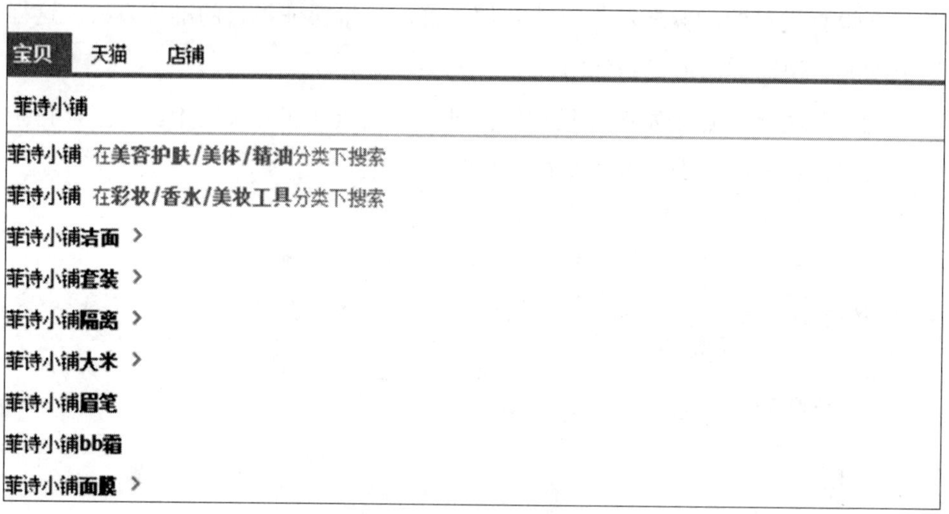

图5-3-6 宝贝词条

商品图片和描述是商品发布的重中之重。

仔细观察你会发现，热销商品的图片与描述往往都下了一番功夫——商品图片清晰简洁，商品描述图文并茂、详尽细致，有的甚至还采用了视频加以说明。

图5-3-7 宝贝描述1

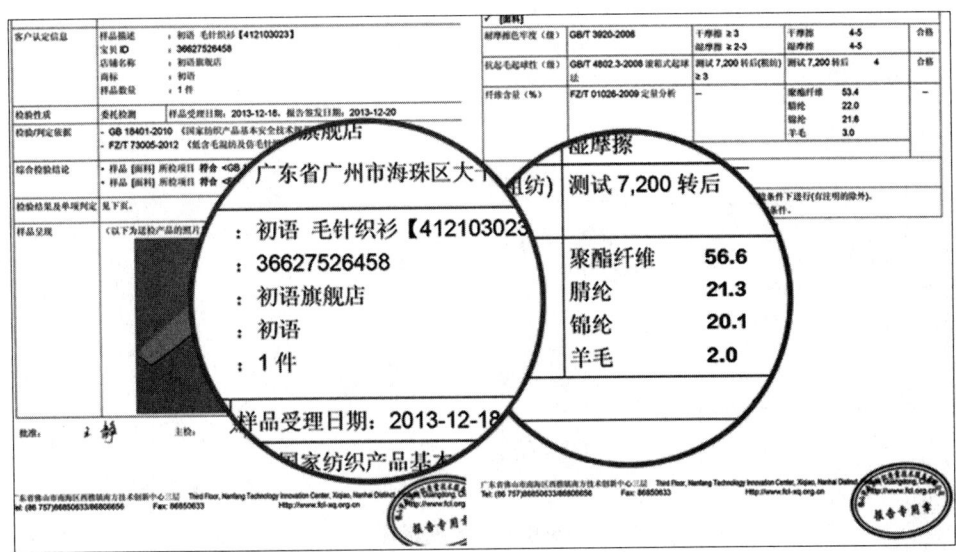

图5-3-8 宝贝描述2

上传商品照片及填写商品描述时,要注意其真实性。为了吸引眼球而过度夸大自己的商品,虽然短时间会有订单数的上涨,但长期来看会大大降低网店的信誉,无异于饮鸩止渴。因此,你要尽可能真实地填写商品描述等信息。

然后来到物流信息页面,填写物流信息时要先设置运费模板。

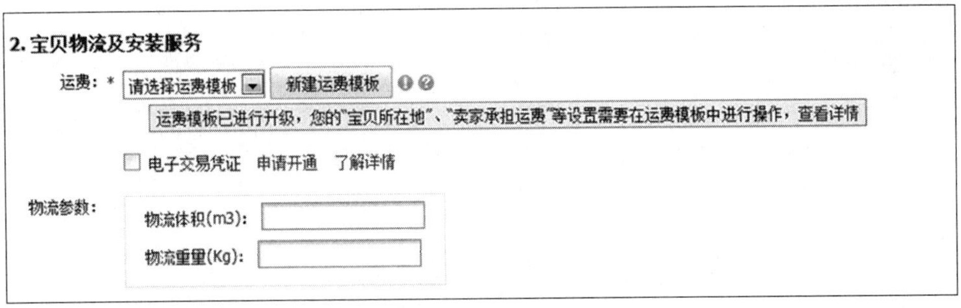

图5-3-9 运费设置

点击"新建运费模板"即可。

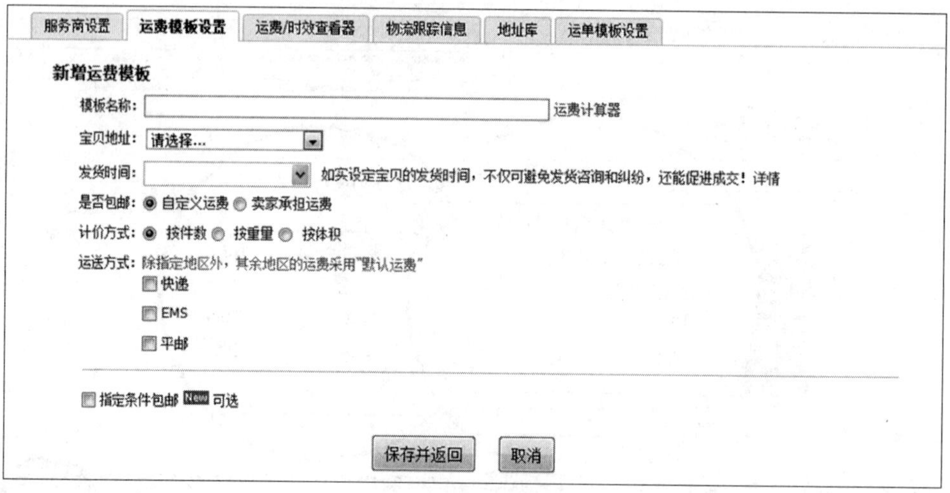

图5-3-10　运费模板

在这里淘宝网提供了一种很方便的功能来计算运费——你可以点击"运费计算器"或直接点击选项卡上的"运费／时效查看器"进入设置页面，来进行运费的设置、计算。

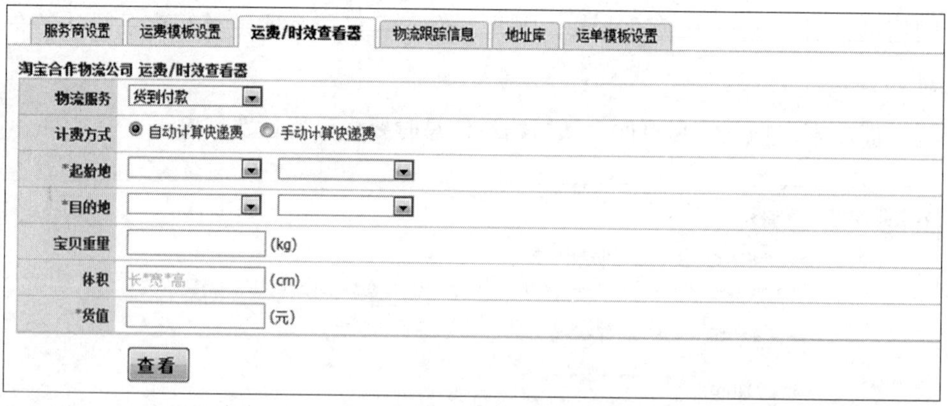

图5-3-11　运费计算

现在的电子商务网站开发出了很多类似的方便实用的功能，这里就不一一介绍了，把它们留给你去发现吧！

在售后信息处，要如实填写信息。如没有发票就要写"无"。不要因为一时的疏忽为日后留下纠纷隐患。

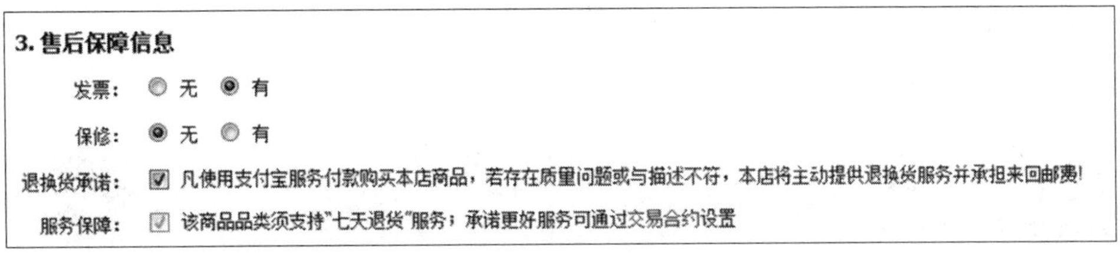

图5-3-12 售后保障

所有商品信息填写完成后,点击宝贝发布页面最末的"发布"按钮,完成商品的发布(如图所示)。

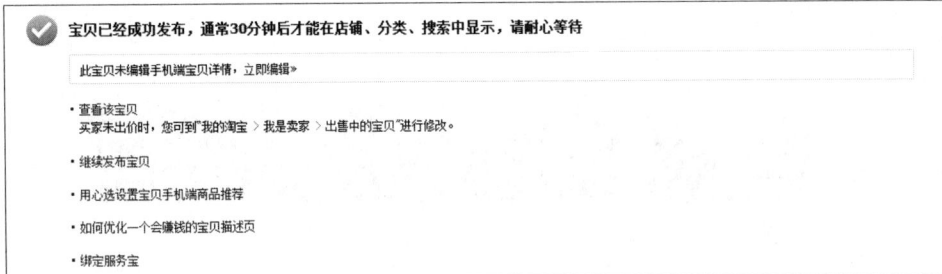

图5-3-13 发布成功

好了,这样就发布成功了!让我们一起期待第一个顾客进店吧!

装修店铺

上传商品之后,我们来装修自己的小店吧!一个美观大方的小店是吸引顾客的利器。

图5-3-14 店铺装修

在店铺管理菜单中选择"店铺装修"。

按照页面中提示的步骤进行操作。

图5-3-15　页面提示

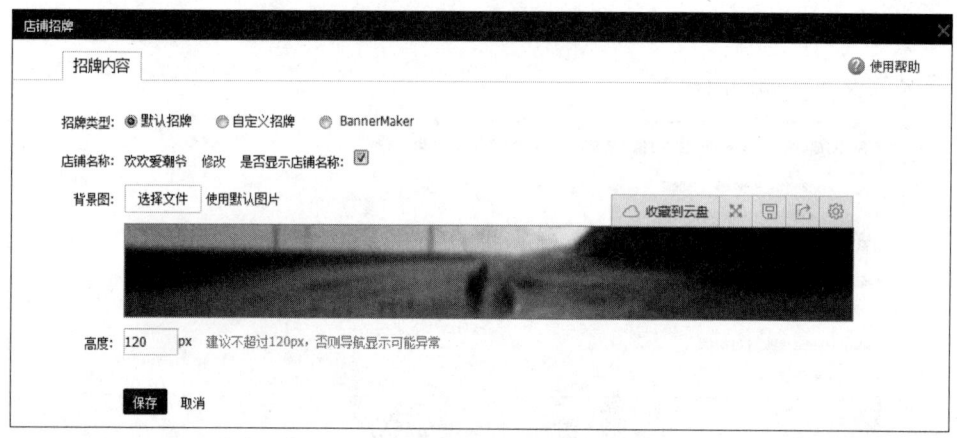

图5-3-16　页面招牌

在这里你可以自定义网店板块、背景图片，甚至可以插入你喜欢的背景音乐，快点去试一试吧！

图5-3-17　页面实例1

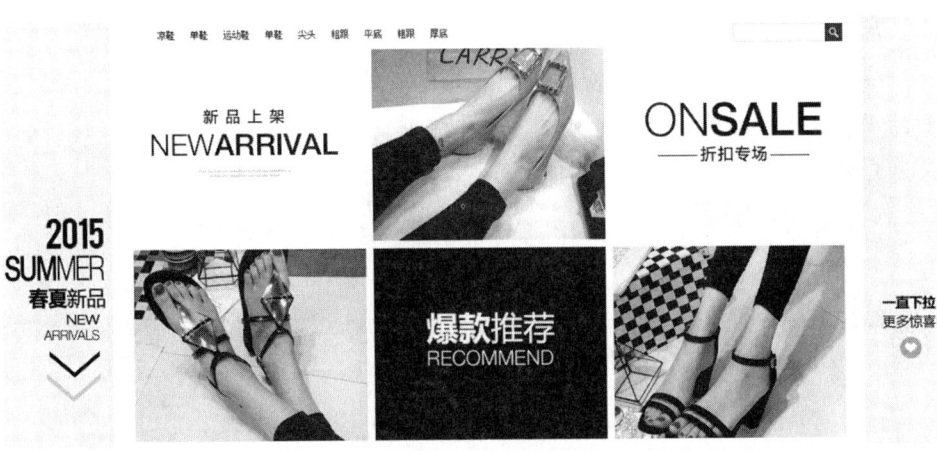

图5-3-18　页面实例2

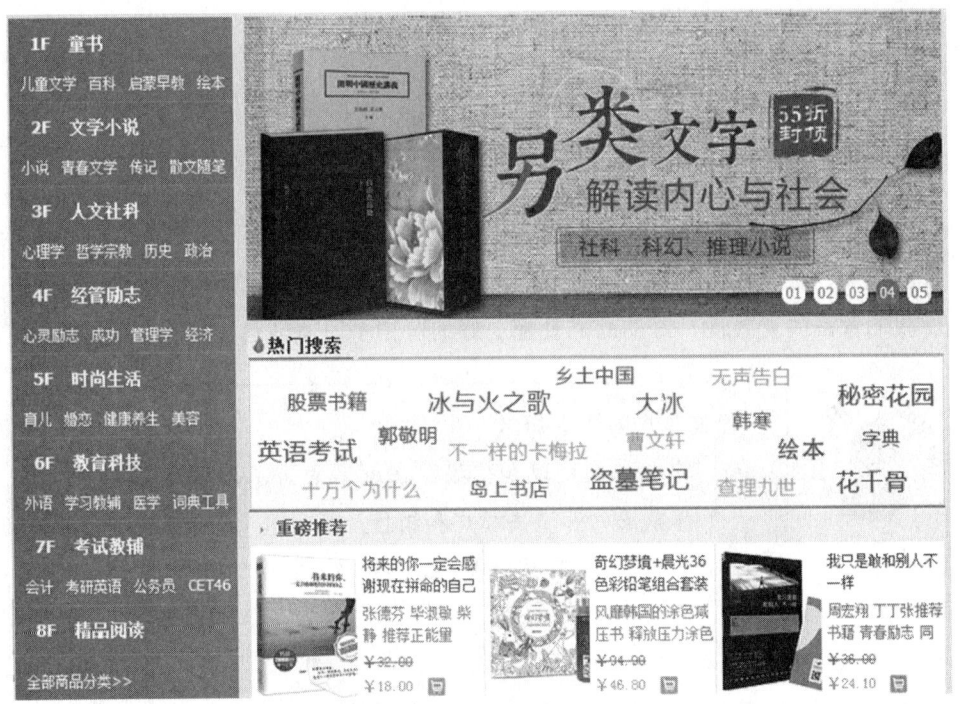

图5-3-19　页面实例3

总结

在这一节中,我们终于将期待已久的商品发布到自己的网店上了,希望我们的步骤说明和讲解对你独立快速地发布销售商品有所帮助!

1. 发布商品
   - 选择宝贝类型
   - 填写宝贝基本信息
2. 店铺装修

第四节　营销推广

在这一节中,你将……
✓ 了解网店营销推广策略

在中国的生意场上,有一句名言叫作"酒香也怕巷子深"。意思是说再香再好的佳酿,如果隐藏在深巷里不为人所知,那么好酒也会卖不出去。这句话告诉我们营销的重要性,好的商品要配上好的营销手段才能会更加畅销。

营销推广的基本知识:
- 其内容是发现和挖掘潜在顾客的需求,从产品本身和整体氛围的营造去推广和销售产品
- 其目的是宣传品牌,吸引新顾客,增加顾客黏性,提高产品销量

对于网店来说,营销尤为重要。网络上的网店如满天星斗,不计其数,仅淘宝网一个平台就有上千万个商家。想想看,在如此众多的商家中,顾客点击你的商品、进入你的店铺的概率有多大呢?只是发现你的店铺就如此不易,更不用说在你的店铺里停留并且购买商品了。在如此激烈的市场竞争环境下,想要脱颖而出,营销推广不可或缺。

在这里我们为你总结了网店营销推广比较有效的方法,可供你参考。

1. 广告推荐

广告推荐是让潜在顾客知道并且了解你的网店的有效的途径。淘宝网为你提供了很多做广告的机会,这些广告能增加顾客看到你的商品的机会,从而增加顾客进入你的店铺的可能性。下面我们将为你介绍在淘宝网上常用的几个广告推广方法,运用这些方法,相信会有越来越多的人进入你的店铺。

橱窗推荐

什么是橱窗推荐呢?如下图所示,那些用图片和文字进行展示的就是橱窗推荐的商品,通常在搜索结果页出现。橱窗推荐可以让顾客在搜索时第一时间看到你店铺的商品,从而增加顾客进入商店并购买货品的机会。

橱窗推荐是一项付费服务,但淘宝网有时会免费赠送一些橱窗推荐的机会,你可以合理运用这些机会对比较抢手的商品进行橱窗展示。你也可以另外购买一些橱窗,为你店铺里更多的商品提供橱窗推荐的机会。这里给大家传授一些橱窗推荐的技巧。推荐时应优先选择一些销量比较好的产品,提高顾客购买的概率。在推荐时间上,最好选择在网页相关产品浏览量比较大的时间进行推荐,不要选择一些浏览量稀少的时间,白白浪费了橱窗推荐的机会。

图5-4-1 橱窗推荐

店铺内推广

橱窗推广纵然好，但大量的橱窗推广要耗费一笔不小的资金，所以往往并不是每件商品都有橱窗推广的机会。那么如何在不花费金钱的情况下，让潜在客户更多地了解到你店铺的商品呢？这里介绍另外一种推广方法——店铺内推广。

店铺内推广是针对已经进入你的店铺的顾客，在店铺的首页或者货品的详细页面加入自己店铺商品的广告。那些原本只对你的某一件商品感兴趣的顾客，在看到店铺内的推广之后，有很大的可能会继续浏览店铺内的其他商品。这样就为店铺内的其他产品提供了更多的展示机会，提高了货品的购买率。

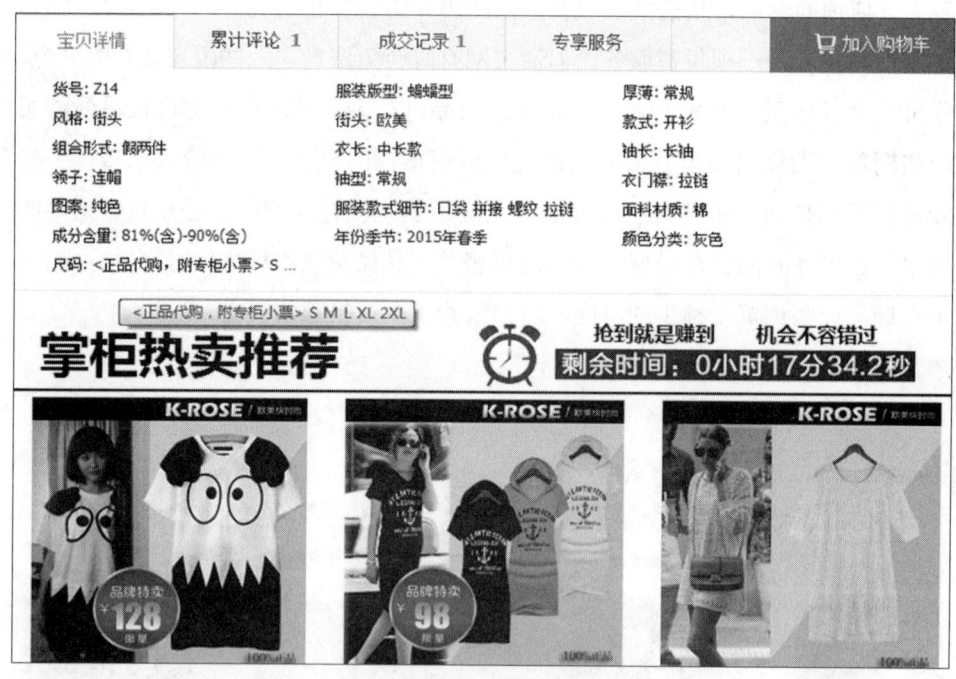

图5-4-2　店铺内推广

2. 打折优惠

消费者都喜欢商品有低于常规价格的折扣优惠。中国的消费者也不例外，打折往往能在第一时间吸引他们的注意。基于这个原因，很多商家会经常举办打折活动，利用折扣达到产品宣传的目的。淘宝网专门为商家准备了许多针对打折优惠商品的推广机会，让我们来了解一下吧。

满就送

"满就送"的意思是只要顾客购物满一定的金额就会收到一定量的优惠或者特定的礼物。这种优惠方式促使消费者比原计划购买更多的商品,不失为一种促销的好办法。

想要开通"满就送"这项服务,店主需要向淘宝网交纳一定的费用。开通"满就送"之后,淘宝网会通过促销活动平台将你的优惠向全网进行推广。你只要在卖家中心的导航菜单中选择"我要推广"便可以找到这项服务了。

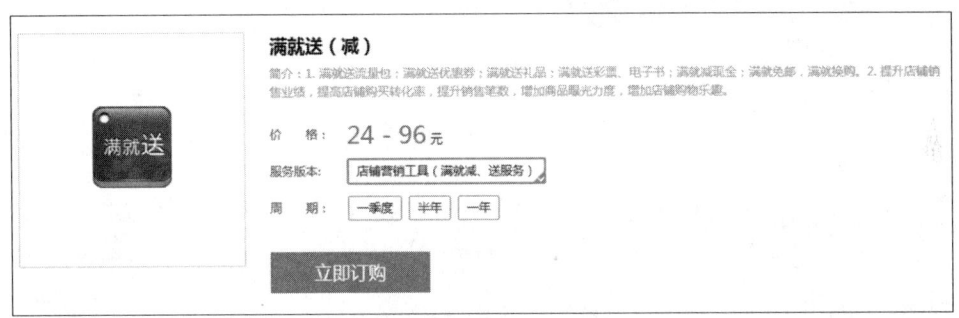

图5-4-3 满就送

当然,你也可以选择不向淘宝网购买这项服务,直接在商品描述中对"满就送"活动进行描述和宣传。不过这种方式就失去了淘宝网为你进行全网推广的机会。这两种方式中的得与失还要自己细细衡量。

优惠券

淘宝优惠券是在买家购物结算时可以使用的电子票券,这种券可以为买家减免一定的最终费用,因此很多买家会因为赠送优惠券而考虑购买这一商品。

优惠券可以由买家领取或者通过"满就送"发放。要注意的是,在向淘宝网支付一定额度的费用开通了优惠券功能之后,这种优惠的成本都是由卖家承担。当然,淘宝网也会为开通了有优惠券服务的卖家提供专门的全网推广机会,大大增加货品的曝光度。

限时打折

"限时打折"是一种在特定时间段增加顾客访问量的很有效的工具,主要是在一定时间内进行的低于市场价的促销活动。这种促销活动的价格往往很具有吸引力,再加上紧迫的促销时间限制,常常会让人产生购买冲动。

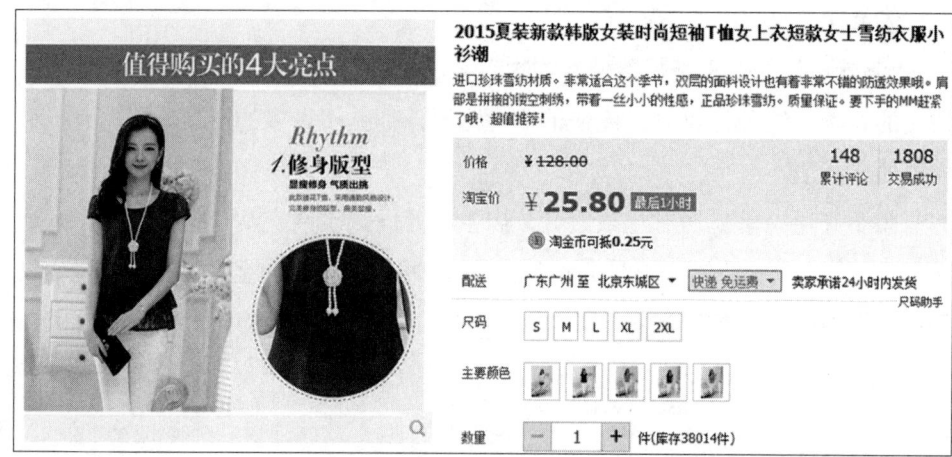

图5-4-4　限时打折

　　为了购买更加便宜的商品,有很多顾客在搜索商品的时候都会勾选"折扣促销"这个筛选条件。如果你开通了这项功能,那么你的商品将会出现在顾客的搜索结果中,大大增加了顾客的购买概率。

3. 评价管理

　　为了买到最合适的物品,顾客通常都会在对比几家同类型的商品之后再做出购买选择。在对比的过程中,让买家最看重的莫过于商品评价了。这些评价都是以往买过此商品的消费者对这个商品发表的评论看法,有时甚至比卖家自己上传的商品图片和商品描述更能反映商品的真实情况。所以,重视评论管理尤为重要。

　　那么如何管理评价呢？这里有一些技巧和大家分享。买家在收到你的货品之后,要及时与买家联系,积极询问他们对网店货品的态度。如果买家觉得货品很好,我们应该积极鼓励买家在我们的货品评论里进行买家秀,有的店家为了让顾客积极上传正面评论,甚至会随商品附赠一些小礼物。如果顾客在收到商品之后不满意,那么我们应该积极与其沟通,弄清其不满意的原因并积极解决,这样可以有效避免很多中评差评的产生。

图5-4-5　评价管理

评价管理虽然开销较少，但它是一项工作量大、对细致和耐心要求很高的工作。如果你持之以恒做下去，赢得顾客好评连连的话，那么评论产生的价值和效果会比巨额投放广告大得多。

4. 其他平台宣传

互联网中有很多访问量密集的平台，在网店推广中，只局限于单一平台的推广有时候会略显乏力。近几年随着论坛、微博和微信等社会化媒体平台的兴起，很多淘宝卖家已将自己的推广范围延伸到了这些热门的平台上。

你可能有类似的经历：在刷微博时看到别人晒出了一个酷炫的耳机——"哇！这个耳机好棒，好酷！"你这样想着，接下去你极有可能会想，"这个耳机在哪里买的？我也想去买一个！"你翻开评论，看到有人在这个微博评论中分享了一条这个耳机的淘宝网购买链接。那么请问这时候你会点击链接去看看这个耳机吗？答案是肯定的。这就是一个顾客从其他平台转移到淘宝平台的例子，这种例子每天会在互联网中以上亿次的频率发生，给类似淘宝网这样的购物网站带来了不可多得的机遇。

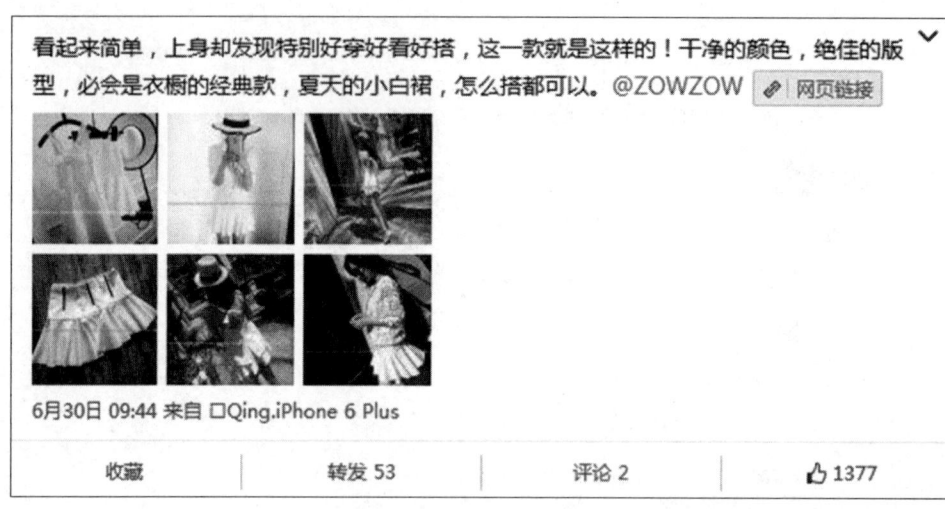

图5-4-6　微博推广

　　流量大的互联网平台蕴藏着巨大的机遇，但是想要在其上做推广可没有想象中的那么简单。一篇好的推广文案可以达到上千的浏览量，为你的店铺增加上千次的点击。但这样的文案只是凤毛麟角，绝大多数推广文案都石沉大海，无人问津。想要做出好的推广，为你的店铺吸引顾客，这需要不断地积累经验和创新。多多思考，多多实践，相信你会在不远的将来做出优秀的推广。

总结

营销推广的种种好方法你都学会了吗？快快来复习一下吧！

1. 广告推荐
- 橱窗推荐
- 店铺内推广
2. 打折优惠
- 满就送
- 优惠券
- 限时打折
3. 评价管理
4. 其他平台推荐

第六章

第一节　做好"抓住"顾客的售前服务

在这一节中,你将……
- ✓ 了解身为一名导购的必备技能
- ✓ 了解与顾客进行售前沟通的各种"小贴士"

不知道大家是否有过这样的网购经历:看中一件商品,查看商品信息后,希望通过聊天工具(如淘宝的阿里旺旺)与卖家进一步沟通了解细节,然而卖家却迟迟没有回应或者答非所问。遇到这种情况,相信大家多半也会和我一样放弃与卖家的沟通,转而浏览其他商品。可见,因为售前服务的不专业、态度的不真诚,卖家会白白流失许多商机。所以身为卖家的你,如果想要留住顾客,首先要成为一名合格的导购!下面,我们就来谈一谈怎样才算是一名合格的导购吧!

做好"抓住"顾客的售前服务

其实,在网店中购买商品时,很多买家挑选到中意的商品时,除了浏览图片、文字介绍和其他买家评价之外,往往还会与卖家"亲切"交流一番——询问商品细节、沟通邮费、了解退换货策略等。例如,下图这位买家,就在咨询以自己的身高体重适合购买哪一尺码的衣服。

图6-1-1

那么问题来了,当你成为卖家,你的顾客在购买前向你咨询时,你该如何做到"专业热情"地回答呢?这里给大家几点"小贴士":

掌握一些与顾客沟通的技巧

1. 认真倾听,准确判断

当一名顾客向你咨询时,一定不要急于回复他/她的问题,先耐心将问题描述听完,明白这位顾客的需求是什么——是要给自己买东西呢,还是要作为礼物送给朋友呢?再明确下这位顾客的问题出在哪里——是怕尺码不合适,还是怕物流赶不上时间?抑或顾客有什么特殊的需求,都有可能通过私聊的方式向卖家提出,卖家你可要接招啦!

2. 积极回复,专业回复

搞清楚以上两个问题后,卖家就不能怠慢,要积极回复顾客的问题啦!注意一定要积极、快速、专业地回复!在这个竞争如此激烈的市场中,顾客是不喜欢等待的,想一下作为顾客时的我们,对于等待总是有那么些许的不耐烦。

顾客与卖家的沟通,往往是从确认卖家在线开始的,所以作为卖家的你一定要给顾客一个积极的信号——是的,亲!我在呢,有什么问题您尽管问!当然,卖家不可能全天候无缝隙在电脑前与顾客进行交流。如果卖家离开或短时间内无法立即回复,则可以选择阿里旺旺提供给卖家的不同状态(图6-1-2),

或编辑自己的在线状态（图6-1-3），或编辑一段自动回复（图6-1-4），告诉顾客无法立即响应顾客的提问，敬请谅解。这样既不会引起顾客的不满，又不失礼貌。总之，记得要在看到顾客的留言后第一时间进行回复！

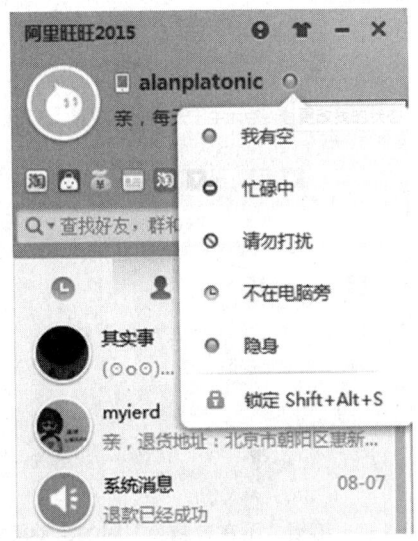

图6-1-2　选择不同在线状态

图6-1-3　编辑个性签名用以提醒

在阿里旺旺页面下端，选择下图中第二个按钮"系统设置"。进入系统设置后，选择"聊天设置"，点击"自动回复、快捷短语"按钮，可编辑自动回复和快捷短语，快捷短语的使用将在本章第四节售后服务中涉及。

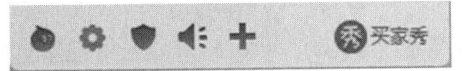

系统设置

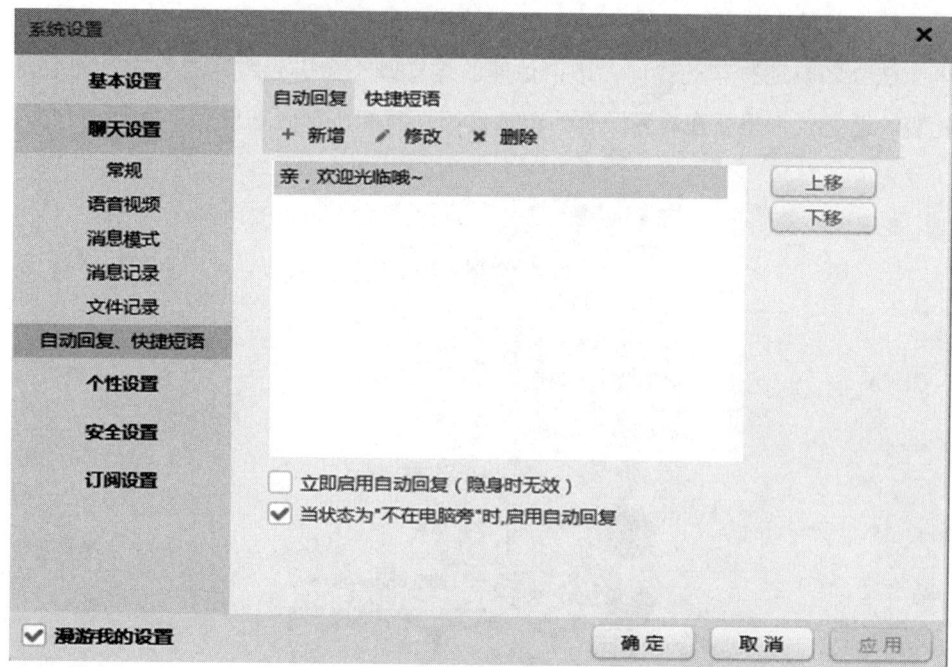

图6-1-4 编辑"不在电脑旁"时的自动回复

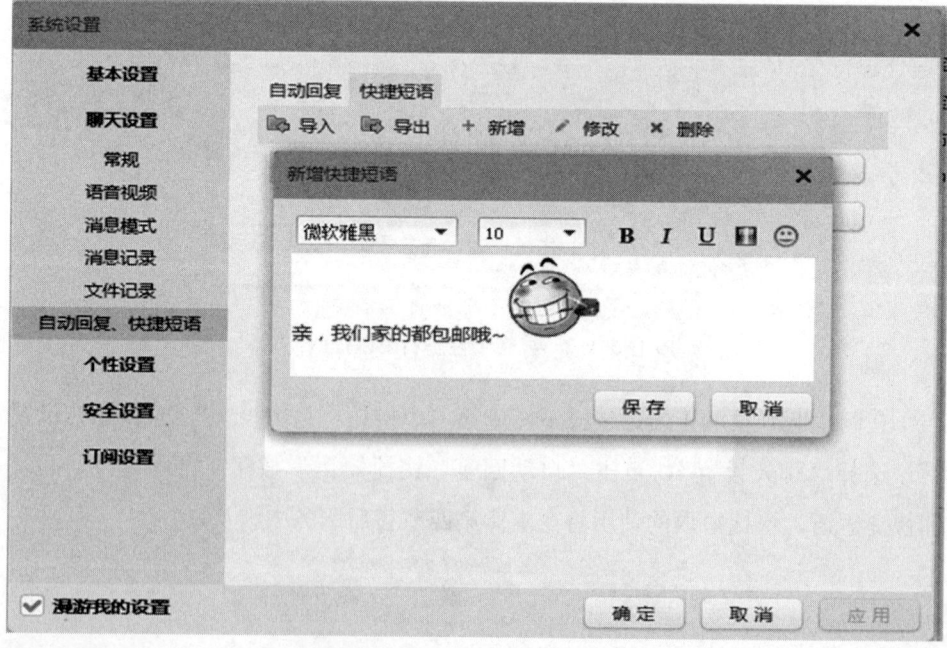

图6-1-5 新增快捷短语

3. 礼貌沟通，换位思考

沟通过程中的礼貌用语是必不可少的，比如"您""请"等。在淘宝网上，卖家普遍使用的打招呼语句——"您好，亲！"就是很好的例子。阿里旺旺还为用户提供了一系列表情，可以使沟通更为自然和亲切，各位卖家朋友们都可以尝试使用。（如图6-1-6）当然，在这一沟通过程中，卖家最好能够站在顾客的角度，想顾客之所想，作出恰当的回答或推荐，这样会使顾客感觉卖家更为贴心，也有助于交易的达成！

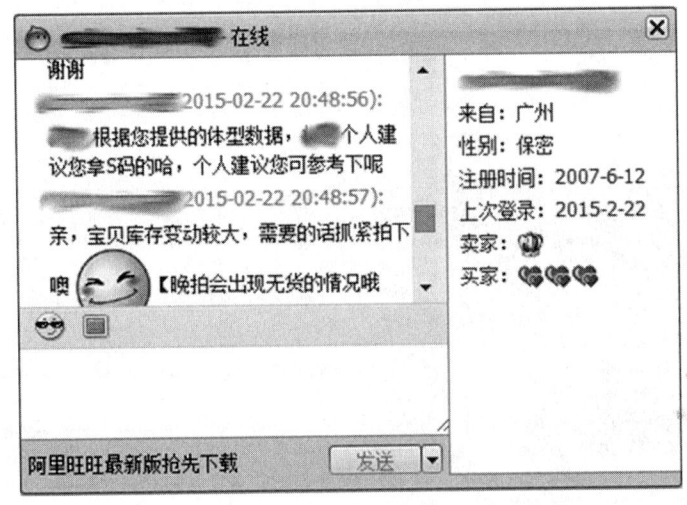

图6-1-6

4. 诚信经营，坦诚相待

无论是线上交易还是线下交易，诚实守信是一条很重要的准则，卖家朋友们一定要与顾客坦诚相待！要明白，没有一件商品是完美的，不要吝于向顾客阐明商品的缺点或使用中的限制条件，全面的信息更有利于顾客做出正确的商品选择，也会让他们觉得这位卖家诚实又靠谱，就买他家的东西啦！拿下交易又赢得信任，诚信功不可没！

专业、客观地介绍商品

顾客在购买前，问题总是围绕商品展开的。除了上述必要的沟通技巧，作为卖家，你也要能够足够专业、客观地向你的顾客介绍店中的各类商品才行。当然，网页上一定会有对于商品的详细描述，以一件衣服为例：

```
产品参数:
主图来源: 自主实拍图          货号: 53140201           品牌: here/所在
厚薄: 常规款                  风格: 通勤               通勤: 淑女
款式: 套头                    组合形式: 单件           衣长: 中长款
袖长: 七分袖                  领子: 圆领               图案: 纯色
毛线粗细: 常规毛线            面料: 棉                 面料主材质含量: 30%及以下
适用年龄: 25-29周岁           年份/季节: 2014年冬季    颜色分类: 绿色 橘红
尺码: S M L
```

图6-1-7 文字描述

```
产品颜色:   橘红
产品成分:   面料:100%棉
产品面料:   精纺棉线

厚度指数:   厚  ○——○——●——○  薄
柔软指数:   软  ○——●——○——○  硬
弹力指数:   弹  ○——○——●——○  无
版型指数:   紧  ○——●——○——○  松

模特 曼旌
试穿尺码: L码        试穿感受: 版型合身
设计点:
舒适圆领/百搭七分袖/下摆开叉/精纺棉线/电脑提花/螺纹收口

洗涤建议  用温水手洗衣物。
         避免阳光直晒,悬挂阴凉处晾干。
         不同颜色衣物分开洗涤,避免染色。
```

图6-1-8 图文并茂

尺码	身长	胸围	摆围	肩宽	袖长	袖肥	袖口
S	69.5	96	74	37	40	25.2	16
M	71.5	100	78	38.5	41	26.2	17
L	73.5	104	82	40	42	27.2	18
-	-	-	-	-	-	-	-

由于尺码是纯手工测量所以难免存在1CM-3CM误差，请亲们谅解。

图6-1-9 尺码详情

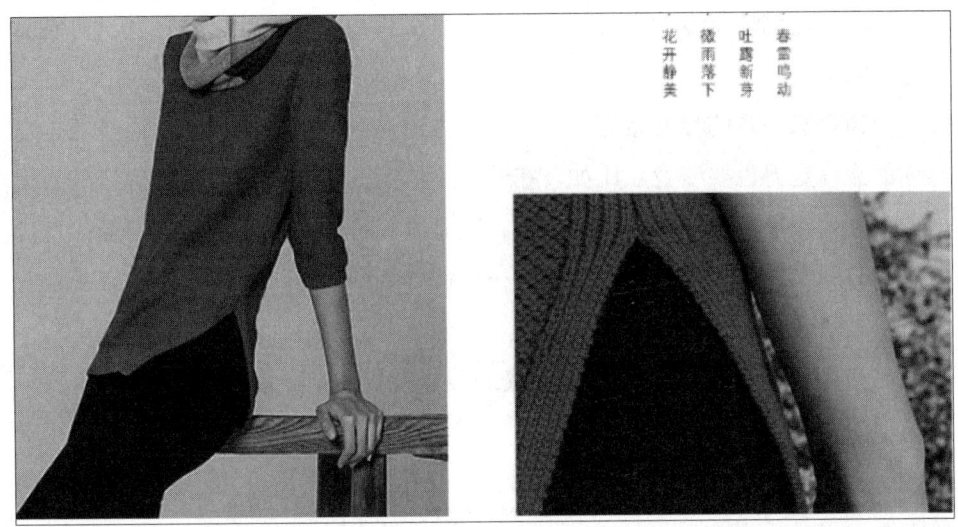

图6-1-10 细节展示

即使有着如此丰富的图文展示，顾客可能还是会有一百个不放心，要和卖家说上几句确认下才好。也有些时候，顾客并不是觉得网页信息有缺漏，而是页面提供的内容太多，反不如和卖家直接沟通来得方便、亲切、有重点。这时，就要看卖家能不能通过自己的介绍，展现出商品的特点，打动顾客的心了。

要将商品描述得客观，就必须熟知一件商品的优缺点。只说优点太完美，总有忽悠顾客的嫌疑；总说缺点——应该没有卖家乐意这么做吧。为顾客呈现一个商品的方方面面，有助于顾客全面了解一个商品，当然也能体现身为卖家的你与顾客坦诚相待，诚信为重。在这里，为各位卖家提供几条能够深入了解产品优缺点的途径。

- 向进货厂商、批发商询问
- 亲自试用、试穿、试吃
- 向销售同一商品的资深人士询问
- 收集用户评价

要将商品描述得专业，首先要具备卖家必备的一些专业素养，其次对商品有详尽的了解。

所谓卖家必备的专业素养，包括我们之前讲到的礼貌用语、沟通技巧。当然你的流程走得也要专业。比如，在顾客下单后，第一时间与顾客确认商品类型、尺寸、数量、价钱、收货人地址、联系方式等信息，避免出现问题；发货后第一时间通知顾客等待签收商品……这些行为都是可以体现一位卖家的专业性，博得顾客好感的！

对商品的详尽了解，当然不仅仅局限于前面提到的优缺点了。具体到商品材质、型号、库存量、适宜人群、使用方法、注意事项、洗涤事项、补货时间、上新时间、相关商品……都能一一为顾客提供。不知这些，你做得如何呢？

其他情况

- 对于一些可以普遍告知顾客的问题，建议各位卖家可以一并放在网页中，不必再在顾客咨询时一一给出，比如下边这两家店的做法：

图6-1-11　海澜之家洗熨小贴士

图6-1-12　佐丹奴购买提示

- 节假日、预售商品发货通知。目前，节假日或预售商品发布时，往往不能及时发货。若遇到这种情况，店家也一定要在店铺网页说明，减少顾客追问。

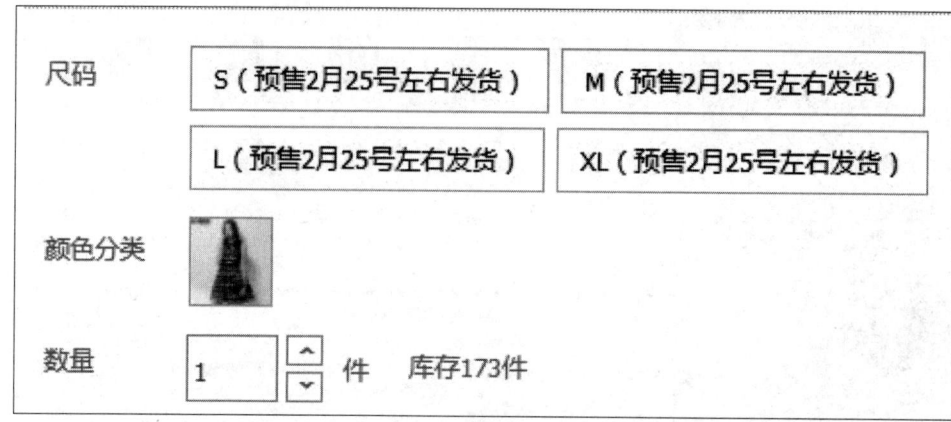

图6-1-13 预售通知

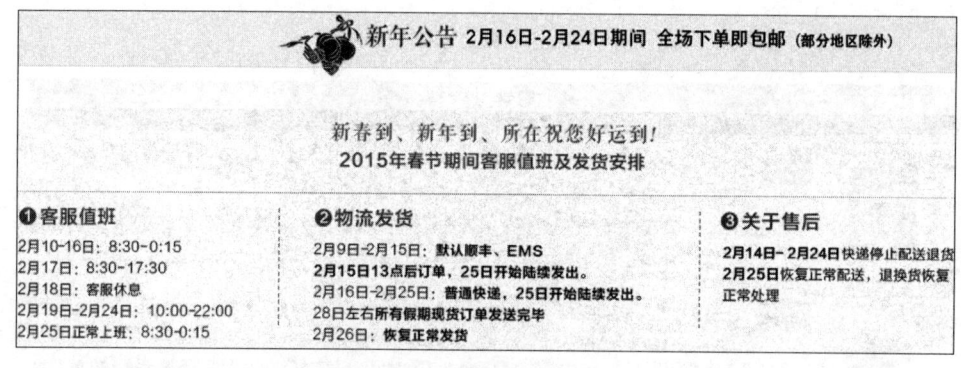

图6-1-14 节假日发货通知

以上各类售前服务技能,不知你掌握了多少呢?本书只是大体介绍,各类细节并不详尽,还需要各位卖家在实践过程中去摸索和补充。

稍事休息,我们的顾客来了,就要进行实战演练了,交易近在眼前!

总结

1. 与顾客沟通"小贴士"

- 认真倾听,准确判断
- 积极回复,专业回复
- 礼貌沟通,换位思考
- 诚信经营,坦诚相待

2. 专业、客观地介绍商品

- 专业性：文字描述、图文并茂、尺码详情、图片细节展示等
- 客观性：坦诚描述商品，不夸大优点，不掩盖缺点与使用约束条件

3. 其他情况（公告、通知等）

第二节　买卖做起来！

在这一节中，你将……
✓ 了解一个完整的商品交易过程

本节，我们将为你展示一个完整的交易过程，帮助你了解和把握淘宝网的交易流程。

你，准备好了吗？

首先，一位买家可能通过淘宝提供的各种方式找到你的商品，并点开了阿里旺旺的对话框，与你进行一番深入攀谈。情景可能是这样的：

图6-2-1

买家经过细致了解和深思熟虑，决定买下咨询的这款产品。自此，一场交易便拉开了序幕！

第一步：收到提醒

买家拍下商品，卖家在第一时间会收到阿里旺旺提醒。为方便各位卖家在第一时间收到交易消息，建议各位卖家与阿里旺旺长期在线。

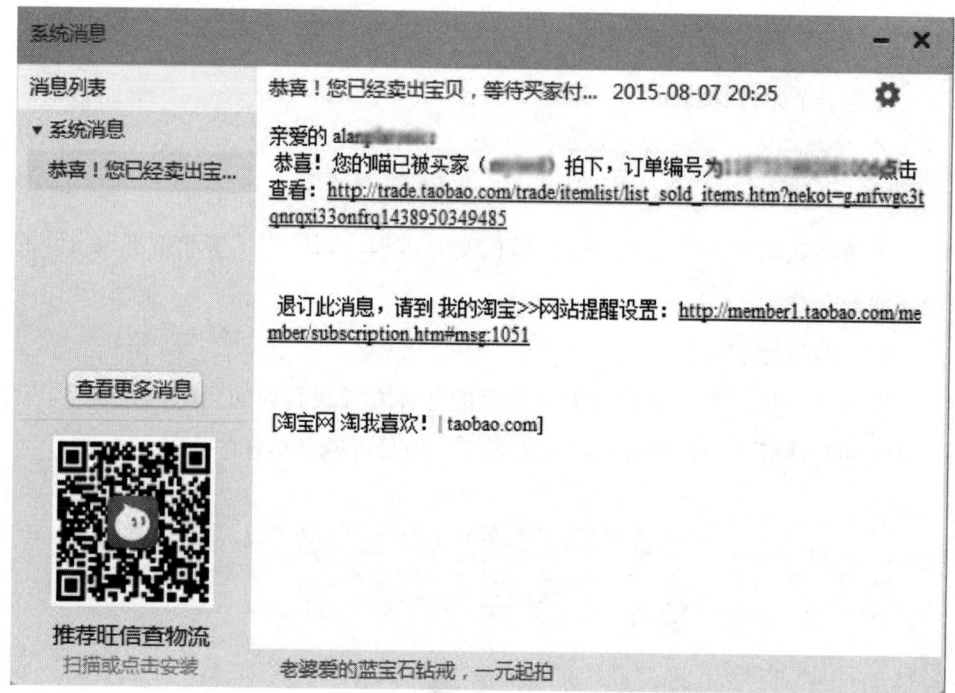

图6-2-2

第二步：查看订单

点击上图第一个链接，可进入"卖家中心"网页进行进一步操作。当然，为确保安全，网页会要求操作者进行安全验证，验证后，便进入到订单页面（图6-2-4）。

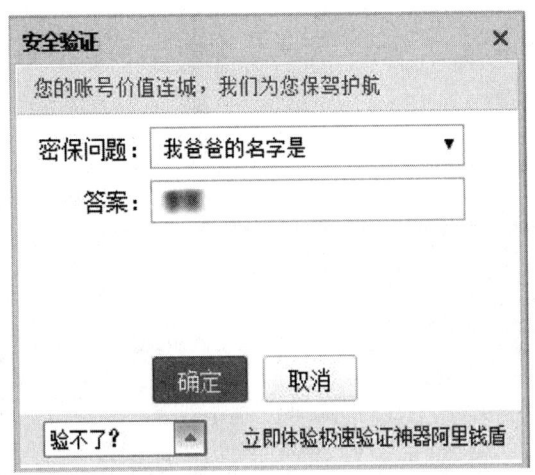

图6-2-3

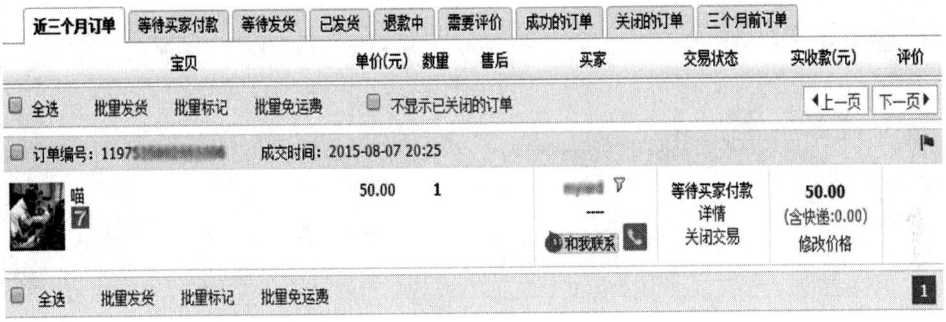

图6-2-4

第三步：修改价格

淘宝网支持买卖双方沟通协商价格，卖家可以在买家拍下商品后、支付前修改标示价格。如果不需要修改价格，且物流模板（下文会说明）已经保存，则本操作可跳过。

以下为买家打 9.4 折为例：

在图 6-2-4 下方，我们可以看到"修改价格"选项。点击"修改价格"，填入折扣和"物流费"（"包邮"即免邮费，为 0.00 元），保存并返回即可。返回订单页面，便会看到价格一栏发生了变化（图 6-2-6）。

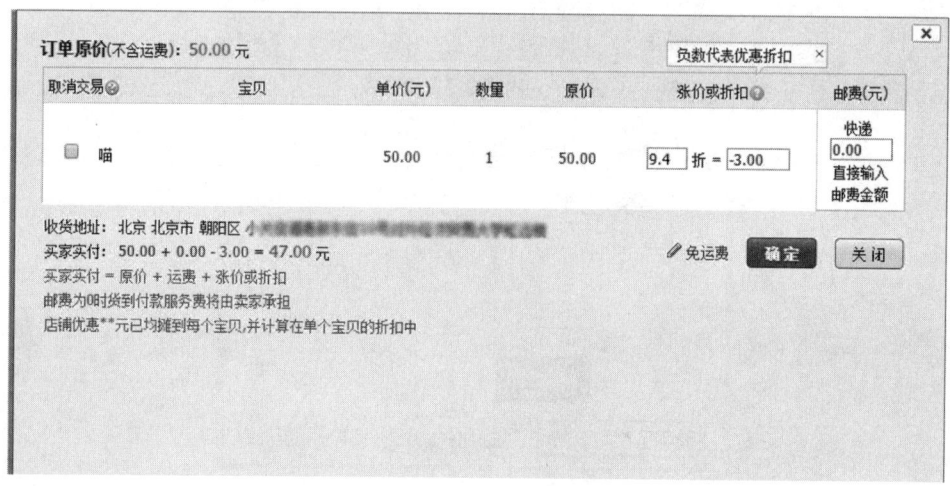

图6-2-5

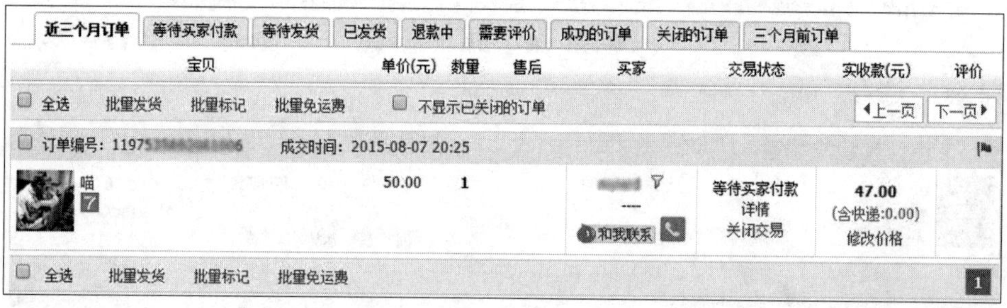

图6-2-6

第四步：等待买家付款

在此后的一段时间里，卖家就要等待买家付款了，这段时间可长可短，取决于买家付款的速度与效率。极为幸运的是，这位卖家遇到了一位高效率的买家，即可搞定付款。

买家付款后，阿里旺旺会在第一时间以系统消息的方式通知卖家，买家已付款，并提醒卖家及时发货（图6-2-7）。

这时，刷新订单页面，会发现"交易状态"发生了变化，由图6-2-6中的"等待买家付款"变为了红色的"买家已付款"。（注意：此时，买家的付款转存在支付宝的第三方平台上，而并非直接转到卖家的支付宝账户。）

图 6-2-7

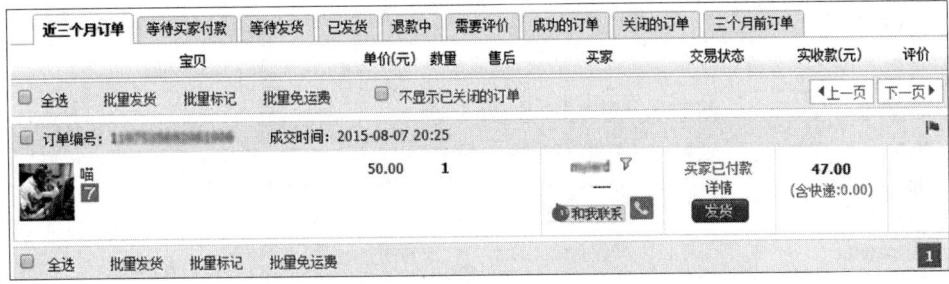

图6-2-8

第五步：卖家发货

一旦买家付款，交易便进入发货阶段。卖家发货时，需要回到订单页面，点击"发货"按钮，填入相应信息。

① 确认收货信息及交易详情

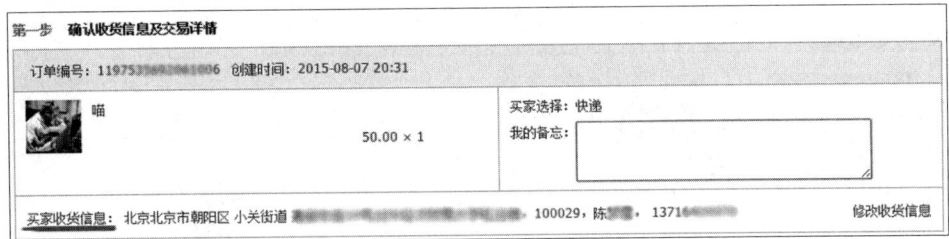

图6-2-9

② 确认发货／退货信息

图6-2-10

③ 选择物流服务

淘宝网为卖家提供了三类可选择的物流服务类型：一类是卖家在线下单、快递上门收货（图6–2–11）；一类需要卖家自己联系物流，并在发货后填入相应的运单号（图6–2–12）；还有第三个选择，用于不需要通过物流运输的商品（如虚拟产品）的交付，卖家直接点击"确认"即可（图6–2–13）。

图6-2-11

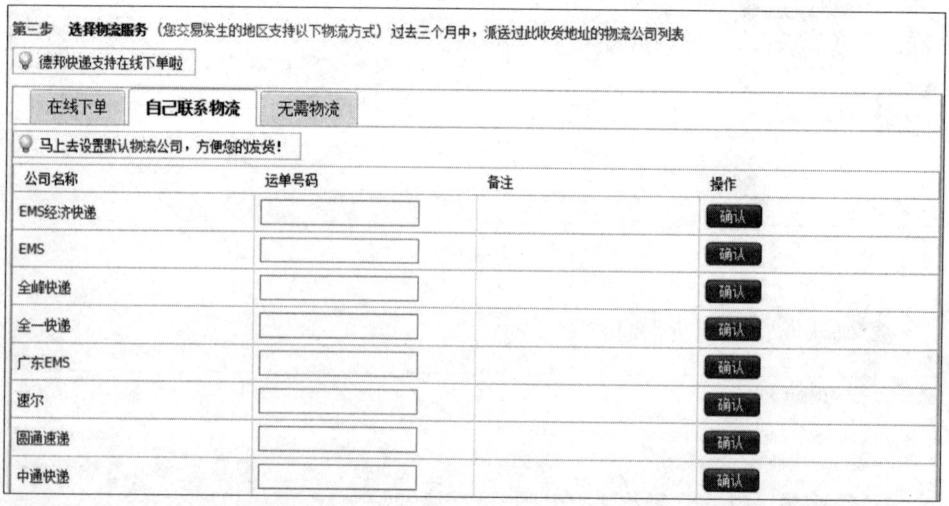

图6-2-12

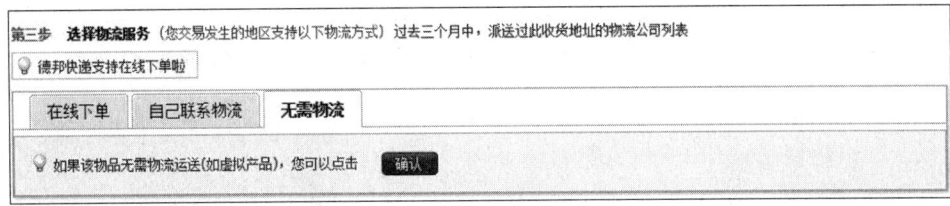

图6-2-13

此时，网页上的发货操作便也结束了，可以看到网页提示如图6-2-14。返回到订单页面，会发现"交易状态"一栏又发生了改变，状态已变为"卖家已发货"（图6-2-15）。

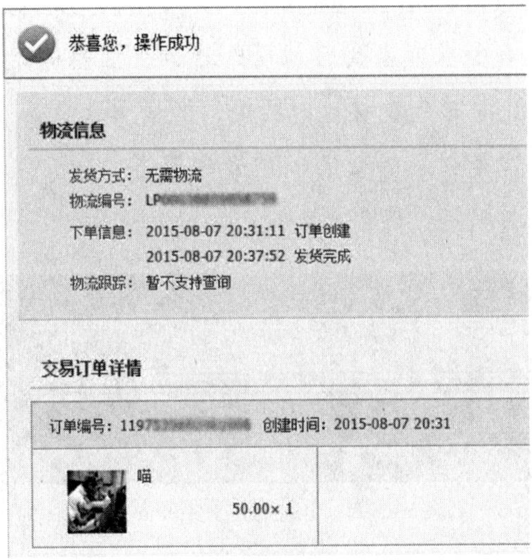

图6-2-14

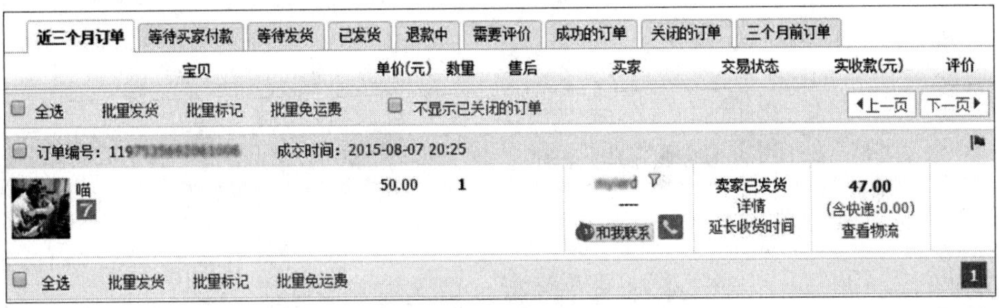

图6-2-15

关于物流选择的补充

1. 邮政运输

邮政运输可以分为平邮包裹、快递包裹、EMS，寄达所需时间依次减少，但费用也会相对增加。

- 平邮包裹——经济实惠，地域要求不是很高，寄达时间比较长，一般需要7天以上。寄达时间长不仅影响顾客的满意度，还会影响资金的回流速度。
- 快递包裹——相对于平邮包裹，费用略高。适合顾客对于收到商品的时间有要求或需要跨地区配送。要注意的是，有些时候快递包裹并不比平邮包裹寄达时间快，要谨慎选择。
- EMS——这是中国邮政的一项专递服务，通常快递会在4天内到达，寄达时间短，费用高。

2. 普通快递

中国主流快递公司一般用"三通一达"来概括。"三通"指圆通、申通和中通，"一达"指韵达快递。下面给大家简要介绍下这四个主流快递公司。

- 申通快递

基本覆盖到全国地市级以上城市和发达地区地市县级以上城市,尤其是在江浙沪地区,基本实现了派送无盲区。

- 圆通快递

服务范围覆盖国内1600余个城市,通达包括港、澳、台地区在内的全球200余个国家和地区,航空运输通达城市达70余个。

业务范围遍及全国31个省(自治区、直辖市)的所有市县乡(镇),营业网点超过4.5万个。

- 中通快递

服务项目包括国内快递、国际快递、物流配送与仓储等,提供"门到门"服务和限时送达(当天件、次晨达、次日达等)服务。

- 韵达快递

总部位于中国上海,服务范围覆盖国内31个省(区、市)及港澳台地区。2013年以来,相继与日本、韩国、美国、德国、澳大利亚等国家和地区开展国际快件业务合作,逐步走出国门,为海外消费者提供快递服务。

第六步:等待买家收货

进行到这里,卖家的工作告一段落,接下来便是等待买家收货了,这一步后续就不需要卖家进行操作了。一般来说,物流状态跟踪到买家签收商品后,买家与卖家的一次交易便结束了。当然,如果买家要求退换货就另当别论了(具体的退换货操作请参考本章第4节)。

你可能要问了,不需要买家确认收货么?否则卖家怎么拿到交易款?由于淘宝网会追踪物流状态,确认买家签收商品后,如买家不主动确认收货,淘宝网会在十日内将款项打入卖家支付宝账户内。所以,卖家在等待的过程中可以进入"交易详情",看看还有多久才能收到买家的钱,等待恐怕是许多卖家都要经历的一个过程。

不过，我们的这位买家还是很积极的，收到货后第一时间确认收货——

图6-2-16

第七步：查收货款

买家确认收货后，款项就会打入卖家支付宝账户了。卖家可通过"卖家中心"的"支付宝专区"查看支付宝余额，并进行"提现"（所谓提现，便是将支付宝余额转入与支付宝账户绑定的银行卡账户中）。当然，如果卖家不急需用钱，也可将余额留在支付宝内。

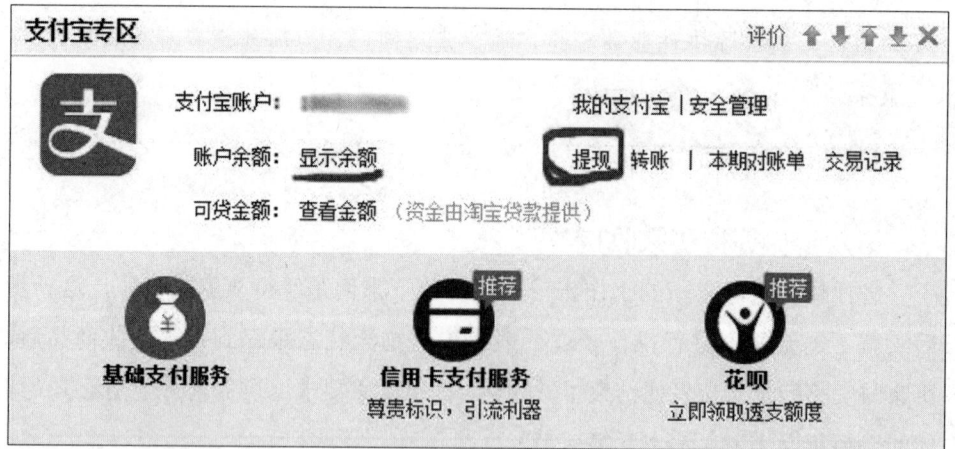

图6-2-17

选择提现后，进入图6-2-18页面，选择相应银行卡，并输入提现金额（注意提现金额不要超过支付宝余额，否则是无法提现的），点击"下一步"，输入密码即可提现啦。这里又要提醒下各位卖家，网页版支付宝支付是"次日到账"，即申请提现后到钱转入银行卡内是需要一定时间的，最快第二天到账。而支付宝的手机 APP"支付宝钱包",提现速度则比网页版快多啦!各位卖家可以下载手机 APP 使用。

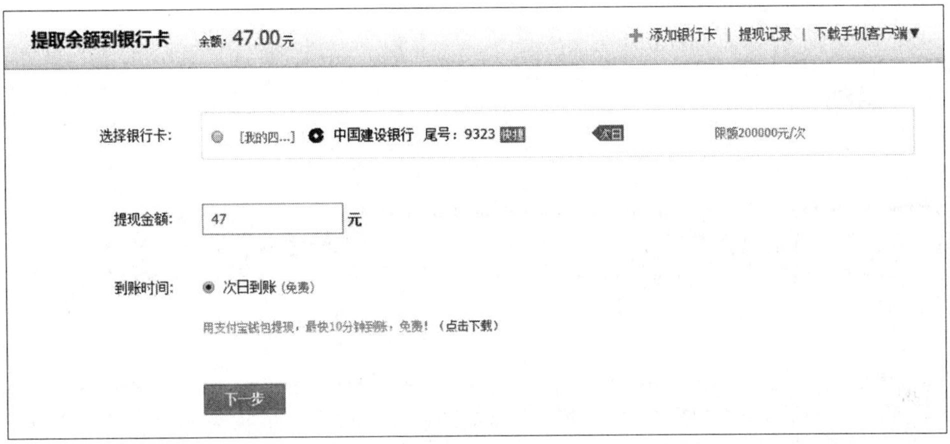

图6-2-18

图6-2-19

完整交易过程的展示到此结束,有没有觉得其实按步骤走下来非常简单呢？在满足用户需求的同时简化用户操作、方便用户使用，是当前各类应用平台的设计目标，所以大家不用担心看不懂、学不会、乱成一团等问题——它们都是非常容易掌握的！

总结
- 一个完整的交易流程

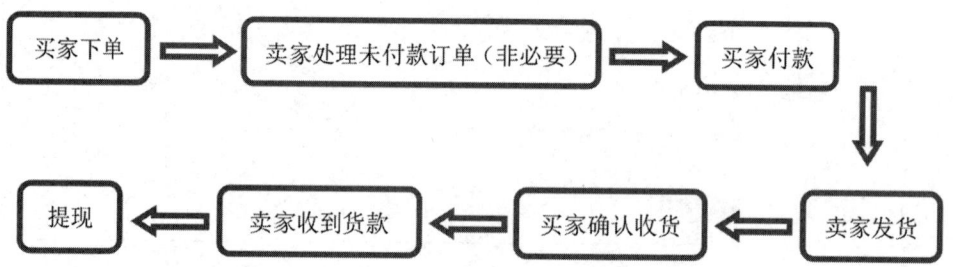

第三节　评价投诉那些事儿

在这一节中，你将……
✓ 了解淘宝网的交易评价体系
✓ 了解影响用户评价的因素
✓ 了解顾客投诉与卖家维权

作为卖家的你一定能发现，在淘宝页面上，你的店铺名后面会展示一些简单的图文信息。点击那些图案，还能进入一个包含更详细的店铺和卖家数据的页面。这些数据是从哪里来的？这一节将告诉你答案。

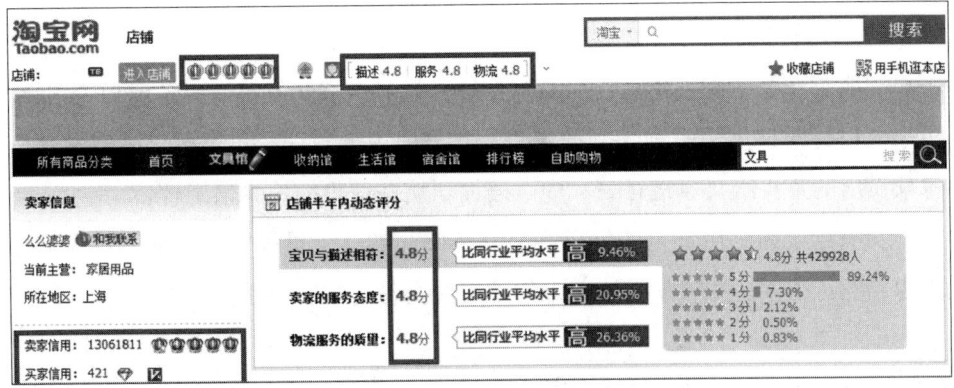

图6-3-1 店铺信息展示页面

交易评价

在上一节中,我们已经为大家展现了一个完整的交易过程。商品交易过程虽然结束了,但是交易还能继续创造价值,那就是淘宝网设立的交易评价体系。

交易评价主要包括两部分内容,分别是信用评价和店铺评分。如图6-3-2,中间进行信用评价,下部进行店铺评分。

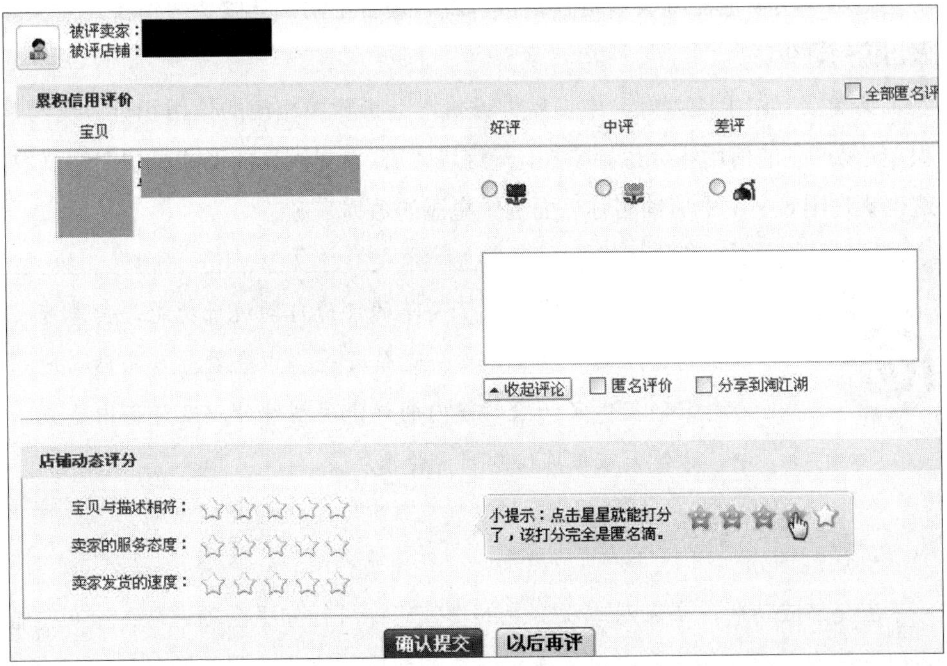

图6-3-2 买家评价界面

- 信用评价

完成每一笔交易订单后,交易双方均有权对对方交易的情况做出相关评价。买家可以针对订单中每项买到的宝贝进行好、中、差评;卖家可以针对订单中每项卖出的宝贝给买家进行好、中、差评。这些评价统称为信用评价。

买家给出的信用评价的评语会显示在商品的"宝贝评价"页面,供之后的顾客参考。图6-3-3就是上一节中的顾客对交易完成的商品做出的评价。

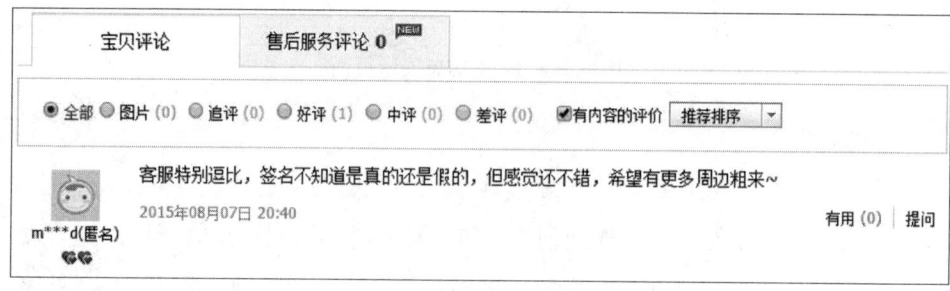

图6-3-3

当然,卖家也能就买家是否积极付款、是否主动确认收货等情况,对买家做出信用评价。

买卖双方做出的"好、中、差"评价,会折算成相应的信用积分。交易累积,交易产生的信用积分也会累加,最终以"心、钻、冠"的形式显示在网页中。这也就是图6-3-1中店铺名称后面五个皇冠的数据来源。

 淘宝网为卖家提供了简单的评价自动统计功能,卖家可以在淘宝网的"卖家中心→评价管理"中查看。页面贴心地为卖家们提供了一段时间内的评价类型统计以及评语内容集中,方便大家根据信息制定营销决策。

- 店铺评分

在交易成功后,买家对本次交易的卖家店铺进行如下四项评分:宝贝与描述相符程度、卖家的服务态度、卖家发货的速度、物流公司的服务。在每个评价维度上取连续六个月内所有买家给予评分的算术平均值为店铺评分。

顾客在淘宝网购物时，不仅可以看到你的店铺的每项店铺评分，还可以与网站提供的行业平均数据进行比较。

店铺动态评分	与同行业相比	店铺动态评分	与同行业相比
描述相符 4.6 ⬇	低于2.64%	描述相符 4.8 ⬆	高于9.46%
服务态度 4.7 ⬇	低于2.47%	服务态度 4.8 ⬆	高于20.95%
物流服务 4.7 ⬇	低于2.22%	物流服务 4.8 ⬆	高于26.36%

图6-3-4

店铺评分和信用评价是并存的，虽然两者的体现内容不一样，但都是为买家提供更多维度的参考价值。同时，作为卖家，你也可以从这些评价维度中看到改进店铺的压力，以及提升店铺品质的着手点，也就是影响用户评价的因素。

影响用户评价的因素

在总结影响评价的因素之前，首先请浏览下面三则关于同一件商品的评论：

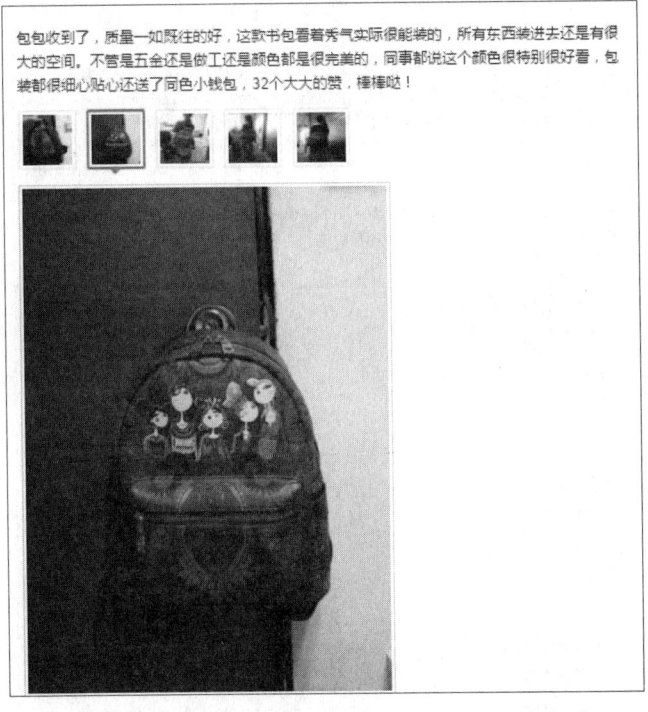

图6-3-5

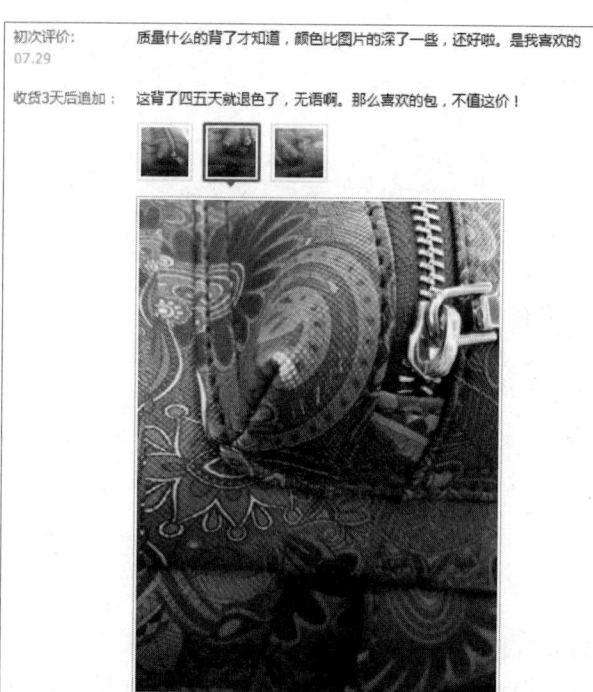

图6-3-6

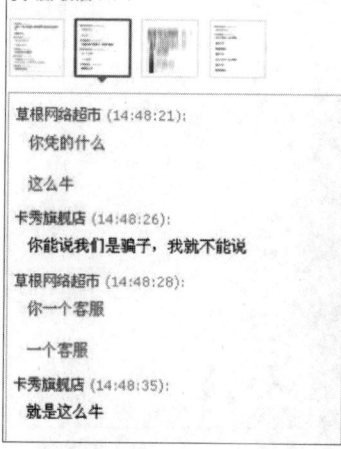

图6-3-7

看到这里,请你不妨思考一下,为什么同一商品,不同的买家评价有着天壤之别,说明了什么?

结合前文提到了交易评价维度,下面为大家简单分析三点:

1. 商品质量

可以看到图 6-3-6 中买家抱怨包包掉色。篇幅有限,这里只为大家提供了一位买家评价的截图,但实际的"宝贝评价"页面中不乏对这一问题的抱怨。这反映的不仅是商品的质量问题,也是卖家在商品销售中不坦诚的问题。

网购这个形式限制了买家只能通过浏览商品图片、与卖家沟通或查看商品评论来获取商品信息,并不能触碰到真实商品。但网购毕竟仍旧是商品交换,顾客最终也会真正接触到实物。那时,在营销过程中的任何假冒伪劣都将无所遁形,对买家造成的伤害也会通过"差评"的形式成百上千倍地扩大为对卖家店铺信誉的伤害。

因此,做一名良心卖家、诚信卖家是相当重要的。为买家提供翔实的商品信息;发货前严格把关,确保发给每一位买家的商品不存在质量问题;用心打包,防止商品在运输途中不必要的破损——总而言之,让买家对商品放心。买家挑不出商品质量问题,自然不会给商品质量差评。

2. 服务态度

图 6-3-7 中,买家对服务态度的抱怨可以说是淋漓尽致了。我们在本章第一节和第四节都在强调服务态度的问题,因为很多差评并不是由于商品本身有质量问题,而是服务上出现了差错。买家咨询许久没有人回复,回复时心不在焉、爱答不理、强词夺理、推卸责任、搪塞顾客,甚至回复时带着强烈的情绪等等,这都是卖家对顾客、对自己不负责任的行为。售前积极、专业地解答顾客问题,售后及时响应买家请求,沟通过程中的积极友好以及换位思考,才能为服务态度加分。

3. 物流服务

在本节图 6-3-2 和图 6-3-4 中我们可以看到,物流服务也是店铺评价重要的一部分。如果一件心仪的商品下单付款后,迟迟不见商家发货,或者发货后物流运输很慢,最后大半个月才收到货,估计当初对商品的好感早已经被等待耗得丝毫不剩了,甚至只剩下了不耐烦。因此物流有时也成为差评的诱因。卖家可以与固定的几家靠谱物流公司合作，保证配送的速度与包裹的安全；也可咨询买家希望由哪家物流配送，按照买家的意愿选择物流公司进行配送。

顾客投诉

相信淘宝网的大部分买家和卖家都是十分理智、通情达理的人，投诉卖家的顾客也是只占少数的，不过在这里还是要科普下顾客投诉。

万一被买家投诉，卖家也不要惊慌，认真判断到底是什么原因导致了顾客的投诉。如果错在卖家，卖家自然要为错误买单，但也应积极与买家沟通，主动承认错误并提出合理的解决方案，看能否让买家撤销投诉；如若沟通无果，买家坚持投诉或者本就不是你的错，卖家也不要着急，淘宝网有一套完整的投诉和申诉机制，辅以人工服务，可以帮助你很好地解决这一问题！

卖家的维权

进入淘宝网的"卖家版服务中心"页面（https://sellerhelp.taobao.com/），我们可以在左侧导航栏看到针对卖家问题的各项服务，如"申诉指南""投诉处罚""消保专区"等，右侧也有常见问题解决规则的链接，供用户参考和使用。在图6-3-9中，我们也可以看到淘宝网为维护卖家权益，提供的各类自助工具，待到所需时，卖家可选择使用这些自助工具维护自己的权益。当然，我们更希望卖家的权益能够自始至终得到切实保障，从而不必动用这些工具去维权。

图6-3-8

图6-3-9

总结

- 交易评价分为信用评价和店铺评分
- 影响买家评价的三个因素：商品质量、服务态度和物流服务
- 顾客投诉与卖家维权

第四节　打造贴心的售后服务

在这一节中，你将了解……
✓ 如何处理网购中最常见的退换货问题
✓ 如何处理售后周边问题并提供贴心的售后服务

售后服务与商品质量、卖家信誉等同等重要，贴心的售后服务能够为卖家赢得好评、积攒人气，从而打造好的口碑和维系客户关系。打造贴心的售后服务，也是卖家一定要掌握的一项技能。接下来我们将介绍几类不同的售后服务以及一些打造贴心售后服务的技巧。准备好了么，学起来吧！

咨询类售后——顾客遇到问题啦!

在新产品或者特殊商品的使用过程中,顾客难免会有些问题。如下图这位顾客,第一次购买某一品牌的裤子,发现味道很重,便去咨询卖家(如下左图),卖家回复如下右图所示。

若您是这位买家,对这样的答复满意么?若您是这位卖家,会给出不同的答复吗?

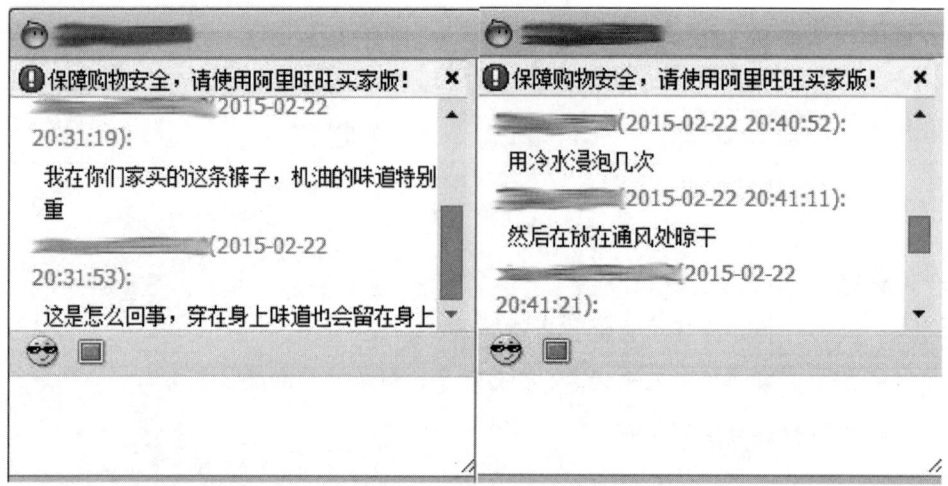

图6-4-1

当遇到售后咨询类问题时,卖家同样要遵循我们在本章第一节售前服务中提及的注意事项——耐心、全面地了解顾客的问题出在了哪里,并为咨询类客户提供较好的解决方案。在这一沟通过程中,认真倾听,礼貌用语,体现专业性是十分必要的。如果卖家能站在顾客的角度,以顾客的思路看待问题,解决起来就会轻松很多。

有一位朋友曾经遇到过样一件事。他在笔记本电脑配件网店做售后工作。有一天,一位顾客买走了一片笔记本电脑防尘网。防尘网本身有磁铁,可以吸附在有磁性的笔记本电脑下方,防止过多灰尘吸入电脑中。然而,这位顾客收货后,询问售后如何使用该防尘网时,才发现她的电脑下方没有磁性,无法吸附该防尘网,最后要求退货。

这虽然是售后才发生的问题,但反映的是售前的不专业。在交易过程中,可能会有许多顾客想不到的点,因此卖家必须思考周全。无论是在网页中展示,还是在与顾客私聊时提醒,都要确保将商品的一些特质或特殊要求向顾客阐释清楚。一方面减少不必要的售后麻烦,另一方面也为自己积攒人气。

还是需要退换货!

当顾客拿到手的商品与自己的期待值相差甚远,存在质量问题或并不符合自己需求时,通常会要求进行换货或退货。面对这类情况,卖家你一定要沉着冷静,与顾客耐心沟通,了解情况。无论出于何种原因(商品质量有问题、商品不符合需求)的退换货,都要进行核实。随后按照各个平台制定的退换货流程进行操作。

以淘宝网为例,用户可选择三种售后退换货服务:仅退款、退货退款以及换货。

下面我们将分别简单阐释这三类售后服务的申请条件和流程。

1. 仅退款

- 申请条件:买家一直未收到货,或买家已收到货且与卖家达成一致不退货仅退款时,买家将选择"仅退款"申请。

- 退款流程:买家申请退款→卖家同意退款申请→卖家退款成功。

下面几幅图便是前面一节中,买下商品的那位买家,在反复查看商品后,发现商品稍有瑕疵,与卖家沟通后,申请售后,卖家退款5元。

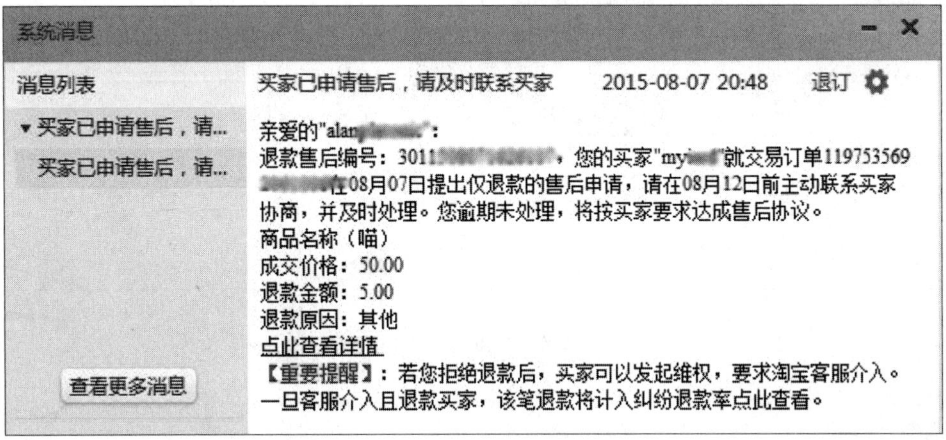

图6-4-2 系统消息——买家申请售后

一旦有买家申请售后，卖家的阿里旺旺便会弹出"系统消息"对话框，提醒卖家收到新消息。若卖家并未登录阿里旺旺，也可在"淘宝网→卖家中心→消息中心"中看到这一通知。

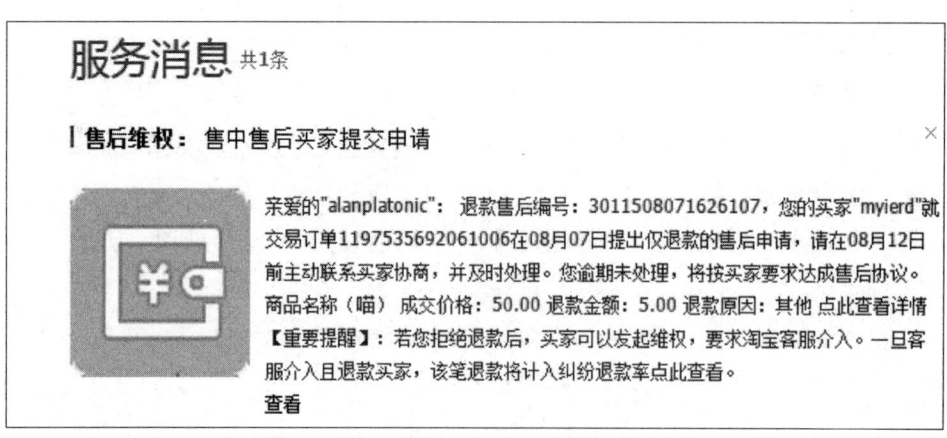

图6-4-3　网页消息中心

看到此消息提示后，卖家可点击消息体进入售后页面，如图6-4-4。

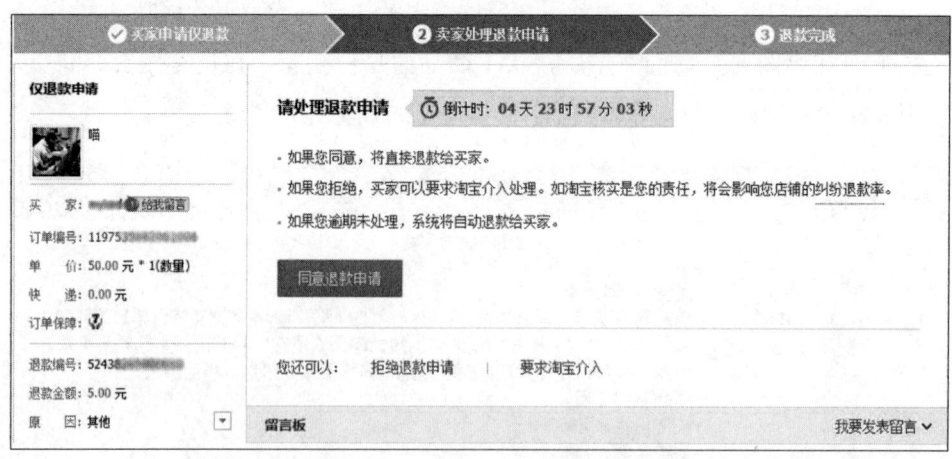

图6-4-4　卖家处理退款申请

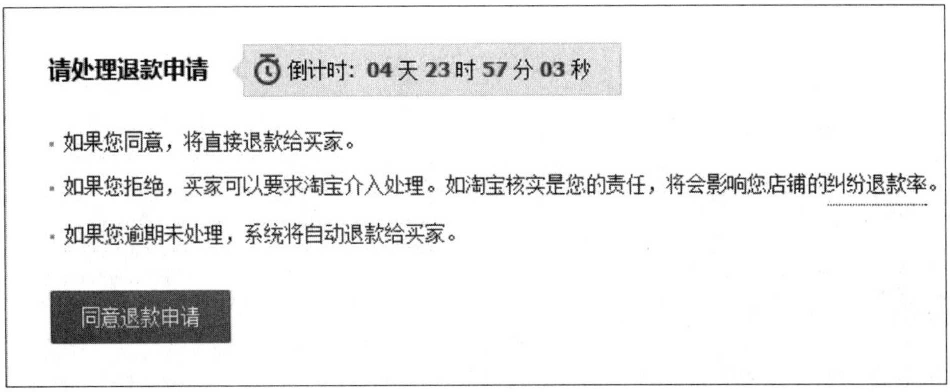

图6-4-5　卖家处理倒计时

买家一般是在和卖家达成协议后才去申请退款的，所以这时卖家往往会选择"同意退款申请"的。当然，卖家也可以"拒绝退款申请"，或者"要求淘宝介入"双方纠纷，这时事情的处理就会变得比较麻烦，需要双方甚至三方进一步的协商。

在这里我们的卖家同意了退款申请，输入支付宝的支付密码即可，如图6-4-6。

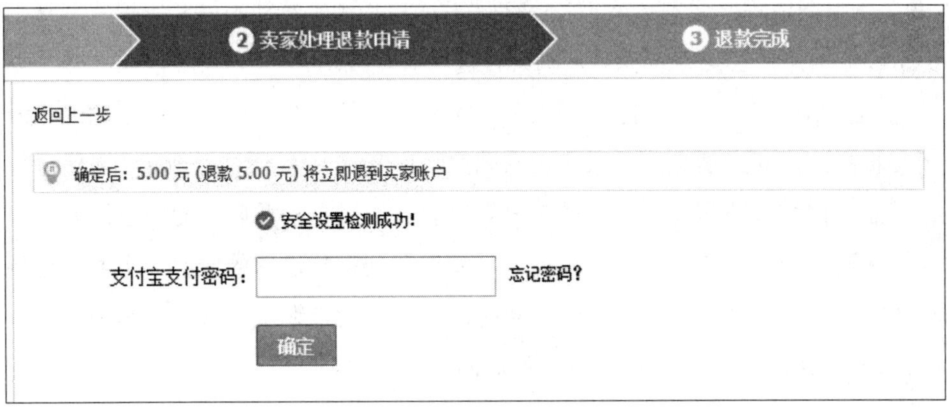

图6-4-6　输入密码，进行退款

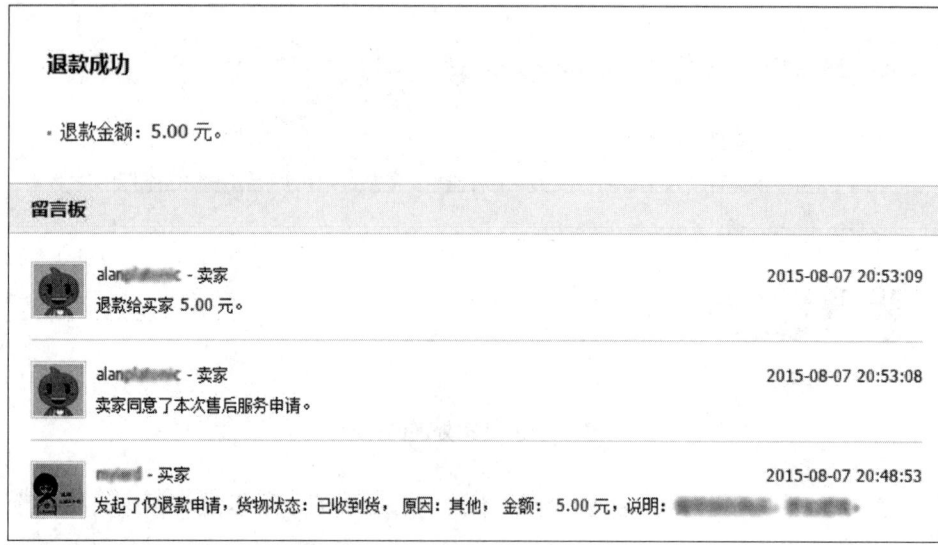

图6-4-7　退款成功

2. 退货退款

• 申请条件：若商品出现质量问题，或者顾客不想要这一商品，且与卖家达成一致退货，买家将选择"退货退款"选项。

• 退货流程：买家申请退货→卖家发送退货地址给买家→买家退货并填写退货物流信息→卖家查看物流，确认收货，退款成功。

"退货退款"与"仅退款"在处理上是有不同之处的——"退货退款"需要买家将商品寄回给卖家。买家在卖家同意"退货退款"申请后，有7天的时间将商品交付物流公司寄回，超过7天售后服务便会自动关闭；而卖家需要在收到买家退回的商品并检验商品后退款。如果遇到退货退款的情况，卖家一定要与买家沟通好时间，避免双方的反应超出淘宝的规定期限；同时，卖家也应仔细检查退回商品，确认退回商品无误后向买家退款。

3. 换货

• 申请条件：买家买到尺码、颜色、款式等不合适的商品，但仍没对这位卖家放弃希望，便与卖家协商一致换货（一定要协商好，尤其是所换商品的型号、尺码、颜色等，不能一错再错了），并发起"换货"申请。

- 换货流程：买家申请换货→卖家发送退货地址给买家→买家退回商品，卖家签收后重新发货（注意不要发错货），买家再次确认收货（线下完成了换货过程）→买家线上确认完成。

◆ 注意：换货过程是不涉及退款的哦！

此外，由于退换货均需要将商品寄回，为各位卖家提供一个小小的贴士：

在阿里旺旺的客户端，可以进行诸多设置。在第一节中，我们也展示了"快捷短语"的设置。为了方便客服和买家的沟通，各位卖家可以将退换货地址、联系人、联系方式、注意事项等编辑成一条快捷短语，在需要的时候轻轻一点，就可以传达消息啦！是不是方便了很多呢？

退换货中的物流费用

大部分的网络购物平台都制定了一套全平台适用的退换货规则，如淘宝网支持7天无理由退换货，卖家也会在服务承诺中标明支持的各项服务（图6-4-8）。但退换货往往涉及快递费用问题，因此对于快递费用应由谁来负担，淘宝网做了如下指导性界定：

退货或换货邮费该由谁承担？

关于退货或换货邮费的问题，由于交易款项中本身并不包含这一部分费用，建议双方积极联系对方进行协商，若双方无法协商一致，进行中的退款请双方就自己的处理意见、退款原因在退款页面内进行说明，并上传有效凭证（如商品存在问题的实物图片，相关旺旺聊天记录截图等），其中一方在规定时间后可以点击"要求淘宝介入"按钮申请客服介入协调处理（退款"要求客服介入处理"介绍）。

因卖家过错导致退货，卖家应当承担相应的运费，如卖家明示不承担退货运费，则本公司有权对卖家账户做出相应处罚；卖家对退货不存在

过错的,退货时的邮费参考如下:
- 商品质量问题、实物与描述不符等卖家责任导致的,邮费卖家承担。
- 关于"七天退货"的运费问题,即买家个人原因发起的退货行为:

商家包邮商品,发货运费需要卖家承担,退货邮费买家自行承担;

商家非包邮商品,来回邮费买家承担。
- 关于"退货承诺"的运费问题,即买家个人原因发起的退货行为:

商家包邮商品,发货运费需要卖家承担,退货邮费的承担以退货承诺设置的为准;

商家非包邮商品,发货运费及退货运费的承担原则,以退货承诺设置的为准。

关于非"七天退货"及"退货承诺"的运费问题,即买家个人原因发起的退货行为:

卖家同意买家无理由退货的要求,包邮/非包邮都由买家承担来回运费,但若买家对发货运费价格有异议,卖家需要配合提供相关运费证明。(如带有价格的发货底单等有效收费证明)

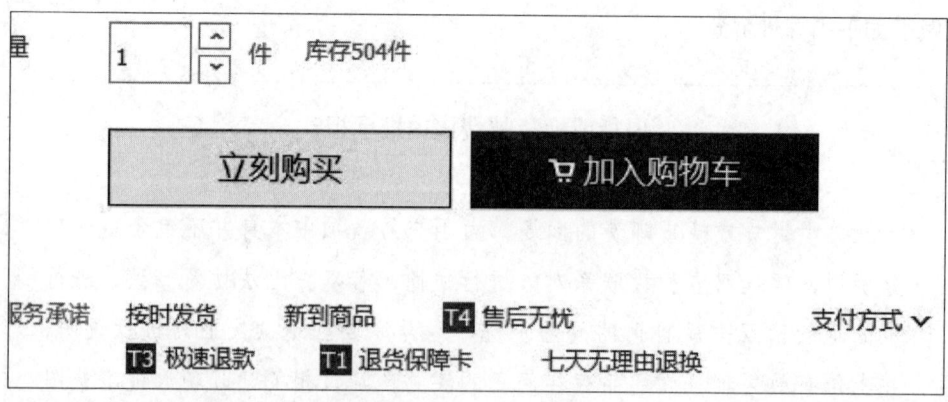

图6-4-8 服务承诺

看到上述规则,是不是有些晕?但是耐心地去阅读和理解,会更了解规则,也能更好地维护权益。

有的卖家在淘宝网统一的指导下，给出了自己的退换货费用规则，比如这家：

7天退换货须知

自收货之日起（以签收日期为准）七日内，货品在未经过穿着、洗涤、熨烫、污损、加工（翘边或自行修改尺寸等）的情况下，吊牌完整，即可享受无条件退换货服务一次，由买家承担寄回货品的邮费。退货时请连同收纳袋/衣服配件，赠品等完整寄回才能办理。如需退货前请先确认收货再联系旺旺客服为您处理。如货品存在质量问题或发错，请马上联系客服为您处理，如属实，我们会为您承担运费退换。提示：贴身货品（如内衣裤、袜子等），不予退换。

**信心保障**

亲，我们已为您投保运费险，退货不花一分钱。注：您需先行垫付运费，当完成退货操作并退款成功后，运费将会自动退还到您的支付宝账户里（最高25元）。但请您务必在线完成全部退款流程并填写正确的物流单号，在没有完成退款前请勿点击"确认收货"。如保险公司认为是潜在高风险的用户将会暂时不能提供运费险服务。

图6-4-9　佐丹奴退换货须知

无论是直接采用通用的规则，还是另立规矩，抑或直接与顾客通过私聊协商，只要能帮助你避免和解决销售中的问题，都值得一试。实践出真知，各位聪明的卖家，一定会在实际运作中更清楚地知道如何处理售后问题，通过贴心的服务和网站提供的标准售后流程，赢得良好的口碑。

其他售后服务与售后问题

售后过程中会出现各种各样的问题，完美地解决这些难题，需要的是各位卖家的细心和机智。这里为大家提供两个容易被忽视的售后视角。

首先是物流的服务质量管理。相信很多人都对物流的暴力现象有所耳闻，也就是在运输过程中，搬运工为了追求速度往往会不那么温柔的投、掷、扔、扫快件。因而快递运达时，可能会出现商品的遗失、磨损或损坏。这虽然是第三方——物流公司的问题，但交易过程中，只要商品没有送到顾客手中，都是卖家负责的范围。所以，卖家需要对自己的物流服务进行管理。建议的做法是选择一家或几家靠谱的物流公司，并签署合作协议，将各种可能的损失、必要的赔偿或补偿措施，一并写入协议。当遇到商品遗失或损坏等情况时，一方面，与顾客解释情况，好好沟通，提出满足顾客需求的解决方案；另一方面，必然是需要与物流公司进行沟通协商,甚至索取必要的赔偿。

然后,和大家分享一则短信通知,见图6-4-10。如果你收到这样的通知短信,会不会感觉很可爱又很贴心,有没有忍不住再做一次它的顾客?智慧的卖家总会找到合适方式在合适的时间向顾客塑造好的品牌形象。

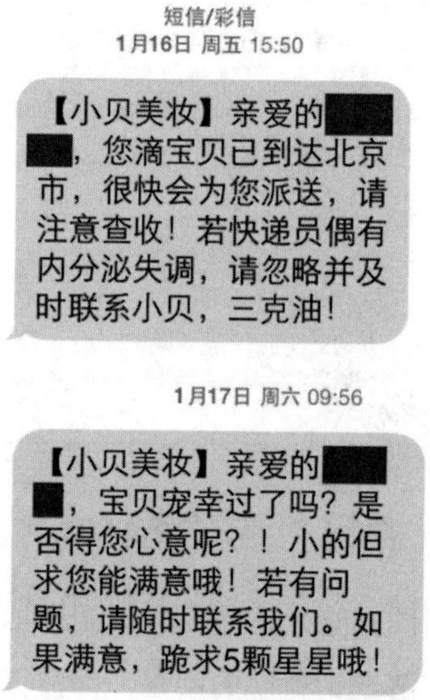

短信/彩信
1月16日 周五 15:50

【小贝美妆】亲爱的■,您滴宝贝已到达北京市,很快会为您派送,请注意查收!若快递员偶有内分泌失调,请忽略并及时联系小贝,三克油!

1月17日 周六 09:56

【小贝美妆】亲爱的■,宝贝宠幸过了吗?是否得您心意呢?!小的但求您能满意哦!若有问题,请随时联系我们。如果满意,跪求5颗星星哦!

图6-4-10 贴心的短信提醒

总结

1. 咨询类售后的应对
2. 退换货的处理
- 仅退款
- 退货退款
- 换货
3. 退换货中的物流费用
4. 其他售后问题

Chapter 1

1.1 Background of China's E-commerce

In this section, you will understand
- ✓ The development of China's e-commerce
- ✓ The development of shopping online in China
- ✓ The trend of China's e-commerce

E-commerce is a popular word today and most people are familiar with the term. With the rapid growth of the internet, a variety of e-commerce websites have sprung up globally in various forms. You can probably list the names of several of e-commerce websites such as Amazon, eBay, and Alibaba with ease.

In China, e-commerce permeates people's lives. Almost everything can be purchased online, from clothes, handbags and cosmetics, to household articles and snacks. There are numerous O2O platforms for people's different needs. If you go out and forget your wallet it doesn't matter—the option to pay using your cellphone will most likely be available. If you need to make changes to your travel itinerary while you are on your vacation, you can do all this online on the move. Nowadays, top international brands you used to only dream of can be delivered straight to your door quickly from international websites. China's e-commerce is developing at an unthinkable speed.

China's State-of-the-art E-commerce

E-commerce in China began to take off in the 1990s. By 2006 development was cruising at top speed and this shows no sign of slowing. In 2014, e-commerce in China entered a new era when Alibaba was listed on the New York stock exchange. This not only made Alibaba known throughout the world, but also injected vitality into China's e-commerce as well.

According to a report released by iResearch, the transaction value of China's e-commerce reached 12.3 trillion RMB in 2014, and had a year-on-year growth of 21.3%, of which the B2B market accounted for over 70% and online shopping for over 20%. The B2B market revenue for middle and small-sized enterprises increased by 30%. The annual penetrance of online shopping broke through 10% for the first time, and the rate of mobile internet shopping increased by over 200%.

Since 2011, transactions have rapidly increased year on year, thus proving that China's e-commerce has great potential.

Fig. 1-1-1

According to an iResearch report, mobile online shopping within China's e-commerce market is developing very quickly, with a consistent Compound Annual Growth Rate (CAGR) of 48%, and now the key impetus to the rapid development of China's online shopping market. Online tourism and the O2O market are set to maintain a consistent CAGR of 20% over the next few years. Mobile online shopping and O2O markets are expected to be the most rapid micro-segment area within the e-commerce market in China in the coming years.

中国电子商务主要细分市场未来发展预期

大类别	小类别	2014年规模（亿元）	2018年规模（亿元）	CAGR（2014-2018年）
B2B电子商务	中小企业B2B电子商务	61358.6	116627.3	17.4%
	规模以上企业B2B电子商务	28782.6	42140.1	10.0%
网络购物	网络购物（移动+PC）	28145.1	73000.0	26.9%
	移动网络购物	9297.1	45039.7	48.4%
	PC网络购物	18848.0	27960.7	10.4%
在线旅游	在线机票	1607.3	3250.0	19.2%
	在线酒店	636.1	1620.0	26.3%
	在线度假	426.5	1286.7	31.8%
O2O	餐饮O2O	941.9	2127.3	22.6%
	休闲娱乐O2O	660.0	1521.5	23.2%
	婚庆O2O	45.2	227.1	49.7%
	亲子O2O	55.7	135.9	25.0%
	美容美护O2O	54.1	88.7	13.2%

来源：综合企业财报和专家访谈，根据艾瑞统计模型核算。
©2015.1 iResearch Inc.   www.iresearch.com.cn

Fig. 1-1-2

Online Shopping, One of the Most Necessary Skills for Survival in China

If you live in China, you will inevitably encounter e-commerce, the most frequent being online shopping. What you can buy online in China is beyond the imagination. How popular is the trend of online shopping in China? Statistically, the report released by iResearch shows that the transaction value of online shopping in China in 2014 reached 2.8 trillion RMB with a comparatively high growth of 48.7%. According to official data by China's National Bureau of Statistics, in 2014 online shopping transactions exceeded 10% of total societal consuption for the first time at 10.7%. Analysis based on this data reported that the typical e-commerce enterprises had expanded their businesses to Tier 3 and Tier 4 cities, and even to rural areas. The enterprises had also adjusted their strategic global layout accordingly. In the next few years China's online shopping market is predicted to maintain a stable CAGR of 27%.

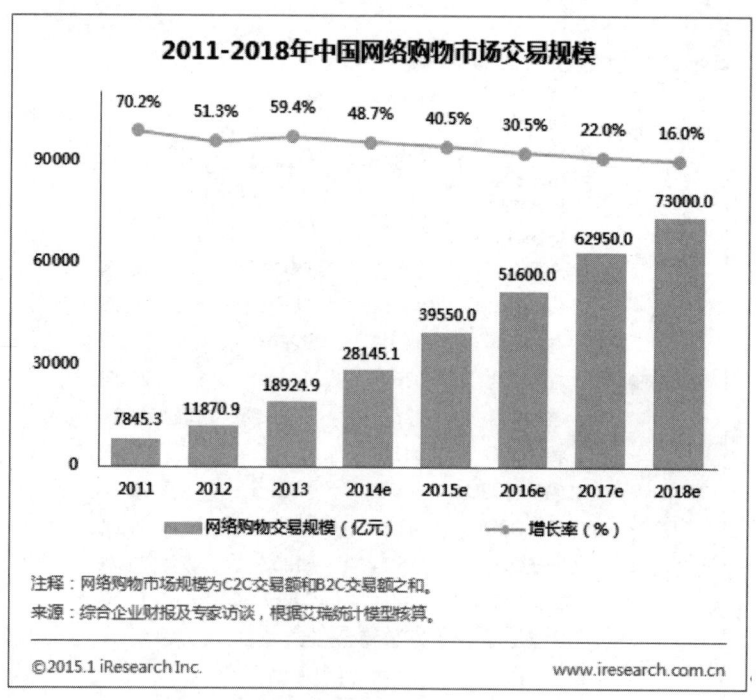

Fig. 1-1-3

At present, the online shopping market in China is shared equally by the C2C market and B2C market. With its great market size and full range of commodities, C2C enjoys the advantage of being able to meet the differing individual demands of online shopping customers, and thus will surely continue growing in the future.

Compared to the stable development of the C2C market, the B2B market, with its access to a variety of foreign businesses and manufacturers, still has plenty of space for development by providing more market opportunities for middle and small-sized enterprises, and individual merchants. From the consumer perspective, concepts have gradually changed to focus on the quality of online commodities. The mode for B2C will follow alongside C2C. Therefore, the market share for the B2C market has been increasing on the premise that quality and service are the two key factors that impact the decisions consumers make of their purchases.

Within the B2C online shopping market, in 2015 Tmall had a 55.6% share and JD a little over 25%. (Fig.1-1-4) Among other B2C enterprises, the year-on-year increase by Suning E-commerce and Vipshop has been higher than the total increase of the B2C market. Within the B2C market's stand-alone retailers, JD accounted for 60%, and Suning E-commerce and Vipshop combined were 10%. The MI official website was the most stable and quick among the B2C enterprises.

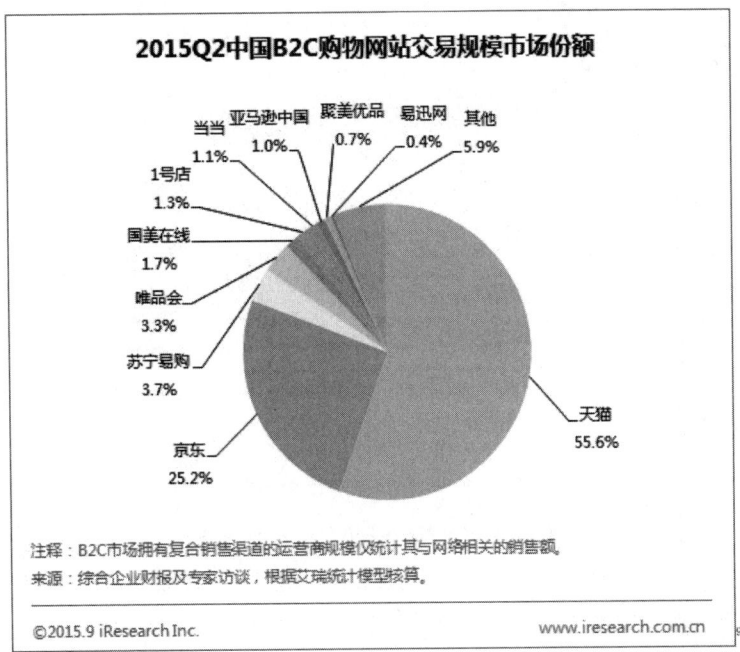

Fig. 1-1-4

In conclusion, based on the market share in 2015, Tmall, which is part of Alibaba, is still in an unshakable first position in the B2C online shopping market.

With the rise of cross-border e-commerce in recent years, and an innovative expansion by the experienced magnates of the domestic e-commerce market, transactions in China's online shopping market have increased with a vigorous momentum and now surpass the United States. Data by iResearch shows that the value of online shopping in China in 2013 was 1.84 trillion RMB, and in the United States the corresponding value was 1.59 trillion RMB. (Fig.1-1-5) That same year, transactions in the mobile online shopping market in China reached 169.6 billion RMB, and 255.9 billion RMB in the United States. It was anticipated that the mobile online shopping market would have exceeded that of the United States by 2015.

Fig. 1-1-5

The Outlook of China's E-commerce Development

I. Great opportunities for cross-border e-commerce

After a few years of development and accumulation, China's cross-border e-commerce has formed a steady industrial structure covering marketing, payment, logistics and financial services. The government has provided comprehensive support to cross-border e-commerce at a policy level, and more than ten cities including Shanghai, Chongqing, and Hangzhou have been authorized to be pilot cities for cross-border e-commerce.

China's cross-border e-commerce has entered a new era of development with enormous support by government policies and the rapid development of e-commerce and spread of globalization.

II. The exciting potential of the mobile e-commerce market with the rapid development of the online shopping market, propelled by mobile shopping, online tourism and O2O

According to the analysis released by iResearch, in China's e-commerce market, the mobile shopping market section has boasted a rapid expansion with a Compound Annual Growth Rate (CAGR) of 48% over the past few years, and have been the main impetus for the rapid development of China's online shopping market. In addition, online tourism and O2O will maintain a rapid growth with a CAGR of over 20%. In the future, mobile shopping and O2O will become the market sections with the most rapid development in China's e-commerce market.

III. The share of diversified value-added services will be enlarged and become the most important revenues for B2B platforms

Because not all enterprises use online transactions due to them having large volumes of single transactions, payment security issues, or the online habits of how consumers pay, services covering payment, guarantees, authentication, and loans provided by suppliers need to be developed further and customers made accustomed to conducting transactions online. Generally speaking, membership fees, commission, insertion charges, and value-added service charges are the main revenue for middle and small-sized enterprises on B2B e-commerce platforms. The share of diversified value-added services will surely enlarge and become the most important forms of revenue and the core advantage of enterprise competition as well.

Summary

• The development of China's e-commerce

E-commerce in China started in the 1990s and its popularity began to rise sharply in 2006. Since then it has been continually developing at top speed.

At present, B2B has the greatest share of China e-commerce market.

Year on year from 2011 to now, the transaction value of e-commerce in China has increased with a comparatively stable growth rate. In the future this can only continue.

• The development of China's online shopping

The transaction value of China's online shopping market has also increased year on year, and there is a lot more room for it to continue alongside the consistent development of mobile shopping.

• The trend of China's e-commerce

I. Great opportunities for cross-border e-commerce

II. Great potential for the mobile e-commerce market propelled by mobile shopping, online tourism and O2O

III. The share of diversified value added services will enlarge and become the most important revenue for the B2B platform

1.2 The Framework of This Book

In this section, you will understand the framework of this book.

In the wake of the high-speed development and extensive use of information technology, human society has gradually informationalized. In such a spring tide of information, the combination of business and the Internet gave birth to a new form of business—e-commerce. China's e-commerce started in the 1990s and developed rapidly afterwards. Since 2006 e-commerce has maintained a steady growth rate and swept the whole nation.

Because of China's special economic environment, its e-commerce has its own features. In order to assist foreigners in their learning about the development of China's e-commerce, certain representative e-commerce websites will be taken as examples to introduce the features of China's e-commerce and how they have been applied.

From the respective of buyers and sellers, this book gives detailed introductions on how to use these representative websites.

The sections from Chapter 2 to Chapter 3 mainly involve the overall procedure and transaction methods from the perspective of buyers.

Chapter 2 — What you have to know before shopping. This chapter is divided into two sections. The first section is about general procedures and what you have to prepare before online shopping. The second section describes some of the features and the adaptability of typical e-commerce websites in China. This chapter leads readers through the door of China's e-commerce.

Chapter 3 — Buying and Payment. Chapter 3 is the important part of the "buyer" section. This chapter is also divided into two sections which respectively explain the processes of "buying" and "payment". In the section covering buying, you will come to have a detailed understanding on the whole process, from how to select commodities, to how to communicate with sellers and to place an order. Several kind tips will be suggested in this section. In the section covering payment, a special introduction is given because of the difference between payment in China and foreign countries. You will understand the main procedure of online shipping by reading Chapter 3, and you should not skip it if you are a buyer.

Chapter 4—After the sale. This chapter mainly involves the processes covering logistics, inquiries, receipt of goods, and exchange of goods. A good shopping experience is closely related to satisfaction after the sale. Remember to refer to Chapter 4 if you have any problems after placing an order.

Chapter 5 and Chapter 6—For Sellers. These two chapters are mainly concerned with the transaction from the seller's point of view.

Chapter 5 gives a complete overview on how to prepare for setting up a shop online, from the shop's inception, applying for its establishment, updating goods, and marketing.

Chapter 6 focuses on expansion and further marketing. How can you attract more customers through marketing? How can you provide an intimate service for customers? How can you retain repeat customers by improving your service after sale?

The book comes to an end at this chapter.

Summary

This chapter is divided into two sections. The first section gives a general introduction on the development and characteristics of China's e-commerce. The second section gives an overview of the whole book so as to help readers to understand the context.

Chapter 2

2.1 Are You Ready?

In this section, you will understand
- ✓ What you need to prepare before starting online shopping
- ✓ How to prepare what you need
- ✓ The procedures of China's online shopping

John is a student from the United States. He has just arrived to study at a university in China this year and needed some school and living supplies. Because he was new to China, he asked his classmate Li Jun for help. Li Jun told him that e-commerce in China was very convenient and reliable, and that almost everything could be obtained by means of the internet. But John was inexperienced in online shopping and didn't know the procedures for shopping online in China at all. What exactly do we have to prepare before shopping online? What is the procedure for shopping online in China? Let's find out about it together.

Hardware Necessary for Shopping Online
  · Electronic devices (computers, smart phones or tablet PCs)

You can visit shopping websites through the browser on your electronic device, or you can download and install an app on your smart phone or tablet PC. (Large shopping websites usually have their own app.)

· Internet

Of course, you will need to access the internet through your electronic device. If you are using a mobile device, it might be better to access the internet via Wi-Fi, as using 3G/4G internet provided by mobile suppliers will consume a lot of data.

· Payment

A Chinese bank card approved for online banking services.

Although many online shopping platforms support payment on delivery, most online transactions have to be paid online. Thus a Chinese bank card that is approved for online banking services is necessary for a buyer to avoid superfluous troubles. You need to go to a bank within China and apply for a bank card with your identity document (e.g. passport). Bank cards can be either debit cards or credit cards. A debit card is required for online shopping in China. The ability for your card to make payments online must be initiated at the bank. If you wish to pay online by credit card, because there are a lot of restrictions on applying for a credit card in China, you will need to call customer service at your bank for a consultation.

> Similar to Mastercard and Visa, China's UnionPay united all banks in China to formulate industrial standards and promote corporation so as to provide convenience for consumers.
>
> It is necessary for you to have a UnionPay card if you live in China. And after you leave China, your UnionPay card can still be used in over 150 countries throughout the world.
>
> You can apply for a UnionPay card at any bank in China. The four major banks are Bank of China, Agricultural Bank of China, Industrial and Commercial Bank of China, and China Construction Bank.

International Credit Card

Certain transactions on China's e-commerce websites can be paid for by international credit card (such as Visa, MasterCard, Discover, JCB, etc).

Take the biggest shopping website in China, Taobao, as an example. At present, transactions on physical commodities can be paid by Visa/MasterCard/JCB issued throughout the world (except in Washington D.C. in the United States). However, buyers need to pay a 3% fee. Only personal cards are accepted, cards in the names of businesses or companies are not. Other shopping websites support international credit cards to varying degrees. Details can be found on the relevant websites.

> 1. Be cautious of phishing sites. Though theft caused by bank security vulnerability is rare, some buyers suffer misfortune by visiting phishing sites. When you open the home page of a bank, add the correct URL in your favorites in order to avoid accessing false addresses or links.
> 2. Protect your online bank login ID and code.
> 3. Regularly query transaction details.
> 4. Use anti-virus software. Set your computer's firewall to a high level, upgrade anti-virus software in a timely manner to avoid online bank thief invasion.

Please refer to Section 2 of Chapter 3 for credit payment details.

Software Necessary for Online Shopping

• A third-party payment account

Third-party payments are managed by reputable independent agencies. They provide a platform to convert transactions by bank account or card to virtual accounts or virtual currency. Third-party payments provide an escrow service connecting the payment and settlement systems of banks domestically and abroad. In transactions paid through a third-party payment platform, a buyer conducts his payment through the account provided by the platform after selecting goods. The third-party informs the seller that they have received the money for the goods and the goods can be delivered. After receiving and checking the goods the buyer then informs the third party to finish the payment, though this will happen automatically after a time. In China, the most commonly used third-party payment platform is Alipay which is similar to Paypal. Now we'll take Alipay as an example and walk through the steps taken in registering and opening a third-party account.

Enter https://www.alipay in the browser address bar to go into the Alipay home page.

Fig. 2-1-1

Click on the top right of the page at "Free Registration". Enter your information according to the prompt to begin registration of a new user.

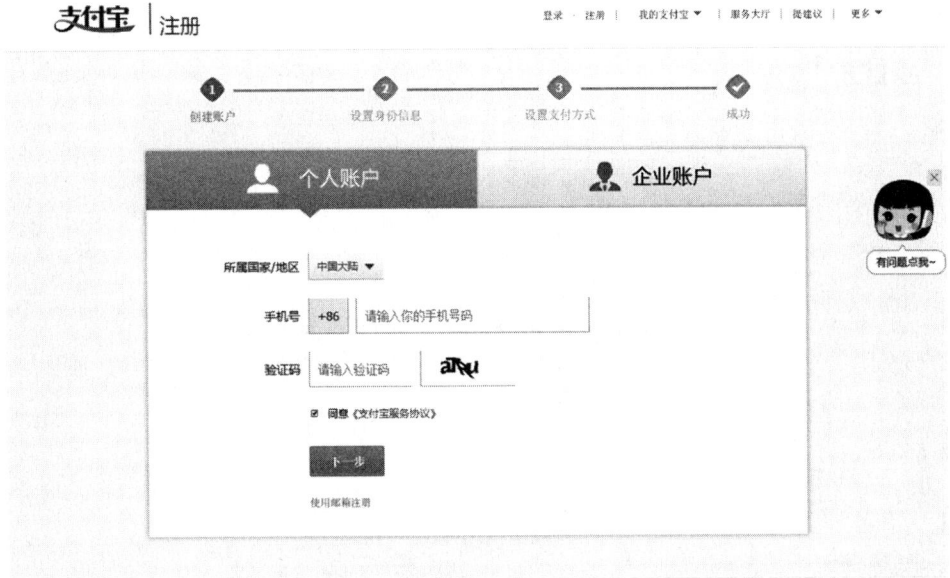

Fig. 2-1-2

You can register through by email or phone. You need to enter an SMS verification code when registering by mobile phone.

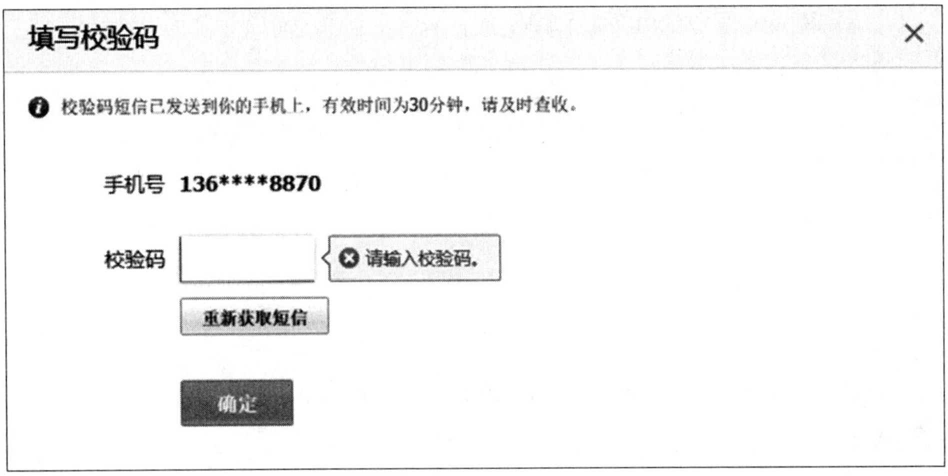

Fig. 2-1-3

You need to verify the e-mail when registering by e-mail::

Fig. 2-1-4

Then continuing to set up your account information to complete registration.

Attention

1. Be sure to remember your Alipay payment password and log in password. You can set the two passwords the same to avoid confusion.

2. Account security is very important when using third-party payment platforms. If it recommends you install a secure digital certificate, do so, as it can ensure security on your computer and protect you from password theft. Do not deposit too much money in your account if it is not necessary in order to avoid theft.

· Ali Wangwang—a bridge of communication with sellers

When shopping online sometimes we need to contact a seller. Different sites provide different ways to do this: some sites use the online customer service, and some proved the seller's QQ account. Ali Wangwang is a free online communication software provided by Taobao. When shopping on Taobao or TMall, you can use Ali Wangwang to communicate with any seller, to discuss for example product information and freight methods, or bargaining, etc. Chat records in Ali Wangwang can be used in cases of litigation or for ensuring legal rights.

For the use of Ali Wangwang, see Section 1 in Chapter 3.

What is mentioned above are the main requisites for opening a new online shopping account. You can start your online shopping journey when you have the right equipment, have connected to the internet, and prepared a bank card and the software for payment.

A Brief Look at the Process of Online Shopping in China

In China, there are many websites that offer online shopping services. Although the focus of their services can be slightly different, the shopping process is much the same. The main process of online shopping can be summarized as follows: register—log in—search for the goods you want to buy—select your favourite goods—add them to the shopping cart—submit your order and pay—follow the logistics information—confirm receipt—give feedback.

Now let's use Taobao to explain things in more detail.

· Register and log in

Enter www.taobao.com in your browser's address bar to go to the Taobao home page.

Fig. 2-1-5

The Taobao homepage is visually jam-packed. Do you think it is difficult to figure out where to register? It is at the top left. Click "Free Registration" and input the relevant information according to the prompts to finish the new user registration.

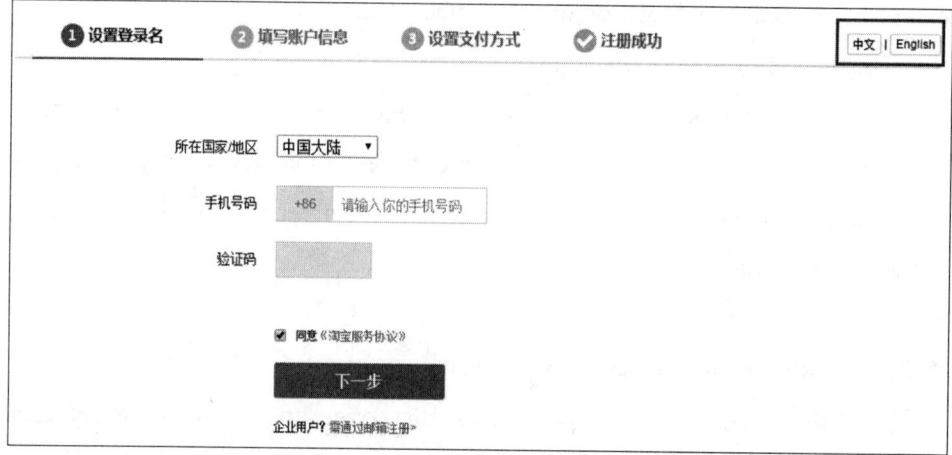

Fig. 2-1-6

 If you are not able to read Chinese, you can switch your registration page to English using the button in the top right hand corner.

· Search for what you want

There is a search bar across the top of the Taobao home page where you can begin to look for what you want to buy. If you are a loyal fan of a specific Taobao shop or brand, you can search for it here also.

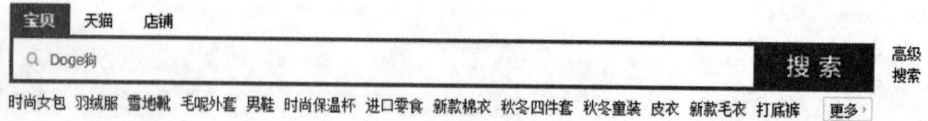

Fig. 2-1-7

· Select your favourite goods.

After you enter what you are looking for in the search bar, it will return a whole page of results. If you are overwhelmed by the possibilities, you can refine the results further by brand, or sort the results by numerous other conditions of your choice.

When you find the goods you are interested in, do not hesitate to click on its picture or text link to read a detailed description about them.

· Add to the shopping cart

If you decide you're going to buy these goods, and if necessary you have chosen the colour, style, quantity, etc., you can now click "Buy Now" to proceed to the payment page. If you want to browse other goods, click "Add to Cart" instead to add the goods into the shopping cart and then continue to shop at your leisure. If there are any further items you wish to buy you need to add them to your cart and check everything out together.

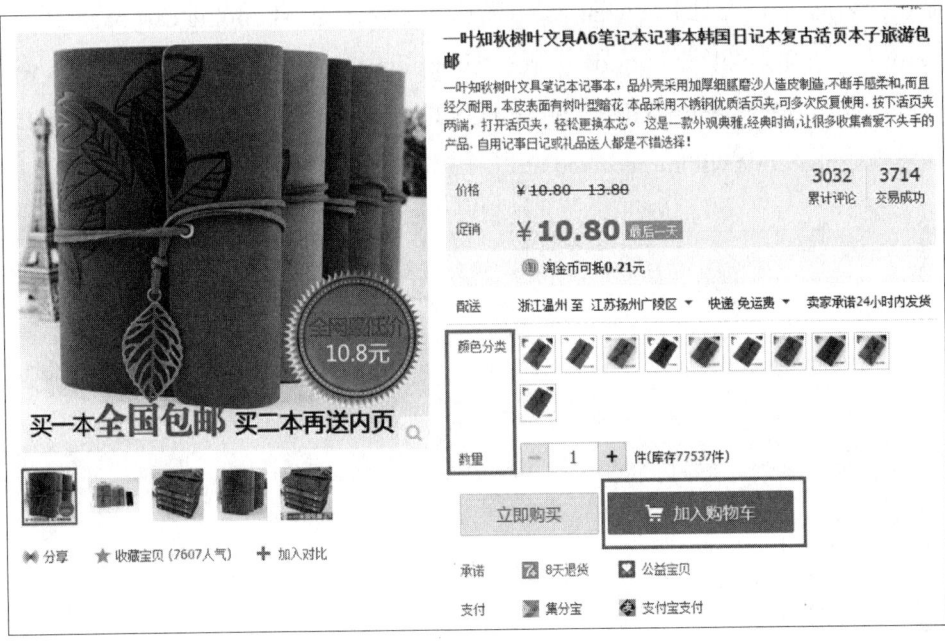

Fig. 2-1-8

· Submit the order and pay

If you have selected goods you want to buy, click at the top right of the page on "Shopping Cart" to see your card and proceed to the payment stage.

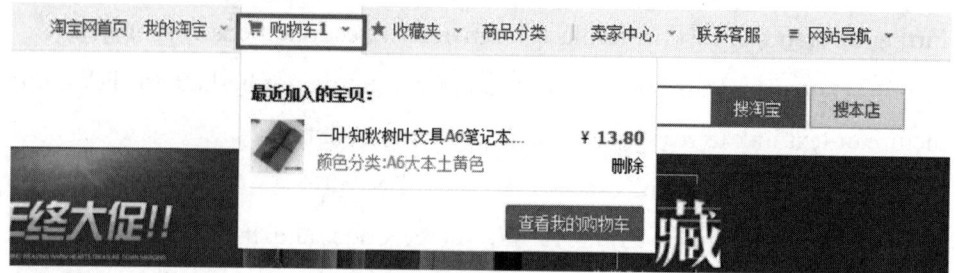

Fig. 2-1-9

You now see all your items listed on the shopping cart page. If you decide you have too many things or realised that you are a bit short and need to ditch some items you can delete what you don't want from the shopping cart page. If you want to purchase all the goods in your shopping cart click "Settlement". This will take you to the page on which you can confirm your order. You need to fill in the address the goods will be received at.

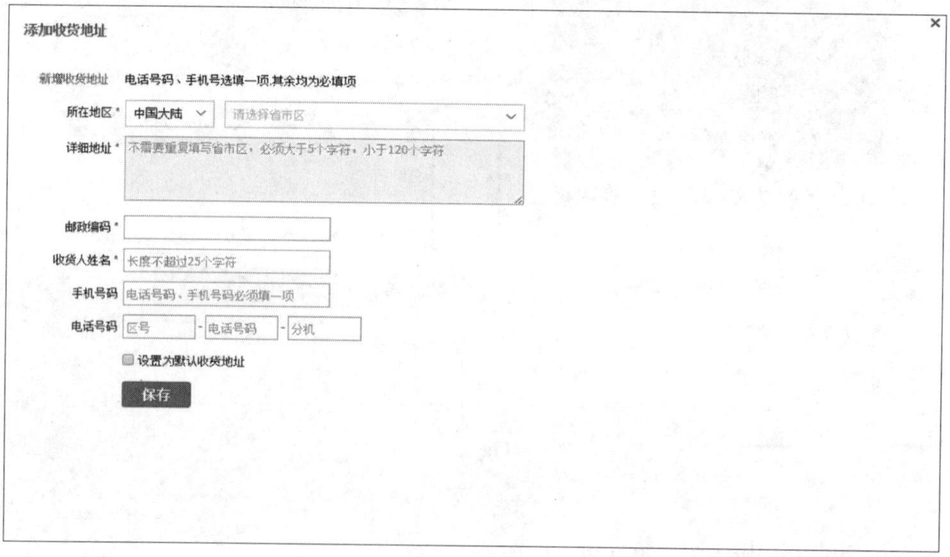

Fig. 2-1-10

Fill in your delivery address and confirm any other relevant information about and then you can submit your order. After submitting the order, Taobao will automatically connect to the Alipay payment page. If the payment page fails to load or you close the payment page by accident, do not worry-just click at the top of the page on "My Taobao" then "Bought Baby", and it will take you to a list of orders you have submitted.

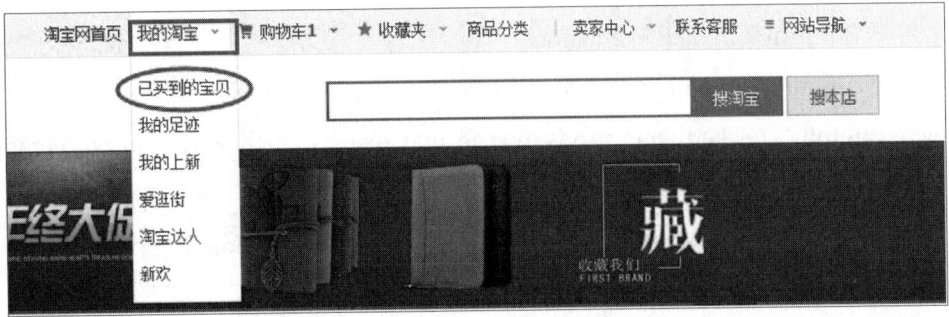

Fig. 2-1-11

Now click "Pay Immediately" on the right hand side of the page and you will be taken to the payment page again.

Fig. 2-1-12

• Tracking logistics information

After your payment is processed successfully, all you need to do is to wait for your items to be delivered. You probably will want to know which step in the dispatching process your goods are at, or whether they are close yet. If you do, you just need to click on "My Taobao" then "Bought Baby" then "Check Logistics Information" next to the order in question. Here the detailed logistics information will be clearly displayed.

• Confirmation and evaluation

Eventually you will get what you have been anxiously waiting for. After you have carefully checked your goods over to make sure that there are no problems and they meet your expectations, log into Taobao and click on "My Taobao/Bought Baby" and click on "Receipt Confirmation" on the right hand side. The payment for the goods will be deposited to the seller's account immediately.

If your goods have not been delivered, or you want to return them, you mustn't click on "Receipt Confirmation" or you will lose both your money and your goods.

Don't worry if you forget the receipt confirmation step—your payment will automatically be deposited to the seller's account a few days later by Alipay.

After confirming receipt you can give feedback on your goods and experience with the seller. After doing this the shopping process on Taobao has ended.

Though it may be complicated, this section has just given an elementary introduction to shopping online with Taobao. The process for returning goods has not been mentioned and will be explained in detail later.

Summary

• What you need before shopping online

Hardware: electronic equipment (computer, smart phone or tablet), internet, bank account

Software: third-party payment account, Ali Wangwang

• Process of online shopping

Register — Log into the website — Look up what you want to buy — Select your goods — Add them to the shopping cart — Submit you order and pay — Track the package — Confirm receipt — Give your evaluation.

2.2 What Do You Want to Buy?

In this chapter, you will ...
✓ Learn what you can buy from China's e-commerce websites.
✓ Learn the characteristics and categories of typical e-commerce websites in China.

After learning about how to prepare for online shopping in China, John looked at his long shopping list and found he had a problem. His roommates dragged in a big box from "yhd.com" which was filled with all kinds of food. The next day, came another box with "Jumei.com" written on it which contained skin care products. There were so many things he had to buy—food, clothes yet there seemed to be so many online shopping websites and they all had similar homepages and his Chinese was not very good. So where would he buy the things he urgently needed for school?

Maybe you face the same dilemma as John, and don't know where to buy different products? Let's talk about how to choose shopping websites.

What Chinese People Usually Buy from the Internet

In 2014, the volume of e-commerce transactions in China was 3.19 trillion RMB (exceeding both the US and world average). Online shopping accounted for nearly 30% of that value. It is expected that by 2020, the value of China's e-commerce transactions will be approximately 50 trillion RMB, making it the world's largest e-commerce market, with the value of online retail over 10 trillion RMB, 16.3% of the country's total retail sales. At the same time, China's logistics systems are also developing, especially in Beijing, Shanghai and other big cities that have plentiful resources. On some large shopping websites, an order placed by a person today can arrive at his home the following day. It is also possible to receive the goods in the afternoon if they were ordered in the morning.

China's e-business culture has penetrated the daily lives of urban Chinese residents. A housewife said that her family used to spend one evening every weekend driving to a large supermarket near their neighbourhood to buy a week's worth of groceries. But since they began shopping online they no longer do and have bought everything from the internet from food bags and toilet paper to an electric cooker and a washing machine. Though she lives in Tianjin, she often buys things on the internet for her father in Sichuan, and sends them directly to his home so he does not need to go the supermarket as he has trouble walking.

Let's now take a look at the classification of goods on the homepage of two large shopping websites:

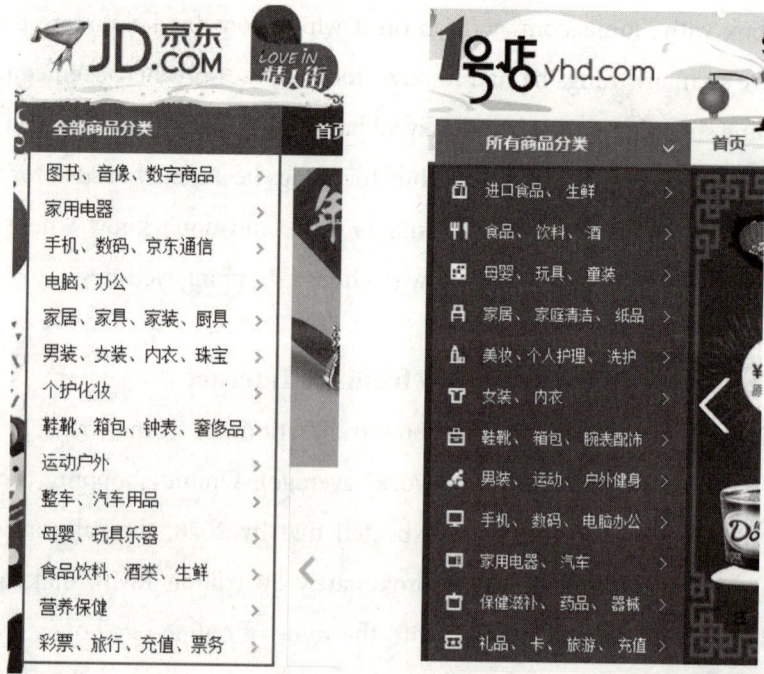

Fig. 2-2-1　Commodity Classification at Jingdong Mall　Fig. 2-2-2 Commodity Classification at Yhd.com

Though they are all comprehensive shopping websites, they put different emphasis on the sale of particular goods. For electronic equipment and electrical products, we usually go to Jingdong, and when it comes to buying food, our first choice yhd.com. This is evident from the sorting of classification of the above two websites.

Typical E-commerce Websites in China

· B2C type

B2C is one of the patterns of e-commerce. Its full name is Business to Customer. Generally speaking, it is commercial retail, i.e. enterprises directly sell products and services to consumers. B2C was the first e-business model in China. Many shopping sites—online shopping malls, department stores, vertical stores and brand stores—all belong to the B2C model. Below are a few large and commonly used B2C websites.

➢ Go to yhd.com for stocking up on grains

Yhd.com was the first online supermarket in China. It was founded by former Dell executives Yu Gang and Liu Junling at the Zhangjiang Hi-Tech Park in Shanghai. Since its establishment in July 2008, with the idea that it is a "cheaper online supermarket than the supermarket", this online shop has maintained a high growth momentum. By the end of 2013, the shop had 57 million registered users and more than 15 million mobile subscribers. At present, it is the largest B2C food business in China.

The website address of the store is http://www.yhd.com/.

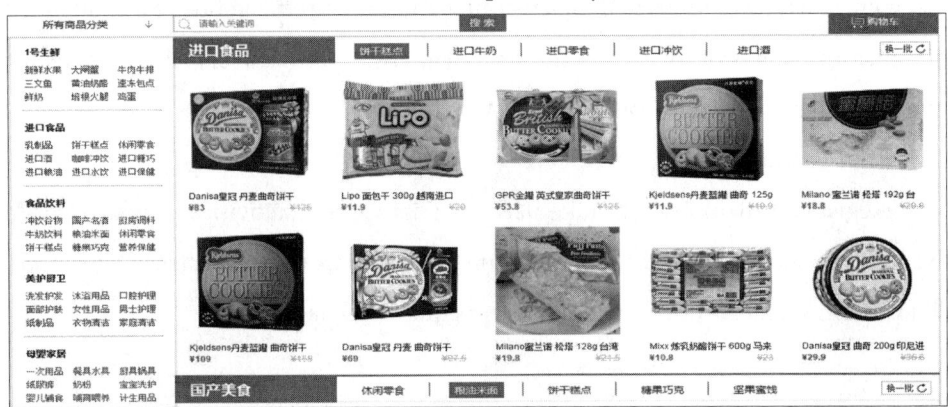

Fig. 2-2-3　Yhd.com or No. 1 Store

Since the shopping process at this shop is almost the same as most e-commerce sites, it's not necessary for us to go into details.

Fig. 2-2-4   Shopping Process of No. 1 Store

This shop provides the following services:

Delivery on a fixed date

If the order is submitted before 20:00 on any day of the week (online payment must be completed), customers can choose to pick up their purchase any day within 7 days of the order.

Punctuality of delivery

If the order is submitted successfully by 20:00 on any day of the week (online payment must be completed), the customer can pick up the goods at a designated time within 7 days of the order. The store will ensure the delivery of the goods for the customer within one hour of requested time.

Trial center

Registered members can take part in 'Trial Center' activities. Click "Website Navigation" at the top right-hand side of the shop's front page, select "Zero *Yuan* Trial" from the drop-down menu bar, and enter the Trial Center.

Fig. 2-2-5

Trial activities are divided into two types: "Free Trial" and "Mail Trial". As the name suggests, "Free Trial" means that members can get free items including free delivery. During the activity, members apply for a trial activity, and, within 10 working days from the end of the activity entry date, some of the customers will be selected to participate. The shop or supplier will send trial goods to these customers. Usually, "Free Trial" products are small quantities of finely packaged high price items.

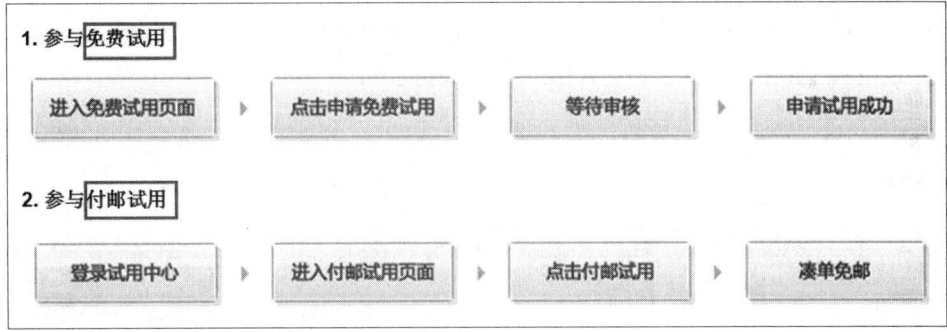

Fig. 2-2-6

"Delivery-paying Trial" means that customers receiver free goods but need to pay a small delivery fee. However, if the customer's orders meet certain rules, they will get the free goods with no additional delivery charges. For example, if the store stipulates that if they make an additional purchase of 59 RMB they can receive the trial products without paying the delivery fee. Delivery-paying trials release small sample products of low unit price in large quantities.

When competition in China's major e-commerce platforms is in full swing, many special services such as fixed day delivery, punctuality of delivery, and trial centers are advertised. These "little tricks" attract business and expand the number of customers.

➢ Go to Jingdong for digital products and household appliances

Jingdong is China's largest self-run e-commerce enterprise. On 22 May 2014, it was listed on Nasdaq as the fourth largest internet company in China, second only to Alibaba, Tencent and Baidu.

As a comprehensive one-stop shopping platform, Jingdong Mall provides a wide range of products: computers, mobile phones and other digital products, household appliances, auto accessories, clothing and footwear, luxury goods, household and family supplies, cosmetics and other personal care supplies, food and nutrition products, books and media products, mother and infant supplies, toys, sports and fitness equipment, and virtual goods, etc. It has 31.50 million kinds of SKU (Stock Keeping Unit) products in 13 categories.

The address for Jingdong is http://www.jd.com/.

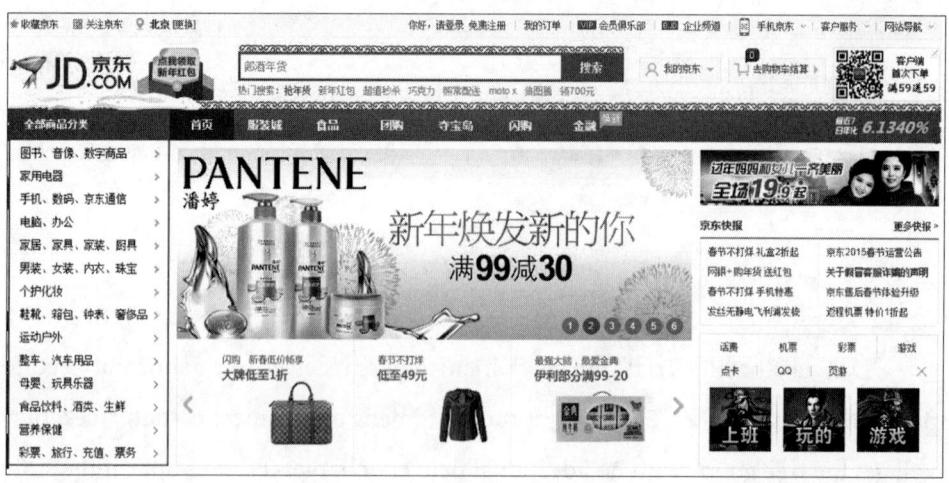

Fig. 2-2-7 Jingdong Mall

In the eyes of Chinese consumers, Jingdong Mall is a seller of genuine and reliable electronic products and household appliances. Jingdong provides authentic product guarantees and a perfect after-sale service policy. For example, it provides installation of large electrical appliances, and customers can apply for repairs or return goods without fuss. Compared to purchasing such items in real stores, Jingdong will not infringe on consumer rights.

售后特色服务	
服务名称	具体描述
7天无理由退货	客户购买京东自营商品7日内（含7日，自客户收到商品之日起计算），在保证商品完好的前提下，可无理由退货。（部分商品除外，详情请见各商品细则）
售后上门取件	客户购买京东自营商品15日内（含15日，自客户收到商品之日起计算）因质量问题提交退换申请且审核通过，在京东自营配送范围内，京东提供免费上门取件服务。法定节假日、停电、天气等不可抗力情况除外。
售后100分	客户购买京东自营商品15日内（自客户收到商品之日起计算）如出现故障，京东售后服务部收到故障件并确认属于质量故障（以国家3包法等有关法律、法规为准）开始计时。在100分钟内（工作时间每周一至周五，上午9:00至12:00，下午13:00至18:00，法定节假日、停电等无法正常处理情况除外）处理完客户的售后问题，处理完的标志为已经为客户提交了换新订单、补发订单、补偿申请或者退款申请（通过邮政等退款要依赖于第三方退款平台服务速度）。注：如客户不同意以上解决方案，协商时间另计。如以上承诺京东未做到，除故障商品全额退款外再给予客户京东账户1000个京豆作为补偿。
售后到家	自商品售出一年内，如出现质量问题，京东将提供免费上门取送及原厂授权维修服务。 温馨提示： A. 售后到家服务仅针对部分指定商品，具体以客户下单时订单详情为准； B. 此服务仅限京东自营商品（京东销售和配送）； C. 法定节假日、停电、天气等不可抗力情况除外。

注：
京东自营商品指在商品详情页明确标识为"京东发货并提供售后服务"的商品，此外为第三方卖家商品。

Fig. 2-2-8　Special After-sale Service of Jingdong Mall

➢ Buy books, go to "Dangdang"

Dangdang, founded in November 1999 as a book retailer, has developed into a leading online retailer selling multiple products. It is China's largest book retailer, also has a third party investment platform. Dangdang was officially listed on the New York Stock Exchange on 8 December 2010. It is the first B2C online mall in China which is totally based on online business to be listed in the United States.

In the category of books, Dangdang occupies more than 50% of the online market share, and a third of the book retail market nationwide. Dangdang's order conversion rate is as high as 25%, which is far higher than the average 7% for the book sector. This means that every four people browsing Dangdang network will produce an order.

The address for Dangdang is: http://www.dangdang.com/.

Fig. 2-2-9　Dangdang Books

➢ For professional beauty and skin care products, go to "jumei.com" or "lefeng. com"

Jumei.com is a limited time sale cosmetics mall. It was founded in March 2010 by Chen Ou and Dai Yusen. It is essentially a B2C website in a vertical industry. On 16 May 16 2014, jumei.com was officially listed on the New York Stock Exchange and became the first vertical cosmetics supplier in China to be listed in the US.

The address for jumei.com is http://www.jumei.com/.

Fig. 2-2-10　Jumei.com

Jumei.com acquires its goods from brand manufacturers, regular agents, and special domestic and foreign stores. They guarantee their goods as authentic and this shouldto a certain extent reduce any doubt you might have in buying cosmetics on the internet. At the end of 2013, jumei.com opened its first flagship store, creating a precedent for the O2O (Online to Offline) in China. CEO Chen explains: "Because the threshold of e-commerce is too low, consumers have a natural distrust of online cosmetics, so opening an offline store will help to solve the problem of consumer trust."

At present, jumei.com is making efforts to develop "offshore purchasing", mainly from Japan and South Korea, supplemented by European and American cosmetics brands. Jumei purchases goods from abroad which are delivered to the Zhengzhou bonded area, where quality inspections are conducted and and sales shipped. Higher taxes incurred through this method of acquiring stock are not inferred on customers but instead borne by Jumei. Therefore, for customers, the price provided by Jumei is close to that of a duty free shop.

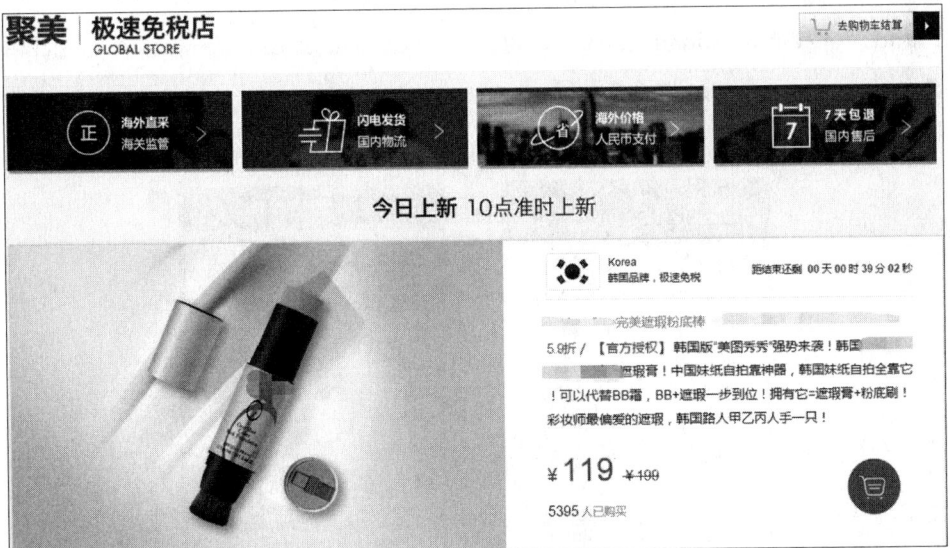

Fig. 2-2-11　Jumei.com's "Fast Duty Free Shop"

Fig. 2-2-12   Lefeng.com

Lefeng.com is also a vertical cosmetics business founded in 2008 by famous television hostess Li Jing with the goal of providing "the first choice portal for hundreds of millions of Chinese women who want to enjoy a high quality life". It is the first B2C website in China to be run by a TV star that has brand authorization and delivers "100% authentic goods". The special feature of website is its star brands—media personalities sign contracts with Lefeng and the website launches their corresponding unique brand.

The address is http://www.lefeng.com/.

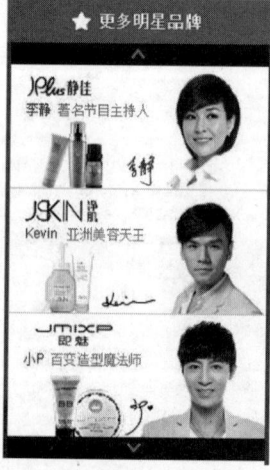

Fig. 2-2-13   Vip.com Star Brand   Fig. 2-2-14   Vip.com Star Brand

From the perspective of popularity, sales, and the number of members, lefeng.com and jumei.com are the largest vertical cosmetics electronic suppliers in China. Therefore, competition between the two is unavoidable. Since 2013, the two suppliers have waged many sales and price campaigns.

➢ "Vip.com" — online outlet

Unlike other shopping sites, vip.com defines itself as "a special site for special sales". It provides a one-stop shopping experience with new products listed on a daily basis, with a very low 90 percent off discount and a fun-filled time limit buying model. As many as 100 brands are authorized to sell on vip.com. Goods include clothing, accessories, shoes, cosmetics, bags, home textiles, leather goods, perfumes, 3C, and products for mother and baby, etc. In March 2012, vip.com successfully landed on the New York Stock Exchange.

The goods on vip.com are directly supplied by the brand's factories, dispensing middle men and multiple-layer sales channels, and thus the price is much lower, even as low as wholesale!

The website address of vip.com is: http://www.vip.com/.

Fig. 2-2-15 Vip.com

Because vip.com's sale model is to "launch new products at 10 a.m. every day", many of its members have formed a habit of sitting in front of the computer at this time to prepare to "snatch goods". There are many enthusiastic customers sharing "strategies for snatching goods on vip.com". If there is a brand that you are particularly interested in, you should pay close attention to vip.com's special sale activities.

· Types of C2C

C2C means customer to customer, and it provides an online trading platform for both buyers and sellers. China's largest C2C website is Taobao, which accounts for more than 60% of China's C2C market share. A more detailed account of Taobao's shopping process and usage will be given in the third chapter of this book.

Apart from Taobao, many large comprehensive shopping websites not only provide self-operated B2C services, but also encourage third party sellers to enter and establish C2C trading. Of the B2C websites mentioned above, lefeng.com, jumei.com, vip.com are all vertical types of B2C, while yhd.com, Jingdong and Dangdang, although each having their own particular features, are comprehensive shopping websites. All have established C2C channels.

If you search for a brand of coloured pencil on Jingdong, you will get many similar search results, such as:

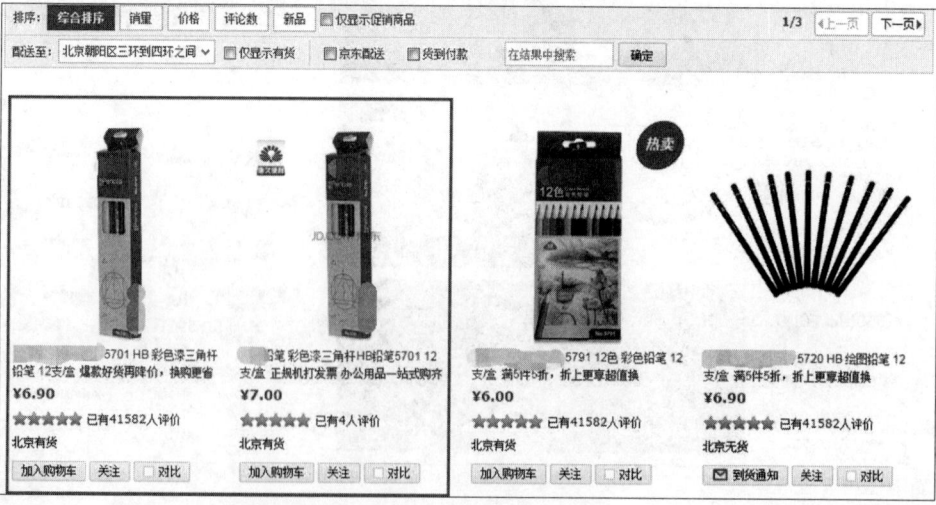

Fig. 2-2-16   Search Results

After finding the prices of identical goods to be different, you will certainly click each item to see further details. The first item is like this:

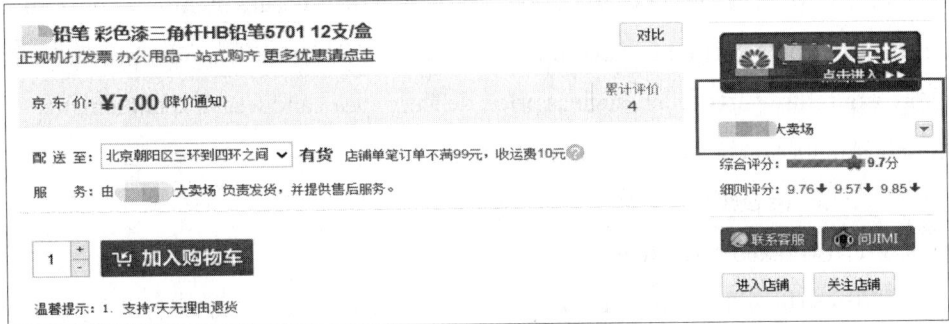

Fig. 2-2-17　Details of the Goods

The second item is like this:

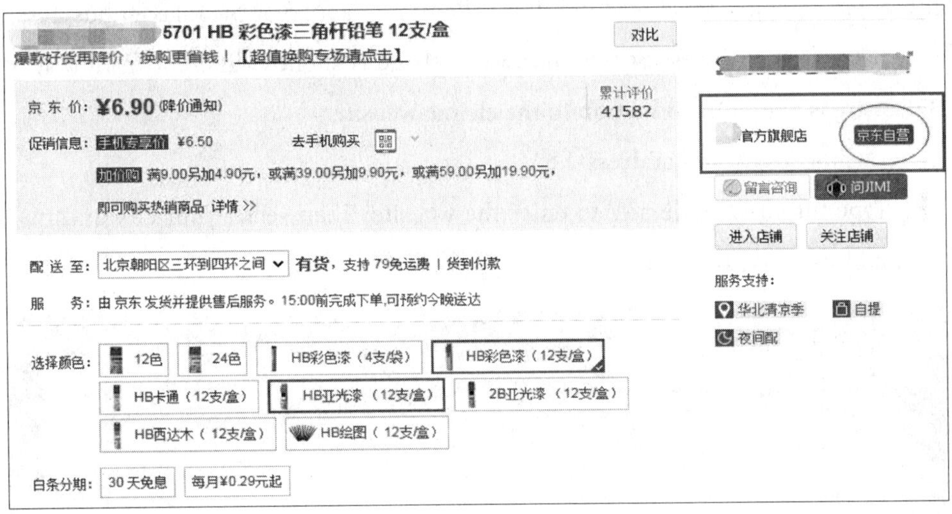

Fig. 2-2-18　Search Results

On the right side of the page, you can see which store the merchandise comes from. The first item comes from "XX Hypermarket" and the second one comes from "XX Official Flagship Store". You may have also noticed that on the right hand side of the shop name for the second item, "Jingdong's Own Item" is written, while these words cannot be found to the right of the shop name for the first item, indicating "XX Hypermarket" is a third party seller not operated by Jingdong.

When buying something from Jingdong, Dangdang and No. 1 Shop, we must pay attention to whether the goods to be bought are from the websites themselves or from a third party. There are often some differences between the goods from the websites and those from third party sellers such as price, delivery speed and fees. It is not a matter of which are superior, but you need to make a choice based on your own preference.

· Types of O2O

➤ Call a takeout — ele.me

Ele.me (literally "Are you hungry?"), founded in April 2009, is one of the largest O2O platforms for delivering food and beverages in China. It integrated food and beverage brands and online network resources so that users can easily search surrounding restaurants, order online through mobile phones and computers to enjoy delicious food. It is called the "Taobao of the takeout business".

Because the process of the takeaway website is slightly different from that of B2C, here is a brief introduction to the ele.me website.

1. Choose city and address

Type http://www.ele.me/ to enter the website. Then select your city and type your address and press enter.

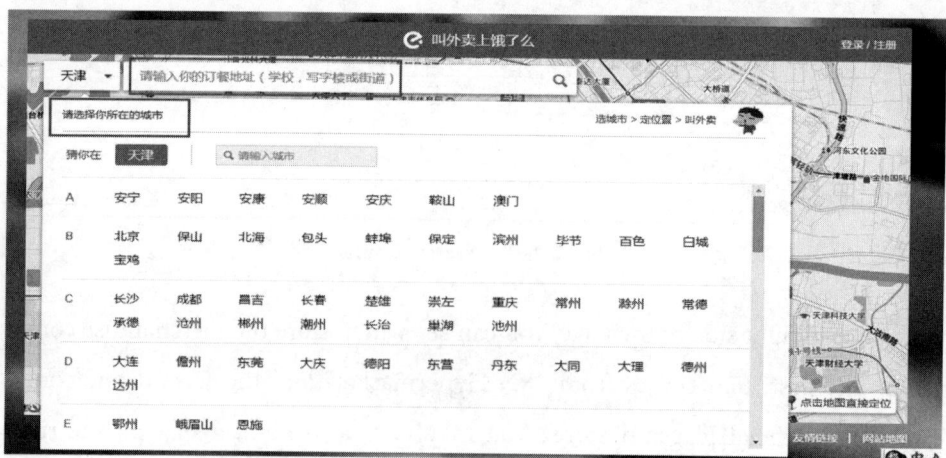

Fig. 2-2-19

Fig. 2-2-20　Ele.me

2. User registration and login

Click "login / registration" on the top right hand side of the page, enter your information according to the prompts, and register as a new user.

Fig. 2-2-21

3. Browse restaurants and menus

After registering, you can begin to choose the dishes you want to enjoy. You can choose a restaurant that you are interested in on the front page and browse its menu.

Fig. 2-2-22

You can also search the restaurants and foods you prefer at the search bar above the page.

Fig. 2-2-23

4. Place yummy foods into the gourmet basket

After selecting the dishes, click the price button to add the dish to the food basket.

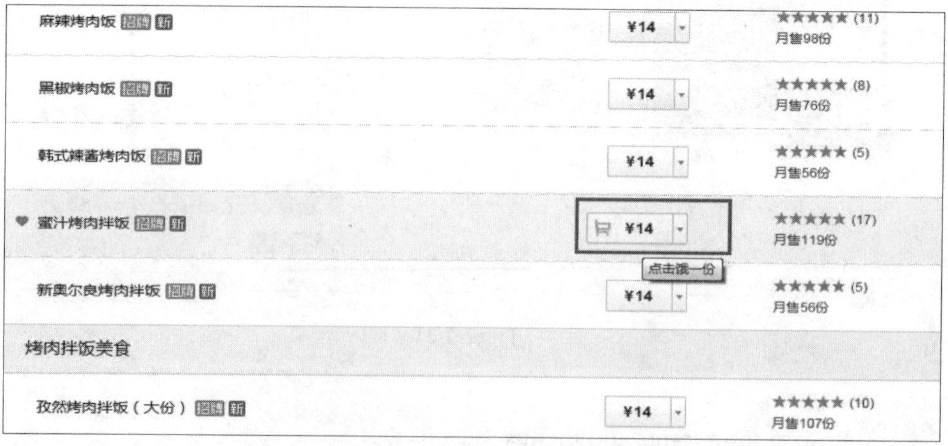

Figure 2-2-24   Click the Price Button

5. Confirmation and payment of order

Click the "Go to Pay" button at the bottom right hand side of the food basket to confirm the order.

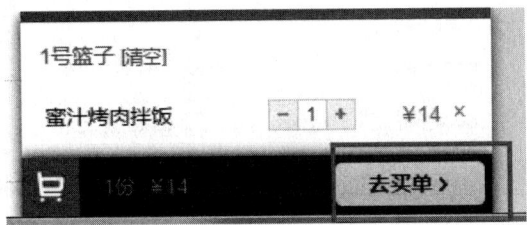

Fig. 2-2-25　Order Confirmation

On the order confirmation page, according to the prompt, enter your address, the delivery time and the payment method. If you have any special requests, such as you'll not accept substitutions for orders not available, that you don't want your order spicy, or you want more vegetables added, etc, you can leave a message in the message box.

Fig. 2-2-26　Order Confirmation Information

Click "Confirm Order" and choose a payment method. You need to complete the payment within 30 minutes otherwise your order will be cancelled.

Fig. 2-2-27   Confirmation and Completion of Payment

6. View order status

After the payment is accepted, all you need to do is to wait for your order. You can click "My Ele List" at the top of the front page to check your order status.

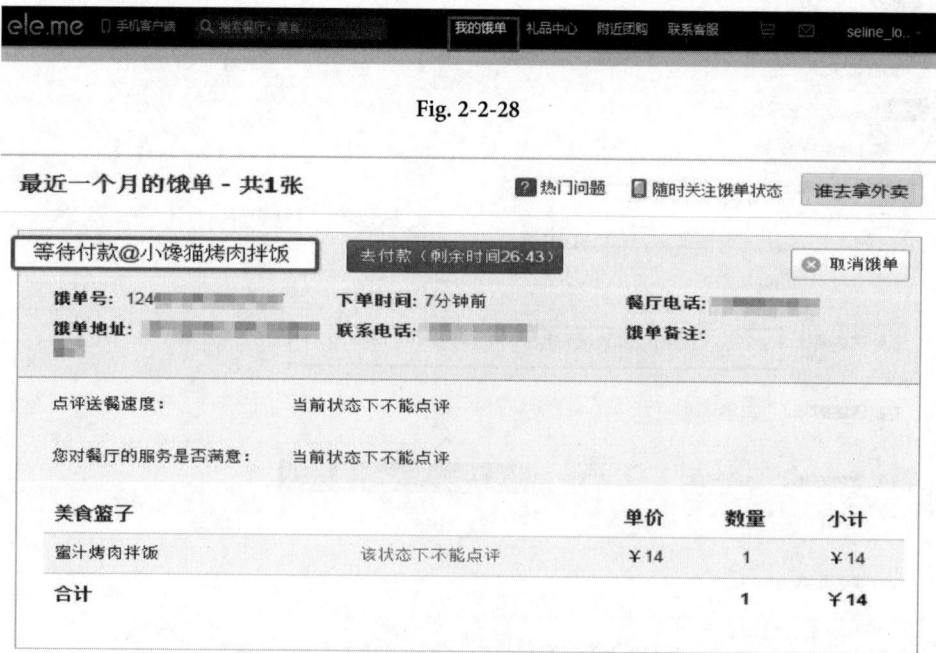

Fig. 2-2-28

Fig. 2-2-29   View Order Status

There are many O2O food and beverage websites of this kind such as waimai.meituan.com and waimai.baidu.com. In the face of competition, major platforms often launch promotional activities. It is suggested that you not forget to pay attention such promotions.

Takeout — The Next Main Battlefield of O2O War

Eating has become a difficult task in the hot summer, being sweaty when you cook by yourself, and being anorexic after insolation outside. So the takeout service becomes hot as the hot weather. However, it is out to collect the cards or call for reserve. The popular on is to order on APP …

Ordering takeout via mobile phone

For Xu Liang who works on Gaoxin Road, where he will eat his lunch every summer is a issue—the small restaurants around his company are so crowded with people at noon. Tables are even placed outside. "Sitting in the hot sun to wait for a bowl of noodles would leave my whole body dripping with sweat." Although there are many comfortable air conditioned places near the company where one can eat a meal, salaried people can only go there once in a while, otherwise a month's worth of salary would go just on meals.

But this summer, Xu Liang's life is much better. Meituan and Baidu have launched takeout apps. If he places an order his meal will arrive at his company half an hour later. Although he has to pay a few *yuan* on a tip for each order, if several colleagues order together the split each has pay is equivalent to a bottle of water. How enjoyable it is to eat a takeout while relaxing in the company's air conditioning before taking a nap!

Like taxi apps, takeout apps seems to have become popular overnight all over the country. However, compared with taking a taxi, eating is a must for everyone, so unlike taxi software that gives customers many discounts, takeout apps, which only launched last year, offer few discounts except for first time use discounts.

Each takes what he needs to make profits for all

Taking a taxi is also nothing new, but since utilising the internet it has become a new fad. Takeout is also not something new either—once a small card inserted in the door at a college student's dormitory, or a telephone number advertised by a restaurant, ordering a takeout has always been an option for many young people needing to solve their problem of needing to eat.

The other day, Xu Liang saw a noodle shop with only six tables downstairs that also had up a sign saying "Meituan Takeout". In his opinion this noodle shop is a typical "mom and pop shop" and joining the takeout ranks should definitely make their business more prosperous.

Yuan Hang opened a cold rice noodle eatery not long ago in the vicinity of Fengchengwu Road. Although the lamp boxes, seats and the overall decor are as exquisite as a Chinese fast food chain, spending on this and the rent took almost all his savings, so he could only hire two bar tenders, three chefs and two waiters. "The cost of labour is too high now. Before we opened the shop, we thought about whether we should engage in takeout, but it was too difficult to recruit the right people. If we hire someone who has not done the job of express delivery before, it would take him one month to find any destination in the surrounding areas; but if we hired a courier, the wages he would demand would beyond what we could afford."

Therefore, when someone recommended that he join Meituan Takeout, he readily agreed because at the time his new business was in a slump due to cold weather. "I pick up orders and sell food, Meituan helps me to deliver. I earn my money by selling noodles and Meituan earns their delivery fees. What a wonderful cooperation."

The secret rivalry between internet giants

"Lots of business choices, a good user experience and great customer service system." These are the features introduced to reporters by Meituan during their release conference." To provide consumers with a one-stop quality local service has always been the goal of Meituan."

However, these words made Yuan Zheng (his assumed name), a college student entrepreneur, feel very bad during the interview. He and his partners started a takeout business in 2009, which expanded to 15 neighbouring universities and 5 CBDs. "To strive to operate their business in 100 cities across the country in 5 years" had been their dream. But in reality, it was unavoidable they would be met with difficulties. Due to limited funds, they could only put their business information on websites and wait for customers to order. They couldn't offer any discounts, nor make enough profit to cover the costs of recruiting delivery staff, so it was difficult for them to imagine tangible profits.

Therefore, encountered with the competition of Meituan and Baidu supported with the investment of the internet giants, it could be imagined what kind of a dilemma Yuan Zheng was in. Just as taxi app quickly replaces local taxi-calling business, takeout app also shatters the local takeout business into pieces.

But infighting over the new model has not stopped, and the battle between internet giants has just begun. Baidu has its own takeout business; Ali group not only holds shares of Meituan, but also has set up word of mouth takeout; and Tencent has taken a 25% share of dianping.com to invest in an ele.me O2O takeout platform.

More importantly, unlike taxi apps that are limited to one car no matter what form it takes, takeout platforms have extended their tentacles from meals to other daily necessities such as flowers, fruit, vegetables, daily necessities, and even medication.

"Little Wang Next Door" was a salesperson at a fruit shop. When he realised that he could apply to be on a takeout platform, he resigned and started his own business. "What I needed to do was upload photos of the fruit I sell to the app, and if when someone places an order I purchase the goods from Hujiamiao and send them to my customer." As a result of his previous work experience he could get fruit from the Hujiamiao wholesale fruit market at a low price and keep the price difference. "Though I don't earn much, it is better than selling it in the street."

The internet has caught everything in one giant net—clothing, home appliances and grocery stores. Meituan takeout said: "Any industry that has not been changed by the internet will be changed by it sooner or later."

Reporter: Pei Lei

Source: Xi'an Daily (Xi'an) 31 July 2015

➢ Participation in group purchasing — meituan.com

Group buying began in China in 2010. Consumers who know or do not know each other join forces to increase their bargaining power with businesses so as to get the best price. Based on the principle of small profits through quick turnover, businesses can offer discounts below retail prices and quality services that cannot be purchased individually.

Meituan was the first group buying website in China.

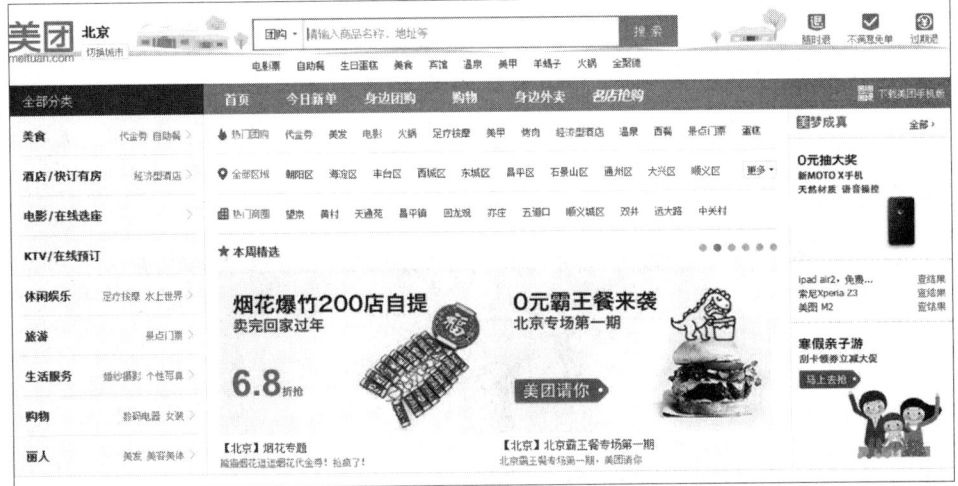

Fig. 2-2-30　Home Page of Meituan

Fig. 2-2-31　Gourmet Food on Meituan Website

The shopping process on Meituan is not that different from other online shopping websites except for in one aspect: when you purchase a business's product you receive an SMS (Short Messaging Service) code or e-coupons from Meituan. The customer can then buy goods by showing this code or e-coupon in an offline store.

① **注册** 点击首页右上方"注册",也可使用第三方账号直接登录

② **抢购** 登陆美团,点击"抢购",购买成功后凭美团券密码去商家消费

③ **支付** 选择您常用的支付方式

账户金额:¥20.00 您的余额不够完成本次付款,

④ **消费** 凭美团券到店消费美团券

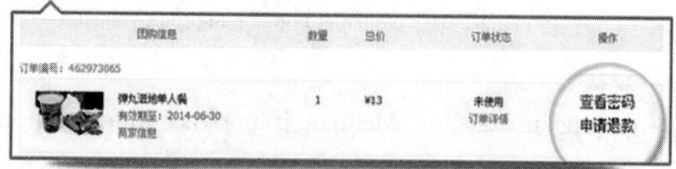

Fig. 2-2-32　Shopping Process of Meituan.com

Fig. 2-2-33 Rich Variety of Products of Group Purchase

In addition to physical goods, a group buying website also provides many types of services. If you want to get your hair done, see a movie, or get photos taken, Meituan group buying is a good way to save money. There are many similar group shopping sites, such as Baidu's http://www.nuomi.com, http://t.dianping.com, http://www.lashou.com, and so on.

Summary

• What to buy from China's e-commerce websites

Everything you can't think of can be bought online.

• The characteristics and categories of typical e-commerce websites in China.

B2C type: yhd.com, Jingdong, Dangdang, jumei.com, lefeng.com, vip.com

C2C type: Taobao, yhd.com, Dangdang, Jingdong

O2O type: ele.me, Meituan.com

Chapter 3

3.1 Compare Prices, Then Order

In this section, you will …
- ✓ Learn how to search and sort goods on Taobao
- ✓ Learn how to shop around
- ✓ Learn how to use Ali Wangwang
- ✓ Learn how to choose the shipping method
- ✓ Learn how to order goods

John has prepared all the things he needs for e-shopping and also has learned the processes and characteristics of many shopping websites. Looking around the dormitory, John feels that the dormitory is too empty and lacks a cozy home feeling. So he decides to buy some wallpaper to decorate, as well as some household items. But where can he get these things conveniently and inexpensively? At this moment, John remembers the website, Taobao, which his roommate mentioned. Taobao offers so many different kinds of goods, and so many distinctive shops from which to select from. John is eager to log onto the website and throw all the things he needs into his bag. But when John logs in Taobao to choose, he is stunned to find that many stores offer similar goods or even the same kind goods at slightly different in prices. John hesitates. He is wondering whether he should choose the cheapest, but maybe they might not be best or most suitable.

You've been in the same situation as John if you've been e-shopping before. So how can you find real, high quality and inexpensive goods on Taobao?

Find your favourite goods quickly and accurately — search and sort goods

The first section of the second chapter has taught you how to register on Taobao. Go and try to register a Taobao account yourself!

Also, in the first section of the second chapter, we have given a preliminary explanation of the search function. Let's apply this knowledge now. For example, you, like John, want to buy wallpapers on Taobao to decorate your dormitory. So enter "wallpaper" in the search box.

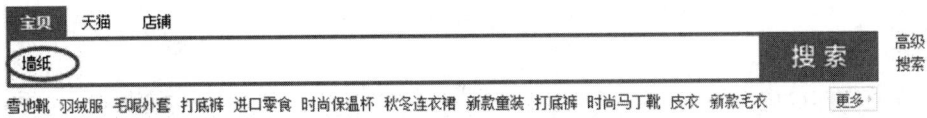

Tip. 3-1-1

There are hundreds of thousands of search results! Isn't it like looking for a needle in a haystack? After navigating a few pages, you're already weary, and still fail to find the wallpaper you like. Here is when the filter function at the top of the screen comes in handy. If you have a preference for certain brands, you can choose the brands you like. If you have prefer certain styles, you can choose the styles you like. It may initially look like Taobao offers only a few types of styles, but click at the bottom on "More". Are there now several kinds of styles that you like? Click on "Multiple" to the right to choose more than one.

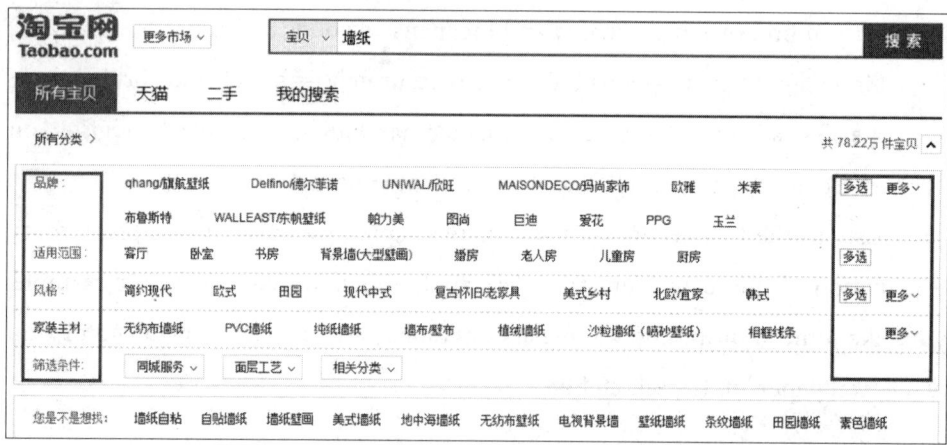

Tip. 3-1-2

By using the above screening method, you have moved one step closer to your favourite goods. Next, we will use the sort function. The sort function will greatly filter out the goods which do not meet your specifications, saving you a lot of time! Taobao provides five sort methods, including "Comprehensive", "Popular", "Sales", "Credit", and "Price". Before sorting, if you have a budget, it is a good idea to input a price range.

"Comprehensive" amalgamates the rating on each aspect of a sellers' goods into one score. After inputting the search words, "comprehensive" is the default sort; "Popular" as its name implies shows the popularity of goods, but popularity does not mean which goods have been purchased the most, it could mean high click rate or collection rate; "Sales" refers to the specific number of goods sold; "Credit" is based on the sellers' reputation to sort (more details on this will be given later in the book); "Price" sorts according to the price.

Tip. 3-1-3

None of the above-mentioned sorting methods is perfect—they all have their own advantages and disadvantages, so choose which you like according to your actual needs.

Shop around—check the description of the goods, check the seller's reputation, and check the overall evaluation

After checking through the above, you should have found some satisfying goods. Still taking wallpaper as an example, you are fond of lots of fancy wallpapers, but you cannot take all of them, right? If you're now planning to pick the cheapest, please wait a moment! It is strongly believed in China that cheap means no good. It of course does not mean goods with a low price must are never good, but in general, cheap goods are more likely to have quality problems. With online shopping a virtual activity, worrying about after-sales services such as returns in the event of a problem can be avoided by buying wisely. Here are some tips about how to compare goods and pick out the best.

· Step one: check goods introduction

Just click and open a goods link, then in the page of "Goods Details", you can learn the detailed information of the goods. In "Goods Details", the seller not only introduces the brand, origin, specifications and other basic information of the goods, but also loads figures of real goods, design sketch and detail sketch, in order to give you a visual impression of goods.

宝贝详情	累计评论 73	成交记录 71	专享服务
品牌:	型号: SE48305		有无图案: 有图案
每卷宽度(m): 0.53m	颜色分类: SE48308米黄色 深卡其...		风格: 欧式
面层工艺: 毛面	适用范围: 客厅 书房 卧室 婚房 老...		产地: 国产
计价单位: 卷	墙纸规格: 5.3㎡ /卷		同城服务: 同城卖家入户安装

Tip. 3-1-4

If you want to buy clothes, shoes or something similar, the sizing table for these items will be on "Goods Details" page. You must carefully check the size table to avoid the trouble of returning goods.

・Step two: check the seller's reputation

The right side of the goods page shows the seller's information. Seller information shows the seller's reputation, how much the goods meet their description, the seller's service attitude and seller's delivery speed. (Full score is 5 points.)

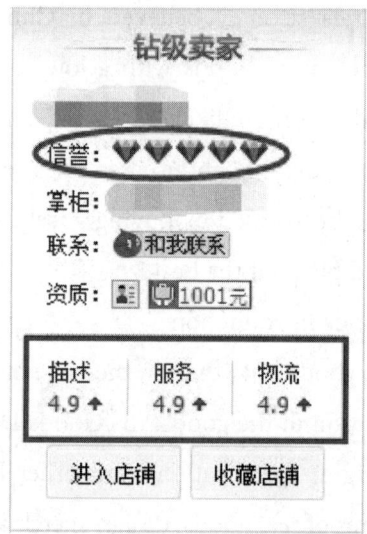

Tip. 3-1-5

Classification of Seller's Credit Rank

When Taobao members finish a payment via Alipay on the Taobao website, they can do an evaluation of the item. Evaluation is divided into three categories, "good", "medium" and "bad", and each evaluation corresponds to a score as follows: "good" means plus one point, "medium" zero points, "bad" minus one point.

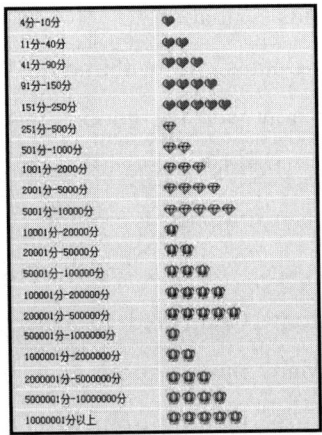

Tip. 3-1-6

A higher point rank is obviously better. Point equate to symbols with the best one being a crown. If a store has a crown it means that many people visit and give praise. If you click on a diamond or crown symbol you will see the seller's stats in comparison to other shops over the last six months, as well the ranking for the last thirty days.

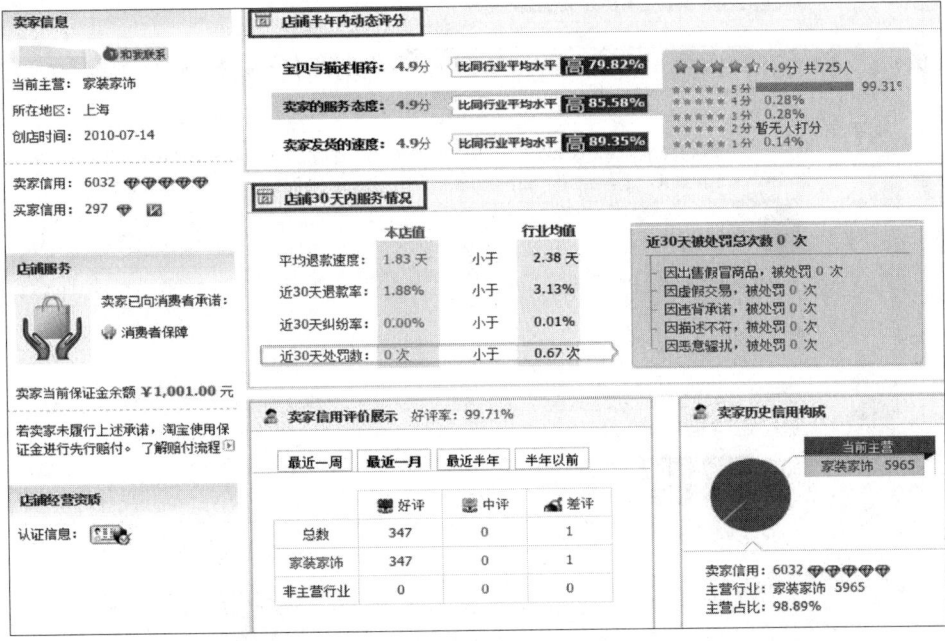

Tip. 3-1-7

· Step three: check goods evaluation

Next to the tab "Goods Details", you will find the tab "Cumulative Evaluation". On this page, the score of how well the goods meet their description is stated alongside an average rating. The higher the score the more the goods are in line with the buyer's expectations. A full score is 5 points.

On the goods details page, you can browse buyers' comments. Most give relatively objective evaluations. Compared to sellers' evaluations, buyers have a greater reference value. Many buyers attach their own pictures of the goods. Compared to the seller's pictures, pictures from buyers are more objective and also disclose more on details such as colour deviation.

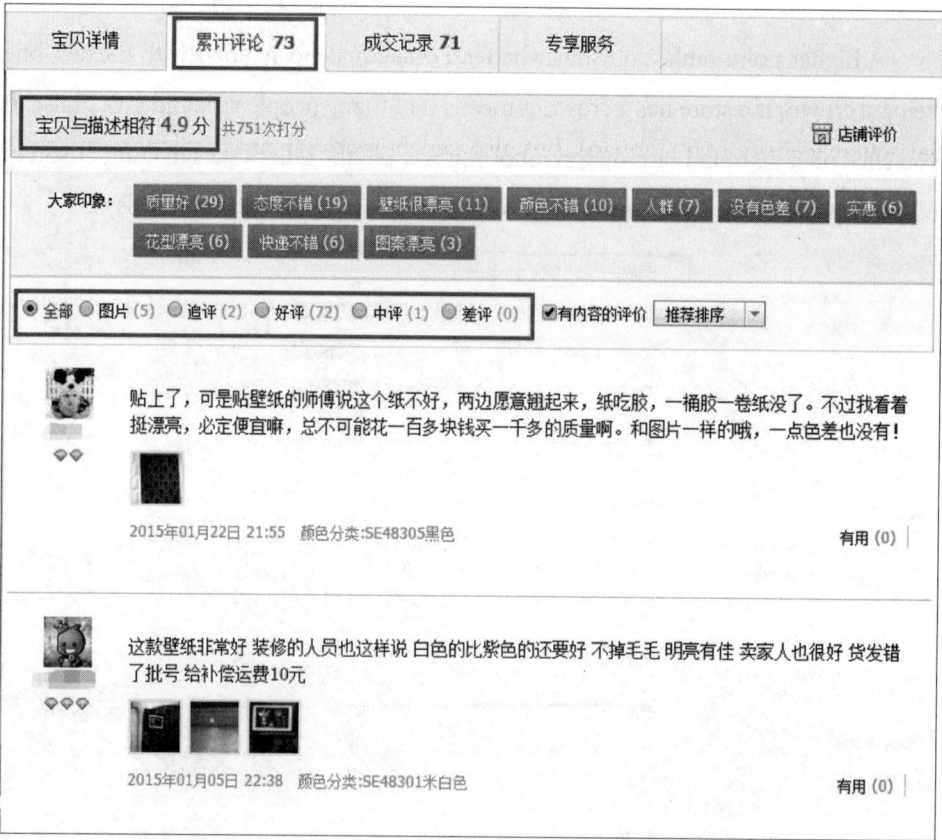

Tip. 3-1-8

Another Tip on Shopping Around—Price-compare Websites

Practice makes perfect when it comes to shopping around. With experience you will find your own way of shopping around.

Although we have said that price needn't be a deciding factor for making a purchase, in real life, the choices the majority of shoppers make is still greatly influenced by it. If the factor influencing your shopping choice is only price, and you have no desire to spend your time shopping around, then a price-comparison website is recommended.

The popularity of e-commerce has generated a large number of online stores, such as B2C and C2C. When users are shopping online, they tend to choose those shopping websites with the lowest price. Under such circumstance, price-compare websites began to emerge. What should be note here is that price-compare websites are not only capable to compare the price of the same kind of products on a particular website (e.g. Taobao), but also can put similar products from multiple shopping websites together for the price comparison. Next, let's take a look at what we on earth need to do with the price-compare websites.

Let us look and see how to use price comparison websites, taking manmanbuy. com as an example.

First, input "http://www.manmanbuy.com/" into the address bar and go to the website.

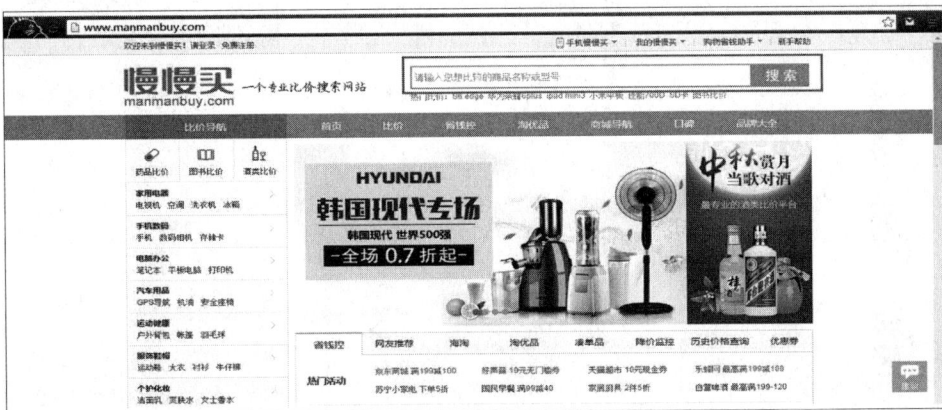

Tip. 3-1-9

With no need to register, you can input the name of goods that you want to compare into the search bar, such as "iPhone6", and click "Search".

Manmanbuy will search through different shopping sites and show them on the results page.

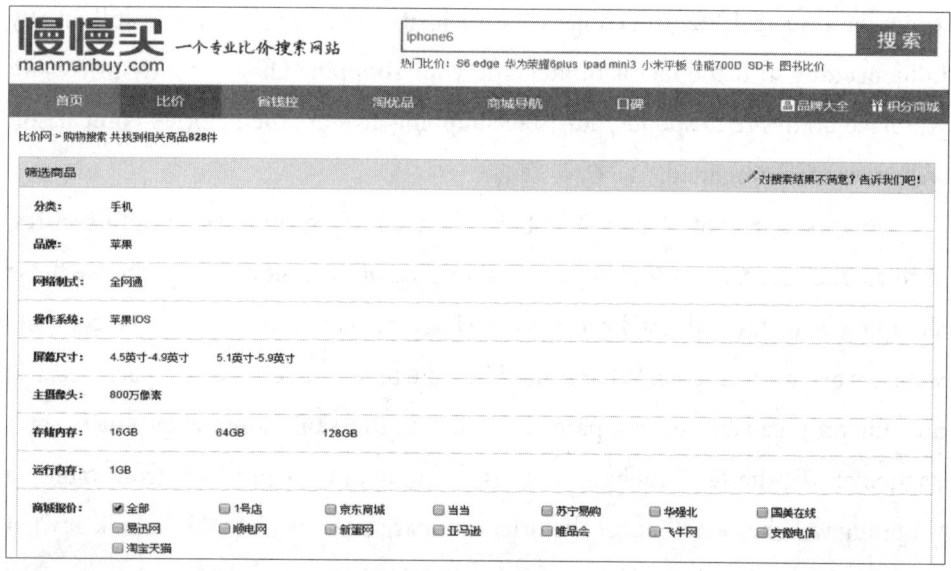

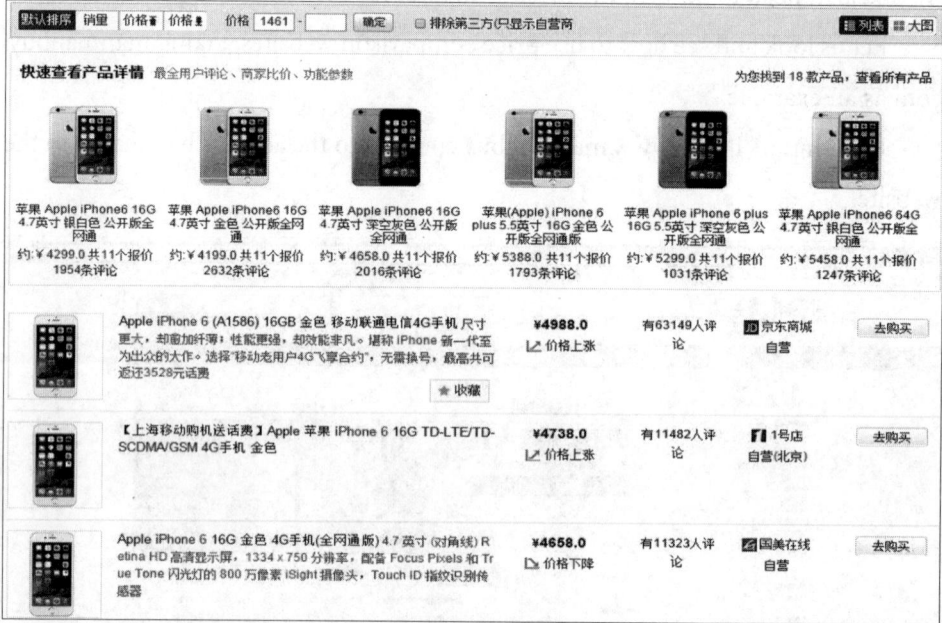

Tip. 3-1-10

You just need to choose the goods you want to look at and the webpage will automatically jump to the site where that item is. You can then purchase it if you like, or you can go back to comparing.

The advantage of price comparison websites is they can compare prices across different shopping platforms, such as JD, Yhd, etc. The problem this causes is it requires you to have registered across multiple platforms and be familiar with the various shopping processes and rules of these sites.

People still have different views about whether price comparison websites are convenient or even necessary to use before shopping. You can make your own opinion on this.

Installation and Usage of Ali Wangwang

After receiving the goods which you had chosen so carefully, what can you do if they don't meet your expectations, for example if the colour is not as described? How can you get free shipping? How do you contact a seller if your goods don't arrive?

From before the sale to after, we always have the need to contact the seller. The tool you can use for this is Ali Wangwang.

Ali Wangwang has a web version which has limited functions, or it can be downloaded and installed on your computer or mobile device. In order to ensure a good shopping mood, and improve the efficiency of shopping, you should install it.

【Installation Steps】

1. Enter http://wangwang.taobao.com/ into your browser's address bar to go to the download page for Ali Wangwang.

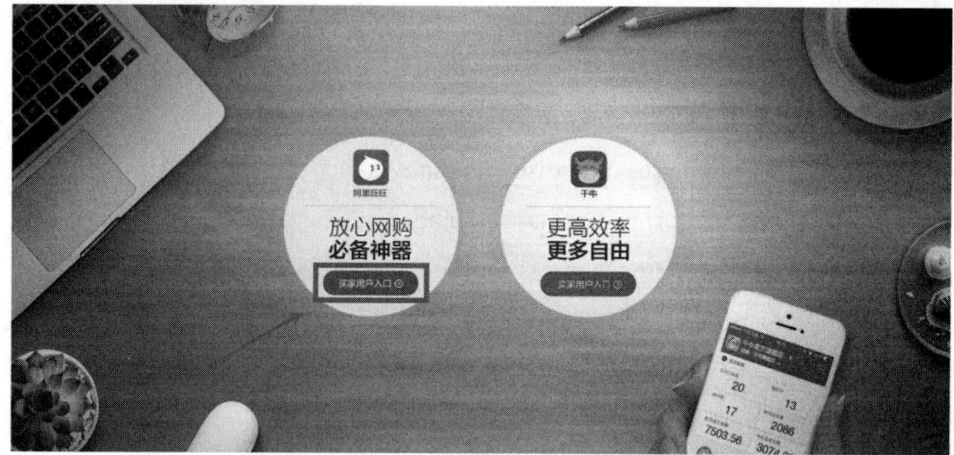

Tip. 3-1-11

We are going shopping, so we click "Buyer Entrance" on the left hand side. If you become a seller, you can go to the sixth chapter and read the guide before clicking "Seller Entrance".

2. To the upper right corner of the page you can select the version according to the operating system of your computer or mobile device.

Tip. 3-1-12

3. Download Ali Wangwang

Tip. 3-1-13

4. Click install package to install

Tip. 3-1-14

· Click "Custom Install" to select the installation path, and then click "Install Now".

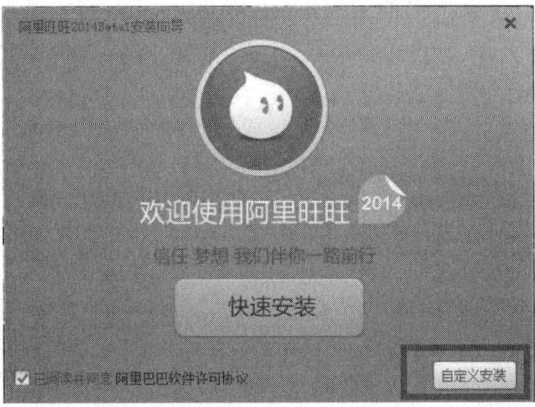

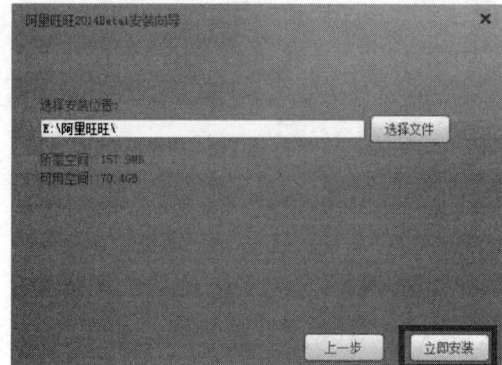

Tip. 3-1-15

· Click "Immediate Experience" on the left hand side to use "Ali Wangwang" immediately, otherwise click "Finish".

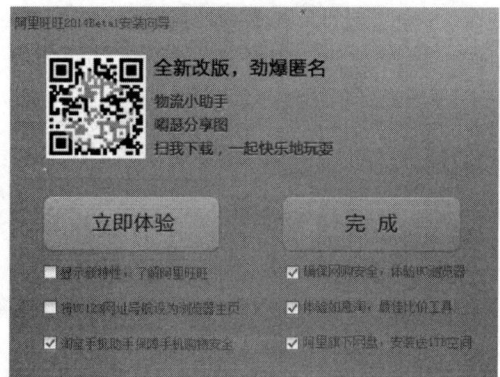

Tip. 3-1-16

【Operating Guide】

1. First, log into your account. You can log into Ali Wangwang with your Taobao username and password.

Tip. 3-1-17

2. On the home page, you will find that contacts are divided into four tabs, including "Recent Chats", "Friends", "Group Chats" and "My Applications", and that the first two are the most used.

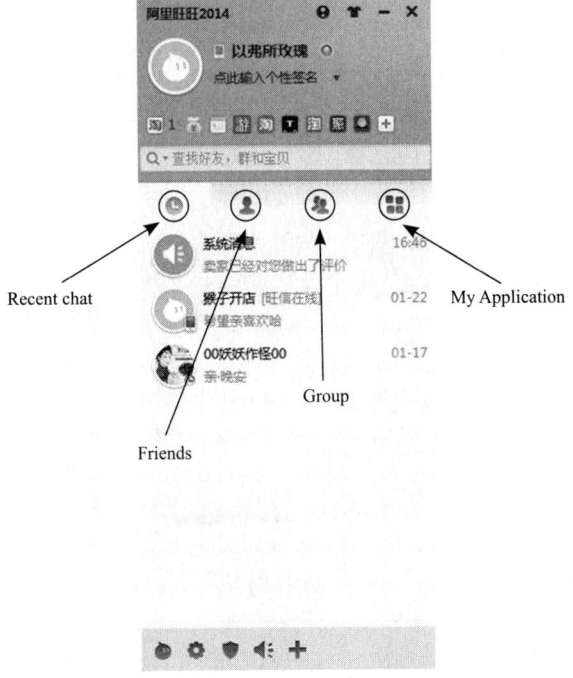

Tip. 3-1-18

3. If you want to contact a seller about some goods you've been looking at, what you need to do is find the "Ali Wangwang" logo and click it, which will open up the Ali Wangwang client on your computer or mobile device.

Tip. 3-1-19

Tip. 3-1-20

Note that the web version and client version of "Ali Wangwang" sometimes conflict.

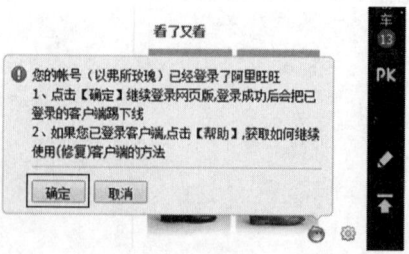

Tip. 3-1-21

When it happens, just click "OK".

After that, you can talk to the seller. If you have any concerns or other questions and need to communicate with the seller, e.g. you want to confirm details of the goods, enquire about shipping fees, or ask if you can have a small gift, etc., you can always do this via Ali Wangwang.

Who Sends the Goods—Logistics Selection

Most of the goods shopped for online in China are transported to the customer across great distances. Thus, choosing a reliable shipping company is very important. In the previous chapters we have introduced the main Chinese shipping companies, so you should already have a general understanding of their characteristics.

Most e-commerce sites today do not require customers to choose the shipping company. B2C sites, such as Jing Dong Mall and Tmall have in-house logistics controlling the quality and speed of distribution services. But on Taobao, buyers need to choose a logistics company which is convenient both for them and the seller.

There are two ways to choose a logistics company on e-shopping sites.

1. Check the "Goods Details" or home page of the store.

2. Communicate with the seller to get information on the logistics company if you do not find the information you need from clearly listed. You can also talk via Ali Wangwang if none of the seller's preferred logistics companies have shipping hubs near to your location and you wish to use another.

After you confirm the logistics information, you can freely order. Note that in the order process, there is a step to choose between "Express" and "EMS", this is equivalent to using a courier or the domestic postal service. You can choose according to your needs. Considering the price and arrival time, the majority choose "Express".

运费　　　江苏常州 至 北京∨ 快递: 10.00 EMS: 30.00

Tip. 3-1-22

All set to order! —order process.

Go to the home page of the goods, and click "Buy Now".

Tip. 3-1-23

Enter the order interface.

Choose the shipping address.

Tip. 3-1-24

You can choose from existing addresses or click on "Manage Shipping Addresses" in the lower right hand corner to add or delete addresses.

Then confirm the order details.

You can choose to buy insurance so you don't have to bear the costs of return shipping. You can also leave a message to the seller here. When you click the red "Submit Order", the order process is completed! The next step is payment.

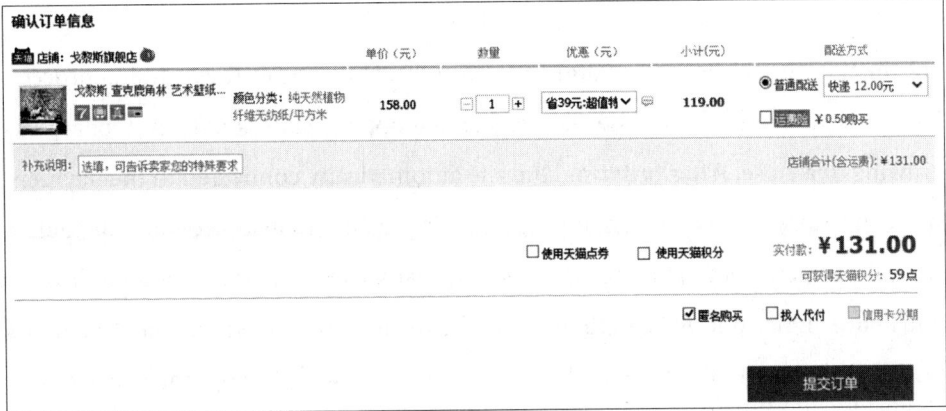

Tip. 3-1-25

Summary

- Searching and sorting Taobao goods

There is "Comprehensive" or "Popularity", according to the popularity of goods, "Sales" according to the specific number of goods sold, "Credit" according to the sellers' reputation, and "Price" accords to the price.

- Shop around: Check the description, rating and evaluation of the goods, check the seller's reputation, and use price-comparison websites to compare prices.
- Use Ali Wangwang: Download and install the software from the official website to chat with sellers in real-time.
- Select shipping method: Check the goods details or shop home page; get the shipping company information from the seller
- Order: Edit or select your own address; confirm the order information; submit the order

3.2 To Pay Finally

In this section, you will ...

√ Learn different payment methods

√ Learn the payment process of e-shopping on Taobao

After shopping around briefly on Taobao, John selected his favourite goods, put them in the shopping cart and ordered successfully. After the ordering process, John was relieved. The online part of his e-shopping experience on Taobao was drawing to a close. After ordering, the site automatically connected to the payment site. John stared at the screen and had no clue again. Taobao provides customers several payment methods, including Alipay, bank card, etc. John thought "Even I don't have choice phobia, it's still difficult for me to choose from payment methods I don't understand." John decided to ask a roommate with e-shopping experience.

Last Step of E-shopping — Goods Payment

The payment process is actually very simple. Usually, after you submit your orders, Taobao will automatically connect to the payment page, where all you need to do is to choose the payment method you prefer and input your Alipay payment code of (note: on the payment page, whatever payment method you choose, you will always input your Alipay payment code in the box shown below, rather than your bank code or other codes). Click "Confirm Payment" to finish the payment process and wait for your goods to be delivered.

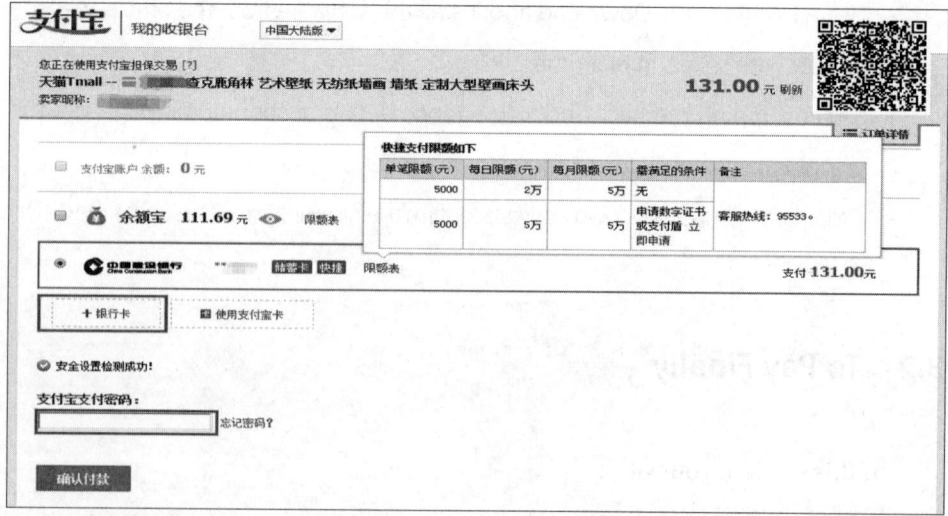

Tip. 3-2-1

If you accidentally close the payment page, or just like John, didn't want to pay right away and closed the payment page, you needn't be concerned. You just need to go to "My Taobao" — "Bought Goods", and find the unpaid orders. After you click on "Pay Now", you can go the payment page again to finish the payment process.

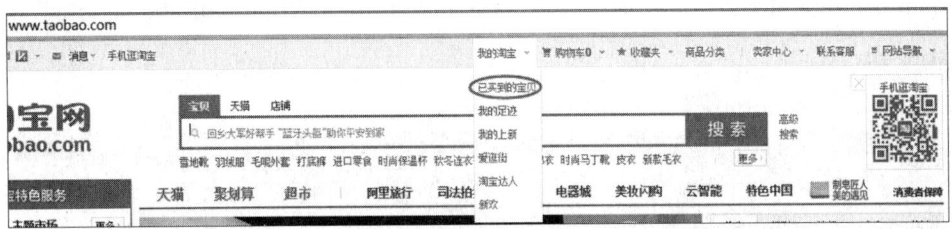

Tip. 3-2-2

Tip. 3-2-3

How to choose from the various payment methods

Taobao provides various payment options, including "Ask Someone Else to Pay", "Alipay Account", "Bank Card Quick Pay", "E-bank", "Alipay Card", "Onsite", "Customer Card" and so on. In order to help you choose the most suitable way to pay, let's learn them one by one.

· Ask someone else to pay

This is for new users who are unfamiliar with online payment or users who are short of money in their own account.

When you have found somebody who is willing to pay for you, what is the process? First you enter "My Taobao", "Bought Goods", find unpaid orders, then click on "Ask Somebody Else to Pay" below "Pay Now" on the right side.

On this page you need to enter a friend's account (their Alipay/Taobao account nickname), and click on "Ask to Pay". The rest of the payment will be handled by your friend.

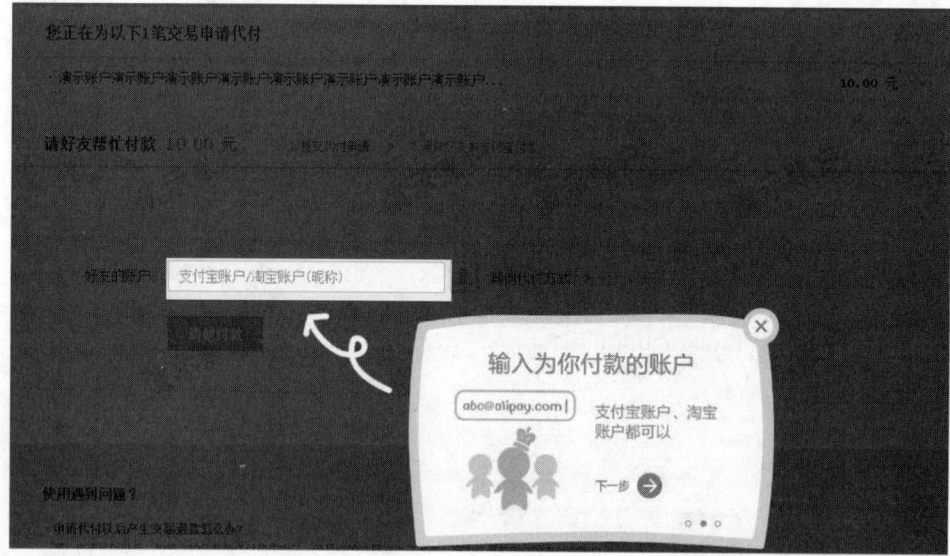

Tip. 3-2-4

If you know someone who is willing to help you, but don't know his account nickname, what should you do? Don't worry, you can do it another way. Taobao can generate a payment link. You just need to send the link to your friend and they can help you complete the payment.

 Make sure you tell your friend before you send them any payment links and also inform them when the payment has gone through.

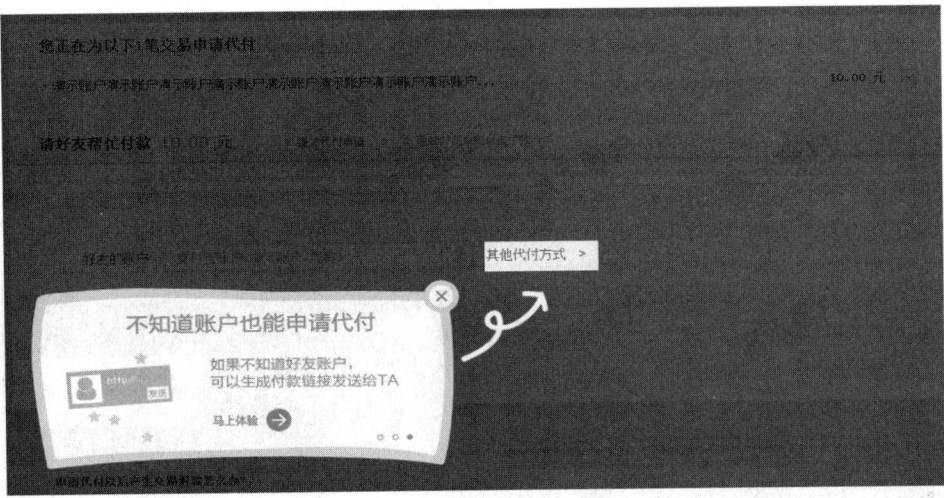

Tip. 3-2-5

Do you think it is very convenient asking someone to pay for you? Certainly it is convenient, but only for you. The best way to pay is to do it yourself.

· Alipay (recommended!)

Alipay and Taobao both belong to the Alibaba Company, so your Alipay account can be directly linked with your Taobao account.

Linking them is very simple. Log into Taobao and click on "My Taobao". On this page click "Account Settings", select "Alipay Linking", and follow the instructions. After successfully linking them, an "Alipay Account Payment" option will appear when you get to the payment stage every purchase. You can now just enter your Alipay payment password and complete the payment operation easily.

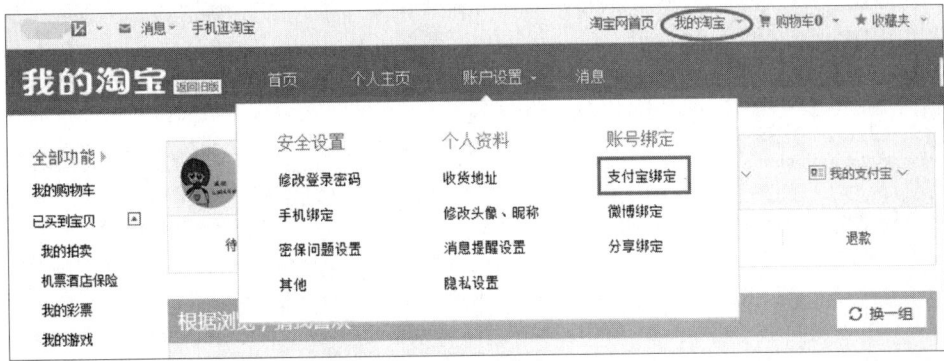

Tip. 3-2-6

If your Alipay account has no money, what should you do? The answer, of course, is that you need to recharge your account. This operation is very easy. First, log in the Alipay website "https://www.alipay.com/".

Tip. 3-2-7

Select the "recharge" operation and follow the instructions (new users need to link a bank card first).

Tip. 3-2-8

When a payment amount is greater than 200 RMB, Alipay will send an SMS verification code to your phone. You just need to enter this verification code onto the payment page and then click on "Confirm Payment". SMS verification codes are a powerful security measure.

If your purchase amounts are always high and you feel it is too much work entering an SMS verification code every time, you can cancel this service.

Cancelling the SMS verification code service is very simple. Enter the Alipay website first "https://www.Alipay.com/" and log in, then select "Security Center" to the top right of the page. On the presence page, you are free to choose whether to allow or deny "SMS Verification Service".

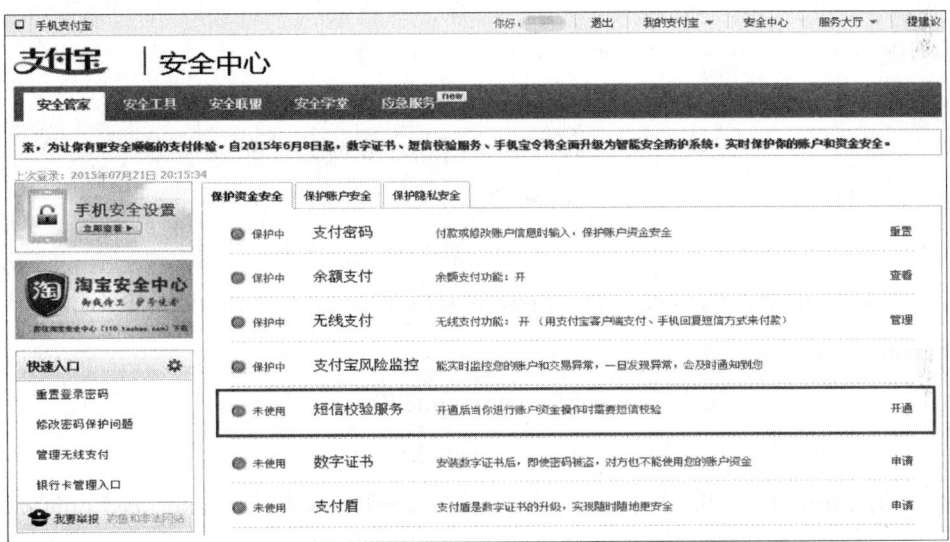

Tip. 3-2-9

Alipay and Paypal

It must be true that people from other countries indeed have a basic understanding of PayPal. Actually, there are certain similarities between Chinese Alipay and PayPal that is commonly used in the international market, both of which are online payment tools as well as a form of third-party payment. If you have ever used PayPal, then there's no need to worry too much about how to use Alipay.

However, there are still two major differences between Alipay and PayPal which are worth noting:

One of their differences lies in their service domains. PayPal is only used for the collection of foreign trades, which allows the circulation of 26 major international currencies including US dollars, Canadian dollars, Euros, British pounds, Australian dollars and Japanese yen only except for RMB, while Alipay, one of the most mainstream payment methods in China, is only available for RMB.

The other difference is the way of receiving payment. On Alipay, the payment will truly enter the seller's account only after the buyer has clicked on "Goods Received" if they received the goods, while PayPal does not require customers to click on "Goods Received" and the payment will be directly transferred to the seller's account as soon as the buyer makes the remittance.

In summary, payment via Alipay is safe, easy and convenient. It is highly recommended to you!

· Bank card quick payment (recommended!)

Suitable your use when Alipay is already linked to your bank card.

The process of linking and using a bank card is as follows and need only be done once:

(1) Enter the payment page, choose "+Bank Card", input your bank card number, which can be a credit card, debit card or other, and click on "Next".

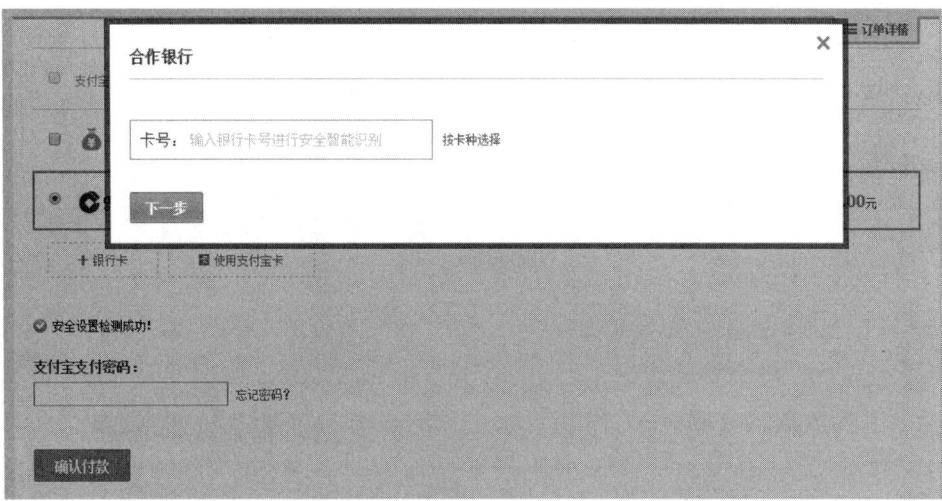

Tip. 3-2-10

(2) Choose "Quick Payment" and click on "Next".

Tip. 3-2-11

(3) Fill in your personal information and pay. Your personal information is the same as the information you provided to the bank when you opened your bank account.

Tip. 3-2-12

Bank card quick payment is also very convenient, and highly recommended!

- E-bank payment (online bank payment)

U shield

U shield is a tool for authenticating digital e-bank signatures. It looks like a USB stick, and its safety features are like a shield, hence the name. The role of U shield is mainly to ensure the confidentiality, authenticity, integrity of online transactions, to protect the security of online banking funds, and to avoid hackers, fake sites, Trojan viruses and other risks.

When you go to the bank to enable your online banking services, bank staff will give you a U shield.

Before every payment you have to insert the U Shield to your computer and check it works. Go to payment page and just like with a bank card quick payment, you need to choose "+Bank Card", input your bank card number, then click on "Next". Choose "E-bank" from the payment methods shown in figure 3-2-11.

Using an e-bank payment will jump directly to the web page of your bank. You just need to follow the instructions to finish the payment, and remember to remove U shield when you're done.

Previously, Chinese e-shopping customers mostly used e-bank payments. But now the number is decreasing with the rapid rise of payment types such as Alipay.

· International credit card payment

Some foreigners who have just arrived in China may not have had the time to get a Chinese bank card yet, so an international credit card can be used.

Next, we will introduce the payment process for international credit cards:

1. After submitting the order, reselect the Alipay checkout region version, either [Overseas] or [Hong Kong]. Under both versions, you can use international credit card to pay.

2. Input payment information on the page, then use your international credit card to pay.

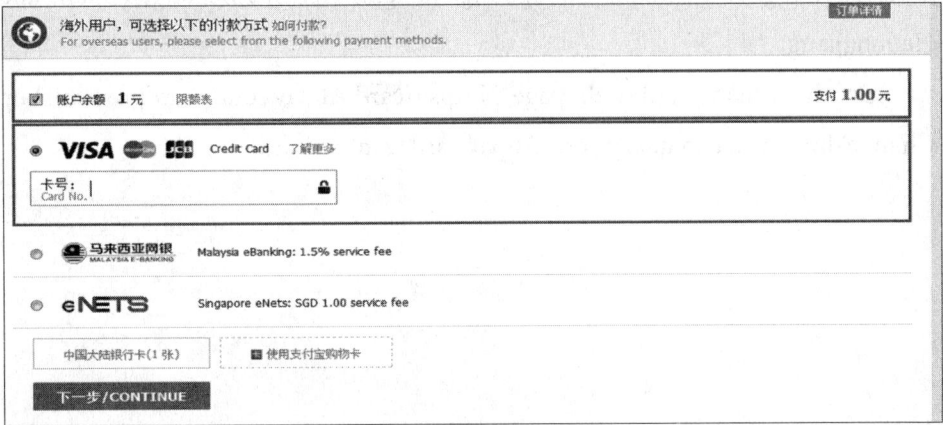

3. If the cardholder has authentication services enabled, you need to enter the code or password as appropriate.

```
Enter Verified by Visa One-Time Password

Verified by Visa One-Time Password (OTP) has been sent to
your mobile phone number in our record (last 4 digits 1010).
Please enter OTP in the field below.
                    Merchant: ALIPAY (WWW.ALIPAY.COM)
                    Amount: CNY 50.00
                    Date: 06/12/2011
        Credit Card Number: XXXX XXXX XXXX 3005
        One-Time Password: 📱 ajB3- [ ][ ][ ][ ][ ]
                    [ Submit ]
Resend OTP?   Cancel OTP   Mobile Number Changed?   ❓ Help
```

Click on "Confirm Payment" to finish the payment.

· Alipay card payment

An Alipay card is a prepaid card issued by Alipay, which can be used when shopping on Taobao and Tmall. The funds on the card can be checked on the Alipay website at "Account Assets — Alipay Card". An Alipay card is anonymous, so if it is lost you will not be able to get the funds back. It is available in a variety of denominations and it is valid for 36 months, though this can be extended.

An Alipay card is currently only available to buy in nine provinces: Jiangsu, Shanghai, Sichuan, Guangdong, Jiangxi, Hebei, Zhejiang, Fujian, and Heilongjiang.

On the Alipay card web page "https://card.Alipay.com/pcardprocess/shop Channel.htm", you can query your Alipay card transactions.

Tip. 3-2-13

For most buyers, purchasing an Alipay card is very inconvenient. In spite of this, an Alipay card is relatively easy to use—choose "Use Alipay Card", input the card number and password into the popup page and that's all. It is important to note that when you use an Alipay card, that card is linked to your Alipay and cannot be unlinked, thus can only be used by your account.

Tip. 3-2-14

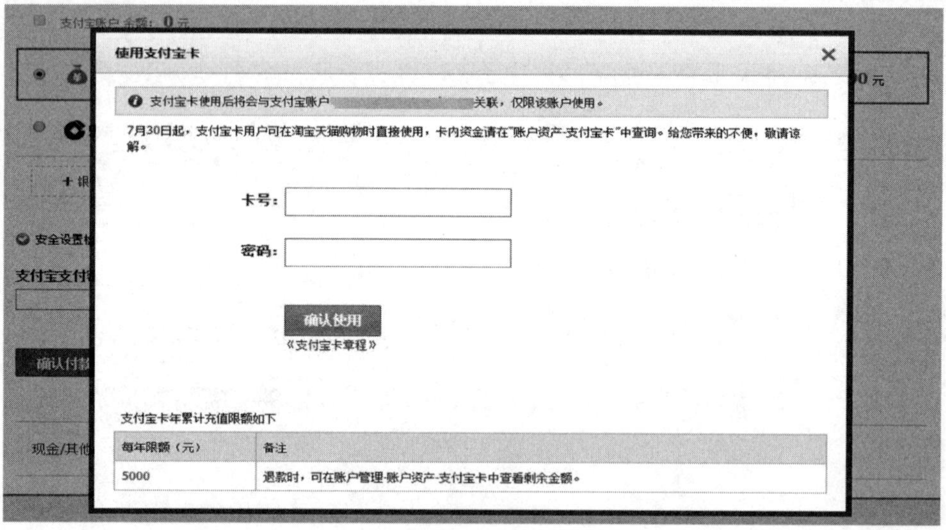

Tip. 3-2-15

· Network payment

Network payment is paying with cash or a credit card offline, which is a new payment method that Alipay provides. It is for users who have no Alipay account or e-bank. All that is required is a payment location nearby that is participating in the Alipay network payment method.

To pay via network payment you need to provide certain information online first. The process is as follows:

Enter the payment page and click on "Case/Others (Consumer Card)".

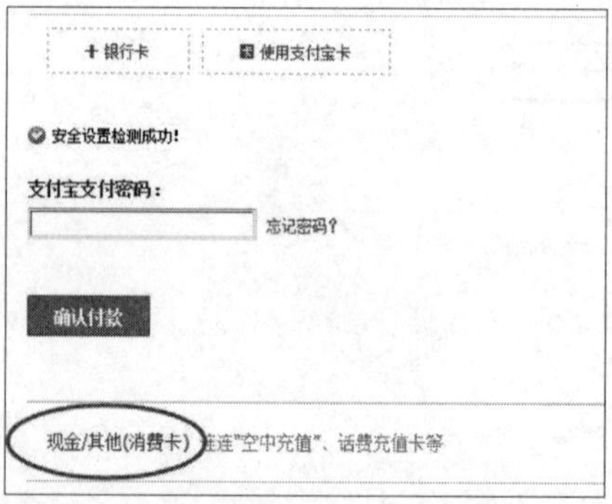

Tip. 3-2-16

Choose your location on the popup page. If the location is correct you don't need to choose. Choose participating locations.

Tip. 3-2-17

After this, make a note of your transation number and the amount you need to pay, go to the nearby participating location and give the information and the money to the teller.

· Consumer card payment

A consumer card payment is basically a phone recharge card, and currently only supports 100 RMB (not including 100 RMB) prepaid recharge cards. Before using a consumer card payment, you need to purchase a China Mobile, China Unicom, or China Telecom prepaid recharge card from any place that sells them.

After buying the phone recharge card, click on "Cash/Others (Consumer Card)" in the payment page. Choose "Others"—"Phone Card" in the popup page, and click on "Next".

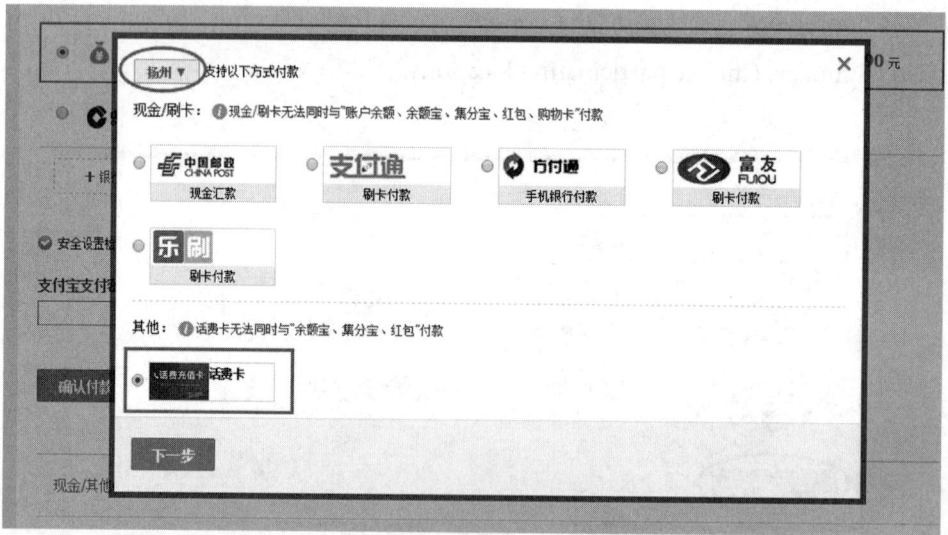

Tip. 3-2-18

Choose the denomination of the phone recharge card according to the instructions, input the card number and password, and click on "Confirm" to complete the payment operation.

Tip. 3-2-19

A consumer card is usually suitable for making small payments. You will be charged a 5% service fee for using a consumer card, so it is not recommended to use this payment method.

So now we have some understanding of the seven payment methods for Taobao. Which payment method will you choose? John's roommate who has experience in e-shopping tells John that most Chinese people usually choose Alipay and bank card quick pay, because these two payment methods are the safest and most convenient.

Besides the above mentioned payment methods, some sellers on Taobao and also some e-shopping sites accept the payment method "Cash on Delivery".

Summary

- Payment process of goods on Taobao

"My Taobao"—"Bought Goods"—"Pay Now" —choose payment method—input payment code for Alipay account – confirm payment.

- A variety of payment methods provided by Taobao

Ask somebody else to pay: Convenient for yourself but troublesome for others.

Alipay account payment: Link your Alipay account with your Taobao account. You can easily complete the transaction as long as there is enough balance in your Alipay account.

Bank card quick payment: The most convenient payment method.

E-bank payment: U shield is required.

International credit card payment: Suitable for foreigners who have just arrived in China and have no local bank card, only an international credit card.

Alipay card payment: You need to purchase an Alipay card from a specified location.

Offline payment: You need to go to a location participating in offline payment and pay by card or cash.

Consumer card payment: You will be charged a 5% service fee.

Some sellers on Taobao and also some e-shopping sites provide the payment method "Cash on Delivery" for consumers to choose.

Chapter summary:

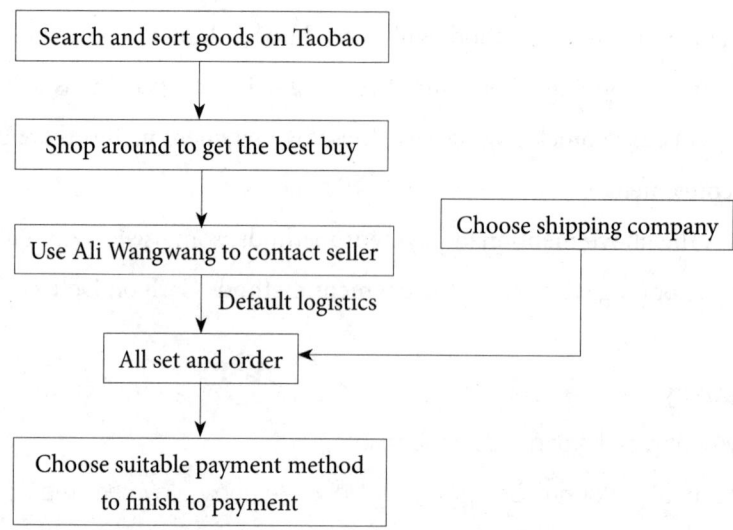

In this chapter, your shopping trip on Taobao officially kicks off. You know how to search and sort goods on Taobao, how to shop around to get the best buy, how to use Ali Wangwang to communicate with sellers, how to choose the shipping company, how to order and purchase, how to successfully pay by choosing the most suitable payment method, all so that you can draw a satisfactory full stop to your online shopping trip.

First of all, Taobao's search function will take you into a world filled with goods you want to buy. By using the screen and sort function you can avoid being overwhelmed and get closer to your favourite goods; secondly, shop around. Check the description of the goods, check the seller's reputation, check the reviews of the goods, use a price-comparison website. If you have any questions and want to communicate with the seller, do not hesitate to use Ali Wangwang! Finally, confirm the courier company and choose the most suitable payment method. Alipay and bank card quick payment are recommended.

After this chapter, you should be good at online shopping.

Chapter 4

4.1 Wait and Wait

In this section you will ...

✓ Learn how to check the status of an order

✓ Learn how to check the delivery status

If you don't know how the order is progressing or where the goods are, you will grow old faster! Fortunately, most e-shopping sites provide a function to check the delivery status.

Check Order Status

The process of most orders is "buyer orders – buyer pays – seller sends – buyer confirms receipt". When each step is accomplished both sides are satisfied.

The processes may look complex, but in fact are not. In chapter three, we went through the order and payment process. The next step for the seller to send the goods and for you to supervise it a bit.

1. First open the Taobao webpage and log into your account.

2. Click on "My Taobao" — "Bought Goods" at the top of page.

Tip. 4-1-1

3. On this page, you can see all the goods you have bought. To check the status of an item, you just need to check the first line of the status bar on the right hand side of the page. In the example we have picked, you can see that this transaction has already been successful—the buyer got the goods and the seller got the money.

和我联系			¥ ⬆ ▶ 🗑
申请售后 投诉卖家	65.00 (含运费：0.00)	交易成功 订单详情 查看物流 双方已评	追加评论 再次购买

Tip. 4-1-2

In this stage, three types of orders may appear:

· Buyer already paid

This means the buyer has ordered and paid the money, but the seller still has the good and has not sent them to the courier company yet.

Shipping speed is one of the most important standards used to evaluate a seller. Most sellers ship goods within 48 hours after they have been ordered. If sellers don't ship goods in time, you can contact them through Ali Wangwang. If communication fails, you can apply to return your goods (you will learn how to do this in Chapter 2 and leave the seller an appropriate evaluation.

· Shipped by Seller

Compared to above, this status states the seller has already passed the goods to the courier company and the goods are on the way. The buyer just needs to be patient, but if you still want to know where the goods are, you should not contact seller. You should check the logistics information with the courier company (how to do this will be introduced below.)

· Transaction is complete

The example shown in figure 4-1-2 shows the status as "Transaction Complete". This status means you have received the goods and seller has got the money. This status is our final aim.

After checking the order status, how do you check the delivery status?

Where Are My Goods?

How to check the delivery status is similar to how to check the order status. Login to "My Taobao" — "Bought Goods", go to the page shown in figure 4-1-3, and look at the lower right hand side of the page.

Tip. 4-1-3

Click on "Check Logistics" and then a new page will appear (figure 4-1-4). You can check where the goods are on this page.

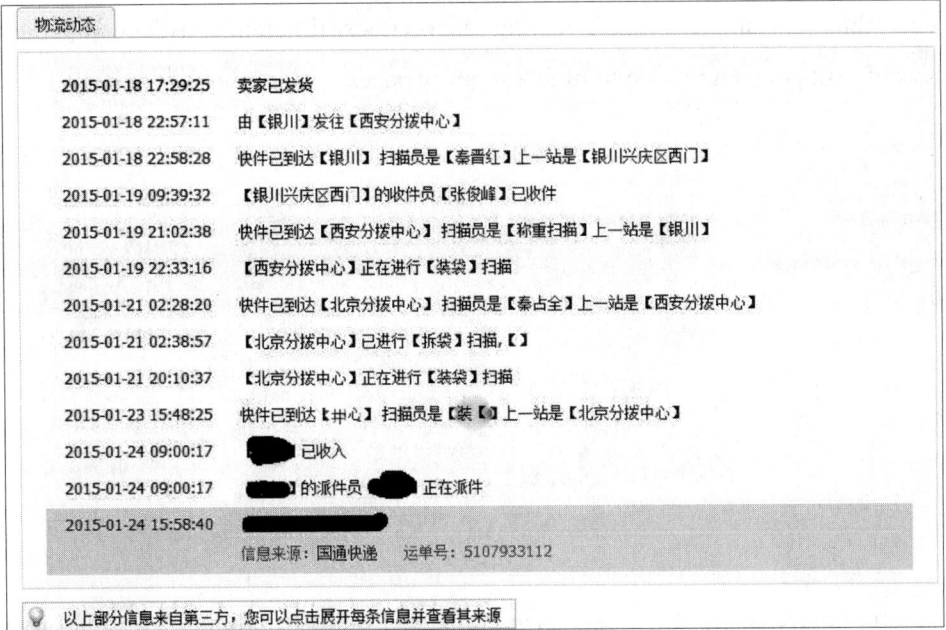

Tip. 4-1-4

 Sometimes, because information is not updated in a timely manner, some delivery information cannot be found on e-commerce sites. Instead you can trace it to its source and check it through the courier company directly.

1. Find the order that you want to check and click on "Check Logistics" to open the page of delivery details.

2. At the bottom of the logistics number on the right hand side of page, find and copy the delivery number.

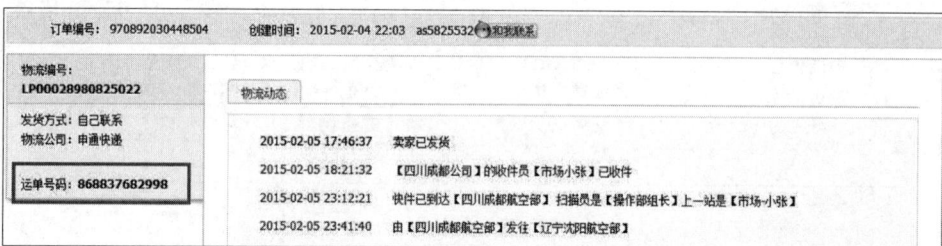

Tip. 4-1-5

3. In the logistics status bar, click the quick link to the delivery company to enter their official query page. Different sellers choose different logistics companies, so different goods might go to different query pages.

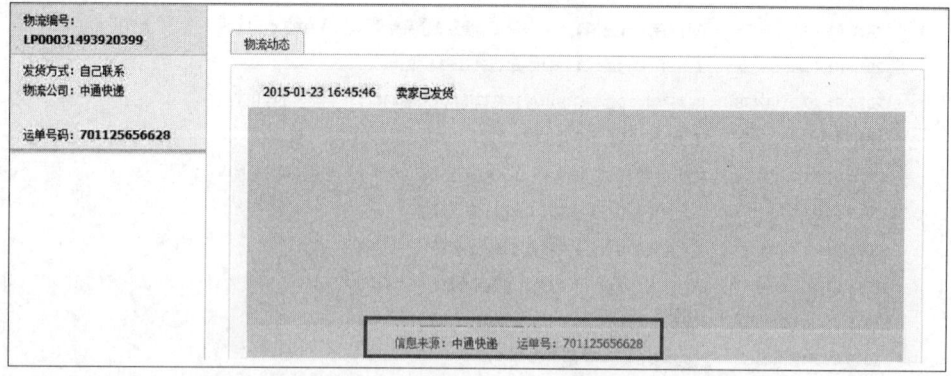

Tip. 4-1-6

4. After opening the query page, input the delivery number into the order number box and click on "Confirm".

Tip. 4-1-7

5. Then, a new popup page displays the tracking status of the order, including the date, time, and current order location, etc. If your query returns no result and your order status says it has already shipped, maybe the logistics company has not received the goods from the seller yet. You can call customer service and consult them.

Now, you know how to check the order and logistics status.

China has developed a logistics distribution system with its own characteristics. Let us take a look!

Logistics Companies with Chinese Characteristics

At present in China, the competition between logistics companies is particularly fierce. China's express delivery industry has maintained three consecutive years of growth of more than two digits, and the long-term growth rate is more than 50%. In all aspects, the influence on commercial and economic value is not to be overlooked. This can also be seen from online public opinion about the important role of express delivery in internet users' online shopping lives.

If you live in the vicinity of an express delivery point, you can take a stroll there to see what the main companies are. The most common are, Yuan Tong, Shen Tong, and Zhong Tong; small scale ones are BEST express, Little Red Hood, and Zhai Jisong Express; SF is one of the best, fast and safe, but is expensive alongside Express Mail Service (EMS).

The first are the "Three Tong One Da" companies, namely "Yuan Tong, Shen Tong, Zhong Tong and Yun Da". Among these four, Yun Da is the most inexpensive. Yuan Tong's prices are not expensive either. The security of Shen Tong is the best. The price and speed of Zhong Tong are mediocre.

SF express has the best reputation among all Chinese express delivery brands. It is known as being fast, safe, and best choice for if you have bought something expensive or urgent. SF staff are high quality, and the turnover rate is relatively low. It is called the courier fighter express company. Of course, their price is high. EMS is an express service provided by China Post. Although the service is provided by China Post, the price is relatively high though the speed is no faster than other express companies. However, when sending to some very remote areas, private express companies often do not have a business point and cannot provide service. This is when EMS is an inevitable choice.

We also mentioned some of the relatively small express companies, such as Tian Tian, Little Red Hood, and BEST… Their biggest feature is that their prices are relatively low. But you get what you pay for. In terms of package loss rate is higher than others and delivery speed is slower, but when buying cheap small things, if you do not want the delivery cost to be higher.

Summary

- Check order status: Login to Taobao, click on "My Taobao" and "Bought Goods".
- Check delivery status: "Check Logistics", check the latest updates from the courier company's official site using the package number.

4.2 I Want to Return It!

In this section, you will …

✓ Learn the return requirements

✓ Learn the return process for Taobao

John finally gets his package. After signing for the delivery and going back to his dormitory, John unpacks the package at once. The wallpapers are the same as how the seller has described on Taobao—really good quality and beautiful. But after unrolling the wallpapers, he finds there is some damage in their middles. It would have been acceptable if the damage was in the corners, but it is right in the middle! As an e-shopping newbie, John thinks returning goods is very troublesome and only does it when it is unavoidable. Although the wallpaper has some flaws, he really likes the wallpapers. After thinking twice, John at last decides to ask the seller if he can return the goods. But how can he do this?

Many buyers, like John, have the same wearisome feeling when thinking about returning goods and make do with what they've been given. This not only wastes money but also influences their mood. In fact, lots of e-shopping platforms, like Taobao, provide the perfect return system. Returning goods is not as difficult as we think. So do not worry. And if you don't believe it, let us continue.

What Kinds of Goods Can Be Returned?

Though most large e-commerce platforms, including Taobao, provide a return service, not all goods are returnable. Some e-commerce platforms clearly indicate that digital products, food, drugs, mother and child supplies, personal care, cosmetics and so on are not returnable if there are no quality problems; some e-commerce sellers believe that precious metals, watches, jewelries and personal accessories should not be in the scope of returnable goods; also some sellers state that underwear, swimwear, and socks etc. are not returnable if there are no quality problems. However, there are some sellers who are easy on returns. For example, Jumei supports returns within 30 days even if the seals of the goods are broken.

Taobao claims that the following goods are not returnable by default: all booked goods or customized special size goods, perishable goods, online downloaded digital goods, service goods and some collection goods. In addition, the return of goods is determined by the seller. If goods are not returnable, generally the seller will state it clearly in the product description.

In general, returnable goods must meet the following requirements:

1. You shouldn't have clicked on "Confirm Receipt" (unless you have communicated and agreed with the seller in advance);

2. The goods have a quality problem when you received them (not including man-caused problems). If the goods have no quality problems and have no 7+ return commitments, you need to discuss with the seller whether or not you can return them. Goods which have 7+ return commitments can be returned within the specified period without a reason, in the premise of not affecting the secondary sale of goods (any reason such as you don't like or don't want them are acceptable);

3. Goods for return are required to be intact in terms of packaging, accessories, tags etc. They are to be unused. Goods washed, used, showing signs of man-made damages are not returnable.

7+ Return Commitments

1. The consumers have rights to apply for return or replacement of goods without any reasons after they signed for the receipt over 7 days (8-15 days) on the premise that its resale will not be affected.

2. The sellers can specify the validity period (8 days minimum, 15 days maximum) of the commitment and who shall bear the freight for the return or the replacement.

3. The buyer's application of refund amount depends on the price

actually paid by the buyer.

  4. The applications must formally comply with relevant laws and regulations of the country.

  Goods with 7+ return commitments display the label "7+" under them on the search page.

Tip. 4-2-1

  You can check the details for "7+" return commitments by sellers, including how many days you have to return, who will bear the delivery cost and so on.

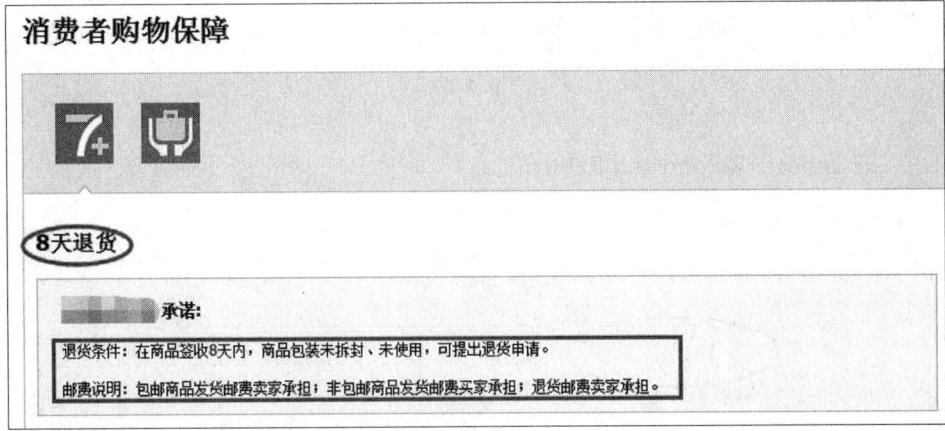

Tip. 4-2-2

With the above knowledge you can start to return the goods. Here is a little tip, if you really are confused by the rights you have in returning goods or the process, then contact the seller. You can even confirm these with the seller in advance of the purchase.

Next, we will introduce the return process details.

Not Satisfied with Goods Received, You Can Return Them.

· Taobao Return Process

(1) Login to Taobao and click on "My Taobao" then "Bought Goods" on the upper right hand side.

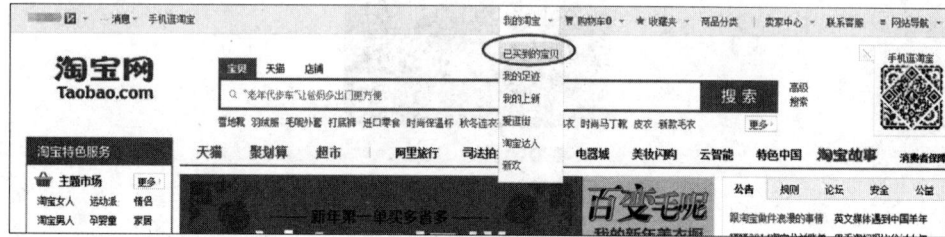

Tip. 4-2-3

(2) Choose the goods you want to return and click on "Refund/Return"

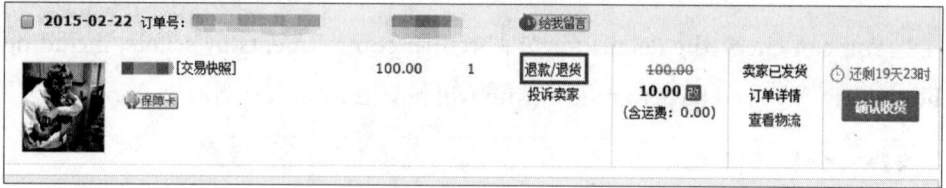

Tip. 4-2-4

(3) Choose "Refund and Return"

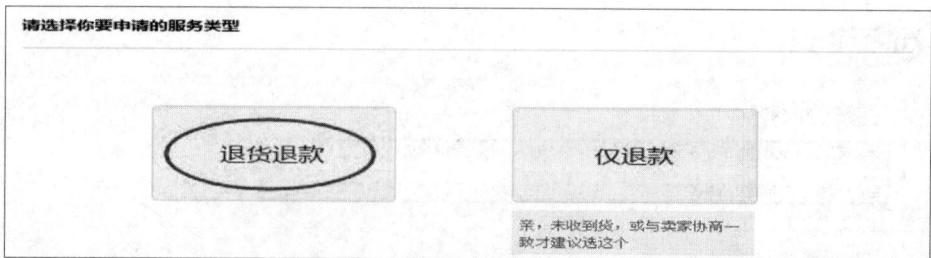

Tip. 4-2-5

(4) Choose the reason for your return (mandatory), also input the refund amount (mandatory). Then input the refund information and upload evidence (such as pictures showing any quality problems, etc.) then click on "Submit Application".

Tip. 4-2-6

(5) After submitting, wait for the seller to deal with your application. If seller does not deal with your application in time the system will automatically refund you. If you and the seller disagree on the refund you can ask Taobao customer service to intervene.

(6) Seller finishes the application and provides you the return address via Ali Wangwang (if the seller does not contact you first, then you should ask seller the to provide you return address and save time.)

(7) You need to send the goods back to the seller. Usually a seller will not want you to use surface mail or receiver pay. Use general express. (Remember to keep the postage receipt. If there is an argument this can prove that you have sent the goods back.)

(8) Seller confirms receipt and refunds successfully.

· Taobao Exchange Process

(1) If you are not satisfied with the goods, you can contact the seller via Ali Wangwang or tell customer service that you are not satisfied and ask for an exchange. (Remember to keep a copy of the chat, because when there are disagreements records will be strong evidence.)

(2) Seller agrees to replace and provides a return mail address. Send the goods back to the seller.

(3) Seller receives the returned goods and resends a replacement. The system will automatically confirm you have received replacement goods after a specified date, so if the seller does not send the goods or if they are slow to arrive, then you can open "Order Details" from and apply to increase the receipt time.

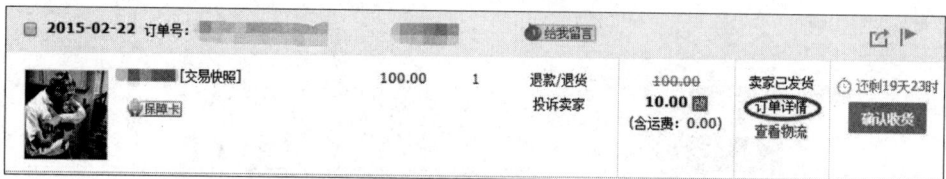

Tip. 4-2-7

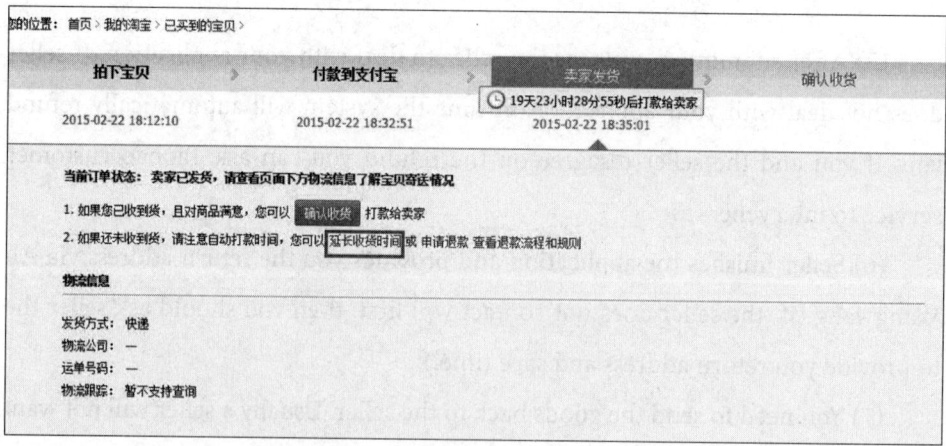

Tip. 4-2-8

4. Sign for the goods and finish the exchange.

So when you receive unsuitable goods, do return/exchange them. Refuse to make do with what you are given if you are not happy with it.

Summary

· Conditions for returning goods:

(1) Goods have not been confirmed as received yet.

(2) The goods have a quality problem when they arrive (not including problems caused by misuse).

If the goods have no quality problems and no 7+ return, you need to ask the seller whether or not you can return the goods.

Goods which have 7+ return commitments can be returned without a reason;

(3) If you return goods you need to ensure any packaging, accessories, tags etc. are as they were when you received them.

· Return process for Taobao goods

Apply to return goods — seller sends return address to buyer — buyer chooses logistics and returns goods — seller confirms receipt and refunds successfully

· Exchange process for Taobao goods

Contact seller to exchange — send goods back to seller — seller receives goods and sends replacements — buyer signs for replacements and finishes exchange

4.3 Confirm Receipt & Evaluate

In this section you will ...

✓ Learn the process of receiving goods

✓ Learn how to evaluate a seller

After a long wait and complex return process, John finally has beautiful and quality wallpapers. But there is still one more thing to do — to confirm receipt and evaluate the seller.

Confirm Receipt

In general, the process for confirming receipt is "Click Confirm Receipt—Confirm Order Information—Approve Alipay Transfer to the Seller—Successful Transaction":

First, login to your Taobao account and at the top of the page click "My Taobao"—"Bought Goods" to see all of your orders. Find the order in question and click "Confirm Receipt" on the right hand side.

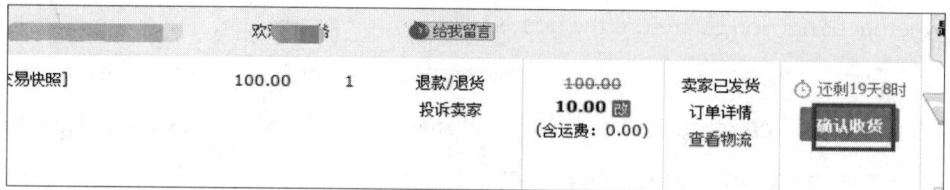

Tip. 4-3-1

The page will redirect, please confirm the order information is correct.

Tip. 4-3-2

According to the tips, enter your Alipay payment password and verification code and click "Confirm".

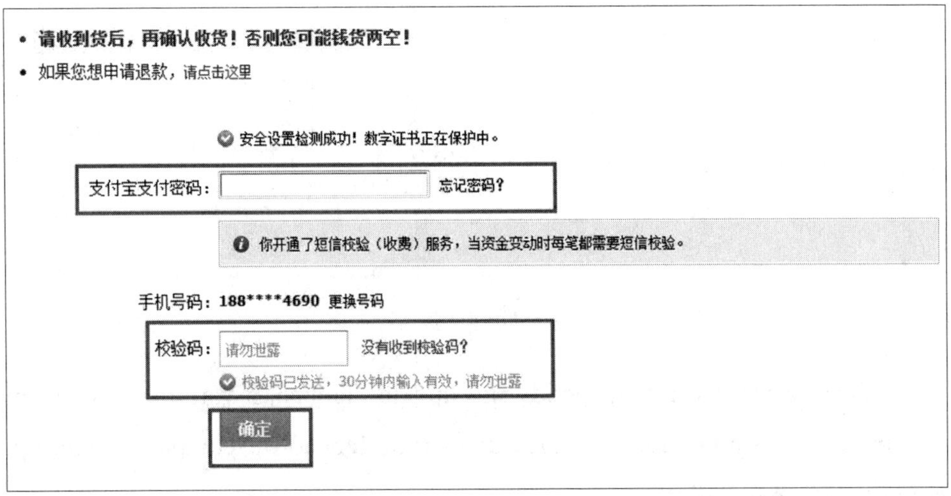

Tip. 4-3-3

After confirming, the money held by Alipay will be transferred to the seller's account. Please pay attention! If you have not received the goods or have any questions, do not confirm receipt. Because confirming receipt means the transaction process has completed successfully. If you want to return the goods, the seller is not obligated to oblige and Taobao will not side in your favour in a dispute. You will risk losing both money and the goods!

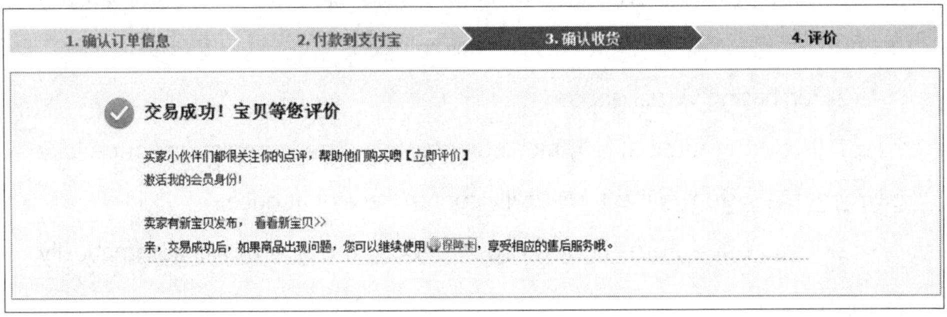

Tip. 4-3-4

After confirming receipt, the transaction status changes to having succeeded.

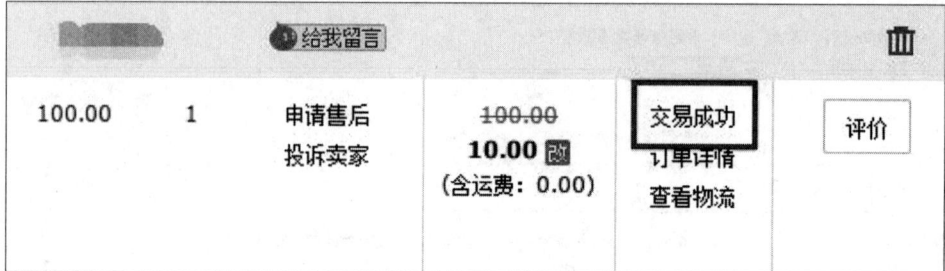

Tip. 4-3-5

After the seller sends the goods and updates Taobao, if you do not confirm receipt or apply for a refund or return, after a time Taobao will complete the receipt confirmation automatically.

How Long until the System Automatically Transfers Money to the Seller If You Don't Confirm Receipt?

1. Purchasing physical goods

1) If you choose "Express, EMS, No Logistics" when shopping, the system will automatically confirm receipt 10 days after the seller has shipped.

2) If you choose "Surface Mail" when shopping, the system will automatically confirm receipt 30 days after the seller has shipped.

3) If you purchase overseas direct mail goods, the system will automatically confirm receipt 20 days after the seller has shipped.

2. Purchasing virtual goods

1) If you buy automatically recharging goods, , after completing your Alipay payment the system will automatically confirm receipt at once.

2) If you buy automatically shipped goods , the system will automatically confirm receipt 24 hours after the seller has shipped.

3) If you buy virtual goods , for some categories of virtual goods, the system will automatically confirm receipt 3 days after the seller has shipped.

3. If the goods are not received within these times, you can ask the seller to extend it.

> 4. You can enter "My Taobao"—"Bought Goods" to find specific orders, then click on "order details" to view transaction delay times.

Seller Evaluation

In the first section of the third chapter, you learnt that comments from other buyers can help you make your own purchasing decisions. After receiving your goods, you can share your experience with the seller and opinion of the goods with other Taobao users, helping other shoppers in the future.

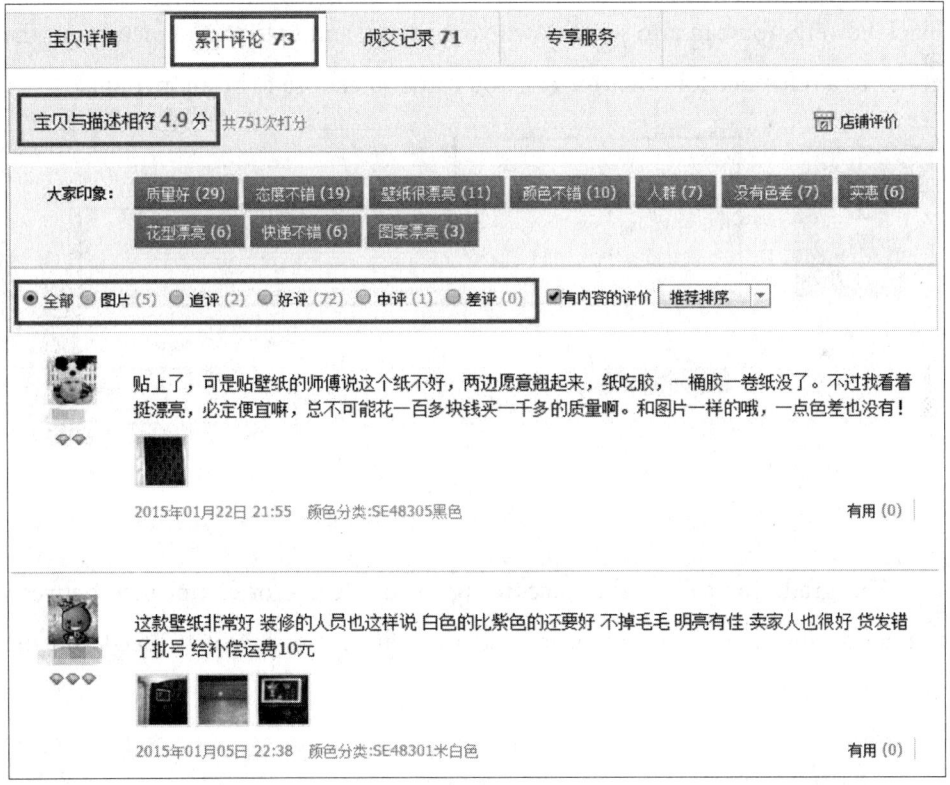

Tip. 4-3-6

So how to evaluate the seller?

After you confirm receipt, the status next to the order will show that the transaction has been successful. At this time you can evaluate the goods and the seller. Click on "Evaluate" on the right hand side next to the order.

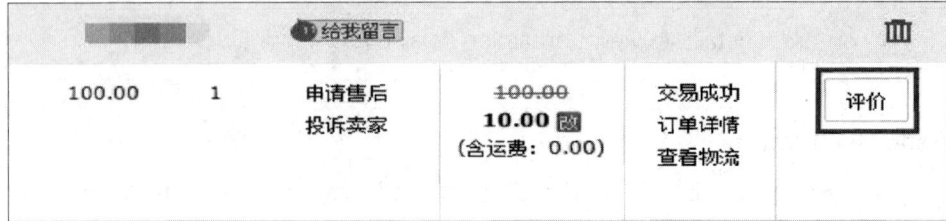

Tip. 4-3-7

You can choose "Good" (a red flower), "Medium" (a yellow flower) or "Bad" (a black flower). You can also write down your views, and upload real pictures of the goods as a reference for other buyers. You can also choose to be anonymous.

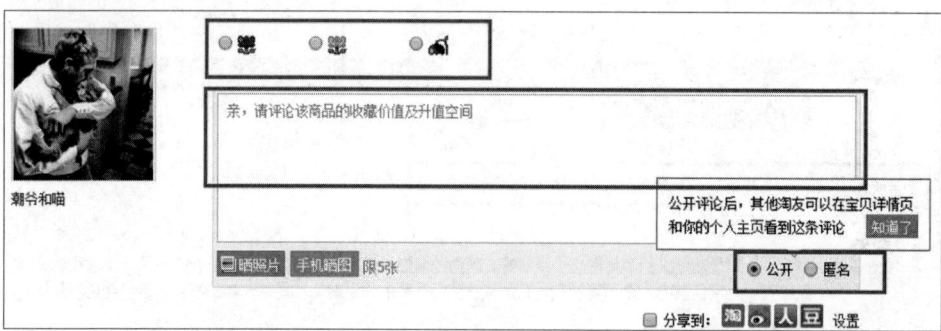

Tip. 4-3-8

You grade the seller's shop according to the degree of compliance between the goods and their description, the seller's attitude, the despatch speed and the delivery speed.

Tip. 4-3-9

After evaluating the seller, the seller's rank will change. At the same time, the seller will evaluate you.

Tip. 4-3-10

Buyer Rating

Both sides of the transaction in Taobao can obtain an evaluation from the order after each transaction. After the success of the order transaction, the seller can make a real assessment of the buyer in terms of each item. The evaluation can be divided into three categories: "Good", "Mmedium" and "Bad". "Good" means plus a point, "Medium" zero, and "Bad" minus one.

Tip. 4-3-11   Buyer rating

Sometimes there is another situation. After receiving the goods, you are satisfied with them and give a high score. However, after using them for a period of time, you find that the quality, durability and so on are far lower than the original description and expected value, which were beyond your expectations. But the evaluation cannot be changed, so what should you do? It doesn't matter. You can "Add Comments", on the right hand side of the corresponding order.

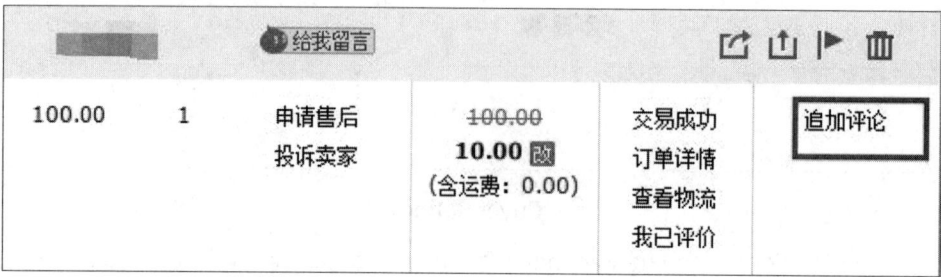

Tip. 4-3-12

Now you have completed the entire process of purchasing goods on Taobao you can't say you're a newbie! However, online shopping in the real world will bring a variety of unexpected problems from time to time. Only by doing it yourself, will you understand what kind of experience online shopping in China is. Go buy something!

Summary

- Learn the process of receiving goods

Click confirm receipt—Confirm order—Approve Alipay transfer to the seller—Transaction successful

- Learn how to evaluate the seller

Score the goods and write your opinion—Score the shop—Add comments

Chapter 5

Aliababa Group listed on the New York Stock Exchange on 19 September 2014. The dot-com company went public in a blaze of publicity and attracted the attention of millions of people.

It is difficult to describe how fast China's e-commerce is developing, though we can easily see in the data. In the third quarter of 2014 (Q3), China's online shopping market transactions amounted to 691.41 billion RMB, accounting for 10.6% of Total Retail Sales of Consumer Goods, an increase of 49.8% compared to the same period the previous year.

Are you itching for a try after reading those figures? Can you smell the excellent opportunity? Our Sri Lankan friend Mike is going to go back home this year after several years studying in Beijing. He has a lot of things to deal with before leaving. It is too inconvenient for him to take all his belongings back home, yet it is too wasteful to throw them away. Some Chinese friends suggested he sell them online. After much consideration, Mike decided that it was a good idea and that he would open an online store.

But, how do you open an online store? Let's learn the details in this new chapter.

5.1 Conceiving

In this section, you will learn ...

✓ The advantages of setting up an online store

✓ Common platforms for online stores

✓ Preparation necessary for opening an online store

What are the advantages of setting up an online store?

Fig. 5-1-1　Online Stores on TMALL

A summary of the main advantages:

1. Broad prospects

We have mentioned above in the summary that the annual growth rate of online shopping transactions has risen by 49.8%. Unlimited internet platforms will promote the continual growth of online shopping.

2. Low cost

Starting a business on a large online shopping platform like taobao.com is completely free. If your goods are relatively small, you can stock according to customer purchases, so need not open a warehouse, you also do not need to employ management or staff; fit out a shop or pay rent or utilities.

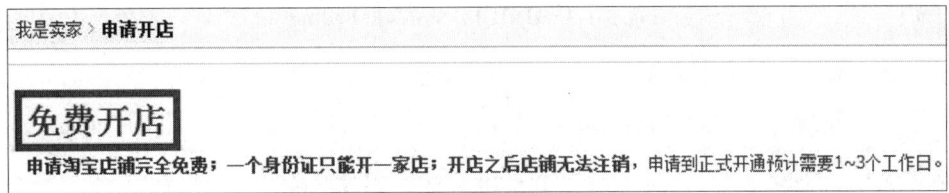

Fig. 5-1-2

3. Wide range of consumer groups

It is an indisputable fact that online shops cater to a wide range of consumer groups. First, online shops break the limitation of time and space. Consumers can buy goods no matter when and no matter where. Secondly, there are hundreds of millions of internet users in China who can independently access the internet to browse shops and become potential consumers.

UNIQLO in Fig.5-1-1 is an apparel brand quite familiar in China, which enjoys a sound reputation and consumer acceptance. In Beijing, Shanghai and other big cities, it is in almost all the large shopping plaza; however, in some smaller underdeveloped cities, the number of its stores is very limited. To a certain extent, geographical location and quantity restrict the consumption of physical store consumer groups.

Fig. 5-1-3　UNIQLO Stores in Beijing

Fig. 5-1-4　UNIQLO Stores in Weifang

The establishment of an online UNIQLO store meant things you couldn't buy in a physical store, whether because there wasn't store in your location or your store didn't have what you wanted in stock, you now could. Logistics could even deliver your goods directly to your home.

Chapter 5

Fig. 5-1-5   UNIQLO Online Store

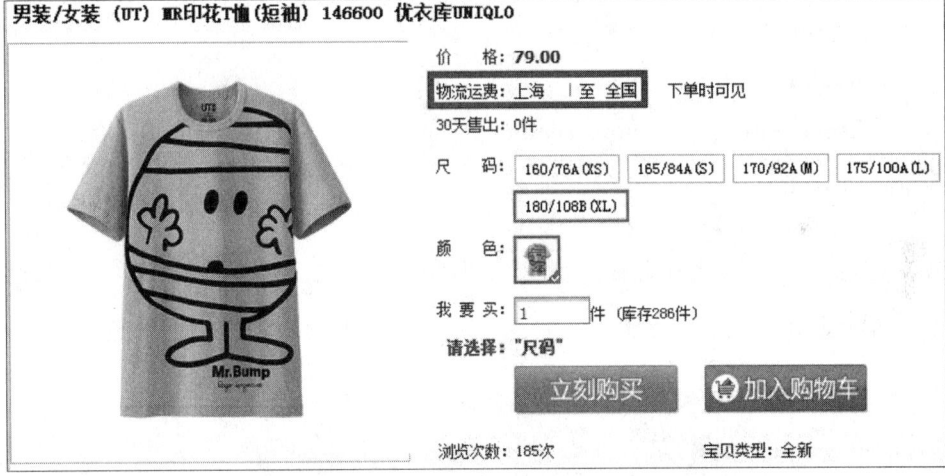

Fig. 5-1-6   Logistics

Online shop's operating modes:

• UNIQLO, as mentioned above, runs a combination of physical and virtual stores.

• Some operators adopt another operating mode — virtual shops only, trading from Taobao.com or Tmall.com, etc.

In this operating mode, some people run an online shop as

281

> their main business and some have an online shop as a sideline or part-time business.

4. Flexible operating time

The time required to run an online store is quite flexible. You need to set opening hours for a real-world business, but an e-commerce platform doesn't care whether you are leaving for the day or going on vacation. Online stores operate 24/7, taking orders at all times.

Which platform can you open an online stores on?

At present, China has three major C2C platforms — Taobao, Eachnet and Paipai.

1. Taobao

Website: http://www.taobao.com/

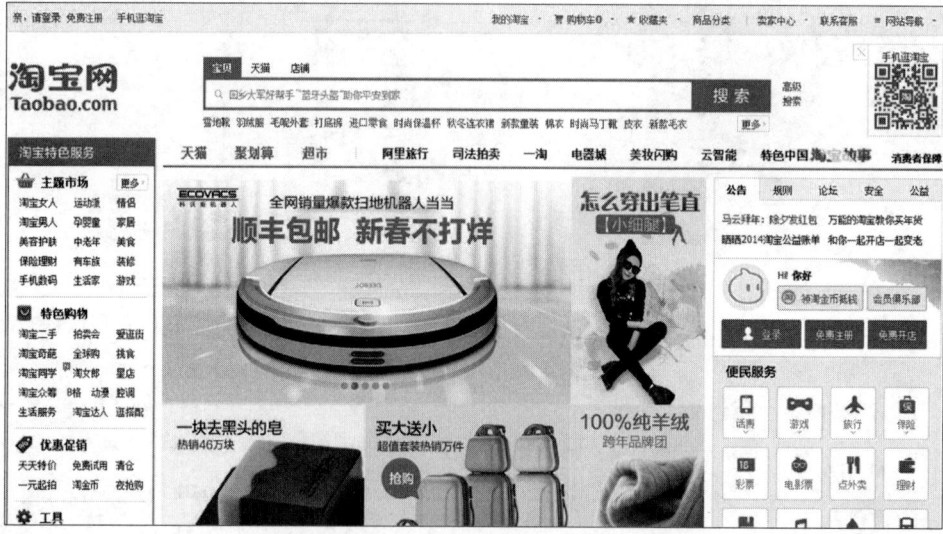

Fig. 5-1-7 Taobao.com

In the previous chapters of this book, we have introduced Tabao from the perspective of the buyer. Taobao's main function is to serve as a platform for C2C, providing trading venues for individual sellers and individual buyers.

The platform function is very powerful, and includes an instant chat tool (Ali Wangwang), payment instruments (Alipay), consumer protection, etc, through which sellers and buyers can be assured.

It is worth mentioning that Taobao is currently China's most popular C2C platform, having the greatest number of users, number of stores, and type of goods.

2. Eachnet

Website: http://www.eachnet.com/

Fig. 5-1-8   Eachnet.com

Eachnet was founded in Shanghai in August 1999. In early 2005, the number of Eachnet users had exceeded 10 million. In 2002, Eachnet joined with eBay, renamed itself eBay Eachnet, and quickly developed into the largest domestic online trading community.

Eachnet runs the business concept of "Global Market". From the picture above, we can see the China Division, American Division and Canada Division are different zones. Users can buy what they want from overseas through Eachnet.

If you want to sell something on Eachnet, you can choose auction or set price, and the product listing lasts a certain length of time. You can also open a store. Eachnet.com provides users with a third party payment platform similar to Alipay—Paypal—as well as a complaints mechanism and violation reporting mechanism to coordinate trade disputes and protect consumer rights and interests.

3. Paipai

Website: http://www.paipai.com/

Fig. 5-1-9   Paipai.com

Paipai.com is an e-business which was initially under the leadership of Tencent, and has since been taken over by JD. Paipai.com went online on 12 September 2005, and officially started to operate on 13 March 2006. It is committed to creating an interconnected C2C platform for both sellers and buyers, who can fully meet the needs of consumers by providing apparel, baby products, food and beverages, home furnishing, electronics and other products. Paipai.com also provides value-added services such as data mining and analysis for third party sellers, which helps them to make an accurate analysis of consumers and the market, thus supporting product planning and precision marketing.

After reading the introduction of the above three platforms, which one do you prefer? Since Taobao currently has the largest amount of users and is used the most frequently, in the following section on opening an online shop, we will use Taobao to illustrate the process. The steps for opening a shop on other platforms is similar and you can explore more by yourself.

1. What hardware do you need? What should you prepare before opening an online store?

· A computer

Nothing can be done without a functioning computer!

· The internet

To open a virtual shop access to the internet is necessary, whether wirelessly or via cable to a network.

Gaining access to the internet can be done through local communication service providers, such as China Mobile and China Unicom.

· A contact telephone number

Sometimes problems cannot be solved online, so you will also need a contact telephone number. It may be a mobile number or landline.

· A high pixel camera

Products in virtual shops are sold to customers by a picture. A high pixel camera is the best option for taking these pictures, through which you can show the full details and quality of your goods..

· A printer

If order volumes are relatively small, you can fill in courier invoices by hand. However, if your business has developed to a certain scale, printing invoices will save time and effort.

· E-banking

Business transactions by online shops take place almost entirely on the internet; therefore, an e-banking account is essential! How to apply for a bank card and how to open an e-banking account and other related details can be found in previous chapters in detail.

2. What software do you need?

· An e-mail client

Everyone has at least one E-mail address, and this can be used to join Taobao. In addition, e-mail is a very important and formal way to communicate. It is likely to be used by the platform providers and platform managers in addition to buyers.

· Ali Wangwang

This is an instant messaging tool provided by Taobao. You can use the web version, or download the application to your personal computer (there is also a terminal version called "Wang Xin"). This tool facilitates communication between buyers and sellers.

· Image processing software

See the two pictures below (Fig. 5-1-10). If you were a buyer and had to choose between the two, which would you choose? Most buyers would choose the first. They are items from spring 2015 and the same brand, but come across completely different. Beautiful photography is the first step in attracting buyers, so using image processing software is essential before uploading to your virtual shop item gallery. Currently, the most popular comprehensive image processing software is Adobe Photoshop.

Fig. 5-1-10

3. What information and materials do you need to prepare?

- Passport

Fig. 5-1-11   Passport

- Entrance Permit (or Residence Permit for Foreigners)

 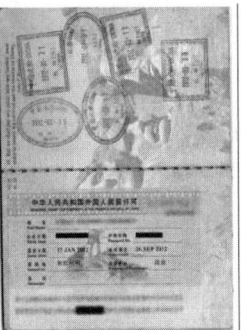

Fig. 5-1-12   Entrance Permit

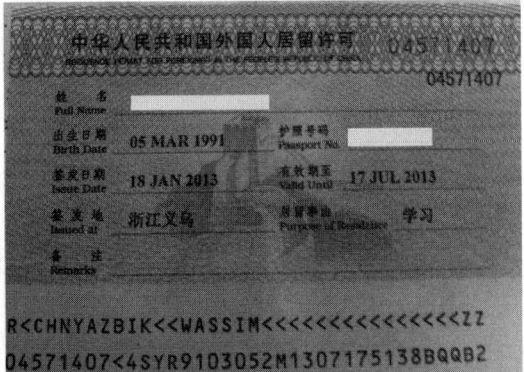

Fig. 5-1-13   Residence Permit for Foreigners

> **Note**
> - The certificate must be the original colour version or a copy of it made with a digital camera or scanner.
> - Pictures must be unedited.

• Chinese bank account

No matter what platform you open your shop on, you need a bank card. On Taobao, your bank account is needed to bind with your Alipay to settle transactions. Currently, Taobao shops authenticate bank cards issued by the following 15 banks:

China Construction Bank (CCB)	Agricultural Bank of China (ABC)	Industrial Bank
China Minsheng Bank	SPD Bank	Industrial and Commercial Bank of China (ICBC)
China Merchants Bank	Bank of Communication	Bank of China (BOC)
China Guangfa Bank	China Citic Bank	China Everbright Bank
Bank of Hangzhou	Postal Savings Bank of China	Ping An Bank

Summary

It is the end of this chapter. In this chapter, we have answered three questions and listed the preparations that must be made before opening an online store. Hopefully it is helpful to you!

1. Advantages of trading online
   - Broad prospects
   - Low costs
   - Wide range of consumer groups
   - Flexible operating time
2. Platforms
   - Taobao.com

- Eachnet.com
- Paipai.com

3. Preparations

- Hardware: computer, internet, contact number, camera, printer and e-banking
- Software: e-mail account, Ali Wangwang and image processing software
- Materials: passport, entrance permit and Chinese bank account

5.2 Application for Opening a Shop

In this section, you will …

✓ Learn the steps for running an online shop

In the preceding section we gave the theory behind running an online shop. Now let's put it into practice and set up an online shop of our own on Taobao.

First, you need to have your own Taobao account. If you haven't got one, go get one.

Fig. 5-2-1　Homepage of Taobao

After you have logged in, look for the orange button in the lower right corner of the screen and click on "Open a Free Shop".

Taobao will usually ask you to enter the password again as a security precaution. After this, you will enter the seller's center.

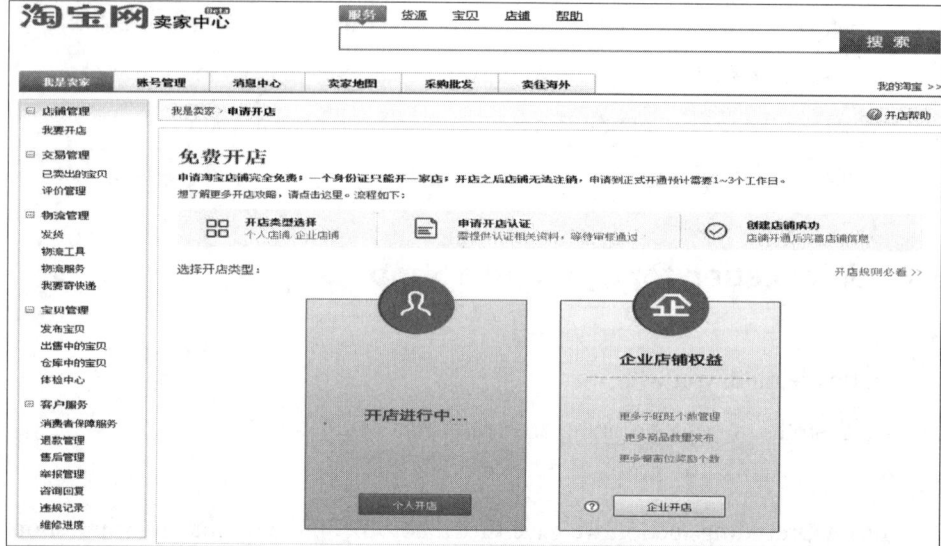

Fig. 5-2-2　Setting up a Free Shop

The picture above is the seller's center page on taobao.com. It can be seen that there is a simple search bar at the top of the screen where you can search for relevant information such as source of goods, commodities, stores, etc. It classifies the related information at the bottom of the screen that covers every aspect of online sales, which we'll explain in detail one by one in the following sections.

There are two kinds of shops: individual and enterprise. If you want to set up a shop by yourself, please choose individual, otherwise, choose enterprise. These two types differ in the application process. In this example we are setting up an individual store. But before that, we will find out about the rules of opening up a shop. Click on the blue text that says "Click Here" to go to the explanation page.

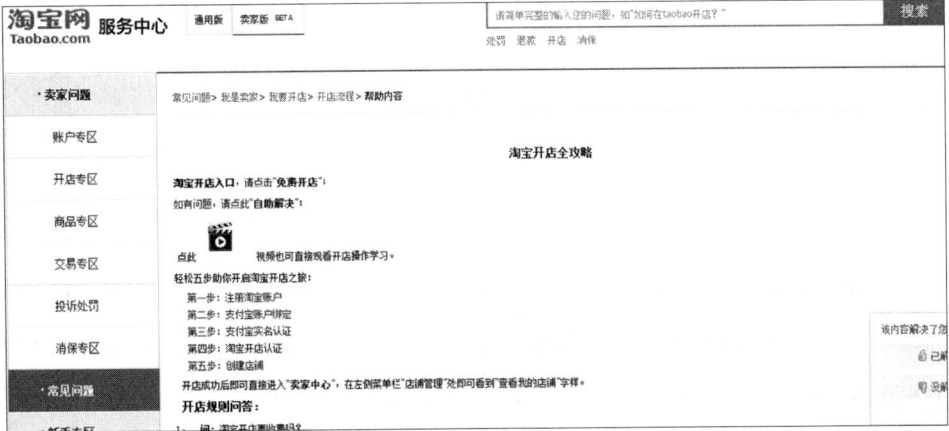

Fig. 5-2-3　Service Center Explanation Page

After reading the relevant rules and procedures you will have a general understanding of the application process and will be more successful in completing the follow-up application stages. You do not need to worry, however, if you choose to skip reading these, because your application will go smoothly from following the steps described in this book.

After reading about what you want to know, go back to the main page of the seller center and click on "Open a Free Shop".

Taobao will automatically check your account to see if you are meet the conditions required to open a store, and if you are, you will be sent to the store authentication process.

In this process you have to go through two authentications before permission to open a shop is given: Alipay real name authentication and authentication for opening a Taobao shop.

Purpose of Alipay real name authentication:

The purpose of Alipay real name authentication is to verify membership information and bank account information. If

> you pass Alipay real name authentication, you will be given the equivalent of an internet ID card, with which you can use set up shops on many e-commerce platforms such as Taobao to sell goods and improve your Alipay account users' credit.

In the Alipay account authentication process, pay attention to the fact that the Alipay account address must be consistent with your geolocation. If you have not registered for an Alipay account, please do it now. We will provide more detailed information in this regard in Chapter 2.

Fig. 5-2-4   Authentication for Opening a Shop

After the completion of the Alipay real name authentication, click on "Immediate Authentication" to go to the Taobao shop authentication.

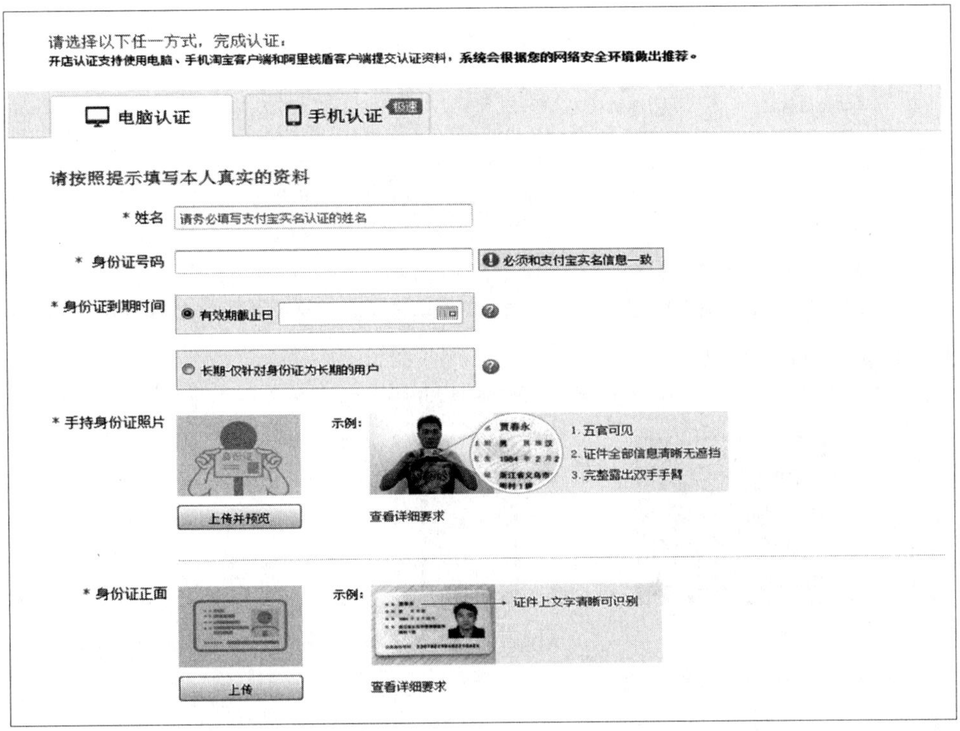

Fig. 5-2-5　Computer Authentication

For identity authentication, Taobao provides two methods: computer authentication and mobile phone authentication.

If you choose "Computer Authentication", you need to upload the requested application documents and a photo of yourself, and also fill in your address and phone number.

If you choose "Mobile Authentication", you need to install Ali money shield and scan authentication before completing two more steps that are similar to the computer authentication process.

Fig. 5-2-6 Mobile Authentication

After downloading the related security software, the subsequent process is basically the same as the computer authentication process.

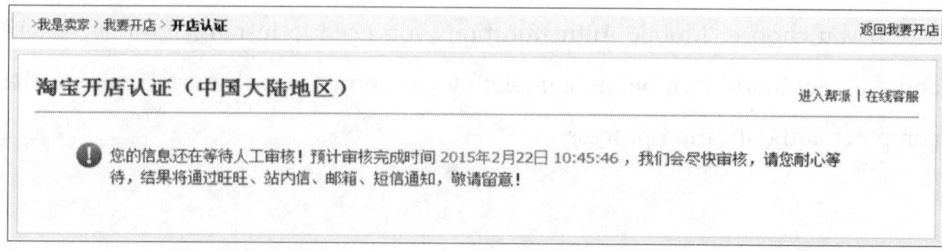

Fig. 5-2-7 Manual audit

After you have submitted the application materials, you must pass a manual audit to be able to finally open your shop. The manual review is generally long. The website will calculate you how long it will take you to complete it. After a few days you will log in to find you have passed the audit and can set up your store.

Fig. 5-2-8　Set up a Shop

Summary

In this chapter, we have walked through the steps of applying to open an online shop. The following is a flow chart extracted from this chapter.

5.3　Displaying Products

In this section, you will …
- ✓ Get to know the steps of uploading goods to an online store
- ✓ Learn the steps for "decorating" an online shop

Displaying goods

In the Taobao navigation bar, click "Seller's Center" to enter your online store admin page.

Let's start publicizing your products!

Fig. 5-3-1　Display babies

You can choose "Display Baby Immediately" by clicking the green box on the store's open the shop page, or "Display Baby" under "Baby Management" on the left menu bar.

Fig. 5-3-2 Classification

You can choose the categories your goods will be classified in through the category menu, or via a category search. In the above picture, there are three search boxes, and the categories gradually become more specific as you move to the right.

Or for example if you search for "U Shield", then click "Quickly Find Categories", the system will find the best matching category for you.

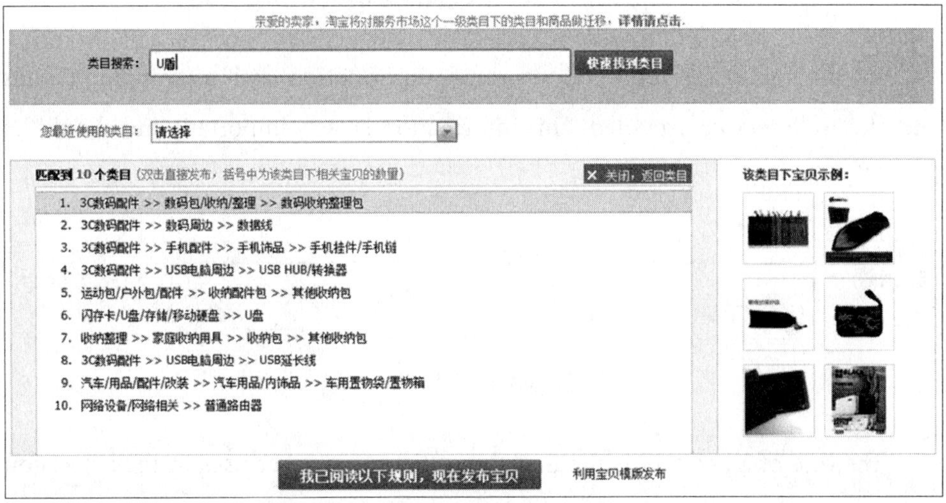

Fig. 5-3-3 Category Search

When choosing your categories, be careful not to set them up arbitrarily and try to ensure their accuracy. In this way, it will be more convenient for customers trying to find products quickly.

After completing classification and categorisation, there is one more stage to complete before publicising your babies (in Taobao, in order to sound amiable, goods are known as babies).

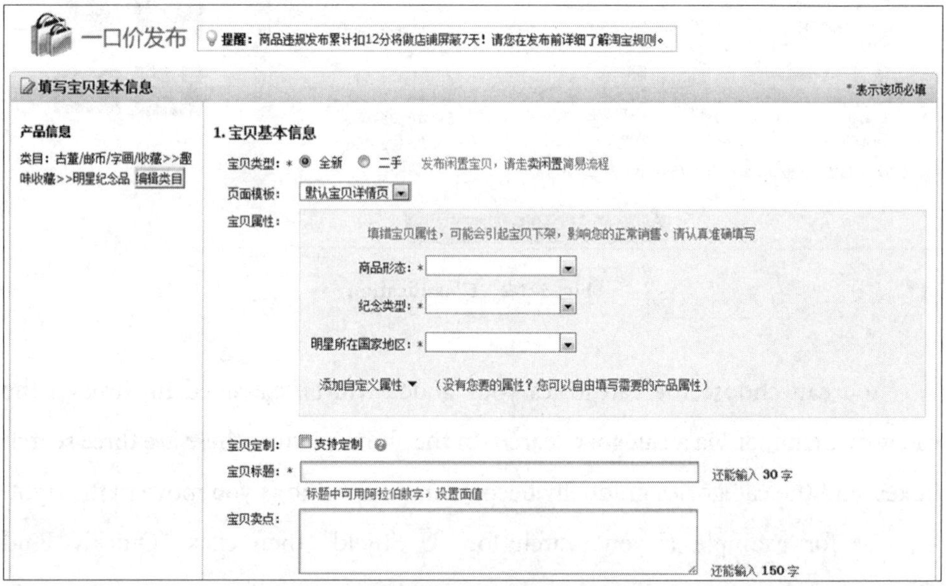

Fig. 5-3-4 Baby Information

In this final stage you need to provide information such as shipping details and after-sale service provided. This information is very important and should be carefully filled in.

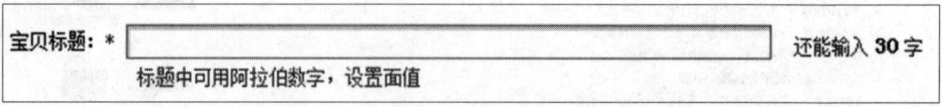

Fig.5-3-5 Baby Title

The title of a product is the first thing that a customer uses in their decision making. It has a great impact on the number of visits and purchases. You can see how the titles or headlines for the same type of products are written for other similar products before filling yours in. You can also use the search bar on Taobao's home page. Some of the key words about the products will automatically appear. These are popular keywords that customers often search for. You can tailor the title of your products according to these.

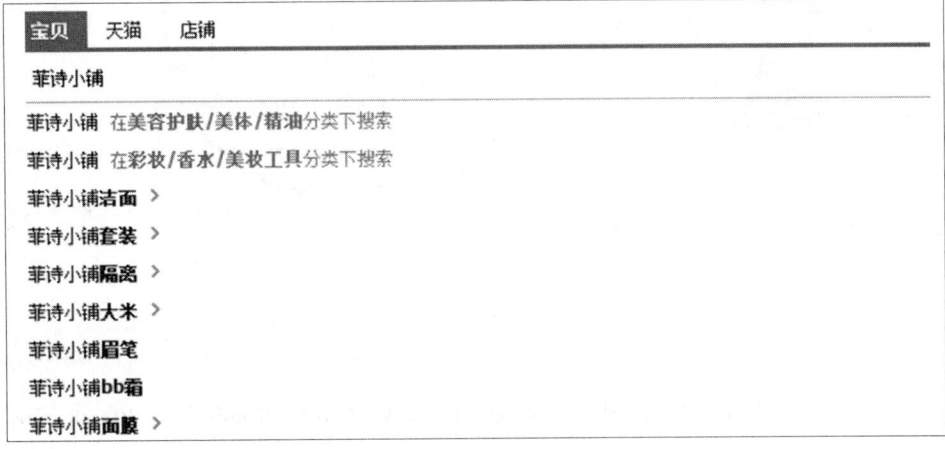

Fig. 5-3-6　Baby Entries

The pictures and descriptions of your goods are extremely important.

The pictures and descriptions of popular goods are often done with tremendous effort—the pictures are clear and concise, the descriptions of the goods are complete and detailed, with some even using videos to explain them.

Fig. 5-3-7　Baby Description 1

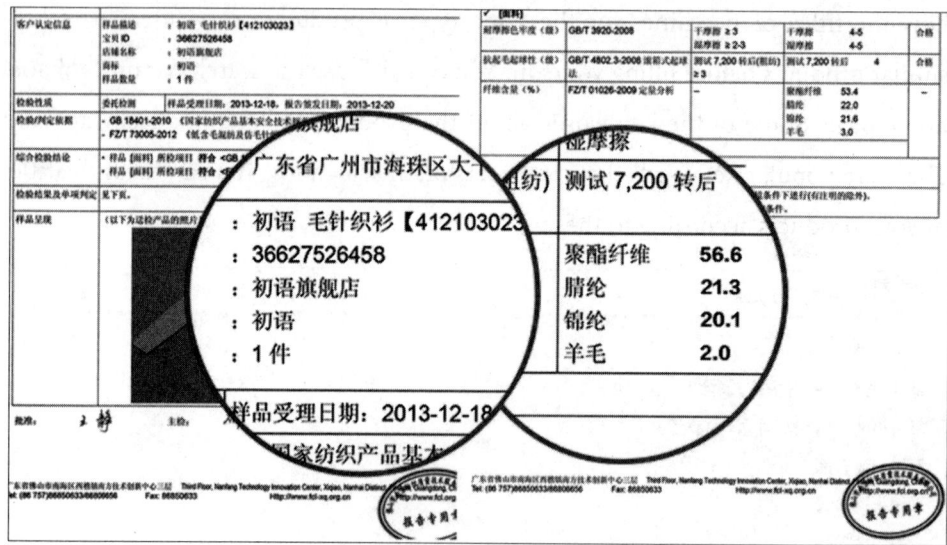

Fig. 5-3-8   Baby description 2

Attention should be paid to the authenticity of the uploaded photos and the descriptions of your products. Attracting visitors by overstating the worth of your goods will greatly affect the reputation of your online store.

Now we have come to the logistics information page. When filling in the logistics information, we need to set up the delivery cost template first.

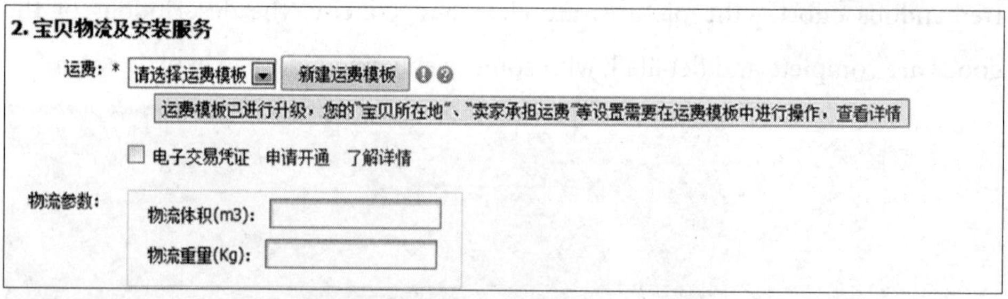

Fig. 5-3-9   Setting up Delivery Cost

Click on "New Delivery Cost Template".

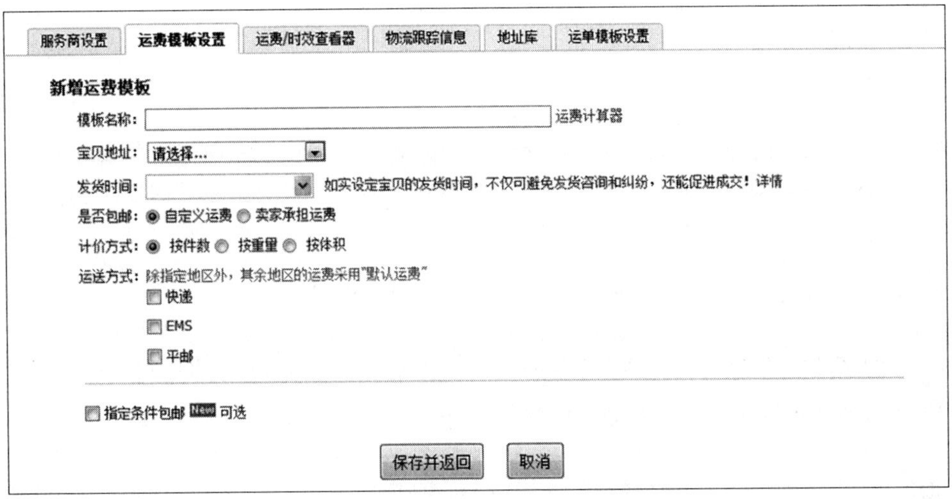

Fig. 5-3-10　Delivery cost template

Taobao provides a convenient tool for calculating delivering costs — you can click on "Delivery Calculator" or enter the setup page by clicking on "Delivery Fee/Time Effect Viewer" tab.

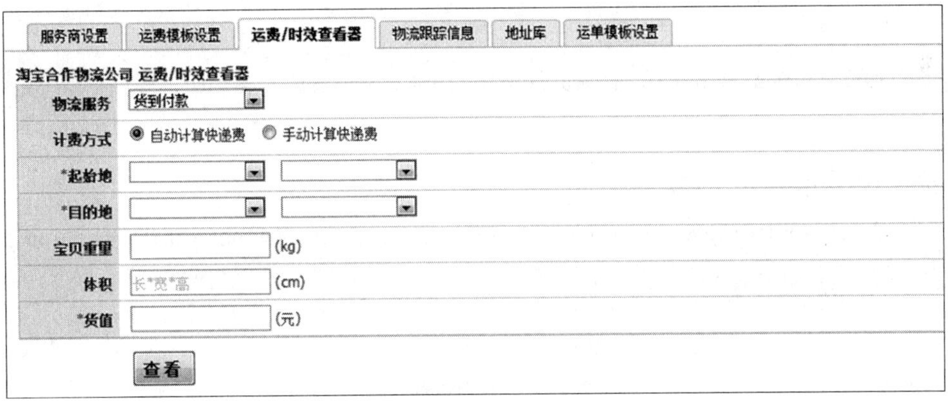

Fig. 5-3-11　Calculation of Delivery Cost

Post-sale information should be filled in truthfully. If there is no invoice, you should write nothing. Do not create troubles for the future through carelessness.

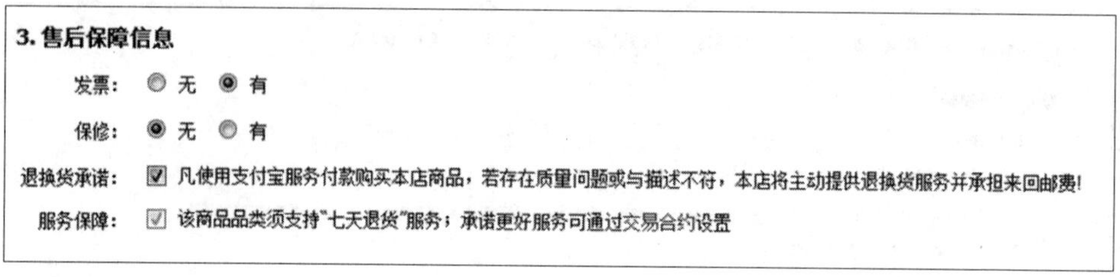

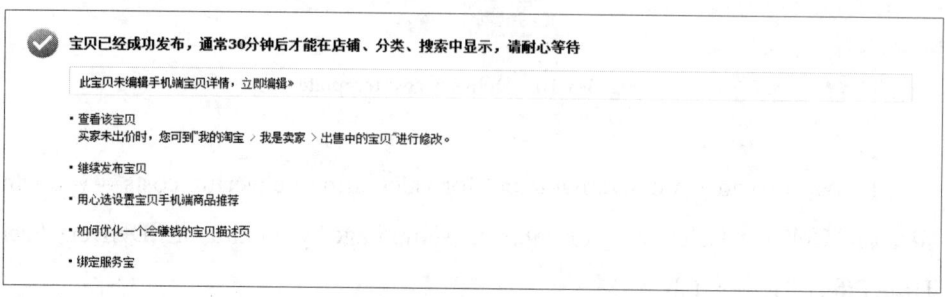

Fig. 5-3-12   After-sale Guarantee

After uploading all of the product information, click the "Display Button" at the end of the baby publishing page to complete the process.

Fig. 5-3-13   Successful Release

OK, so it's a success! Let's wait for the first customer!

Decorating your shop

After uploading your goods, let's decorate the shop. A beautifully decorated shop is a good way to attract customers.

Fig. 5-3-14   Shop Decoration

Select "Shop Decoration" in the store management menu.

Follow the steps that are prompted on the page.

Fig. 5-3-15　Page Prompts

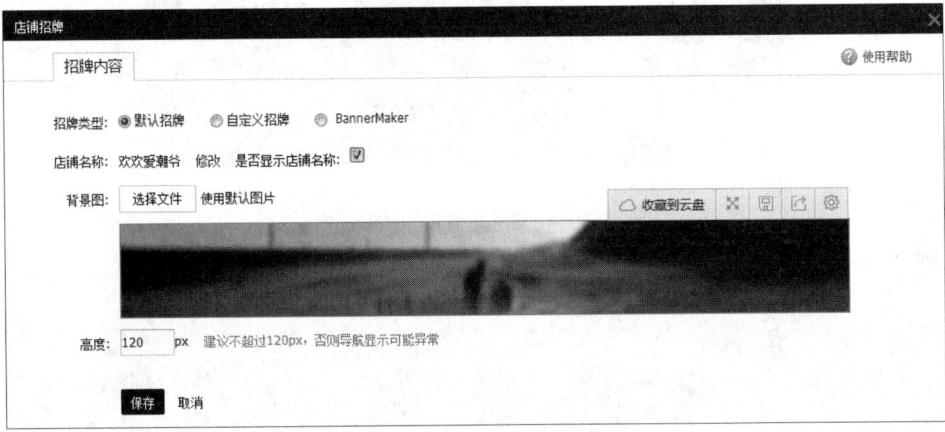

Fig. 5-3-16　Page Signboard

Here you can customize the shop's template, background picture, or even upload background music that you like.

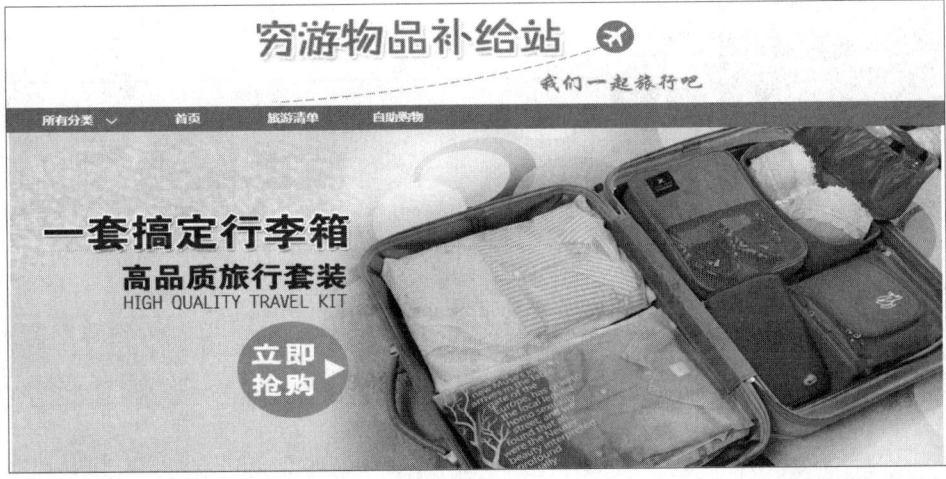

Fig. 5-3-17　Example Page 1

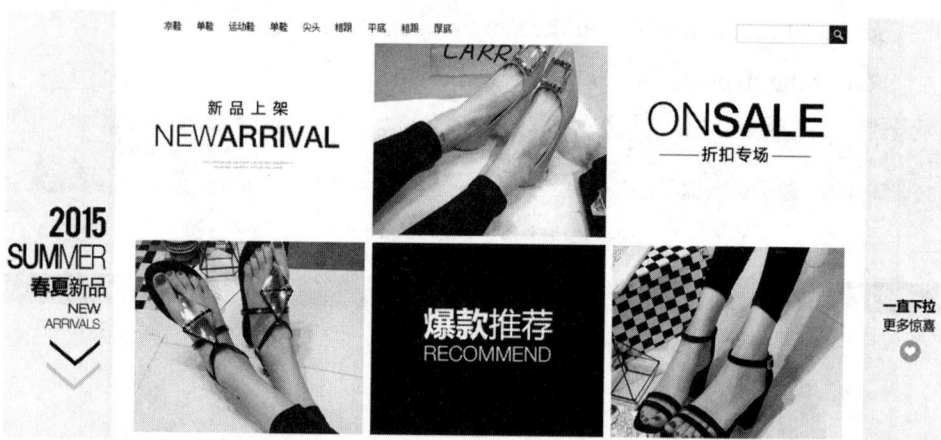

Fig. 5-3-18　Example page 2

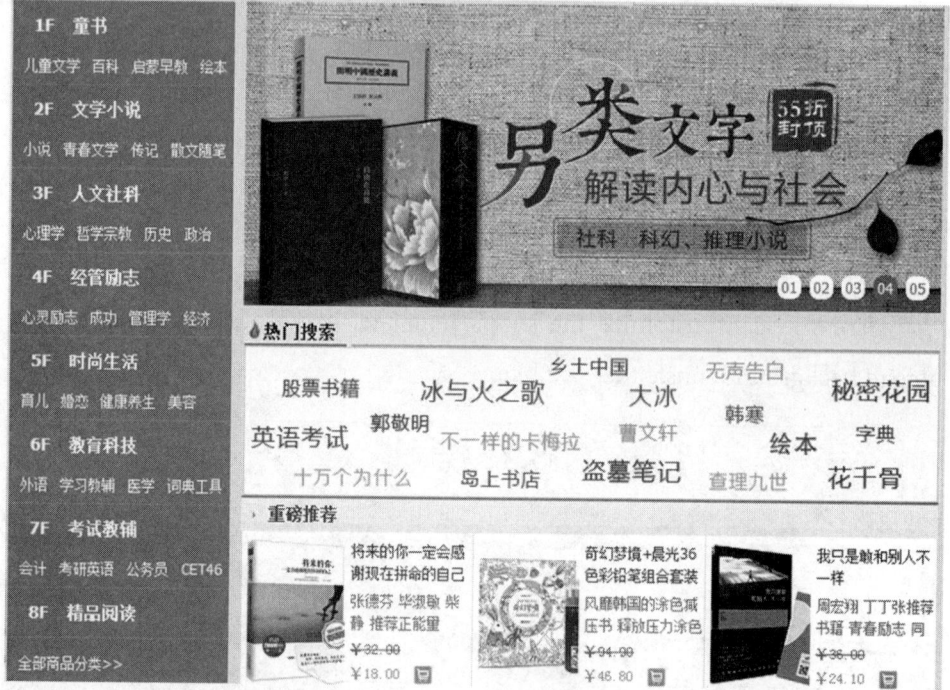

Fig. 5-3-19　Example Page 3

Summary

In this chapter we have finally added the long-awaited products to our shop.

1. Displaying goods

Chapter 5

- Choose baby type
- Fill in the baby's basic information

2. Shop decoration

5.4 Marketing and Promotion

In this section, you will ...

✓ Learn the marketing strategy for an online store

In China, there is a famous saying called "Good wine not necessarily needs no bush / Deeply buried gold cannot shine" in business, which means that if the wine is hidden in the deep lanes, it cannot be sold out even though it is the best wine. This word tells us the importance of marketing, and good products will be more salable if combined with good marketing methods.

Basic knowledge of marketing:

Discover and tap the needs of potential customers, and promote and sell products based on the quality of the products and the overall atmosphere.

Publicise brands, attract new customers, retain old customers and increase product sales.

For online stores, marketing is particularly important. On the Taobao platform alone there are tens of millions of businesses. Think about how many customers are likely to click on your products and enter your store with that much competition. It's hard to find your shop, let alone stay there and buy something. In such a fierce environment, if you want to stand out, promotion is indispensable.

We have summed up some effective ways of marketing for your reference.

1. Advertisement

Taobao provides a lot of opportunities for advertising. We will introduce several advertising methods commonly used on Taobao below. By using these methods, we believe that more people will visit your shop.

· Window displays

What is a window display? As shown in the chart below, it is a display of pictures and words created by a shop that usually appears on the search results page. A window display allows customers to see your store's products on their initial search, thereby increasing the chance they will enter and buy goods from you.

Window displays or promotions are a service you have to pay for, but Taobao sometimes offers some opportunities for free. When displaying you should give priority to products with better sales so as to increase the chances of a purchase. In regard to displaying duration, it is best to choose a period with the largest page view to promote related products.

Fig. 5-4-1   Window Display

• Shop promotion

Although window promotion is good, it costs a lot of money. So, how can you let potential customers know more about your store's products for free? In-shop promotion.

In-shop promotion is aimed at customers who have entered your shop. Add store and merchandise advertisements on the front page or the detailed goods page of your store. Those who came only interested in one of your items are likely to continue to browse other items in your store this way. This provides more display opportunities for other products in the store and improves the purchase rate of goods.

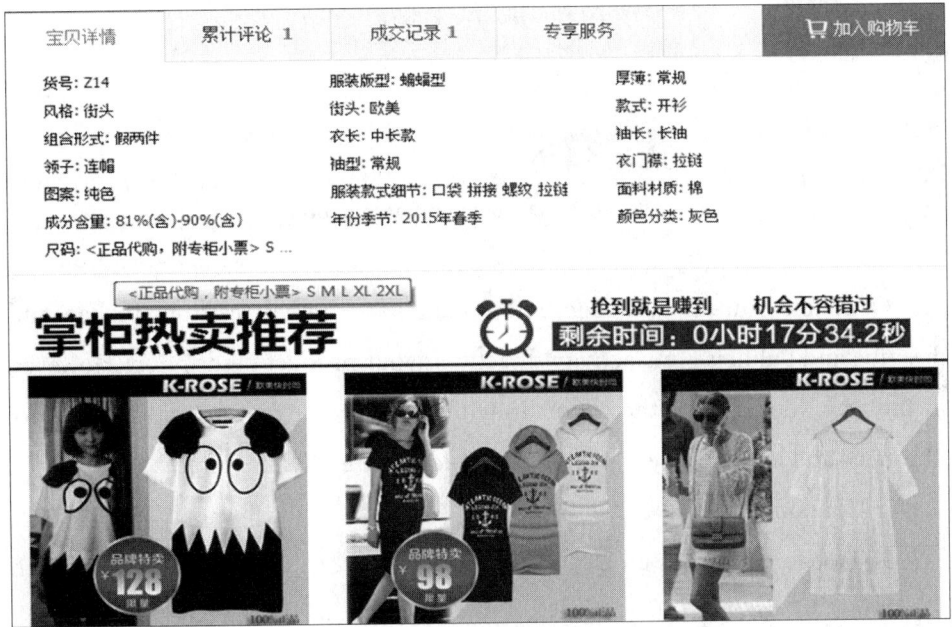

Fig. 5-4-2　In-shop Promotion

2. Discount

Consumers like goods with discount rates below normal prices. Discounts often attract attention. For this reason, many businesses often hold discount activities to promote products. Taobao provides a lot of opportunities for shopkeepers to offer discount promotion.

· Discount on consumption

"Discount on consumption" means that discounts or gifts will be received as long as the customer spends a certain amount of money. It encourages consumers to buy more products than originally planned.

In order to activate this service, shopkeepers need to pay a certain fee to Taobao after choosing "I Want to Promote" in the navigation menu. After opening this service, Taobao will promote your discount across its platform.

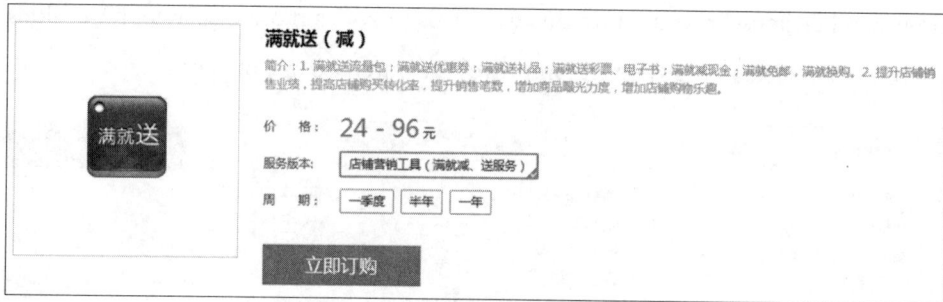

Fig. 5-4-3   Discount on Consumption

Of course, you can also choose not to purchase this service from Taobao, and describe and publicise this activity directly in your product description. However, in this way, you will lose the opportunity to promote our products across Taobao. The gains and losses of these two ways should be carefully measured.

· Coupon

A Taobao coupon is an electronic coupon that can be used by buyers when they come to checkout. It can reduce the final cost for the buyer, so many will consider buying a certain product in order to get the gift of the coupon. Coupons can be picked up by buyers in numerous ways including through "discount on consumption" offers.

Taobao provides a full network promotion opportunity for sellers who have acquired the coupon service to greatly increase the exposure of their goods.

· Deadline discounts

"Deadline discounts" is a very effective tool for increasing customer visits in a given period of time during which products will be sold at a lower than the market price. The price of such promotions is often very attractive, which, coupled with the urgent time limit, often leads to impulse buying.

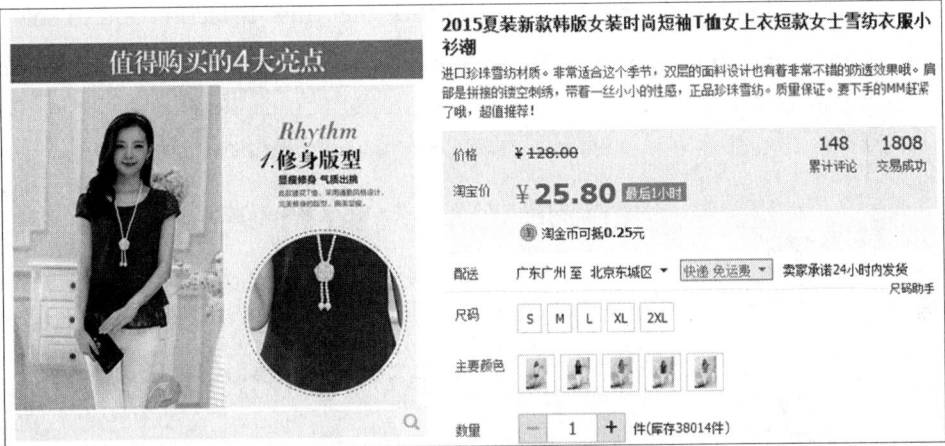

Fig. 5-4-4　Deadline Discounts

In order to buy cheaper products, many customers will look for "Discount Promotion" in their search. If you enable this function, your product will appear in the customer's search results, greatly increasing the customer's purchasing probability.

3. Evaluation management

In order to buy the most suitable items, customers usually make a purchase choice after comparing several similar products. In the process of comparison, the most important thing for buyers is the evaluations of the products by other buyers. These comments sometimes paint a more realistic picture of the goods compared to the seller's own photos and descriptions. Therefore, it is particularly important to attach importance to evaluation management.

But how do you manage the evaluation? Here are some tips. After a buyer has received your goods, you should contact them promptly and ask them about their attitude towards your online store. If the buyer thinks they are very good, you should encourage them to write a positive review. Some stores even give some small gifts along with the goods in order to incentivise the leaving of positive comments. If the customer is not satisfied after receiving the goods, we should communicate with them to find out the reason or reasons for their dissatisfaction and to solve any problems instantly. This can effectively avoid many negative or bad comments.

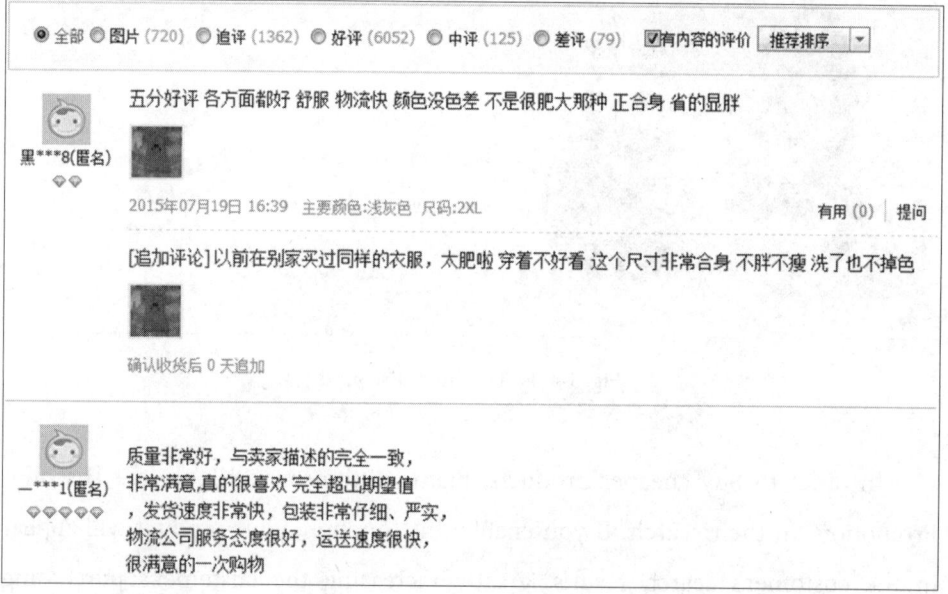

Fig. 5-4-5   Evaluation Management

Although evaluation management is not expensive, it is demanding work that requires patience. If you keep on doing it and win customer praise, then the value and effect of their comments will be much greater than that of costly advertising.

4. Other platform promotion

There are many places on the internet that get a lot of visits. In online promotion, promotion on a single platform is sometimes a not enough. In recent years, with the rise of social media platforms such as forums, micro-blogs and WeChat, many Taobao sellers have extended their promotions to them.

You may have had a similar experience. While browsing a micro-blog, you see someone with a very cool pair of headphones. "Those are great, really cool!" you think to yourself and you wonder where did this guy buy those headphones? You read the comments and see someone has shared a Taobao link where you can buy them too. This is an example of a customer moving from another platform to the Taobao platform. This occurs more than 100 million times a day on the internet, bringing many opportunities for shopping sites like Taobao.

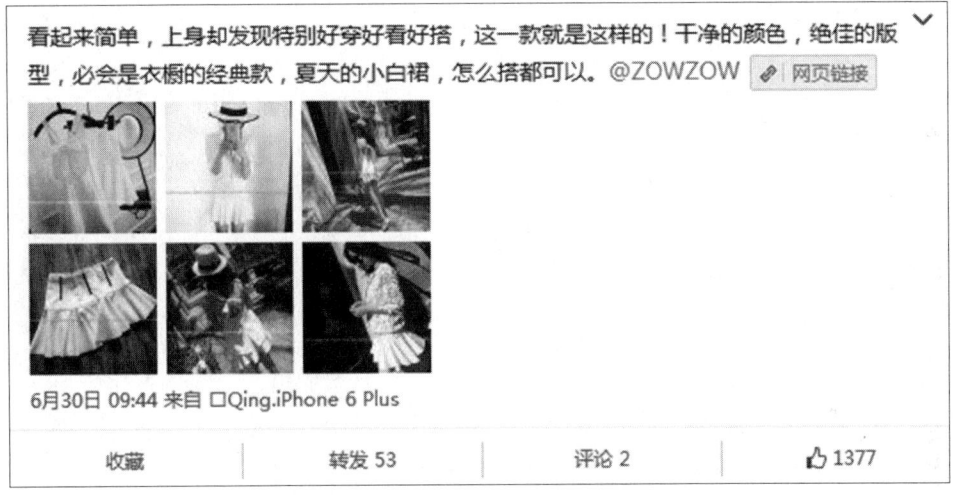

Fig. 5-4-6   Micro-blog Promotion

Internet platforms with huge information flows provide huge opportunities, but popularising your products is not that simple. A good promotional article can reach thousands of viewers and add thousands of clicks to your store. However, such articles are rare, and most drop like stones into the sea. If you want to promote well and attract customers to your shop, you need experience and continuous innovation.

Summary

Have you learned all the ways of marketing? Let's review!

1. Advertisement
  - Window displays
  - In-shop promotion
2. Discounts
  - Discount on consumption
  - Coupons
  - Deadline discounts
3. Evaluation management
4. Other platform promotion

Chapter 6

6.1 "Attract" Customers Through Good Pre-service

In this section, you will …
- ✓ Learn the necessary skills to become a shopping guide
- ✓ Learn all kinds of "tips" for communicating with customers before sales.

Say you like an item online, you look at the information and hope to communicate with the seller through a chat tool for further details. But the seller is slow to respond or gives you an irrelevant answer. In this situation, you will probably give up talking with the seller turn to other products because of their unprofessional and insincere attitude. So if you want to retain customers, you must first become a qualified shopping guide. Now let's talk about how to qualify as a shopping guide.

Do a good job with pre-service to "attract" customers

In fact, when buying goods on an online store, many buyers like to have a "friendly" exchange with the seller to inquire about other details, delivery fees, and rules for cancelling the order. For example, the buyer below is consulting the seller on which size clothes will fit his height.

Fig. 6-1-1

Then the problem is: when you become a seller and your customers consult you before buying, how do you respond professionally and enthusiastically? Here are some tips:

Mastering skills to communicate with customers

1. Listen carefully and judge accurately

When a customer consults you, do not be so anxious to rush to respond to his or her questions. First, be patient and listen to the question and understand the customer's needs. Does he want to buy something for himself, or is he looking for a gift to give to his friend? Then clarify the problem. Is he worried about the size? Or that what he has bought cannot be delivered on time? Does he have any special requirements? All of these are possible questions and as a seller, you have to be able to answer them.

2. Prompt and professional reply

The seller cannot ignore the customer's problems but must reply to them quickly. Be sure to respond positively, quickly and professionally. In this competitive market, customers don't like to wait. Think of yourself as your customer, aren't you always a little impatient when waiting.

The communication between the customer and the seller often starts from the fact the seller is online, so, as a seller, you must give the customer a positive signal—"Yes, sweetie! I'm here! Got any questions? Shoot!" Of course, sellers can't communicate with customers in front of the computer all day. If the seller is off the line or cannot reply immediately, in Ali Wangwang he can choose from one of the default statuses provided (Fig. 6-1-2), edit his own online status (Fig. 6-1-3), or edit an automatic reply (Fig. 6-1-4), telling the customer that he is unable to respond immediately to the customer's questions, and ask their forgiveness. This politeness will not cause customer dissatisfaction, but remember to reply to the customer's message as quickly as possible when you can.

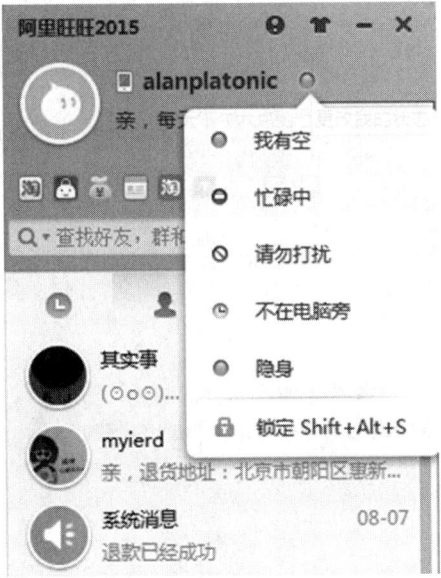

Fig. 6-1-2   Choose Different Online Status

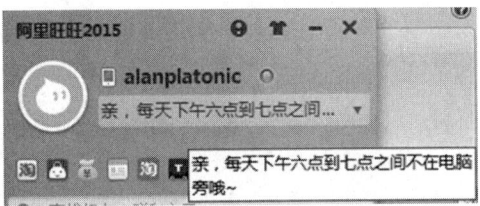

Fig. 6-1-3   Edit Personality Signature

At the bottom of the Ali Wangwang page, select the second button "System Setup" as shown in the chart below. After entering the system setup, select "Chat Setup", click "Automatic Reply and Short Message" button, and then edit this automatic reply and short message. The use of this will be described in the after-sale service section of this chapter.

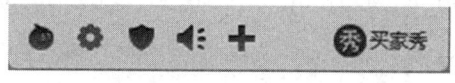

System Setup

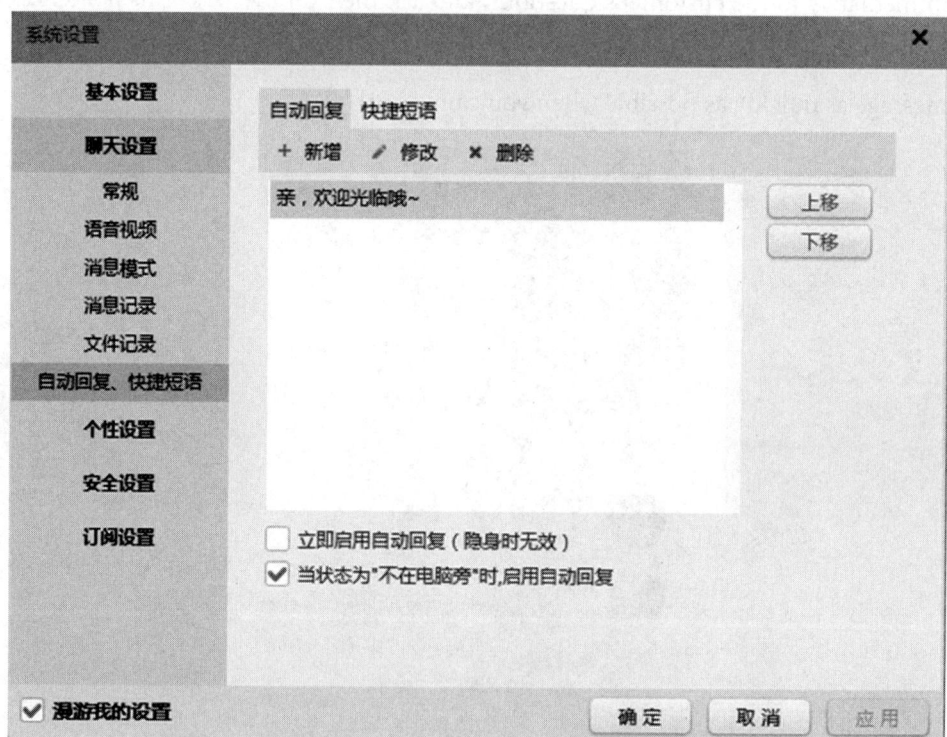

Fig. 6-1-4 Edit the Automatic "Not at the Computer" Reply

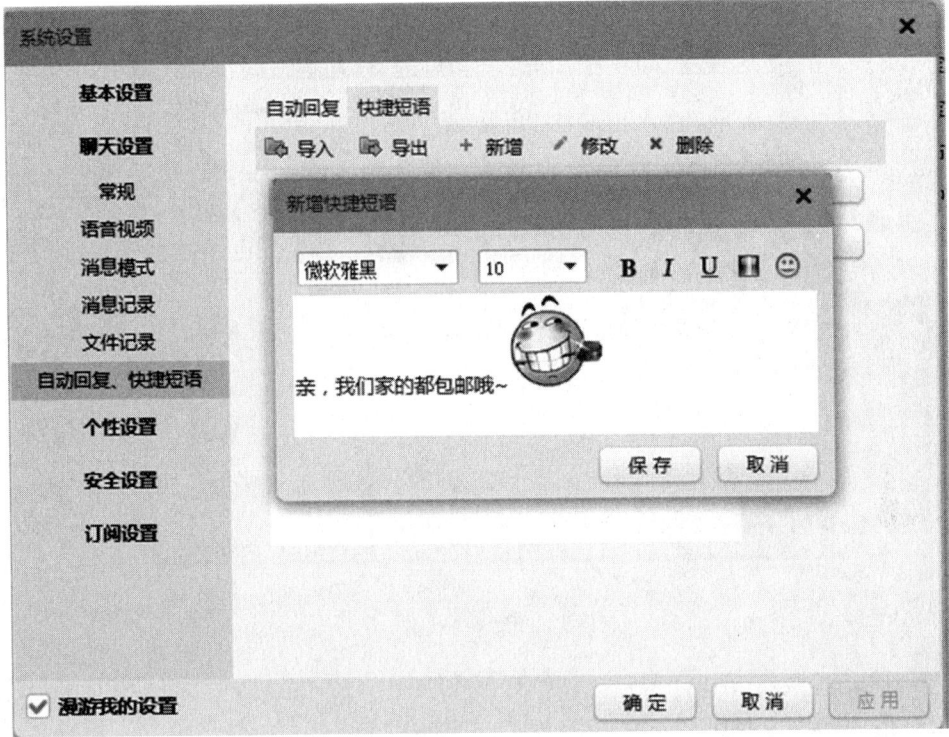

Fig. 6-1-5 New Short and Instant Message

3. Polite communication and understanding

Polite expressions in online communication, such as "please", are essential. On Taobao, one greeting commonly used by sellers is "hello, dear!". Ali Wangwang also provides users with a lot of emojis, which can make communication more natural and friendly and all sellers try to use them (see Fig. 6-1-6). Of course, in the communication process, the seller should make appropriate answers or recommendations by assuming the customer's point of view, which will have the customer feel that the seller is very considerate, facilitating the completion of the transaction.

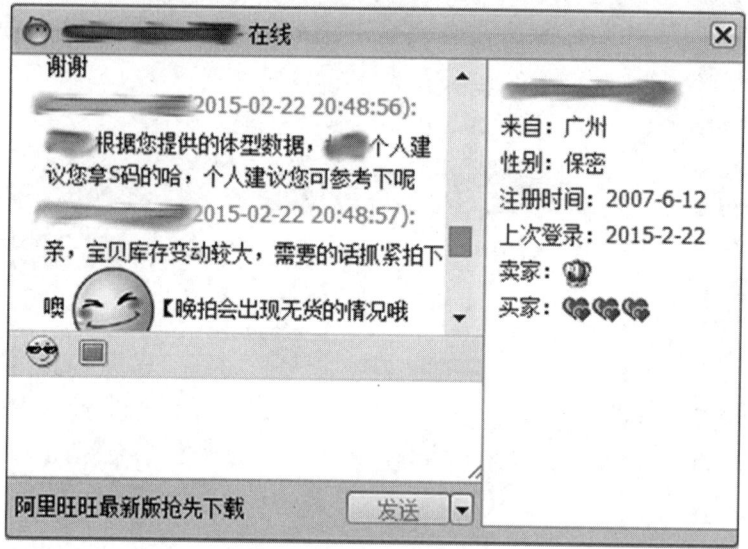

Fig. 6-1-6

4. Honest business and frank with customers

Whether online or offline, honesty and trustworthiness are very important criteria for doing business. Sellers must be honest with their customers. No goods are 100% perfect, so do not hesitate to explain to customers the shortcomings of your goods or the limitations of their use. Complete information can better help customers to make the right purchase. (You should provide information on material, model, what other customers think it is suitable for, the method of use, precautions, washing requirements, stock volume, inventory replenishment time, related goods... are you aware of these?) If a customer thinks that the seller is honest and reliable, he will buy something from him. Clinching the deal and winning trust depends on integrity and credit.

Introduce goods professionally and objectively

Before buying, customers always have questions. In addition to the necessary communication skills mentioned above, as a seller, you should be able to professionally and objectively introduce all the goods in your store to your customers. Take a piece of clothing as an example:

```
产品参数：

主图来源：自主实拍图        货号：53140201         品牌：here/所在
厚薄：常规款               风格：通勤              通勤：淑女
款式：套头                组合形式：单件           衣长：中长款
袖长：七分袖              领子：圆领              图案：纯色
毛线粗细：常规毛线         面料：棉               面料主材质含量：30%及以下
适用年龄：25-29周岁       年份/季节：2014年冬季    颜色分类：绿色 橘红
尺码：S M L
```

Fig. 6-1-7　Description

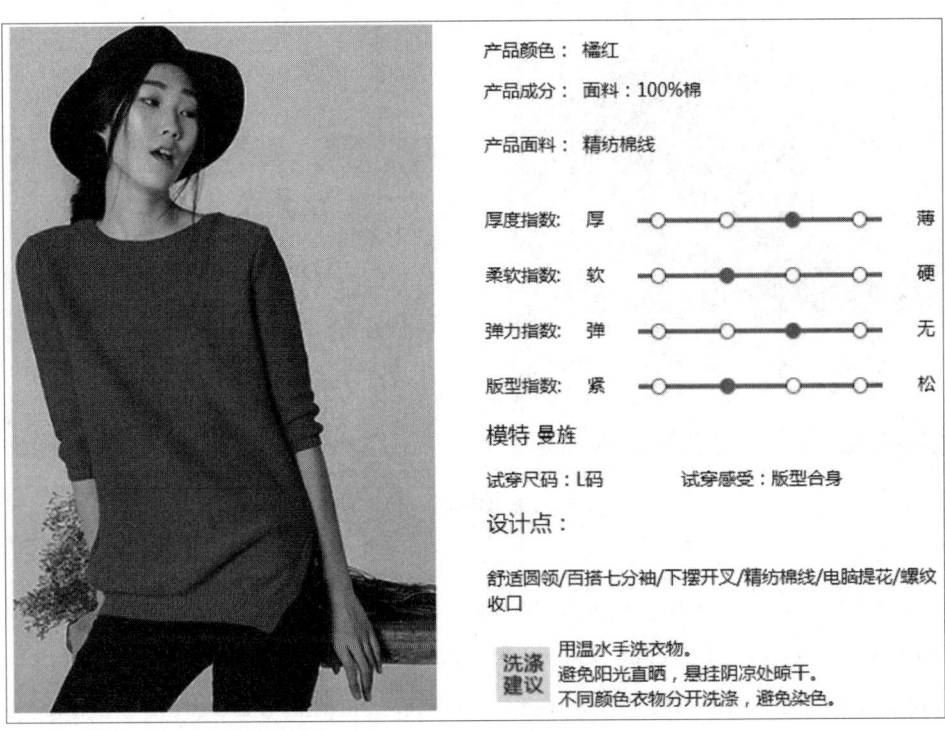

Fig. 6-1-8　Graphic and Description

尺码	身长	胸围	摆围	肩宽	袖长	袖肥	袖口
S	69.5	96	74	37	40	25.2	16
M	71.5	100	78	38.5	41	26.2	17
L	73.5	104	82	40	42	27.2	18
-	-	-	-	-	-	-	-

由于尺码是纯手工测量所以难免存在1CM-3CM误差,请亲们谅解。

Fig. 6-1-9　Details of the Size

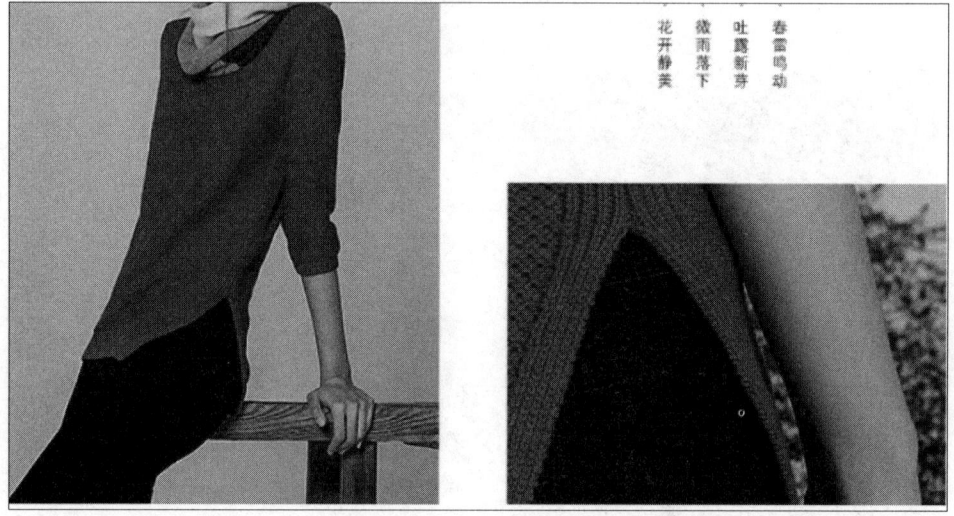

Fig. 6-1-10　Display of Details

  Even with so many graphic presentations, customers may still be worried and have to talk to the seller so they can rest assured. Sometimes a customer does not feel that information is missing from a page, but that there is too much to go though, so they think it is better to talk to the seller to get to the point. Then it is necessary that the seller can introduce the characteristics of the products concisely and in such a way as to impress the customers.

  To describe the product objectively, we must know the advantages and disadvantages of the commodity well. If you only say that your goods are perfect, you will cause your customers to be be suspicious or leave them feeling fooled. On the other hand, no seller should be willing to constantly talk about the shortcomings of their goods. Presenting a commodity in all aspects can really help a customer, while it also shows that you are honest and attach importance to good faith. Below are several ways you can understand the advantages and disadvantages of the products.

- Make queries to the suppliers and wholesalers
- Use, wear or eat for yourself
- Ask other more experienced seller of the same commodity
- Collect user evaluations

To describe commodities professionally, we must first have some professional qualities and a thorough understanding of the products.

A seller's professionalism includes the polite language and communication skills we mentioned above. After a customer places an order, a seller should immediately confirm with the customer the type, size, quantity, price, the address of the consignee, best contact method and other information in order to avoid problems; after shipping they should instantly notify the customer.

Other circumstances

If there are problems that customers frequently ask about, it is suggested that sellers put together a complilation that can be referred to so that they do not have to give customers one to one advice, such is the practice of the following two stores.

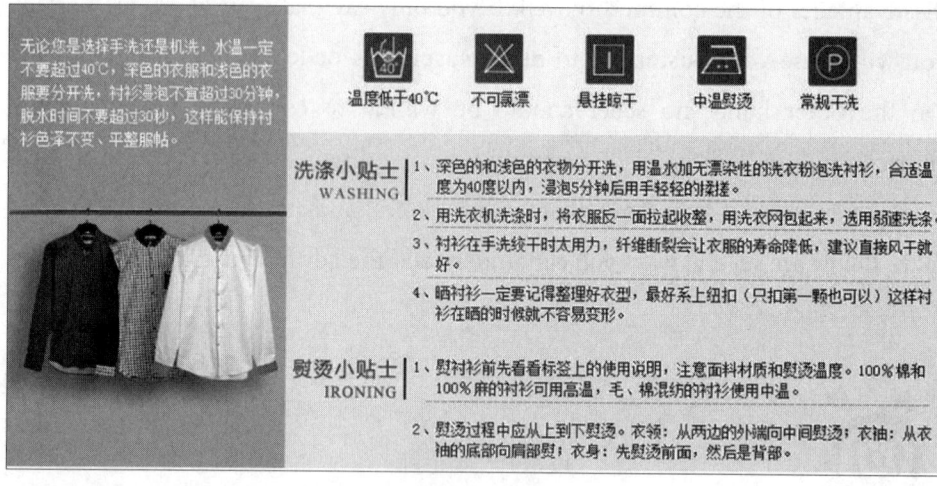

Fig. 6-1-11　Tips for Washing and Ironing from Hlamall.cn

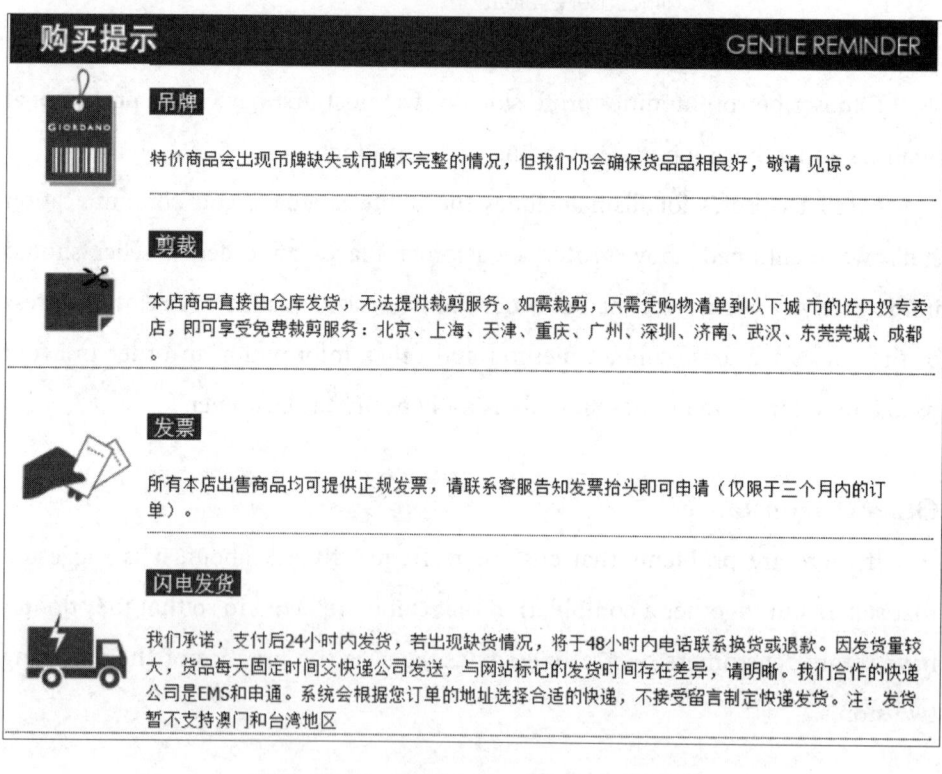

Fig. 6-1-12　Purchasing at Giordano Tips

Goods delivery notice during holidays or for advance sales. At present, pre-sale goods are often not delivered in time, and the same goes for during holidays. If this happens, the store must also explain it on the shop's homepage to reduce questions from customers.

Fig. 6-1-13 Notice of Pre-sale

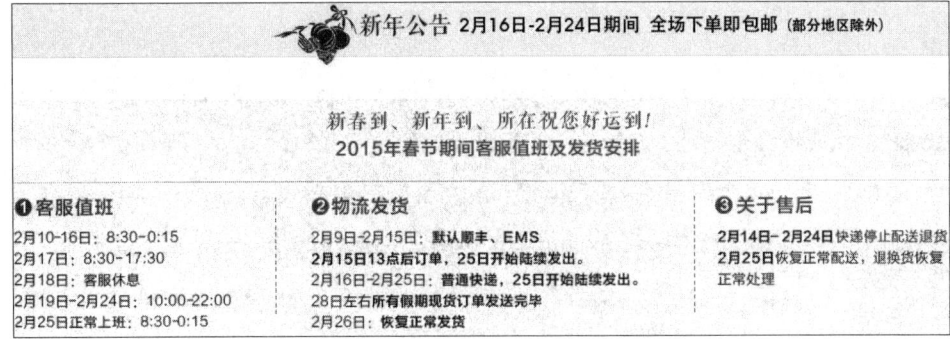

Fig. 6-1-14 Holiday Delivery Notice

How much do you know about the above pre-sale service skills? This book only presents a general rather than a detailed introduction, so sellers need to explore and supplement them in their practice.

Summary

1. Tips for communicating with customers

- Listen carefully and judge accurately
- Reply instantly and professionally
- Talk politely and show understanding

- Be honest in business and frank with customers

2. Professional and objective introduction of goods

- Professionally written descriptions, page graphics, a detailed photo gallery, etc
- Objective and honest description of goods, no exaggeration, no concealment of defects and limitations

3. Others (Bulletin, notice, etc)

6.2 Do Business!

In this section, you will …

✓ Learn the complete process of commodity trading

In this section, we will show you a transaction end to end to help you understand and grasp the process on Taobao.

First, a buyer may find your goods in a variety of the ways Taobao offers, click at the Ali Wangwang dialog box and talk to you. The situation may go like this:

Fig. 6-2-1

After careful questioning and consideration, the buyer decides to buy a product. So, a deal has begun!

Step 1: Receive a cue

After a buyer has decided to buy the products, the seller will receive a notification from Ali Wangwang. To receive this transaction notification in good time, we suggest that sellers should be online or near their computer or mobile device at all times.

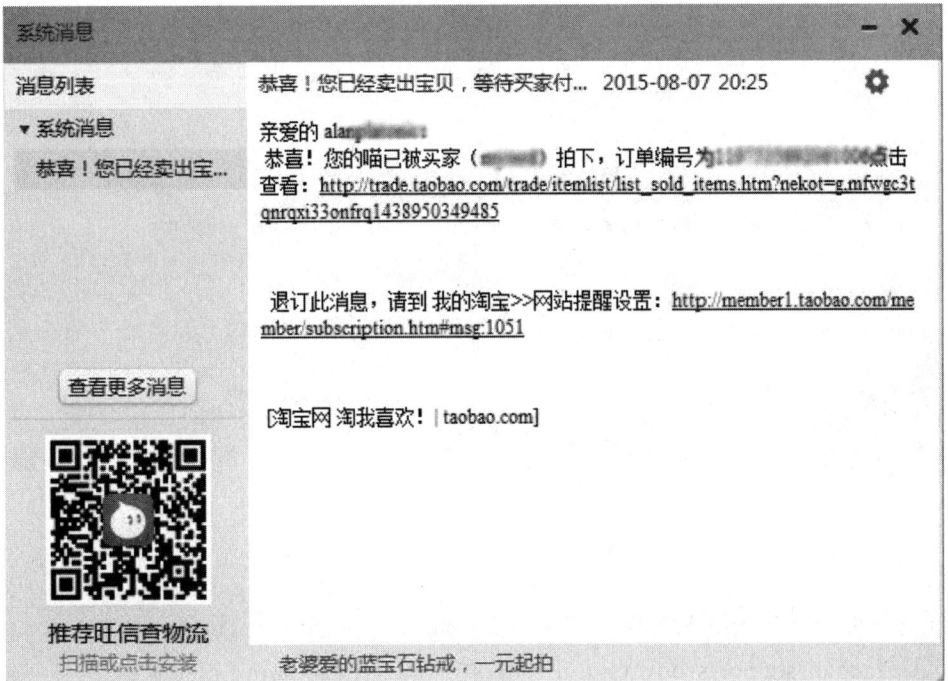

Fig. 6-2-2

Step 2: Check the order

Click on the first link in the above chart to enter the Seller Center for further actions. Of course, in order to ensure security, the webpage will require the user to go through verification (Figure 6-2-3).

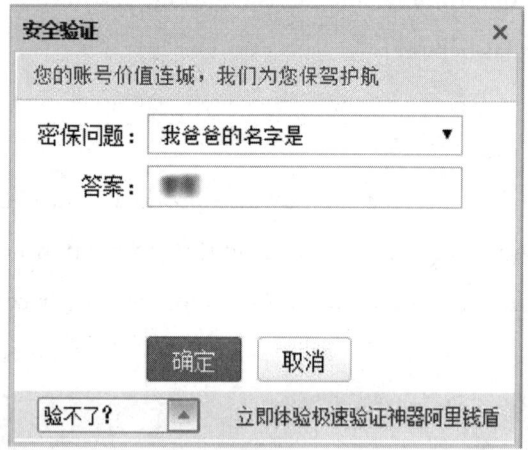

Fig. 6-2-3

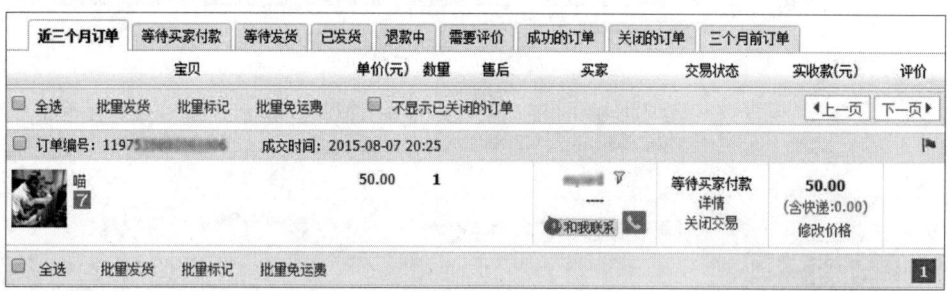

Fig. 6-2-4

Step 3: Modify price

Taobao supports buyers and sellers in their negotiating of prices. Prior to payment a seller can modify the marked price after the buyer has decided to buy it. If you do not need to modify the price, and the shipping template (described below) has been saved, this operation can be skipped.

The following is a case offering 6% off for buyers:

In figure 6-2-5 below, we can see the "Modify Price" option. Click on it, fill in the discount and "Shipping Fee" ("Free Delivery" is zero RMB), save and return. When you return to the order page, you will see a change in the price column

(Figure 6-2-6).

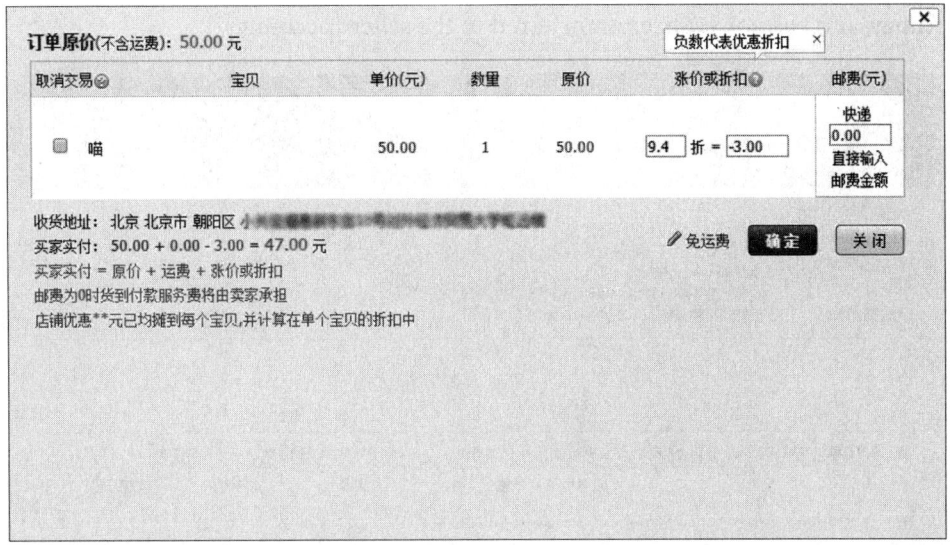

Fig. 6-2-5

Fig. 6-2-6

Step 4: Wait for buyer to pay

After this, the seller has to wait for the buyer to pay. This can be a long or short wait, but luckily the seller here had a highly efficient buyer who made their payment instantly.

After payment Ali Wangwang will notify the seller immediately and remind them to dispatch the goods promptly (Fig. 6-2-7).

If you refresh the order page at this time, you will find the "Transaction Status" has changed, from "Waiting for Buyer's Payment" in Figure 6-2-6 to the red-coloured "Buyer Has Paid". (Note: the buyer's payment is currently held with Alipay, and has not yet been transferred to the seller's account.)

Fig. 6-2-7

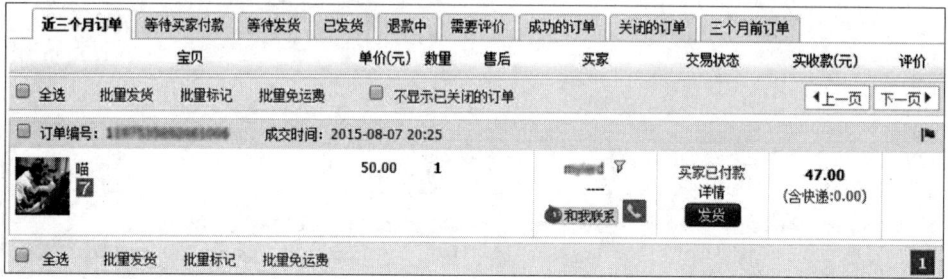

Fig. 6-2-8

Step 5: Seller delivers goods

Once the buyer pays, the transaction will enter the delivery stage. When the seller dispatches the goods, he needs to return to the order page, click the "Delivery" button and fill in the corresponding information.

1. Confirm receipt information and details of the transaction

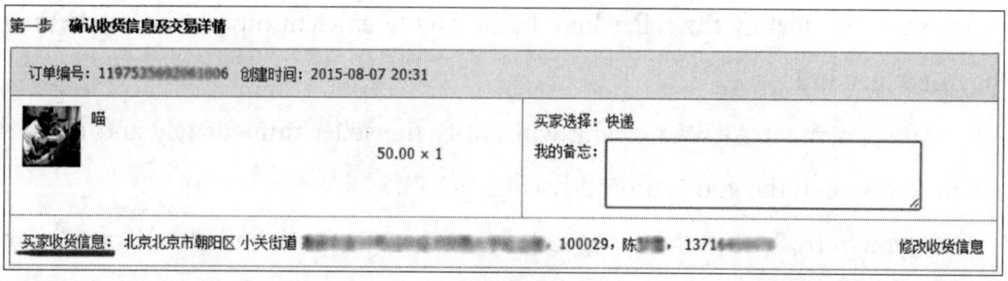

Fig. 6-2-9

2. Confirm dispatch/return of goods information

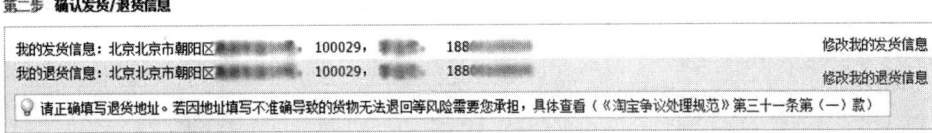

Fig. 6-2-10

3. Select logistics services

Taobao.com provides the seller with three delivery options: the first is the seller's online order and express delivery to the door (Fig. 6-2-11); the second needs the seller to contact the delivery company himself and input the shipment number after dispatch (Fig. 6-2-12); and the third is used for goods that do not need to be delivered (such as virtual products). The seller can simply click "Confirmation" (Fig.e 6-2-13).

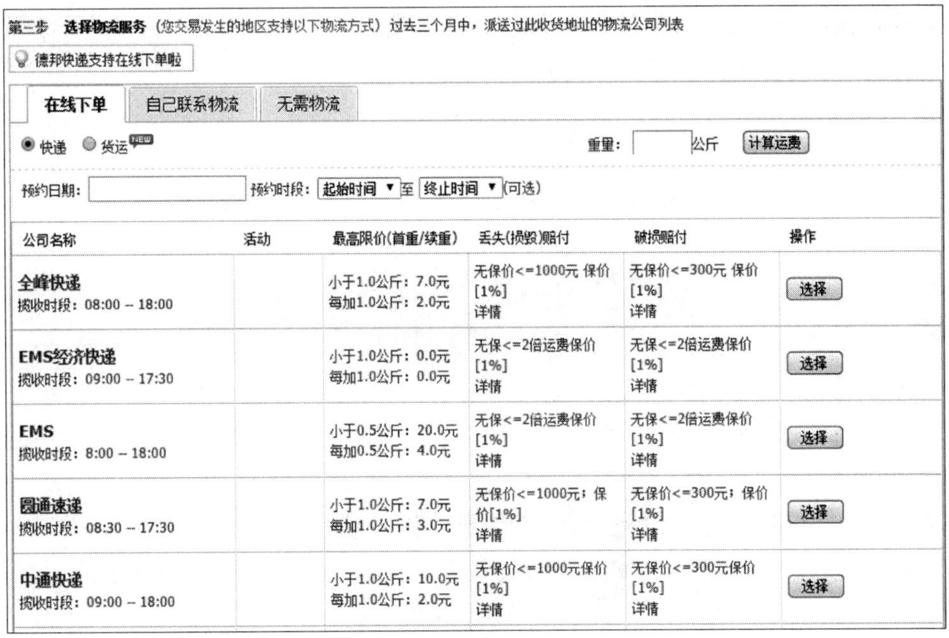

Fig. 6-2-11

Fig. 6-2-12

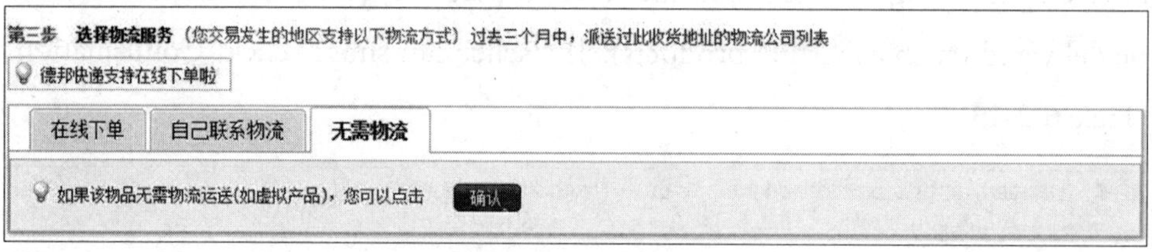

Fig. 6-2-13

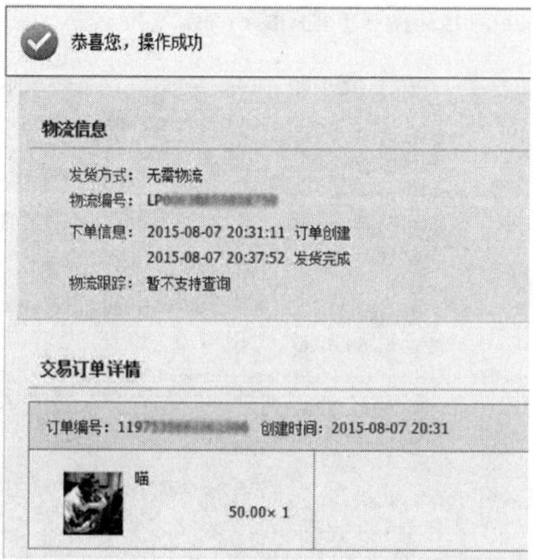

Fig. 6-2-14

At this point, the delivery operation is over. You can see the web prompt as shown in Figure 6-2-14. Return to the order page and you will find that the "Transaction Status" has changed again to "Seller Has Dispatched the Goods" (Figure 6-2-15).

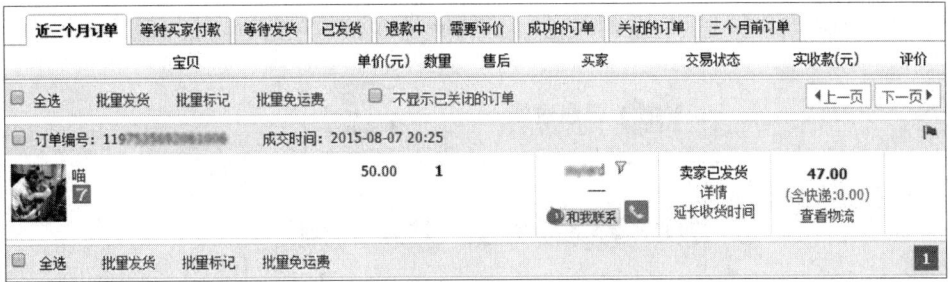

Fig. 6-2-15

More Information on Logistics Selection

1. Postal transportation

Postal transportation can be divided into standard parcel, express parcel and EMS.

• Standard—this is economical and practical. The geographical area covered is widest, though the delivery time is relatively long, usually more than 7 days. This long service time not only affects customer satisfaction, but also the rate of income.

• Express package—the cost is slightly higher than the standard option. It is suitable for customers to have a time requirement for their goods or who live outside normal delivery zones. It should be noted that sometimes express delivery is no faster than standard. So the choice should be made carefully.

• EMS — this is a special courier service provided by China Post. Items usually arrive in 4 days. It has a short delivery time and high cost.

2. Ordinary express

STO, ZTO, YTO and Yundaex are China's main express companies. We would like to give you a brief introduction to these companies.

• STO

Basically covers cities above the prefectural level as well as cities above the county level in developed regions, especially in Jiangsu, Zhejiang and Shanghai. It covers nearly every part of the country.

• YTO

Their range of services covers more than 1,600 cities, including more than 200 countries and regions around the world (Hong Kong, Macao and Taiwan included), and its air transportation covers more than 70 cities.

Its business covers all the cities, counties, townships in 31 provinces, autonomous regions and municipalities directly under the central government, and it has more than 45,000 outlets.

• ZTO

Their service includes domestic express, international express, logistics delivery, warehousing, and more. They provide a "door to door" service and time frame delivery (arriving the next morning or the following day, etc.) service.

• Yundaex

Headquartered in Shanghai, China, the service covers 31 provinces autonomous regions, municipalities, and Hong Kong, Macao and Taiwan. Since 2013, it has carried out international express business cooperation with Japan, South Korea, the United States, Germany, Australia and other countries and regions, providing an express service for overseas consumers.

Step 6: Wait for the buyer to collect the goods

Now, the seller's work has come to an end, and the next step is to wait for the buyer to receive the goods. Generally speaking, after the delivery status is tracked to the buyer, the transaction between the buyer and the seller is over. Of course, if the buyer asks for a replacement, it's another matter (see the fourth section of this chapter).

As Taobao automatically tracks the logistics status, after it has confirmed the goods have been received by the buyer, if the buyer does not confirm receipt, within ten days Taobao will send the money to the seller's Alipay account. The seller can look at the "Transaction Details" page to find out how long it will be before they receive the buyer's money. Waiting is a process that many sellers have to experience.

However, this buyer is very cooperative. After receiving the goods, he confirmed it immediately.

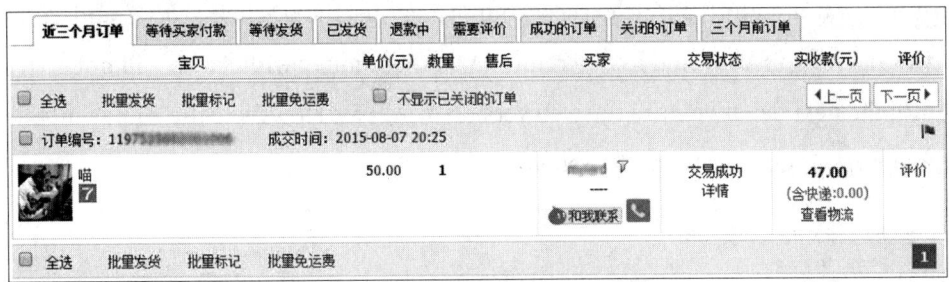

Fig. 6-2-16

Step 7: Check the payment

After the buyer confirms receipt, payment will be sent to the seller's Alipay account. The seller can look at his balance at the "Alipay Area" of the "Seller Centre" and withdraw cash to his account. Of course, if the seller does not need that money at the moment he can leave it in his Alipay account.

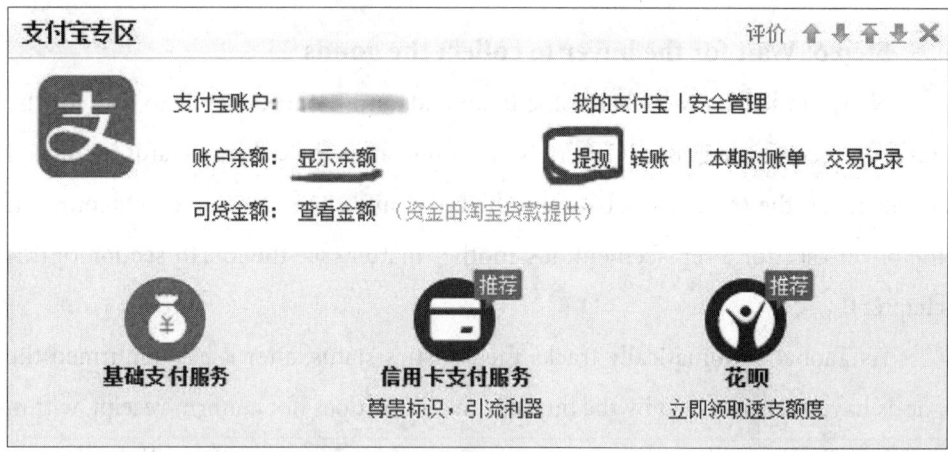

Fig. 6-2-17

After choosing to withdraw, enter the page shown in Figure 6-2-18, select the bank card you want to withdraw to, enter the withdrawal amount (note: the withdrawal amount cannot exceed your Alipay balance), click "Next" and enter your password. We would like to remind you that money withdrawn will not arrive until the next day if you use the web version of Alipay. However, the Alipay mobile phone app is quicker than the web version.

Fig. 6-2-18

Fig. 6-2-19

The complete transaction process is over. Do you think the steps are very simple? The goal for platform and application developers is for them to be simple and intuitive to use. So they are all very easy to master!

Summary

· A complete transaction process

Buyer places order — seller deals with non-paid order (optional) — buyer pays — seller dispatches goods — buyer acknowledges receipt of goods — seller receives payment — seller withdraws cash.

6.3 Evaluating Complaints

In this section you will learn …
- ✓ The transaction evaluation system on Taobao
- ✓ Factors affecting user evaluation
- ✓ Customer complaints and the rights of the seller

You will find some simple picture and text information displayed after your shop name. Click on them and you will enter a page containing detailed store and seller data. Where does the data come from? This section will give you the answer.

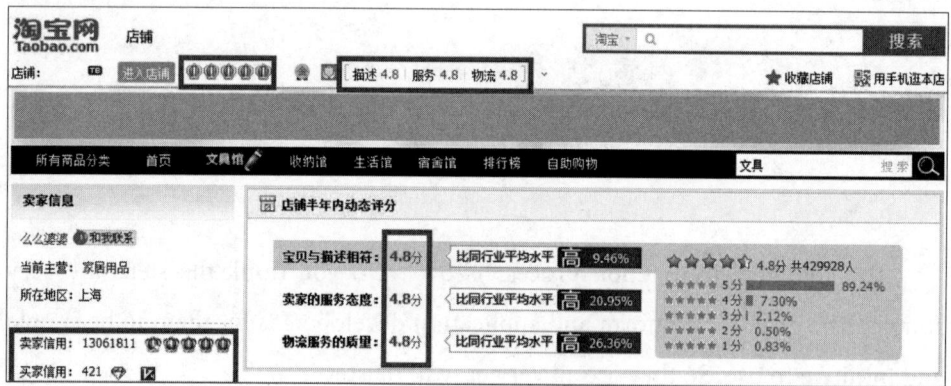

Fig. 6-3-1   Store Information Display Page

Transaction evaluation

In the previous section, we ran through the transaction process. After this process ends it continues to create value through the Taobao transaction evaluation system.

Transaction evaluation mainly includes two parts: credit evaluation and store rating. As shown in Fig. 6-3-2, the credit evaluation part is in the middle, and the shop rating is near the bottom.

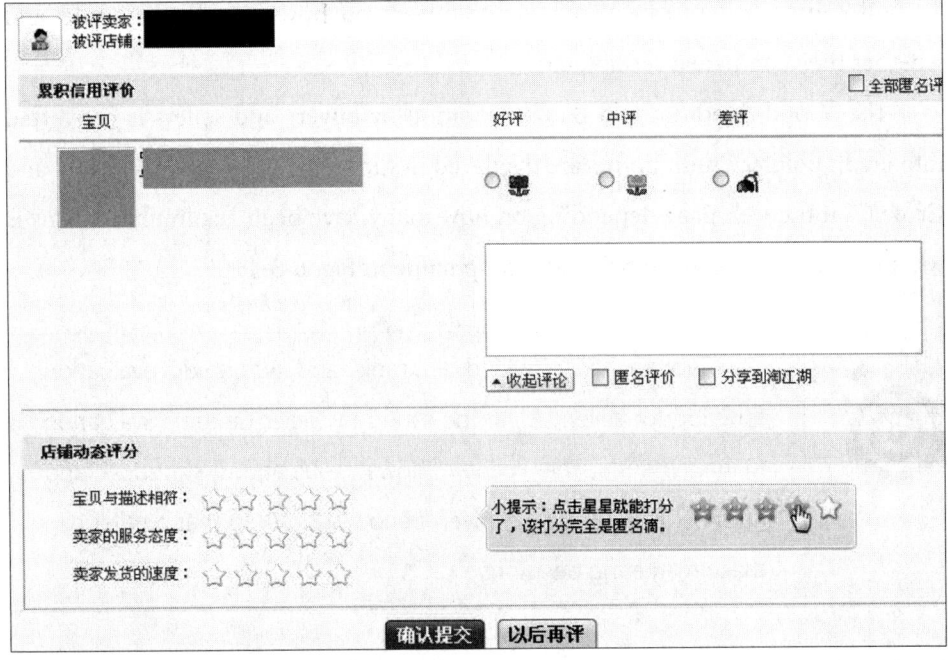

Fig. 6-3-2   Buyer Evaluation Interface

➤ Credit evaluation

After a transaction is completed, both parties have the right to evaluate each other's performance. The buyer can give good, medium and bad feedback for every item bought. The seller can do the same. This feedback is referred to as credit evaluation.

Evaluation given by buyers will be displayed on the merchandise "Baby Evaluation" page for reference by future customers. Fig. 6-3-3 is the customer's evaluation of the products we described in the previous section.

Fig. 6-3-3

Of course, sellers can also evaluate buyers on how quickly they paid and whether they confirmed receipt, etc.

The "Good, Medium and Bad" evaluation by buyers and sellers is converted into credit points. Credit points are displayed in the forms of "Heart, Diamond and Crown" on the web page depending on how many have been accumulated. This is what the five crowns mean below the shop name in Fig. 6-3-1.

> Taobao has provided a simple and automatic evaluation function for sellers. It can be found in "Seller Centre→Evaluation Management". The page shows evaluation statistics and comments written for a given period of time, so that a seller can make marketing decisions.

➢ Shop score

A buyer can evaluate a seller's shop in the following four aspects: consistency between the item and the description, the service attitude of the seller, the speed of the seller's delivery, and the service of the logistics company. The average score from all buyers over six consecutive months will constitute the shop score.

When shopping on Taobao, customers can not only see the score of each item in your store, but also compare it with an average of other similar stores.

店铺动态评分	与同行业相比	店铺动态评分	与同行业相比
描述相符 4.6 ⬇	低于 2.64%	描述相符 4.8 ⬆	高于 9.46%
服务态度 4.7 ⬇	低于 2.47%	服务态度 4.8 ⬆	高于 20.95%
物流服务 4.7 ⬇	低于 2.22%	物流服务 4.8 ⬆	高于 26.36%

Fig. 6-3-4

Store score and credit evaluation coexist. Although the contents of the two are different, they provide more reference value for buyers. At the same time, as a seller, it can provide the impetus to improve your store.

Influencing factors of user's evaluation

Before summarising the factors affecting evaluation, please first see the following three comments on the same commodity:

包包收到了，质量一如既往的好，这款书包看着秀气实际很能装的，所有东西装进去还是有很大的空间。不管是五金还是做工还是颜色都是很完美的，同事都说这个颜色很特别很好看，包装都很细心贴心还送了同色小钱包，32个大大的赞，棒棒哒！

Fig. 6-3-5

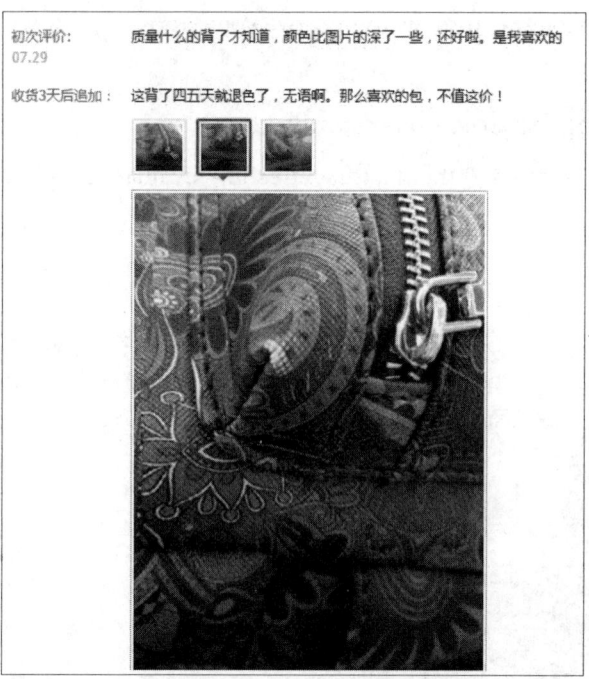

Fig. 6-3-6

Fig. 6-3-7

After reading the comments, consider why there is such a great difference between comments on the same product? What does it mean?

Based on the previously mentioned transaction evaluation dimension, we will analyse three simple aspects:

1. Quality of goods

You can see the buyer in Fig. 6-3-6 is complaining about the bag losing colour. The evaluation page for this item does not lack complaints about this particular problem. This reflects not only the quality of the goods, but also that the seller is not honest.

Online shoppers can only get the information they want by browsing pictures, communicating with a seller, or reading reviews, as they are not able to touch the real goods. But customers will eventually come into contact with the real objects. Any counterfeit or inferior goods will be exposed through "Poor Evaluation" and the credit of the shop will also be exponentially undermined.

Therefore, to be a conscientious seller is quite important. Make sure to provide full and accurate information; before dispatching goods ensure that they do not have quality problems; pack them carefully to prevent unnecessary damage in transit—assure buyers of the quality of the goods and your service.

2. Service attitude

In Figure 6-3-7, the buyer's complaints about service attitude are incisive. In the first and fourth sections of this chapter we emphasised the importance of service attitude, because a lot of bad reviews come due to mistakes here. Not replying to the buyer for a long time, indifferent and absent-minded responses full of lame arguments, shirking responsibility, stalling, or even replying with strong emotions—all are irresponsible behaviour to a customer.

3. Logistics service

In Fig. 6-3-2 and Fig. 6-3-4 of this section, we can see that logistics service is also an important part of store evaluation. If goods have been paid for but are dispatched slowly, or logistics transportation is so slow that half a month passes before the goods are received, any good feelings a buyer will have had toward the store will have faded leaving irritation. Therefore, logistics is sometimes the cause of poor evaluation. A seller can cooperate with a number of logistics companies to ensure the speed of delivery and the safety of the package. Also, he can consult buyers on which logistics they prefer.

Customer complaint

Most of the buyers and sellers on Taobao are rational and reasonable people, and customers who complain about them are few, but there is still the need to say something about customer complaints.

If a buyer lodges a complaint, the seller should not panic but work to find out what has caused it. If the seller is wrong, he should admit the mistake and also immediately propose a reasonable solution that can persuade the buyer to revoke their complaint; if communication is fruitless and the buyer insists on the complaint even though it is not your fault, the seller should not worry either, as Taobao has a complaint mechanism which can, supplemented by manual services, help solve the problem.

Seller's rights

Enter the "Seller Help" page and you will find various services for the seller on the left navigation bar such as "Appeals Guide", "Complaint Punishment", "Consumer Protection Special Zone" and so on. The right side also has links to ways to solve common problems. In Fig. 6-3-9, you can also see the various self-help tools provided by Taobao to maintain the rights of the seller. Of course, we hope that the rights and interests of sellers can be effectively guaranteed from beginning to end, so that they do not need to use them to safeguard their rights.

Fig. 6-3-8

Fig. 6-3-9

Summary

- Transaction evaluation is divided into credit evaluation and store score
- Three factors affect buyer evaluation: commodity quality, service attitude and logistics service
- Customer's complaints and the rights of the seller

6.4 Provide Considerate After-sale Service

In this section, you will get to know …
✓ How to deal with the most common problem for rejected goods
✓ How to deal with after-sale problems and provide the best after-sales service

After-sales service is as important as the quality of the goods and the reputation of the seller. The best after-sales service can win praise and popularity for the seller, building a good reputation and maintaining customer relationships. After-sales service is a skill that sellers must master. Now, we will introduce several kinds of after-sales service and some skills to provide intimate after-sales service.

Advisory after-sales service—customers have problems!

When using new or special products, customers will inevitably face some problems. For example, the customer in the following chart bought a brand new pair of pants for the first time, which he found to be very smelly. He consulted the seller and the reply the seller gave is as follows (see Fig.6-4-1 below).

If you were the buyer, would you be satisfied with such a reply? If you were the seller, would you give a different answer?

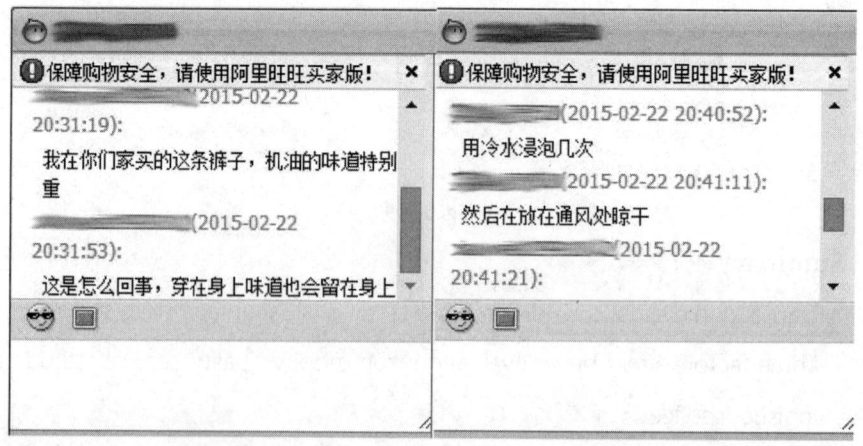

Fig. 6-4-1

When encountering after-sale problems, a seller should follow the dos and don'ts of pre-sales service that we mentioned in the first section of this chapter— be patient, try to thoroughly understand where the customer's problem is coming from, and provide a good solution. In this communication process, it is very necessary to listen carefully, use polite expressions and exhibit professionalism. If a seller can look at a problem from the perspective of the buyer, it will be much easier to solve.

One of my friends had encountered such a thing. He did after-sales work at a laptop computer accessories shop. One day, a customer bought a laptop computer anti-dust sheet. The sheet attached under the laptop with magnets to prevent excessive dust from being sucked in through the fan. However, later the customer came back to say she couldn't use it because the bottom of her computer was not magnetic, so asked if she could return it. Although this is an after-sales problem, it shows unprofessionalism in the pre-sale. There may be many unexpected aspects in a transaction process that the seller knows but a buyer may not think of. No matter on the webpage or in a private chat with a customer, we must make sure to clearly explain any special characteristics or requirements.

Insist on exchanging or returning goods!

When customers receive goods that don't meet their expectations either due to a quality problem or just that they aren't suitable, they'll usually ask to exchange or return them. No matter what the reasons may be, they must be verified according to the process for the platform.

On Taobao users can choose three kinds of after-sales service: refund only, refund and return of goods, and exchange.

We will briefly explain the application and procedures for these three types of after-sales service.

1. Refund only

· Application condition: the buyer has not received the goods, or the buyer has received the goods and has agreed with the seller they will not return the goods but will receive a refund.

· The following pictures show the buyer we mentioned in the previous section who had bought an item.

After repeated inspection of the commodity, he found a slight flaw and after consulting with the seller filed an after-sales application and was refunded 5 RMB.

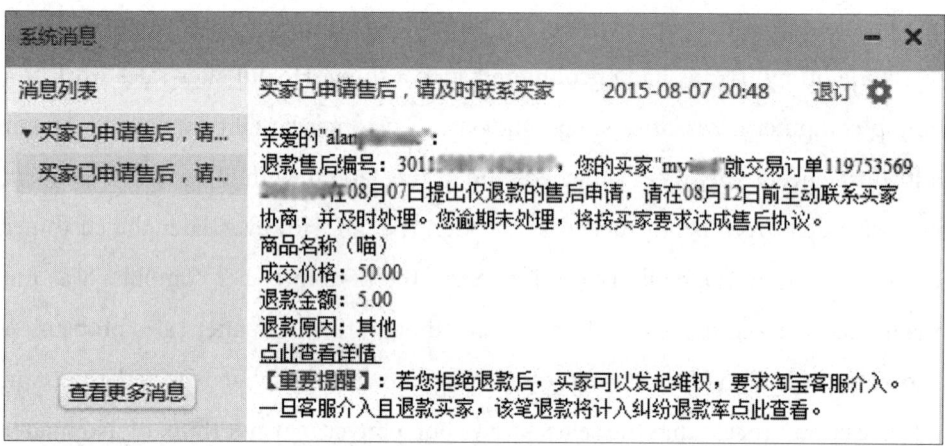

Fig. 6-4-2   System Message—Buyer Files an After-sale Application

Once a buyer sends an after-sales application the seller's Ali Wangwang will send notification of a new message. If the seller does not log in to Ali Wangwang, he can also see the message in the seller center message center.

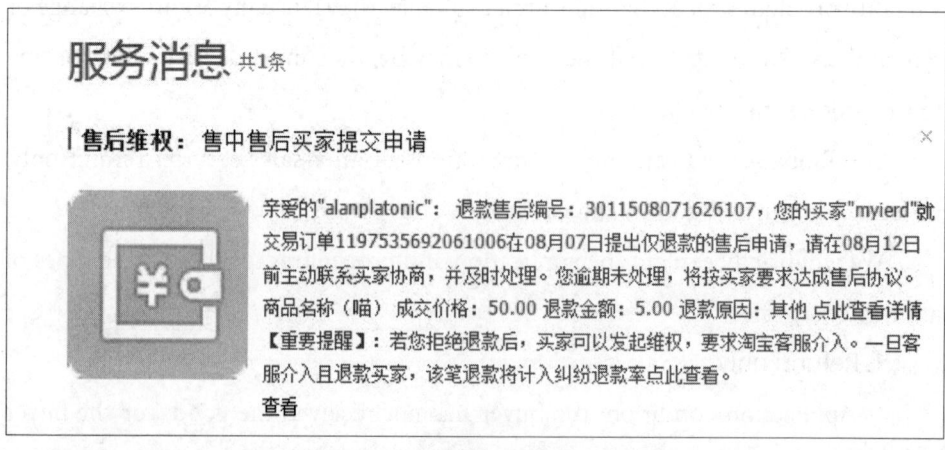

Fig. 6-4-3   Webpage Message Centre

After seeing the notification the seller can click the message to enter the after-sales page as shown in Fig. 6-4-4.

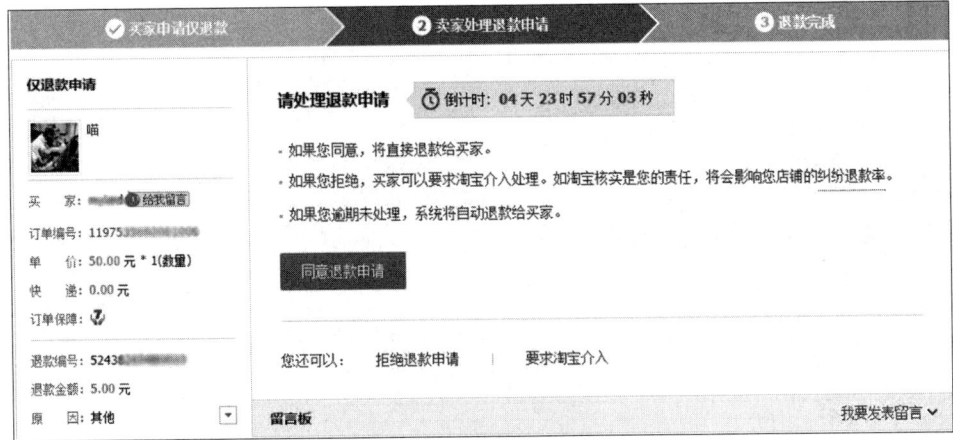

Fig. 6-4-4　Seller Deals with a Refund Application

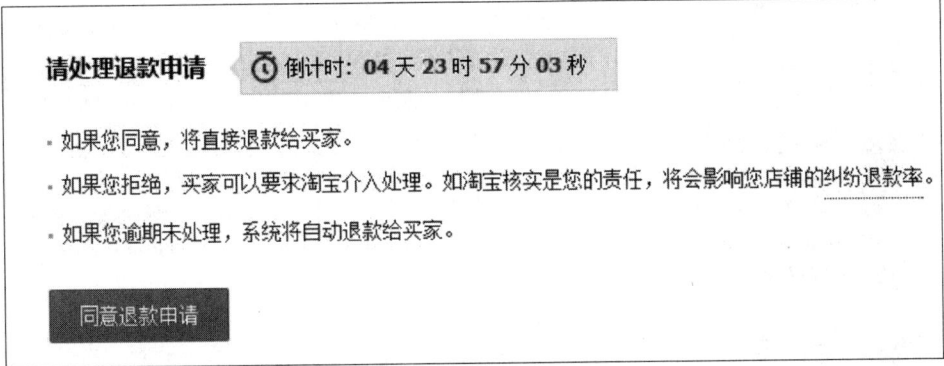

Fig. 6-4-5　Refund Countdown

Since buyers usually apply for refund after they have reached an agreement with the seller, sellers often choose "Agree to Refund Application". Of course, the seller can "Refuse Refund Application", or "Ask Taobao to Intervene" in the dispute, but things will become more troublesome and require further consultation between the two parties, or even the help of a third party in addition to Taobao.

In our case, the seller agreed to refund the payment, so he can simply enter his password as shown in Fig. 6-4-6.

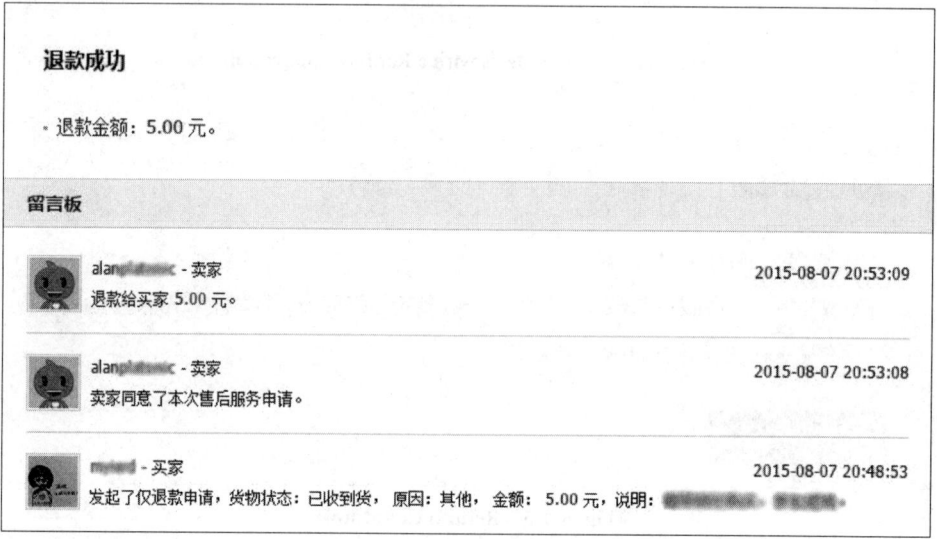

Fig. 6-4-6　Enter Your Password to Refund

Fig. 6-4-7　Refund Success

2. Refund and return of goods

・Application conditions: If the quality of the commodity is questioned or the customer does not want the item and has reached an agreement with the seller to return goods, the buyer can choose this option.

・Return process: Buyer applies to make a return→seller sends the return address to the buyer→buyer returns the goods and fills in the logistics information → seller checks the logistics, confirms receipt and issues the refund.

There is a difference between "Refund and Return of Goods" and "Refund Only"—the former requires the buyer to send the goods back to the seller. After the seller agrees to the "Refund and Return of Goods" application, the buyer has 7 days to send the goods back through a logistics company; after that time limit, the after-sales service will automatically close. The seller needs to receive the goods returned by the buyer and check them before refunding the money. If this kind of application is made, the seller must communicate with the buyer to set up a a time to return the goods in order to avoid exceeding the prescribed period; the seller should also carefully check the returned goods before issuing the refund.

3. Exchange

· Application conditions: Buyers have bought goods unsuitable in terms of size, colour, style, etc., then they can negotiate with the seller over an exchange and file an "Exchange of Goods" application. (The buyer must be very careful in choosing the replacement to avoid making a mistake again)

· Procedure for exchange: buyer applies for exchange → seller sends the return address to the buyer→buyer returns the goods and seller dispatches the replacement after receiving the unwanted item(s) → buyer confirms receipt of the replacement goods→buyer confirms the exchange as complete online.

◆ Note: The replacement process does not involve refunds.

In addition, since the exchange of merchandise requires sending things back, here are some tips for sellers:

In Ali Wangwang, many smart messages can be set, which we demonstrated in the first section. In order to facilitate customer service communication between seller and buyer, sellers can include return address and contact information into instant messages and send them when needed. The following is an image of this in use.

Logistics cost for returning or exchanging goods

Most online shopping platforms have a complete set of rules for returning and replacing goods, such as the unconditional return of goods within a certain number of days on Taobao. Sellers will also state their commitment to various services (Fig. 6-4-8). But the refund or return of goods often involves delivery fees. Who should bear responsibility for delivery fees? Taobao has the following guidelines:

Who Should Pay the Delivery Fee for Goods Returned or Replaced?

On the issue of express fees of return or replacement of goods, it is suggested that both sides consult each other to decide who will pay. If the two sides cannot reach an agreement, they will have to state their opinions and reason for the refund and upload valid evidence to the refund page (such as photos showing flaws, screenshots from Ali Wangwang, etc.). One of party can click on the "Request Taobao's Intervention" button to apply for mediation by customer service. This will take place within the required period.

If the desire to return the goods by the buyer was caused by the seller, the seller should bear the delivery cost. But if the seller says that he should not have to bear the costs, then the platform has the right to mete out a punishment; if it is not the seller's fault, the cost can be paid in the following ways:

Where product quality problems and the goods and descriptions are not consistent, the seller will bear the responsibility.

Where goods can be "Returned within Seven Days", if the return of goods was caused personal problems of the buyer's, the seller is responsible for sending the goods, while return costs should be covered by the buyer; if the purchase does not include delivery costs, the buyer pays both the delivery and return costs.

If the return is initiated by the buyer because of personal reasons:

The seller is responsible for sending the goods, while the cost of returning the goods shall be assumed by the return promise;

If the purchase does not include delivery costs, the delivery and return costs shall be based on the return promise.

When there is no "Return within Seven Days" or "Return Promise", and if the return of goods is initiated because of the buyer personal reasons:

The seller agrees to the buyer's request to returning the goods without question. The buyer is responsible for the return cost, regardless of whether or not cost is included in the purchase. But if the buyer objects to the cost, the seller should cooperate by providing evidence of this cost (such as an invoice from the courier company).

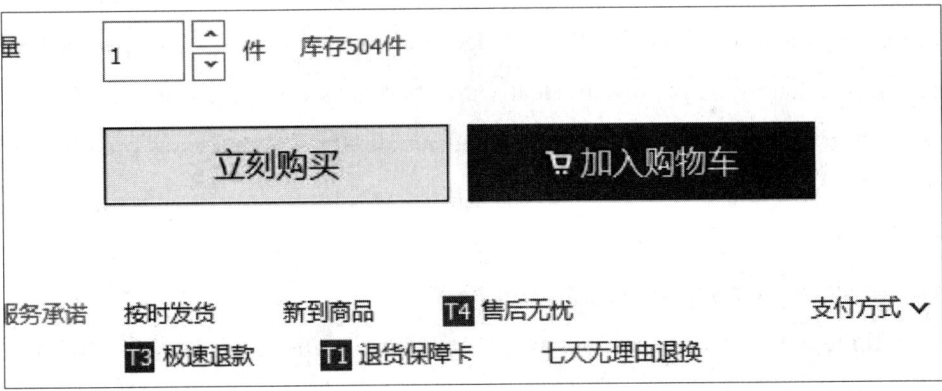

Fig. 6-4-8 Service Commitment

Some sellers, under the guidance of Taobao, work out their own rules and costs for returning and exchanging of goods, such as this one:

7天退换货须知

自收货之日起（以签收日期为准）七日内，货品在未经过穿着、洗涤、熨烫、污损、加工（翘边或自行修改尺寸等）的情况下，吊牌完整，即可享受无条件退换货服务一次，由买家承担寄回货品的邮费。退货时请连同收纳袋/衣服配件，赠品等完整寄回才能办理。如需换货前请先确认收货再联系旺旺客服为您处理。如货品存在质量问题或发错，请马上联系客服为您处理,如属实,我们会为您承担运费退换。提示:贴身货品（如内衣裤、袜子等），不予退换。

信心保障

亲，我们已为您投保运费险，退货不花一分钱。注：您需先行垫付运费，当完成退货操作并退款成功后，运费将会自动退还到您的支付宝账户里（最高25元）。但请您务必在线完成全部退款流程并填写正确的物流单号，在没有完成退款前请勿点击"确认收货"。如保险公司认为是潜在高风险的用户将会暂时不能提供运费险服务。

Fig. 6-4-9 Notes on the Return and Exchange of Goods by Giordano

It is up to you whether you use the general rules, work out your own, or negotiate each time with customers. As long as it helps you avoid and solve sales problems, it is worth a try. Real knowledge come from practice — as smart sellers, you will certainly learn how to deal with after-sales problems and win a good reputation through good service and the general after-sale processes provided by the website.

Other after-sales services and problems

There will always be various problems with the after-sales process. To solve these problems, care and resourcefulness on the part of the seller are needed. Now, we will show you two easily neglected after-sale problems.

You've probably heard that in the course of delivery couriers tend to throw and hurl the parcels in order to meet speed targets. So when an express delivery arrives, there may be loss, wear or damage to the goods. Although this is a problem caused by a third party, in the transaction process it is still seller's responsibility. A proposed solution is to choose one or a few logistic companies and sign a cooperative agreement wherein all possible losses, necessary compensation or measures are written. When goods are lost or damaged you must communicate with the customer to meet their needs and communicate with the logistics company ask for necessary compensation.

> 短信/彩信
> 1月16日 周五 15:50
>
> 【小贝美妆】亲爱的▇，您滴宝贝已到达北京市，很快会为您派送，请注意查收！若快递员偶有内分泌失调，请忽略并及时联系小贝，三克油！
>
> 1月17日 周六 09:56
>
> 【小贝美妆】亲爱的▇，宝贝宠幸过了吗？是否得您心意呢？！小的但求您能满意哦！若有问题，请随时联系我们。如果满意，跪求5颗星星哦！

Fig. 6-4-10 Warm Message Prompt

If you had received this message would you think it was lovely and want to be their customer one more time? A wise seller always knows the right way and time to create a good brand image.

Summary

1. Response to after-sales consultation
2. Handling the return and replacement of goods
   - Refund only
   - Refund and return of goods
   - Exchange
3. Logistics costs for the return and exchange of goods
4. Other after-sales problems